UTOPIAS ON PUGET SOUND, 1885–1915

Utopias
on Puget Sound,
1885-1915

CHARLES PIERCE LeWARNE

UNIVERSITY OF WASHINGTON PRESS
Seattle and London

This book was published with the assistance of a grant from the Andrew W.
Mellon Foundation.

Library of Congress Cataloging in Publication Data

LeWarne, Charles Pierce, 1930-
    Utopias on Puget Sound, 1885-1915.

    Bibliography: p.
    1. Collective settlements—Washington (State)—
History. I. Title.
HX655.W2L48   335'.9'7977   74-13862
ISBN 0-295-95343-8

To Pauline

Acknowledgments

Near the turn of the present century, a half dozen or so communitarian experiments, commonly called utopian or socialist colonies, appeared near the inland waters of western Washington that embrace Puget Sound. Part of a long communitarian tradition and of a contemporary revival, they drew together radicals, reformers, and generally good and well-meaning people in a common search for a better life. The experiments disappeared, and their settlers merged forgotten into the general populace. Later residents of Washington remained generally unaware of them, and few scholars noted them as a written history of the state developed. Alongside the records of more dominant groups, those of the colonists were few and scattered. But the records were there, in old newspapers and periodicals, libraries, archives, state and county records, and in the childhood memories of persons growing old. Thus, the search to rediscover these colonies has relied heavily upon many persons whose contributions are gratefully acknowledged and appreciated. Yet the final responsibility for errors and misinterpretations must remain that of the author.

Much of the research for this book was aided by the helpful and efficient staff of the University of Washington Library, where a special thanks is due Richard C. Berner and Karyl Winn in the archives and manuscripts division, Robert D. Monroe and the staff of the Northwest Collection, Georgia Kloostra of the Newspaper and Microcopy Center, and Ruth Kirk in the Interlibrary Loan Service. I also visited and received assistance from the Washington State University Library, the Stanford University Library, the Washington State Library, the California State Library, the Washington State Historical Society, the Oregon Historical Society, the Seattle Historical Society, the Kitsap Regional Library, and the public libraries of Seattle, Tacoma, Port Angeles, Bremerton, and Portland, Oregon. Help with specific colonies came from Ruth Olsen of the Kitsap County Historical Society, and Dot Lonn and Wilda MacDonald of the Clallam County Historical Society, who have a contagious interest in preserving the histories of their localities. Other libraries and societies aided me through correspondence. The assistance of the Federal Records Center, National Archives, Seattle, and the State Archives and Records Center, Olympia, as well as other federal and state offices, is appreciated. Individuals in several county offices interrupted routine and sometimes pressing business to retrieve old records from rarely used files.

Permission to quote from materials has been granted (sometimes provisionally) by the following individuals, libraries, and publications:

For use of portions of my article, "Equality Colony: The Plan to Socialize Washington," from *Pacific Northwest Quarterly* 59 (July 1968):137-46. For use of portions of my article, "The Anarchist Colony at Home, Washington, 1901-1902," from *Arizona and the West* 14 (Summer 1972):155-68.

For poem on page 211, from International Publishers Co., Inc., publishers of William Z. Foster, *From Bryan to Stalin.*

For quotations from Robert E. Wynne, *Reaction to the Chinese in the Pacific Northwest and British Columbia, 1850-1910,* from Robert E. Burke, Professor of History, University of Washington.

Quotations from the autobiography and letters of Cyrus Field Willard, insofar as they hold them, by permission of the Harvard College Library and the Olive Kettering Library, Antioch College.

Quotations from the Roland E. Muirhead diaries, from Edinburgh University Library. Quotations from materials held by Mina Saari, from Jessie M. Jensen. Quotations from materials held by Robert Hitchman, from Mr. Hitchman. Quotations from School

Board Records of District 12, from Kitsap County Historical Society. Quotations from letters of Norman W. Lermond, from Dorothy M. Burnham.

Quotations from letters of G. E. Pelton, from Florence Clark. (The State Historical Society of Wisconsin also granted permission to the extent that it holds the rights for the above items.) Quotations from writings of Harry E. B. Ault in University of Washington Library, and from interview with Gladys Ault Gray, by Gladys L. Gray. Quotations from *History of the Puget Sound Cooperative Colony*, from Kathleen Coventon Mills. Quotations from interview made by Henry W. Stein, from Katherine Anderson. Quotations from diaries of Alonzo A. Wardall, from Cedric Wardall and Dee Wardall Raible. Quotations from "Notes on the Equality Colony, at Bow, Washington," including quotations from the diary of George Savage, and "Do You Remember Equality Colony?" from Catherine J. Pulsipher.

Perhaps my greatest pleasure has been making the acquaintance, and in several cases the enduring friendship, of persons whom I interviewed. These people never failed to unfold recollections and impressions from long ago. Their names are listed in the bibliography; with sadness I note that several are since deceased. Some of these persons loaned photographs or other materials in their possession, as did Robert Hitchman, Bert Kellogg, Mina Saari, and Fred Smith. Valued correspondence was received from Carolyn Ashbaugh, Sac City, Iowa; Florence Malony Bowler, Woodburn, Oregon; Dorothy M. Burnham, Escondido (since moved to Saratoga), California; Macie Govan Cope, Inglewood, California; D. Stanton Hammond, Paterson, New Jersey; Marvin Sanford, San Francisco; Ellis Spear, Newton Centre, Massachusetts; Ray S. Spencer, Lopez, Washington; Harry Swofford, Chehalis, Washington; and Albert Whitmore, Warren, Maine.

Thanks are inadequate to the good friends, relatives, and acquaintances who have helped over several years in numerous and surprisingly varied ways, but always with their interest and their willingness to hear about yet another development. I cannot list all by name or by contribution, so I shall list none. But they know and I know, and it is greatly appreciated. June Larrick skillfully taped an important interview based on sketchy information I sent her. Several persons read portions of this work, but I would especially like to note Carol Anderson and David Gerlach, who at one point made more perceptive criticisms than one has a right to expect from high school seniors. Professor Arthur Bestor, whose book on New Harmony is a model for all who study communitarianism, and Professor Robert E. Burke, who is a fund of knowledge of the twentieth-century West, made helpful comments, as did fellow students in my University of Washington seminars.

There remain those singularly important persons without whom this book would never have appeared. My parents helped to instill an interest and a curiosity about the region where he lived for half a century and of which she is proudly a native daughter. Happily, my mother, Angie Pierce LeWarne, will see the book in print. Professor Vernon Carstensen, who expects of his students the same high standards of research, scholarship, and writing style that he demands of himself, has mused over problems and benefited me with his insight since the day the topic was first proposed as a doctoral dissertation. Most of all, I am grateful for his constant interest, assurance, and encouragement. Along with being a busy wife and mother, Pauline Nelson LeWarne has been so completely a part of this book from the earliest research to the final proofreading and indexing that it is her book as well as mine. My portion, however, has tended to include more that was fun and hers more that was tedious. And now there are Charles, Anne, and David, constant reminders that utopias still appear on Puget Sound.

Contents

Illustrations

UTOPIAS ON PUGET SOUND, 1885-1915

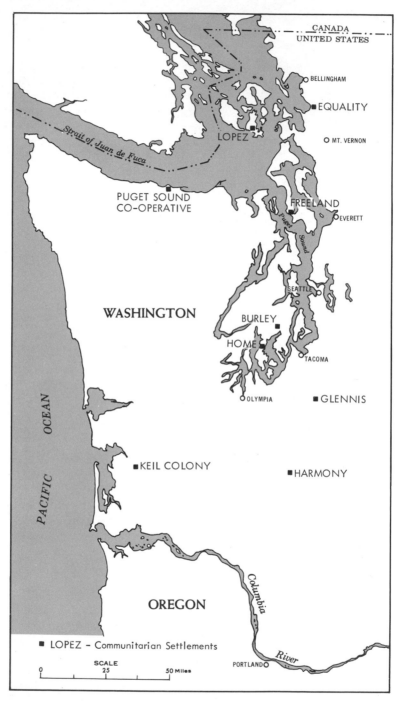

Communitarian settlements of western Washington

1. Introduction

THE COMMUNITARIAN IDEAL
AND THE CHOSEN STATE

In the middle 1930s, so the story goes, Postmaster General James A. Farley visited Seattle and offered a toast: "To the forty-seven states and the soviet of Washington." No one in his audience could have missed the point. For a quarter century the farthest northwest state had nurtured a reputation for radicalism and reform. This was the era of the Industrial Workers of the World, with free speech fights in Spokane and other cities, the Everett and Centralia massacres, and the Seattle General Strike woven into the political and social fabric. Such progressive reforms as woman suffrage, industrial compensation, and direct legislation measures were adopted early in Washington. During the 1920s and 1930s, the state witnessed the rise of strong labor organizations, the Farmer-Labor party, the Washington Pension Union, and the Washington Commonwealth Federation. Novelist John Dos Passos drew upon the lore of Washington radicalism for vignettes in his *Nineteen Nineteen*.[1]

Long before this reputation became established, however, the young state had harbored a different form of radicalism. Late in the nineteenth century, half a dozen communitarian experiments appeared in western Washington. At Port Angeles in 1887, and in Skagit County, on the Kitsap Peninsula, on Whidbey Island, and in Lewis County a decade later, separate groups of visionaries constructed utopias and disseminated radical doctrines. They represented the union of a long-standing communitarian tradition with recent economic and political reform movements in the United States.

3

Despite individual variations, the communitarian ideal has certain general characteristics. Experiments were usually small, isolated but rarely monastic, self-contained units of people who held certain ideals in common. The term "colony" came into popular use to describe them. The political goal was often a pure democracy with broad participation, although this sometimes existed on paper rather than in fact. A strong leader could be an advantage. Many experiments assumed a communal nature as members practiced social or economic activities in common. It was an article of the faith that some functions could not be performed alone as effectively as they could through union of similarly minded persons.   Land could be owned and goods produced and distributed efficiently and beneficially by cooperative efforts among equals who shared profits. Groups that performed most of their activities on such a basis tended to be communistic; those which allowed members to own personal property or retain some profits were considered socialist. Occasionally a group maintained only a thread of the communal practices and did little to regulate its members or to enforce demands.

The communitarian ideal transcended immediate internal programs to include a belief that could be characterized as utopian. Adherents professed a vision, in some cases a religious fervor, which afforded unusual insight into the problems of society and their solutions. They would point to the future by establishing a working model of the perfect society for others to copy. The communitarian effort offered a unique method to accomplish basic change without rejecting traditional American values. The idea of class struggle was rejected in favor of brotherhood and cooperation. A fundamental belief confirmed man's ability to affect his environment and the world; progress was possible, if not inevitable. Advocates of communitarianism valued experimentation. They would strive toward a better life for mankind, not with written treatises, piecemeal reforms, or revolution, but by taking constructive action, by creating a "patent office model" that was a microcosm of the better society.[2]

The communitarian tradition originated in theological controversies and population displacements in Europe during the Reformation. As small religious sects splintered from larger bodies, some of the devout drew together in communal practices. Feeling persecuted, many sought the more hospitable atmosphere of America. The first of these, a party of Dutch Mennonites who established themselves on the Delaware River in the 1660s, was followed in later decades by other sectarian groups, including Shakers, Moravians, and Rappites. Economic necessity often acted with religious tenets to bind participants firmly to communal and cooperative practices. These communitarian settlements paved the way for later religious groups and for secular ones as well.[3]

American communitarian efforts achieved their fullest fruition in the second quarter of the nineteenth century. In the 1820s the British manufacturer Robert Owen excited interest with his attempt to provide a wholesome community for laborers in New Harmony, Indiana. Brook Farm, Massachusetts, which adopted the productive principles of the French philosopher Charles Fourier in the 1840s, was noteworthy because of the writings and general luster of certain members. That decade witnessed the emergence of two dozen other Fourierist colonies and other communities, mostly located in the old Northwest and New England, including Hopedale, Fruitlands, Oneida, and Icaria. The most enduring religious group of the period was the Church of Jesus Christ of Latter Day Saints, the Mormons, formed in a bond of piety, discipline, and economic unity.[4]

Communitarian activities diminished during the next half century. Reformers of the post-bellum years favored conventional methods, and it was not until the 1890s that interest in communitarian activities was renewed and new colonies appeared. The economic transformation of American society after the Civil War had wrought problems of a new kind, scope, and intensity. The growing dependence upon machines and the apparent helplessness of the individual, the urbanization of life, the discomforts and hazards of the factory system, and the increasingly unequal distribution of wealth were among the factors that increased demands for reform. By the early 1890s, many Americans expressed grievances by proposing, exploring, discussing, and agitating for a variety of panaceas; some were specific and limited, some broad.[5]

New theories from Europe were influencing American attitudes, but the socialist preachings of Karl Marx, Friedrich Engels, and Ferdinand Lassalle found relatively few followers in the United

States. By the 1890s the Marxist oriented Socialist Labor party had fallen under the discipline of Daniel DeLeon, whose rigid conformity to the class-struggle thesis retarded open discussion and narrowed the appeal of the party. Notwithstanding socialist groups of German immigrants in the Middle West and Jewish workers in New York City, most Americans discovered socialism in diluted forms which did not seem alien and which emphasized a progressive evolution toward a better life. The mainstream of American socialism and the revival of communitarian ideas flowed directly from the efforts of three men—a Chicago lawyer, the son of a prominent Massachusetts minister, and a Colorado land speculator turned editor.[6]

Laurence Grönlund, who had emigrated from Denmark as a young man, practiced law briefly, but preferred exploring and spreading socialist theory. In *The Cooperative Commonwealth*, published in 1884, he attempted to explain Marx in the American idiom; yet he shied away from predicting an inevitable class struggle and anticipated instead a society of brotherhood and cooperation. Grönlund provided impetus and rhetoric for the American socialist movement.[7]

Like Grönlund, Edward Bellamy abandoned an unsatisfying law practice for writing. His early novels went unnoticed, but *Looking Backward, 2000-1887*, first published in 1887, attracted wide attention. The story described a wealthy, self-satisfied nineteenth-century Bostonian who awoke from a mysterious sleep in the year 2000 to find his city marvelously transformed. Want in the midst of wealth had been replaced by economic equality. Mechanical devices saved manual labor while providing comfort and entertainment. A central government functioned powerfully and smoothly. Culture and refinement abounded. A pleasant, clean, secure, and contented city that resembled Grönlund's "cooperative commonwealth" had been achieved through brotherhood. The book captured the public imagination. Over two hundred thousand copies were sold by 1890. Bellamy or "Nationalist" clubs were established in twenty-seven states; newspapers and lecture bureaus spread the doctrine. The author was celebrated as an apostle of the future who had shown Americans the good life available through a home-grown socialism.[8]

The Bellamy movement was largely urban, but the promise of

socialism was delivered to the rural population through two newspapers originally published by Julius A. Wayland. Restless with a fortune acquired early, Wayland established several Populist papers in Colorado before he returned to Indiana to publish *The Coming Nation* in 1893. Despite his success, mere advocacy did not satisfy Wayland, and he established Ruskin Colony in Tennessee as a practical demonstration of socialism. When this effort disintegrated, Wayland left the paper to the quarreling colonists and moved to Girard, Kansas, where he initiated *The Appeal to Reason*. Both papers attacked present iniquities and preached socialism, and were read on farms and in small towns throughout the country.[9] Grönlund, Bellamy, and Wayland were not the only exponents of socialism in the United States, but their distinctly American ideology profoundly affected the revival of communitarianism.

Other diverse reformers and activities composed the general ferment. The single-tax doctrines of Henry George, attacks upon moneyed interests by Henry Demarest Lloyd, and a flurry of reform literature and journalism were making an impress. Utopian novels appeared each year in America and Europe. Labor unions wrestled with socialist ideology, and the Granger and Populist movements focused on cooperation. Seeking to increase social awareness and responsibility in the church, radicals among clergy and laity advanced principles of Christian Socialism.[10]

Parallel with these developments, exponents of anarchism had emerged in the United States by the 1880s, perhaps as strong numerically as the socialists. Anarchists advocated a total reshaping of society and the economy. In their desire to extend individual freedom, they rejected dependence upon government and authority. Although there were other spokesmen in America, Johann Most was generally acknowledged as the leader after he arrived in 1882. American anarchists were divided into two major groups, reflecting the schism in the European tradition. Anarcho-communists rejected ownership of private property in favor of autonomous collectives, and they advocated a massive effort to destroy government through agitation, propaganda, and sometimes "propaganda of the deed," as acts of assassination, bombing, or terrorism were called. Individualist anarchists, on the other hand, believed that individual rights should be supreme and free from interference by laws or authority, including that of their own leaders. Their consummate weapon was passive resistance rather than violence. They recognized private ownership of property that represented the fruit of one's labor. Individualist anarchists who joined communal societies acted voluntarily to escape pressure and oppression from society. Uppermost was the retention of individuality.[11]

Early individualist anarchists in the United States included Josiah Warren, who rejected the submergence of the individual he experienced as a New Harmony colonist and later founded colonies offering extensive individual freedom with labor the basis of wealth. By the 1890s, the leading American individualist anarchist was Benjamin R. Tucker, who synthesized previous doctrines in his journal *Liberty*. With Tucker's approval, the tenuous links between individualist anarchists and anarcho-communists were almost completely severed over controversies involving origins, goals, methods, and personalities. [12]

Advocates of communitarianism appeared throughout this plethora of philosophies, methods, and goals. Outside the mainstream even of their particular movements, they reflected earlier days and simple solutions. If the believers were to practice ideal lives and if they were to mold the future, they must abandon eastern industrial centers and the expansive farmlands of the Middle West for those areas where frontier conditions still existed. And so they looked to undeveloped parts of the South, to valley pockets in the Rocky Mountains, and to the Pacific states— including the state of Washington.[13]

The first settlers had established on Puget Sound as recently as 1845, and Washington Territory was thirty-six years old in 1889 when it became a state. The 1880 population was 75,116, but the next census count showed 349,390. Thick forests touched Puget Sound and surrounded lakes and rivers. Sawmills dotted the region, spawning settlements that aspired to become towns. Timber was the mainstay of the economy, but mining and fishing accelerated economic growth. Farms were usually small and isolated, the people depending upon Oregon and eastern Washington for most foodstuffs. Yet the high productivity of certain riverbeds and the possibility of diking tidelands prompted agricultural growth. Remote and largely undeveloped, western Washington was dependent upon extractive activities and was just beginning to encounter the pressures of economic change by the middle 1880s.

Railroads were altering conditions in the territory. Short lines constructed with local capital drew towns, mines, and mills together, although communities on Puget Sound relied heavily upon water transportation. Early in the 1880s the Northern Pacific Railroad connected the sound with the rest of the nation. The effect was immediate and direct. Newcomers were attracted to emerging settlements. In 1880 Seattle, with a population of 3,533, was only one of several towns on the sound; a decade later there were 42,837 inhabitants. Tacoma, site of the original railroad terminus, increased from 1,098 to 36,006. In Centralia, Olympia, Port Townsend, and Bellingham, the future looked promising. New industries, many related to lumber, invigorated the economic climate, and shipping activities increased.[14]

Such growth brought complex new problems, and discontent nurtured demands. Although Washington remained safely Republican until the Populist upsurge in the middle 1890s, signs of protest were appearing in labor and agriculture. In the 1870s there were eight labor locals in the state, most of them in the railroad industry, and other workers were starting to organize. The Knights of Labor had one chapter by 1880. Anti-Chinese sentiments in several cities helped to reinforce the Knights' organizational efforts and to establish a local People's party in Seattle. Class identities were solidifying. Farmers' discontent directed at railroads and other monopolies became apparent with the formation of farmers' clubs (of which Washington had more than sixty in the 1870s) and farmers' alliances, and the rise of the Grange movement. The grange reached a peak of membership in Washington in 1875, with the State Grange being formed in 1889; the organization was an important element in developing social consciousness in the state.[15]

There were other reform causes. In the early 1890s, a semisecret political society was promoting direct legislation. Woman suffrage, defeated by a single vote in the first territorial legislature in 1854, was granted in 1883, only to be ended by a court decision four years later. Closely linked was the crusade for prohibition.

Delegates to the state constitutional convention in 1889 encountered strong pressures in behalf of liberal proposals. Some, including restrictions on railroads and upon the seizure of property for debts, were enacted into the document. [16]

In 1892 the Farmers' Alliance led other reform organizations in establishing a state Populist party which became a major political force. A Populist paper appeared in Seattle, and a speech there by presidential candidate James B. Weaver aroused great enthusiasm. Weaver received over 21 percent of the popular vote; eight Populists were sent to the 1893 session of the legislature and twenty-three to the 1895 session. The national fusion with Democrats and Silver Republicans prompted a similar union in Washington, and the 1896 Fusionist platform was mostly Populist. That year, Washington gave a plurality of twelve thousand votes to the Democrat-Populist presidential candidate William Jennings Bryan, and the Fusionists captured state offices. Populists alone controlled a majority in the legislature. Thus in 1897 Washington appeared to be a state attuned to reform and led by a governor, John R. Rogers, with a demonstrated interest in agrarian and humanitarian betterment.[17]

Washington showed other liberal tendencies. The Puget Sound area was one of several starting points for units of the Industrial Army, often known as Coxey's Army. Most of the reportedly eighteen hundred unemployed who formed the Puget Sound contingent got no farther than Puyallup, although a few proceeded to the national capital in commandeered railroad cars. The Pacific Coast generally was a stronghold of the Bellamy Nationalist movement. [18]

Washington was even identified with a few utopian writings. *The Rice Mills of Port Mystery*, published in 1891, described mythical mills located on Puget Sound that benefited the economy of the nation even though they were nonexistent. The argument was for a greatly reduced cost of exchange of goods, the free flow of commerce, and the judicious use of labor-saving machines. In 1896 a Seattle publisher issued *The Light of Eden: Or, A Historical Narrative of the Barbarian Age, A Scientific Discovery*. The author described a journey to a utopian republic where labor was the unit of wealth and the government protected individual interests. The contrast of beneficent labor policies in

Eden with exploitation in the United States was obvious. Governor Rogers had written a utopian novel during his Kansas publishing days. Reissued in 1898, *Looking Forward: The Story of an American Farm* depicted agrarian life as it could be. And a Buckley socialist, E. L. Robinson, proposed a scheme with an elaborate government designed to initiate the cooperative commonwealth.[19] Thus organizers of utopian experiments, especially after 1896, came to Washington anticipating a hospitable political, social, and economic atmosphere.

Actually, Washington's first encounter with communitarianism had occurred many years before. During the 1840s William Keil, a German immigrant, had founded a mystical sect laced with communistic idealism. In Bethel, Missouri, the group's religious and communal practices were formalized and a colony grew and prospered. But Keil found Missouri wanting, and in 1853 he sent scouts to find a new location in the West. Arriving at Fort Vancouver in late summer, the party first moved north to Olympia and then seaward. A few miles inland from Willapa Bay, they secured a claim, planted crops, and built log houses in preparation for the coming of the entire colony. The valley was ample, well forested, and fertile, with the ocean close enough to provide seafood and to promise transportation facilities.

On 23 May 1855, led by a hearse carrying the leader's recently deceased son, a twenty-four wagon party departed Bethel on the two-thousand-mile journey. Arriving 1 November, Keil surveyed the Willapa site and was dissatisfied. The forest was too thick. Roads were poor, full of holes, and muddy, and the river required constant and difficult fording. The weather, wet and depressing, slowed building. Keil conceded that the land was fertile, but crops without markets meant nothing. He doubted that the country could support industries, and transportation costs from Oregon made prices high. All in all, Keil could foresee small success in such a place, and he determined to search for land in Oregon. Soon he moved his colony to a Willamette Valley site which he named Aurora.[20]

Nevertheless, William Keil made some concessions to the Willapa settlement. He purchased the two land claims already secured by his scout, as well as additional claims, which he turned over to families that wanted to stay. The burial of his son there in a lamplight ceremony against the singing of German hymns gave an old-country finis to a trek that would have created a communal settlement near the Washington coast. Most of those who had come to Willapa followed Keil to Aurora, although several families remained, and a tiny rural settlement developed around them. Thus the first attempt to establish a communitarian experiment in western Washington died almost before it began. [21]

About a dozen years after Keil turned away from the Willapa, a religious colony was started east of the mountain divide. In 1867, William W. Davis, a Welsh convert to Mormonism who had forsaken those beliefs, led some forty followers into the Walla Walla Valley. Davis became a mystic whose visions and communions with God strengthened his hold over a small circle of believers. When his first son was born, the father announced that he was Christ reincarnated. The next son was proclaimed to be God the Father, and Davis the Holy Ghost. Except for a belief in reincarnation and the sanctity of the Davises, the theology of the sect was weak, but Davis maintained a paternalistic leadership. As administrative head of the colony, he controlled land holdings, supplies, crops, and occasional profits, all of which were held in common. The colonists depended for sustenance upon their own labors and upon gifts from sympathizers.

The colony encountered trouble. One of Davis' lieutenants increasingly irritated members with his officious personality, and fights and arrests in nearby towns brought disrepute to the group. The deaths of both sons from diphtheria raised doubts about their divinity. As a result of economic setbacks, three members took legal action against Davis in 1881. Despite testimony from several who professed to believe in Davis and his sect, the judge allowed claims of thirty-two hundred dollars, forcing a liquidation of assets, which destroyed the venture fourteen years after its founding. Davis' subsequent marriage to a teacher who he claimed was the reincarnation of his first wife disheartened most of the remaining believers, and he moved out of the state to an obscure conventional life. [22]

Some colonization efforts in Washington involved groups of similarly inclined persons who migrated together. Late in the 1890s, three middle westerners, all members of the Progressive Brethren Church, formed the Christian Cooperative Colony and laid out the town of Sunnyside in the Yakima Valley. Despite its moral and religious standards, this colony was less a communitarian effort than a land development scheme by like-minded persons. [23]

In a similar vein, the Washington Colony that brought about twenty-five families to Bellingham was a mutually convenient arrangement between local promoters and Kansans who wished to come west. Members paid one hundred dollars a share for stock in the company, which was capitalized at seventy-five thousand dollars. They built homes and constructed a sawmill and a wharf. In a short time the economic climate of the town seemed to improve; the mill was turning out shingles, and newcomers were arriving. But land title arguments and disputes among members disrupted the colony. In 1883 the membership arrangement was changed to a capital scheme, which created even more confusion, especially after a Kansas investor who secured half the stock made some dubious transactions and disappeared. When the land fell to a creditor as the result of a lawsuit in 1884, Washington Colony was ended. [24]

Other so-called colonizing efforts were more accurately mass migrations to particular settlements. Railroad lines, steamship companies, and local and federal government agencies sometimes joined in propaganda efforts and land promotions to establish colonies in mutually advantageous areas. Occasionally, national groups united to settle a specific area, such as the Dutch settlement at Lynden in Whatcom County. [25]

Other parts of the Pacific Northwest shared in the communitarian revival near the turn of the century. Mormon colonization spread north from Utah into Oregon and Idaho but did not penetrate Washington. Ruskin Colony, near Hastings, British Columbia, was large, but it endured only a few months early in 1899. From 1901 to 1905 a Finnish socialist headed a colony of 230 persons on a Canadian island he called Harmony. To the south, Oregon had several experiments after Keil's notable one at Aurora. California had experimental colonies of many kinds, and a large socialist colony was started at Fallon, Nevada, in 1916. [26]

Although Idaho seems to have had no secular experiments, a widely publicized utopian novel of the 1890s was set in that state. Co-opolis, a fictitious city located in a fertile Idaho valley, was

settled by about three hundred persons who practiced cooperation. Their success attracted newcomers, and the city became a
major political force, rapidly converting neighboring states and
then the nation to Co-opolitan ideals.[27]

The Co-opolitan dream was shared by real people who hoped to
better life in the United States. When considering actual sites for
realizing their dreams, some were attracted to the natural benefits
and the political promise of Washington.

The earlier experiments and the literary utopias were fore-
runners of several communities in the Puget Sound region. Most of
these were started during the last half of the 1890s, but the first
appeared a decade earlier on a wooded shore along the Strait of
Juan de Fuca.

2. The Puget Sound Co-operative Colony

THE MODEL COMMONWEALTH
OF THE OLYMPIC PENINSULA

The first modern communitarian experiment in Washington was the Puget Sound Cooperative Colony, located at Port Angeles in 1887. In many respects this colony stands apart from later ones. Despite national pretensions, it was essentially a local movement derived from working-class agitations in Puget Sound cities. More than any other colony of western Washington, it helped to establish a modern and permanent city.

Seattle and Tacoma were but a generation old in 1880. As they emerged from pioneer conditions to develop industries and commerce, they attracted skilled and unskilled laborers. Among them came the Chinese. Originally imported to work in California mines, many of them later shifted to railroad construction, fish canneries, or other unskilled jobs. By 1880 an estimated 3,186 Chinese lived in Washington Territory, fewer than in either California or Oregon, but enough to disturb white laborers who feared that wages and employment opportunities would be undercut. The Caucasian laborers, unorganized, frustrated, and increasingly bitter, were ripe for agitators.[1]

One of the first to exploit the situation was Daniel Cronin, who had come from the timber country around Eureka, California, to organize the Knights of Labor. He recognized that latent anti-Chinese feelings could provide the catalyst to draw workers into his union. Some business and political leaders in Seattle suspected that Cronin's activities concealed efforts to organize divisions of the International Workingmen's Association, a radical branch of

15

the Knights of Labor that advocated violence and challenged the union's conservatives. Whatever Cronin's role in the IWA, he organized the Knights by creating secret interlocking cells of nine members each. Following the establishment of a Knights chapter in Tacoma early in 1885, anti-Chinese activity increased in that city. Meanwhile, Seattle workers were organizing a Liberal League to agitate against the Chinese.[2]

During the autumn and winter of 1885-86, tensions reached a climax with mass meetings, demonstrations, threats, arrests, and ultimately the expulsion of several hundred Chinese and a major riot. Martial law was declared in Seattle, and leading citizens were indicted for conspiracy. On one side were the workers, on the other the "law and order" business and civic leaders, some of whom profited from employing Orientals. Seattle events were paralleled in Tacoma.

Although Cronin organized meetings and inflamed audiences, much of the leadership passed to others, including George Venable Smith, recently arrived from California. Born in Kentucky in 1843, Smith had come with his father to the California gold fields as a small child. In Sacramento he received his general education and studied law. Admitted to the bar at twenty-one, he first practiced in Portland, Oregon. In time he returned to California and was a delegate to the 1879 state constitutional convention, where he helped draft the judicial system. This prominence led to his election as district attorney for Kern County. He moved to Seattle in 1883 and was soon appointed acting city attorney, charged with codifying city ordinances. And he became involved with the Chinese problem.[3]

Smith agreed that the Chinese must go, but he counseled caution. Nevertheless, he presided at mass meetings, and plans of attack were laid in his office. Acquitted of conspiracy charges, Smith was the object of unsuccessful disbarment proceedings. His power and influence mounted as the Chinese issue unified Seattle labor elements. According to one student of the affair, the Smith group "showed signs of becoming the masters of a well disciplined movement separated from the rest of the community." They were beginning to take upon themselves "functions normally belonging to the realm of civic administration." Once the Chinese were gone, might there be other purposes for which this organization and energy could be used, "other worthwhile causes for which to fight?" In fact, several leaders of the anti-Chinese element were at work organizing a utopian community. Besides Smith, these included John J. Knoff, Mrs. Laura E. Hall, and Peter Peyto Good. [4]

If Smith was chief organizer and promoter, Good was the instigator and first martyr. The Harvard graduate had practiced law in his native New York and in Plainfield, New Jersey, where he was a city judge for four years. During that time he became interested in reform, and a European tour awakened him to working-class needs and to the ideal of utopian cooperation. Visiting the cooperative community of ironworkers at Guise, France, Good was inspired to found a similar experiment in the United States. He had that objective in mind in the summer of 1885 when he moved to Seattle where his relative, Mrs. Hall, lived. Admitted to the bar on Smith's motion, Good readily became involved in local issues. He spoke at the organizational meeting of the Tacoma Knights of Labor and at Seattle anti-Chinese rallies, where he once digressed to call for what conservatives interpreted as a revolution of the masses against the federal government. Along with several other agitators, Good was imprisoned for ten days in November 1885. Shortly after the Chinese riots, he became sick with pleurisy, and he died on 21 February 1886. Friends blamed his death on the rigors and embarrassment of his recent imprisonment.[5]

Judge Good had talked enthusiastically about a model city. He showed Smith "illustrated maps of a city beautiful with cooperative homes, cooperative hotels and all industries upon a cooperative system, which so captivated Mr. Smith that he was at once seized with the determination to organize another such colony. . . ." Before the judge's death, plans for a colony were under way. In October the friendly *Daily Call* outlined the Guise community and promised that cooperation offered not only economic necessities but luxuries and comforts: ". . . as mankind grows better, juster, kinder and more confiding of each other, that idea will spread and grow." Organizational meetings were held in Smith's office, and a formal announcement in February described a "society... of persons who propose to establish upon a convenient harbor on Puget Sound a cooperative colony." The group elected officers on 5 February (two days before the Chinese riot) and made plans to incorporate. Publicists extolled the potential of Puget Sound, remarking the need for workers and outlining methods of finance. The group produced a book containing plans that placed the experiment in the tradition of Guise, of the Albert K. Owens colony at Topolobampo, Mexico, and of the Fourier phalanxes of the 1840s. Smith claimed that inquiries arrived every day. At least in the minds of its originators, the ideal community was taking shape.[6]

Such developments were not unnoticed by Seattle conservatives. The *Times*, established as the businessmen's spokesman during the recent riots, denounced the founders as socialists "in the mind-poisoning business" and lackeys of the hated Cronin. "George Venable Smith, you self-styled brains of the lawless movement, you dupe of worse wire-pullers . . . you are a socialist and an active socialist [and] a traitor to your country." After 21 May, the colonists could respond with their own newspaper, *The Model Commonwealth*, edited by Mrs. Hall. An introductory article contained greetings and statements of intent: "THIS PAPER is devoted specially to the interest of THE PUGET SOUND COLONY, and generally to the practical solution of the subject of entire Co-operation, e.g., a separate community of collective industry, means, utilities, public and private, and of persons under a single management and responsibility for health, usefullness, individuality and security of each and all."[7]

Claiming to have five hundred members, fifteen thousand dollars, and a colony site, the leaders hoped to incorporate in six months when stock and sales receipts should reach 150,000 dollars. Each colonist could subscribe for one or more lot interests or for shares of stock, the latter bearing 10 percent interest. The company would "issue 100,000 shares of stock at $10 per share, and sell 3,000 lot interests in six series." Lot prices would range from twenty dollars to two hundred dollars with the advantage to first comers. Private enterprise and competition would be prohibited, and there would be no individual taxes. Each laborer would work at his preferred trade; by some undefined balancing, all necessities should be achieved. Basic industries, such as a sawmill, farms, and a dairy, would operate early, with additional industries, stores, and hotels coming in time. Although residents might live in private homes, model homes, or resident hotels, all would enjoy the advantage of cooperative kitchens. Schools, lecture halls, music halls, and libraries were intended, but the community would tolerate neither "saloons, nor churches, nor any private societies." By paying initiation fees and dues, noncolonists might join the Central Society in Seattle or one of the branches being formed across the nation. Open to rich and poor, the colony system was the "hope of the future, especially for the laboring masses; the only release from the tyranny of monopoly and the only method of preventing a repetition of the French Revolution in America."[8]

The *Times* quickly denounced "A CO-OPERATIVE SWINDLE" that made "preposterous and impossible propositions to the dupes." Its editor predicted little success locally where the organizers were known, but he feared the effect of the newspaper on distant persons "who can be deceived by the honeyed words of a lot of socialists."[9]

Judge Junius Rochester and District Attorney J. T. Ronald supplied generous recommendations of colony leaders. But these gentlemen had liberal sympathies, and Mrs. Hall acknowledged that such commendatory letters were not available from other leading citizens. Nevertheless, the colonists continued to plan. And correspondence, publicity, and appeals poured into Smith's office. Special compaigns were presented to unions such as the Knights of Labor, and some members joined. [10]

George V. Smith embarked on a lengthy tour to publicize the scheme and seek members. After two weeks in San Francisco where he organized a local society, he proceeded to the Middle West. "I have now been at such work nearly two months here in Ohio," he wrote in December, "and I have made many speeches. . . . My meets are generally crowded and my audiences . . . seem to be held spellbound, and when at the conclusion of my address I offer them papers, circulars, and pamphlets, . . . they rush for them without dignity like hungry wolves, always wanting more than I have. I have been told that the Colony plans have created such interest that the balance of the night would frequently be exhausted in talk on the way home. . . ." Smith was surprised and pleased by the response shown in

Cleveland among "the better class of mechanics, and the middle classes. . . ." His itinerary included other Ohio cities as well as stops in Chicago, St. Louis, and Kansas City; he spoke and organized branch societies wherever possible. In Chicago he set up headquarters at the Commercial Hotel and was quoted at length in the *Sunday Telegram.* Smith also visited the Union Colony established by followers of Horace Greeley in Colorado.[11]

But the trip was not all smooth. Expenses were greater than initiation fees could support, and Smith discovered that when he asked for subscriptions, some listeners would back away "and at once conclude that I was traveling to make money out of them." Other promoters were experiencing the same problem. For example, Mrs. Nellie M. Beck wrote from Fossil Station, Wyoming:

We have met with so much opposition and discouragement from everyone to whom we have mentioned the colony that, sometimes, I have been tempted never to mention the subject again, but let each go his own way and work out his own salvation.

Some tell us it is a visionary scheme, which can never be put into practice; others call it a swindle, and say that Mr. Smith is a fraud, and only after the working man's dollars, and still others have quarreled with us for sending away our hard earned savings, and called us cranks and fanatics behind our backs.[12]

Smith appointed other agents in the Middle West, one of whom, Venier Voldo, was particularly active until he finally moved west. There was interest in more distant places. A London editor sought information, and sympathizers in Toronto held regular meetings.[13]

Early in 1887 a thirty-two-page pamphlet outlined intentions more comprehensively than had previous statements. The membership had passed one thousand, with two to three hundred new members joining each month. But actual operations would require a thousand stock purchases. By May the colony could probably incorporate and select the "pioneer corps" from among members already living on Puget Sound. It was hoped that more persons could join the colony by fall, although leaders were wisely cautioning against overoptimism and possible crowding. The pamphlet listed twenty branch societies in Illinois, Ohio, California, Colorado, Wisconsin, Oregon, Indiana, and Missouri, as well as those in Seattle and Tacoma.[14]

On 4 May 1887, convention delegates assembled in Seattle to draft the articles of incorporation and bylaws. Thirty-five delegates were included in a compiled photograph, with Smith featured prominently in the center. Smith praised the "character, intelligence and fine appearance" of people drawn from all parts of the Union, although most were from the Middle West and Washington Territory. Territorial Governor Eugene C. Semple, an old acquaintance of Smith's, visited the convention briefly.[15]

The Puget Sound Co-operative Colony incorporated with a capital stock of one hundred thousand dollars for a fifty-year period with rights of renewal. One hundred shares were authorized with par value of ten dollars each. The articles of incorporation listed extensive purposes: "For manufacturing, mining, milling, wharfing, docking, mechanical, mercantile, building and improvement purposes, and for the building, equipping and managing water flumes, and for the transportation of wood and lumber, and for the building, equipping, and running railroads and constructing canals, and for the purpose of engaging in any other species of trade and business to do and perform other things and business matters incident to or which may assist in carrying on, performing and conducting all business and industries aforesaid. . . ." [16]

There were eleven trustees. Smith was president; Mrs. Nellie Wood, a veteran of the Seattle anti-Chinese agitation, was chosen treasurer; and Albert E. Sanderson became secretary. Sanderson was from St. Louis, Missouri, where he had earned degrees from Washington University. A lawyer and high school principal in Missouri, he became interested in communism and was attracted to the Puget Sound Colony. Despite his office, he would eventually return to St. Louis to become active in both the Socialist Labor and Social Democratic parties. Of those associated with the colony, Sanderson was the most prominent national figure. [17]

The directors now announced the site of their colony, which an early pamphlet had described as one of "the many safe and commodious harbors within the magnificent waters of the Straits of Juan de Fuca and Puget Sound . . . if not the best harbor." The founders had been secretive as to its whereabouts, even though the location had been selected more than a year before, payments were being made, and a few members were already residing there.

The tiny community of Port Angeles lay on the Olympic Peninsula sixty miles inland from the Pacific Ocean, where a natural harbor was formed by Ediz Hook, a curved sandspit that jutted into the Strait of Juan de Fuca. Ennis Creek created a small ravine as it flowed from heavily wooded hinterlands to empty directly opposite the tip of the hook. The funneled opening at its mouth and the beach stretching west provided land for the colony.[18]

More than twenty-five full blocks in the previously platted townsite had been purchased in April 1886 from Norman R. Smith, son of the founder of Port Angeles. John J. Knoff, the colony president, had secured this plus two hundred acres of timberland for an initial payment of ten thousand dollars; the balance of five thousand dollars was due within the year. A few weeks after its incorporation, the colony received the deed from Knoff, and the move to the property was under way.[19]

Port Angeles had been discovered, named, and mapped by Spanish explorers in 1791, but the first white settler did not establish his claim until 1857. During the next decade, Port Angeles experienced its initial growth spurt when customs collector Victor Smith got the port of entry transferred there from Port Townsend in 1862. The colorful Smith devoted his private life to developing his city and protecting it from its older and larger neighbor, Port Townsend. But after Smith drowned in a shipwreck in 1865, the customs house was returned to Port Townsend, and Port Angeles lay dormant until 1883-84. A wharf attracted fishermen and traders, and homes for between two hundred and three hundred people were constructed. The colony founders chose this community to be their nearest neighbor.[20]

Colonists began to arrive at Port Angeles long before the formal transfer of colony headquarters from Seattle in June. By 1 January 1887, twenty-two members were on the townsite, including local residents who were enticed to join. Among these were E. B. Mastick, Jr., who had represented Norman R. Smith in the land purchase, and eleven members of the John Church family. The only colony official present was Philo W. Gallup of Greeley, Colorado, but during January the William Becks arrived from Wyoming, and a few others came in February and March. Then on 9 April, a party of thirty-four arrived from Ohio and Chicago. During the spring, arrivals were regular and included officials such as Mrs. Hall, Sanderson, Smith, and Knoff. By the end of June, there were 239 colonists at the Port Angeles site, mostly from Washington, the Middle West, and Greeley. There were two other "arrivals"; the colony recorded its first birth on 29 April and a second on 8 June. By fall there were reportedly four hundred persons on the site.[21]

The arrival in Port Angeles was vivid and memorable. Six-year-old Madge Haynes had come with her family from Greeley in a cramped railway car heated by a stove at one end. After a brief stay in Seattle, they embarked on the final leg of their journey:

> The only transportation to Port Angeles then was a little steamer "Dispatch," which went from Seattle to Neah Bay and back, taking a week for the trip.
> Eventually we stopped at Old Dungeness. Captain Morgan left the boat to go up and have a sociable drink and a game of poker. The game lasted all night, and meanwhile the tide went out, leaving the ferry [sic] slowly tilting over on one side. Mother stowed us all away in bunks for the night, however, the tide returned in the morning and righted the boat, and so did Captain Morgan. He tooted the whistle, and we pulled out for Port Angeles.[22]

Many of the colonists who arrived in Port Angeles lodged temporarily at David W. Morse's hotel. Some of the newcomers never did move to the colony, although they participated in its meetings. An intense rivalry shortly developed between the West End, as the older Port Angeles came to be called, and the East End, the colony. The original trail between the settlements was along the beach, but that first summer colonists cut a road up the gulch and through thick timber.[23]

There was much to be done. The aim was to give every new arrival "shelter, food and occupation"; men and women were busy as loggers, blacksmith, carpenters, surveyors, shoemaker, plowers and planters, cooks, and waiters. Laborers were clearing land, planting crops along the creek, bringing logs down the hill, and erecting buildings. A mill brought from Seattle provided crudely finished lumber. By early June several buildings were completed or under construction. Temporary sheds and shops appeared.[24]

The first achievements were creditable. By late summer the sawmill had turned out about 250,000 feet of lumber and had demonstrated the capacity to saw 20,000 feet a day. Most finished lumber went for colony needs; some was sold. A planer and a scantling machine were installed, but the shingle and lath machine which had been purchased had not yet arrived. One gang was cutting shingle bolts. Beach logs provided the first wood, but some 250,000 feet of new-cut timber awaited sawing alongside the mill. A tramway road under survey would bring additional timber from a logging camp still under construction. Still, the mill failed to satisfy needs, and about twenty-five tents were set up. As fall approached, settlers who could not wait for the mill lumber began to construct private temporary housing.[25]

Bricks were another potential construction material. Lorenzo T. Haynes experimented with beach sand and local clay, and a kiln near the wharf produced "100,000 fine bricks" that summer. Plans for a machine shop were under way, and trustees ordered construction of "a blacksmith and wagon makers shop, a tin and shoemakers shop, a butcher shop and stables, all badly needed. Platforms for moving and storing lumber, a dry house, wharf and other improvements are very pressing necessities at the mill site."[26]

Meanwhile, John M. Grant, a trustee, used stock from his Tacoma nursery to start a garden and greenhouse along the creek. By August this garden was providing "vegetables of many kinds, such as potatoes, beans, currants, cabbage, etc.; work in abundance for men and women." At first fishermen caught only dogfish, which provided no food although the oil was useful to the fledgling logging industry. An expedition south to Hood Canal to catch and salt down salmon was more successful.[27]

If editor Hall is to be believed, work was performed in a cheerful and optimistic spirit. A week after her arrival she wrote:

> ... I cannot forbear to speak of the general air of cheerful content that is shown by all the people here. The men go about their work and apply themselves diligently at whatever is given them to do by the directors, and when the eight hours, which constitutes a days work is done, they show good results of their labor.
>
> The women, so far as I know, submit cheerfully to the deprivations necessary in a new location, where all the conveniences of life are yet to be made or otherwise procured.

Nevertheless, a group of Ohioans arriving a few weeks later decried the insufficient housing and the futility of trying to build new homes fast enough.[28]

As the colony faced its first winter, accomplishments were offset by obvious weaknesses. Expenses were not borne evenly.

Less than a third of the money subscribed had been received. Yet, Smith wrote that most of those who had come had put in all they had, often several times their pledge. Expenses were nearly two hundred dollars a day, "a very heavy drain upon our finances." There was a growing realization that overselling the colony may have attracted too many people too soon. Eventually, leaders would try to prevent persons from coming until called, but the first objections were merely plaintive. "It is the workers that we want at present," wrote the head of the public works department, "men who understand the handling of ax, pick and shovel, and who do not shrink to do hard work of any kind."[29]

Soon there was dissension. A Seattle printer and organizer for the Knights of Labor, John J. Knoff, had become first president of the colony. The property was purchased in his name, and he had arrived on the same day as George Venable Smith, his wife and two children coming a few weeks later. But the ensuing three months dampened his enthusiasm and ended his participation. With a dozen followers, Knoff returned to Seattle where he denounced the colony, its program, and its leader. Decrying "scheming" and secret decisions made by the "Smith crowd," Knoff reported widespread disillusionment and called the movement "nothing more than a land speculating scheme by Smith." The *Model Commonwealth* promptly responded to "MR. KNOFF'S MELANGE OF LIES," but the facade of harmony was broken. Ominous signs of internal strain had appeared in this Puget Sound utopia.[30]

The experiment was designed to enable laboring men to produce and distribute goods on a cooperative basis, dividing profits among themselves rather than siphoning them off to owners or managers. At the same time the workers would create a model community for themselves and future generations. From the beginning, the plan had hallmarks of a land promotion. The test of its success would be whether the general cooperative spirit would prevail or a power struggle would develop, and whether land sales would harmonize with over-all development or speculation would dominate. The final test would be whether the colony could endure.

Colony government was never as democratic as its promoters

implied. Officers had extensive control over colony affairs. Stockholders could only approve basic policy and elect and remove trustees, while dues-paying members had little more than the right of expression. The founding convention issued a Declaration of Principles and bylaws. In twenty-six clauses, the Declaration of Principles dealt with basic philosophy, and also governed the conduct of members and of business. On a referendum the first summer, members were directed to accept the Declaration, "else they cannot be considered colonists, because these principles are the test of our entire co-operative union and basis of first action." [31]

Members had more choice on the bylaws, which defined the responsibilities of governing bodies. Objections were permitted and amendments offered, but discussion was scant. One voter who questioned overcentralization and the power of officials obtained partial and evasive answers from President Smith. The Declaration of Principles and the bylaws were approved almost unanimously. [32]

Colony affairs were directed and managed by an eleven-man board of trustees, which was empowered to create subordinate officers, agents, and committees. The president headed the board but was chosen separately by the stockholders, who elected the remaining ten trustees from among themselves. Trustees served three-year overlapping terms, with three or four members elected annually. The president was general manager of the colony. He could call special meetings and vote upon all matters; he signed official instruments, withdrew checks and warrants, and made appointments subject to approval by the board. Generally he oversaw the affairs of the colony and performed whatever duties the board might assign.

The secretary handled recording, registering, and reporting, and supervised accounts; the treasurer was responsible for funds and their disbursement. Each of the trustees was also the overseer of an executive department, although this arrangement was not specified in the bylaws. These executive departments had stated responsibliities in the areas of finance, public works, law, public utilities, public safety, commerce, manufactures, education, agriculture, and health. Trustees could establish additional departments or alter or transfer functions of existing ones. Although annual board reports were required and records were always open, the general membership had little control over the organization or its officials. Those who did not agree with the adopted bylaws could resign and withdraw money invested, but only upon specified terms and advance notice.

One egalitarian feature was that trustees were to receive the same monthly wages as "the highest skilled mechanic, who is a resident colonist, and that he [the official] be required to do some labor." The president alone was allowed expenses and was exempt from performing other labor. The board, however, could extend special monetary awards for "skills, merit or inventive genius in any member," including, presumably, themselves. And the bylaws specifically granted five thousand dollars in stock and lot interests to George Venable Smith "in consideration of, and for past services rendered and money expended. . . ." After the first election, trustees and the president were required to have lived at least one year at the colony site.[33]

The original board, chosen in May 1887, was to serve only until October, when permanent trustees would be selected. Smith, however, had been granted a five-year term as president. Stockholders were to convene in Port Angeles on 13 September for nominations, with elections set for 23 September. Distant stockholders objected to the requirement of being present to vote, and a dispute erupted over proxy voting. The *Model Commonwealth* rationalized that persons not on the site would be unfamiliar with candidates' qualifications and that Washington corporation laws provided for proxy votes; so they would be honored. But absent stockholders were cautioned to take care to whom proxies were sent.[34]

Although candidates were not supposed to solicit nominations or election, campaigning and criticisms of incumbents appeared early. In July, Trustee Louis Williams warned of a tendency toward office seeking. A fellow trustee, William Beck, in declining to run for reelection, called for leaders "who are not so self important as to utterly disregard the opinions of others, who are equal in authority and responsibility. . . . There has been inharmony on the board ever since all Trustees arrived on the townsite. . . . We all know how contemptible chronic office-seekers make themselves upon the outside. Shall we allow such characters to control us here? I hope not."[35]

Thirty persons were nominated, and the general election brought changes in the board. President Smith, as candidate for trustee, led the count with 257 votes. Frank McGill, active earlier but not a board member, was elected, as were E. B. Mastick, Jr., M. C. Dwight, and Julius E. Krueger. Three incumbents were defeated and, with Beck, were replaced. Well down the list was John Knoff, whose departure may have been triggered by this rebuff. Of interest is the rise of Mastick, who had recently become business manager of the *Model Commonwealth*, and of Krueger. Both men would become major figures in the colony.[36]

At "simple and unassuming" ceremonies on 3 October, the new board was installed. Absent were Mrs. Wood, who continued to live in Seattle, and Dwight, a Chicago physician expected shortly. In a shuffling of duties, Smith added the department of public works to his responsibilities, and Mastick headed the department of commerce.[37]

But this reorganization changed neither the leadership nor the dominant group. More far-reaching dissension was growing among the workers, who were chafing at their lack of influence. One discussion concerned the selection and control of department foremen. A plan to choose the foremen through both examinations and election by the workers in each division was never practiced. Trustee Francis Hinckley argued that foremen should be appointed by department heads "who can be impartial judges of efficient and good men. It is not wise to give [that power] to unexperienced boys and men who may take a dislike to a foreman simply because he *is* efficient and will not allow shirking or poor work the right to combine against such foremen and elect a new one."[38] He complained that a "chronic habit of fighting" prevailed. Calling Hinckley's statement "arrogant and incongruent," a colonist implied that trustees, despite colony rulings, gained big wages while laboring men drew less, and that leaders stultified free discussions of ideas: "Because a man holds different views from the management he is selfish; because he will not acquiesce in everything some Trustee or foreman says, he is selfish; because he does not believe in a subsidized press he is selfish; because he will not kick down two trustees that have been calumniated, buffeted and filled with reproaches, he is selfish;

because he will not say 'Yes' to everything the management say or do." [39]

In February 1888, when Smith had been east seeking funds to construct a logging railroad, the dissidents maneuvered to unseat him and his associates. Gallup and Mastick led several other trustees in resignations from the board. Harmony, progress, and success, they argued, were unattainable without major changes. Mastick, Sanderson, and Dr. Dwight sought the resignation of all trustees and an investigation by a special board. When the faction leaders failed to resolve the deadlock, a closed meeting of foremen and workers demanded a reorganized board, and their action brought results. Although five trustees from the rebel faction declined to run, twenty-two candidates were nominated for the eleven positions. George Venable Smith was among those eliminated. In accordance with the wishes expressed, the retiring board met on 9 March and was reconstituted by alternate resignations and appointments. The new board was headed by Fred R. Thompson as president and Thomas Maloney as secretary. [40]

To the victors, theirs was the triumph of practical men over theorists. Integral cooperation was not wrong, they contended, but realistic measures had become obscured by theory and propaganda. Nonworkers had been attracted to the site, then left to fend for themselves. Too many tradesmen had come instead of the "farmers, woodsmen and fishermen [needed] to develop the industries indigenous to this country." Newcomers were disheartened when the refinements they expected turned out to be only goals. Many had left, but intelligent management could draw them back. The colony idea, the location, the property, the starts made were assets that new leaders could build upon. With an additional thousand dollars, debts could be paid and the logging railroad finished. The board claimed "non partisan" support from the former trustees and urged colonists to heal differences and move forward. [41]

Many of the former leaders stayed nearby and kept an interest in the colony. Bidding farewell, former president Smith confirmed that new good feeling and harmony prevailed, although he denied that conditions were as serious as his opponents had claimed. To him, the problem was that most colony assets were in land, and profits could not be realized quickly. The colony's founder made one final appeal for continued assistance from distant sympathizers, but the new directors had already determined to cease propaganda efforts and to concentrate on local development. [42]

George Venable Smith opened a law practice in Port Angeles, shortly becoming probate judge and then prosecuting attorney. He was Port Angeles city attorney for many years before his death there on 1 October 1919, at the age of seventy-six. His ambitions as a developer of cooperatives had lingered, for in 1893 he issued a pamphlet proposing *A Co-operative Plan for Securing Homes and Occupations at Port Angeles, Washington.* Mrs. Hall stayed on and Francis Hinckley also remained in Port Angeles, where he was soon a Republican office seeker, embarrassed by his reputation as a radical. [43]

Despite promises, the new colony leaders made no immediate alterations in the government. With further individual changes in the board, leadership centered around Mastick, Thomas Maloney, and Herman Culver, who became president in October 1888. The firm but friendly Culver seemed to promise respite from past antagonisms, but it was Maloney who would dominate future affairs. Energetic and many-sided, this native New Yorker had grown up in Indiana and attended a Quaker college in Michigan. He was homesteader, editor, farmer, mining prospector, and contractor in the Middle West and Southwest before moving to Tacoma in 1885 and then to the colony. Politically he was Greenbacker, Populist, and eventually a prominent Democrat in Washington and Arizona. [44]

These men broadened colony enterprises. Real estate transactions, construction, and experiments with the wage system were initiated in succeeding months. Such changes of direction during 1888 would fundamentally alter the philosophy and the history of the colony.

The opening paragraph of the Declaration of Principles described social as well as political objectives: ". . . to establish a system which will foster and secure ethical culture, correct and progressive life in all grades of society, without class distinctions or special privileges or advantages to any one and to secure to all comfortable homes and the blessings of home-life under all its most-favored conditions as keystone of human happiness." Early propaganda reveled in anticipation of comfortable homes, libraries, and other evidences of the good life: "Social Palaces" one page was headed.[45]

Prospective colonists who arrived by water first encountered a long, two-story, wooden structure with "East End Hotel" painted above the main door. One tenant tempered his dream of the ideal with an acceptance of reality. On the beach there was, he wrote,

what we call a hotel, it is a building 25 x 75 feet in size, merely a rough shell. In this building cooking is done for about one hundred people, here we eat our meals, those of us who choose to board, instead of keeping house by ourselves, we have seven long tables in this dining room, and . . . if every person in the United States has as good, starvation will never be heard of on this continent. Around this "hotel" we have about twenty tents in which families are making their homes, some keeping house, and others coming in the house to board. [46]

Communal houses, hotels, kitchens, and dining rooms never developed beyond initial stages, but the cluster of buildings near the beach provided some taste of communal life.

A two story building 40 x 60 feet in size—built of upright boards contains on the lower floor, the printing office and general offices, and the public hall; the upper floor is divided by board partitions, into rooms, which are occupied by several families. This is not our ideal associated home, and were it not for future possibilities would be extremely unpleasant, but this like the tents is only a place for the time being and is therefore endurable. Another two story building 28 x 100 feet in size, of a better and more permanent character, is under course of construction. The upper floor of this building will be divided into living rooms for families, for this winter, two other houses in which several families live, is all we have at present at the eastern side of our townsite.[47]

Four or five small private dwellings bordered the gardens along the creek. In November, the Cyrus Armbrusts, late of Greeley, Colorado, moved into the first house built on the bluff, a cozy home among stumps with a beautiful view of the strait. The model community never developed beyond these starts. [48]

The colony set few membership qualifications and left decisions on admittance to the board of trustees. Each member was expected only to be "devoted to the principles of Integral or Entire Co-operation and the plans and principles set forth. . . ."[49]

The Alfred Ware family had left England about 1870 and lived in Canada before Ware became chief draughtsman for the Northern Pacific Railroad in Milwaukee. Railroad construction brought him to Yakima and then to Tacoma, which he left to move to the colony as chief engineer in 1887. Dr. Freeborn S. Lewis received his M.D. in Detroit in 1874 and practiced in the Middle West before taking a position with the Burlington Railroad. As colony physician, he brought his family to Port Angeles in September 1887. John Henson operated shoe stores in St. Louis, and Alexander Mason had kept a hotel in Ohio. John M. Grant had owned a large nursery which offered a popular Sunday outing for Tacomans. Others were skilled tradesmen. W. W. Maltby and Harvey Pellerin were carpenters. "Mr. [Elliot] Beaumont was a first class machinist and . . . interested in mining," and L. D. Stewart was architect and builder. Critics recognized that an overproportion of professional men and skilled artisans was disadvantageous if there were insufficient laborers, farmers, and woodsmen. [50] Yet Smith, Maloney, Knoff, Sanderson, Dr. Dwight, and several others had professional backgrounds.

The number of nonworkers, especially women and children, caused concern. Although some fathers came before their families, there was dismay at the many children who contributed little but who required housing, food, and schooling. A list of residents published in the *Model Commonwealth* on 1 July 1887 may indicate general ratios. Although almost half of the 239 persons present were men over 21, a few were elderly or unable to work. Seventy-three residents were under sixteen, including thirty-four children under six. There were forty-eight women, twenty-one and over, and only ten young people between the ages of sixteen and twenty who might have been considered productive. One might wonder at the welcome received by the Ohio parents who brought their twelve children.[51]

Officials repeatedly warned members not to come until called. In July, Smith mused that: "Much of the enthusiasm for pioneer life is based upon romance rather than a realization of its hardships." He even saw value in the "rather disparaging" complaints of a departed invalid couple, for they might discourage the "weak-kneed" and the "drones." The board authorized a fifty-dollar fine and rejection of any subscriber who arrived to claim labor and support before being officially called.[52]

One ideal prospective colonist might have been J. B. Pritchett, who wrote from Applegate, Oregon: "I would like to join your colony and will, if I can see my way clear; am a blacksmith by trade; have followed repairing and running machinery. I am at present engaged in fitting up a hydraulic mine which I am interested in. I like to wrestle with Nature's forces, but it seems like putting one's knowledge to poor use—washing away land that would make homes for the needy." [53]

It was assumed but not stated that members would be Caucasian; nothing indicates that persons of other origins applied. Reflecting western labor attitudes and its Seattle origins, the colony paper denounced the Chinese in articles and editorials. Advertisements carried the notation "White Labor," and an appeal from a Seattle cigarmakers union local asked, "Who shall be victorious, the Chinese leper or the Honest American Citizen? We . . . apply to the public and place them to decide whether Chinese filthy scab cigars shall be used in this Territory or Cigars made by honest white men who do not send to China for their Clothing, etc., but leave their money at home and live as God intended them to live." [54] The paper recounted with satisfaction a visit by Governor Semple, who entered the kitchen of a competitive hotel in Port Angeles to place his breakfast order. Discovering a Chinese cook, the indignant governor "went back and told his friends he proposed to go to the Colony Hotel, he would not patronize a house that employed Mongolians." [55]

More commonplace were Indians, for a Clallam village was just across Ennis Creek from the colony. Soon after the colonists arrived at Port Angeles, the *Model Commonwealth* reported:

The East End looked like a large soldiers camp on Monday night. The Indians returning from potlatch at Clallam Bay, had come to our shores to spend the night. There were eleven large canoes of them, each canoe holding several families, and the occupants of each had their own tent, it was interesting for colonists lately arrived from the east to go from one tent to the other and watch the dusky visitors, as they were hudled [sic] together around their camp fires baking their evening meal. They left in the early morning while most of us were still in the land of dreams. [56]

Indians provided color as their canoes beached near the colony to bring in fish. Chief Norman was long remembered for his great "potlatch," with a ceremonial fire, Indian dances, and canoes that had come long distances around the inland waters. Occasionally Indians sold fish, clams, or fruit to colonists and townspeople. During the hop-picking season distant tribes stopped en route to fields on the lower sound and on their return they bought provisions at community stores. Yet there were few solid contacts as each group went its way. Early colony leaders informed newspaper readers that the "beach lands, which six months ago were the habitation of Indians only, now hums with the voices of nearly 300 people ... when the neighboring Indians in their numerous canoes came, as they were long accustomed, to land, found no place to pitch their tents as of yore, looked and wondered for awhile and then moved on, only a remnant remaining." Thus Indians were mostly a curiosity. Obviously apart from the colony, they were neither a hindrance nor worthy of serious attention.[57]

But women's rights were not ignored. The American crusade was forty years old in the 1800s; women could vote in several states and territories. In 1887 Washington Territory ended a four-year experiment giving women suffrage. The colony's liberal attitude toward women's rights was stated in the Declaration of Principles: "That the emancipation of women from the slavery of domestic drudgery and narrow opportunities shall be our first care, and to see that she may be given useful and pleasant opportunities suitable to her sex, freed from the conditions which circumscribe her opportunities and deny her equitable rights and just rewards for services rendered."[58] The bylaws stipulated that "he" included the feminine, and they specifically allowed women the "privilege" of working a full day with pay equal to a man's. Women could vote in colony matters and hold office. The first board of trustees included Nellie Wood, treasurer, and Laura Hall, editor of the *Model Commonwealth* and superintendent of education. In Seattle, Mrs. Hall had participated in a movement of women to activate reforms with their recently won franchise. Involved in later efforts to regain suffrage, she became state vice president of the Society for Equal Suffrage. Other former colony women held local political offices. Mrs. Minerva E. Troy, daughter of Dr. Lewis, was among the first Washington women to run for the United States House of Representatives. Yet the colony apparently took no stand on woman suffrage generally, nor, for that matter, on other large political issues. And the women who participated in colony affairs were greatly outnumbered by men.[59]

Marriage, said the Declaration of Principles, was "the moral and physical foundation of the home, and the anchor of stable upright conduct." Although heavy burdens were "almost crushing it under prevailing social conditions," marriage was sacred, "and every man should have one wife and every woman one husband and no more."

Yet, the Puget Sound Co-operative Colony was accused of being a free-love colony. A few members, including certain leaders, provided ground for this reputation, although they denied promiscuity, considering themselves to have accepted marriage responsibilities without formal pledges. Several divorces and remarriages took place among colonists. Mrs. Hall divorced a Seattle judge and married Charles Peters, a colonist from Texas, in 1886. More sensational was the divorce of the George Venable Smiths and Mrs. Smith's immediate remarriage to Norman R. Smith. Here was a younger, more dashing man stealing the wife of the father figure who had founded the colony. The Norman Smiths moved to California, soon to return to Port Angeles; in 1890 George V. Smith married Ione Tomlinson, the colony schoolteacher.[60]

Yet there was little to indicate moral looseness. One member later recalled: "Like all movements that are antagonistic to the profit system the Colony had its detractors and calumnists. Among its almost 500 members there were several divorces (perhaps 5 or 6), these people all married others shortly after, and lived conventionally the rest of their lives. But in the small and close community, this gave rise to malicious gossip, and an excuse to its enemies of calling it a 'free love' colony."[61]

In other matters, the colony professed an almost puritanical concern for the morality of members. The Declaration of Principles enunciated "That our mission is peace and useful example to mankind. Each of us must be courteous to all, be plain but artistic in dress, correct in speech, modest in conduct and our teachings should be pronounced in the deportment of our every day life one with another and our courtesy and fair dealing with the world." Everyone was expected to "act as a civilized being;

... avoid excesses; be just, respectful and undeceiving to all."
Intoxication and the sale of liquors offered grounds for dismissal,
as did "indecency, immorality, rebellion to the objects and
purposes of the colony, and dishonesty. . . . " Gambling, lotteries,
and "occupations, of a questionable character" were likewise
prohibited. Yet nothing indicates that colony fathers, busy with
other matters, acted against violations.

Skeptics viewed the colony as a haven for agnostics, atheists,
and freethinkers. Although no religion was established, there was a
willingness to provide worship and religious opportunity in a
nonsectarian atmosphere. "In the matter of conscience, belief of
religion," stated the Declaration of Principles, "such liberality of
sentiment should prevail that the private religious opinion of each
should be respected by all." Halls would be open for discussions of
all creeds, but regular clergy and church establishments were
prohibited. Nevertheless, religious groups did organize. From
colony Sunday schools the First Congregational Church of Port
Angeles and later the First Methodist Church developed. Colonists
also established Baptist and Episcopal churches in Port Angeles.
There were probably no Roman Catholics among colonists, but
there were a few Jews, and several members were Spiritualists.[62]

Values of a society may be reflected in the extent of its
concern with education. The Declaration of Principles spoke of
the "education and the moral and material welfare of our
children" and called for "public nurseries for children, kindergarten, eclectic, industrial and ethical schools as rapidly and to as
advantageous a scale as the public funds will permit." The colony
hoped to emulate the kindergartens and nurseries of the Guise
Familistrie in France, which sought mental and moral development. In place of sectarian training there would be opportunities
to learn a trade or "useful calling."[63]

Such ideals faded with the realization that almost a third of the
population was under sixteen. Nevertheless, colonists impelled
expansion of local educational facilities. Port Angeles had a school
as early as 1865, but the school population had declined to only
fourteen by 1887 when the sudden influx of colony people
created unexpected pressures. Colonists rather than the local

district moved to provide facilities. In August Miss Tomlinson, an experienced teacher, started a kindergarten for twenty-five children between the ages of three and eight; afternoon school sessions were held for older children. Official colony support was given grudgingly: "A school house will be built as soon as time will permit; houses for shelter, must come first in order." The school at the colony site lasted only two years, until Central School was built in Port Angeles. Meanwhile the election of three colonists to the Port Angeles school board in November 1887 foresaw that "the colony could have things just about its own way." Although these schools did not attempt political or social indoctrination, the schooling had innovations. The kindergarten was believed to be the first in Washington, and the colony added adult education programs and trade training. The first August, classes were announced in natural history, mathematics, vocal music, and elocution. Although A. E. Sanderson claimed seventy enrollees in his nightly elocution classes, the venture soon withered. Such attempts suggest that the colony might have innovated further with a longer life span. [64]

The broadening of man's interests and mind was part of the original design: "Large libraries, reading rooms and lectures and music halls will be furnished," the Seattle *Daily Call* had stated. About a dozen books formed the scant nucleus for a library, and a lecture-discussion group was established. The latter provided a platform for President Smith to enunciate his ideas, a forum for discussions of socialism and other timely topics, and a stage for musical offerings and readings. Rarely, a visiting speaker appeared. Samuel Putnam of New York stopped during a lecture tour and spoke on "The Ideal Republic" to a crowd he praised as "adventurous reformers in this remote corner of the world." [65] Late in 1887, a twenty-two member band was organized, and then Pioneer Theater, the first theater in Clallam County. This was the forerunner of things to come, for in its declining days the colony constructed the Opera House at the West End, a gingerbread structure that remained the center of Port Angeles social and cultural life for three decades. [66]

Strictly social events had been held since the Seattle days. President Smith's daughter recalled that at the colony the "grown people had some kind of entertainment every night the first year, mostly dances in the cook house dining hall, later the Potlatch was built. . . ." Potlatch Hall, so named because the material and labor were donated, held most social and intellectual activities. During one week in October 1887, the paper described a dance to honor persons leaving for the winter, a ball club, a camp fire, an amateur theatrical class, and donations for the library. A few colonists, however, viewed such things as unnecessary and frivolous. Dancing was a dangerous pleasure that "makes us forget the graveness of our undertakings," warned one. [67]

Critics who doubted the patriotism of these radicals would have been reassured by the Fourth of July festivities in 1887, the "largest celebration ever witnessed in Clallam County." Music, readings, dinner, games, running and sailing races, were followed by an evening concert and dancing. There was propaganda as well. A reading of the Declaration of Independence prompted comparisons between the young nation and this struggling colony. A highlight was the presentation of a Massachusetts newspaper from 1776 that pictured "four coffins representing the first four martyrs of the revolutionary cause in America. . . . The paper will be framed in a double glass frame in order that it may be read on both sides, and at the same time be preserved." [68]

But colonists were concerned less with former revolutions than with current crusades. Like radicals the world over, these followed the fortunes of the Chicago anarchists condemned to death after the Haymarket riot. When the four men were executed, the *Model Commonwealth* appeared bordered in black. "Murder Most Foul," it editorialized. Alongside news columns appeared letters from the prisoners renouncing clemency. A box covering half the front page was conspicuous:

OBITUARY

DIED AT CHICAGO

NOV. 11th, 1887

FREE SPEECH!!!

FREE SPEECH!!!

Rights of Americans peaceably to Assemble and Discuss their Grievances!!!
Rights of Americans Against Unreasonable Search and Seizure
Without Warrants!!!
Rights of Americans to a Fair Trial and Impartial Jury!!!

FOR THESE WE MOURN!!! [69]

A local history labeled this action the "ugliest scar" on the reputation of Port Angeles and denied that it reflected general colonists' views, blaming it on Venier Voldo, foreman of the paper. But the *Model Commonwealth* reported that George Venable Smith, Voldo, and others denounced the executions before a packed indignation meeting "in the light of justice and the Constitutional rights of American citizens." Resolutions proclaimed that the crucial issue was the rights of all Americans, not anarchism, and ordered the *Model Commonwealth* to be draped in mourning. Such concern and the critical reaction from conservatives might have been anticipated.[70]

Many persons were drawn to the colony by promises of social welfare and care "from the cradle to the grave." The prospective member was promised work, living accommodations, and insurance benefits, with special provisions for orphans, widows, and the elderly. The insurance plans, in which a percentage of profits would provide for individual needs and which promised an annuity to those who had worked in the colony for twenty-five years, never materialized. A healthy, clean city with a doctor available was also envisioned. A department of health would be responsible for "medicine, surgery, pharmacy, hygiene, commissariat and baths," and a sanitary division created. But the colony discovered early that it would have to charge for attendance by the sanitary division and for doctors' calls from outside the colony. Nevertheless, a person injured while doing colony work received free nursing care and a continuation of his wages.

The first colony physician arrived in June, but his official practice was short-lived, and he was replaced by Dr. Freeborn S. Lewis, who soon practiced to the entire county. The politically active Lewis became Port Angeles postmaster in 1915 and later mayor. Dr. M. C. Dwight was briefly a colony trustee, and in 1888 a homeopathic physician arrived in a group of colonists. Perhaps as important was "Auntie" Mackay, nurse and midwife. The widowed mother of five children, three of whom died young, she had given the others up for adoption before coming to the colony. The end of a brief, unhappy remarriage—hers was the first colony wedding—left her alone again, and for many years this "quaint little elderly lady with bright sparkling eyes and a friendly smile" nursed the ill and assisted at births in colony and community.[71]

This closely knit settlement escaped the epidemics that sometimes threatened communal living experiments, but there were illnesses, injuries, and deaths. Great misfortune touched the family of Paul Land, whose wife, Luella, died four days after giving birth to their third daughter. This was the first colony death, and the large funeral presided over by "Father" Alexander Mason included a eulogy from President Smith. A few weeks later the newborn baby, named for her mother, also died. That autumn Paul Land officiated at the burial of "Father" Mason. Seventy-four and long in ill health, Mason was a founder of the colony and its most venerable personage.[72]

As an experiment in communal living, the Puget Sound Co-operative Colony never got started. The first months were hurry and hustle and crowded living conditions, and even the most devoted colonists succumbed to the attraction of owning private property in rejuvenated Port Angeles. Social contributions and accomplishments centered on the caliber of persons drawn. Because of the colony, Port Angeles developed with a nucleus of citizens already welded together with common interests and directions.

Plans for trade and industry were ambitious. In time such ventures would extend in directions the founders did not foresee: to land sales and construction in adjacent Port Angeles. Of earliest importance were activities that met immediate colony needs, such as lumbering, brickmaking, and agriculture.

During the first summer, sawmill equipment was installed on the beach just west of the "hotel." Each day brought progress in the mill construction. The smokestack was erected one Tuesday in August; on Wednesday belts were put into place and the boilers filled with water; perhaps if the boilers could be bricked in, the mill would be working by Saturday. A ditch brought water from the creek, and initial operations began. "The first log was sawed in our mill on Friday last; it was found necessary to make some readjustments in machinery and gearing, but it is working now satisfactorily. Our day of waiting for lumber is a thing of the past; as we look out of our window we see sheeting which has been sawed by our mill, being placed upon the roof of the new building. . . ."[73] Although it was working, the mill consisted only of machinery and framework which was never completely enclosed. The cutting capacity was estimated at thirty thousand feet of lumber a day, a goal never realized. The colonists hoped to extend the wharf and build a breakwater to enclose a logging pond.

Property behind the colony was purchased for its timber. By September, 77 acres above the bluff had been slashed and 113,000 feet of logs were in the boom awaiting milling. It was hoped that the lumber derived would pay for the land. Meanwhile President Smith recommended spending five thousand dollars to purchase over a thousand acres of "fine timber lands" adjoining the colony, land containing cedar, red fir, and "other first class varieties of timber." In an hour and a half colonists subscribed almost half the cost. An expansion of the logging and lumber potential, this action was also the first move toward acquiring land for purposes other than direct colony development.

A logging camp was built on the most distant property, and a tramway road constructed to bring the logs down. A year later the road was gravelled so as to enable larger loads. By now lumber was also for sale, with the colony sloop delivering cedar to Seattle. Hopes were so optimistic that stock was offered in the Port Angeles and West Railroad Company, a logging road organized by Grant and Maloney. But competition from larger, less isolated mills thwarted sales on the outside market. Several times the mill was leased to private parties, but financial difficulties forced its return to colony hands, the first time as early as June 1889. Ultimately, the mill was destroyed by fire during the period of colony receivership. During its existence, it had provided lumber, laths, shingles, and shakes for colony buildings and for other construction in the area. [74]

The colony's most unique enterprise was the building of the steamship *Angeles*. At the outset the colonists needed boats for fishing, transportation, and trade: "When we first came here, in May last, the colony was the happy owner of one skiff—at present our fleet, consists of the sloop *August*, one fishing schooner, three large and one small fishing skiffs, a scow, the before-mentioned skiff—and a skiff is now on the ways, which will be finished this present week, besides these boats, there are three or four belonging to private parties." [75] The role of the *August* is suggested by its activities in a single week. On 13 July it brought lumber from Port Townsend; on the fifteenth and sixteenth it traveled to the mouth of the Elwha River and back with household goods; two days later it took President Smith to Port Townsend on business. Mainstay of the fishing fleet, it was also seen as the "entering wedge" for trade in lumber, shingles, tinwares, and household goods throughout the sound.[76]

Organized by Krueger and others, colony members and outsiders subscribed forty-two hundred dollars worth of stock to construct a propeller-driven steam schooner. The necessary machinery was purchased; lumber and labor came from the colony. Completed in April 1889, the vessel was fifty-eight feet, five inches long with a seventeen-foot, seven-inch beam. Named after her home port, the *Angeles* plied the inland waters for many years before being abandoned in 1920. The *Angeles* was the first of many early ships built at Port Angeles but the only such achievement of the colony itself. Later ships were constructed by colony members, most notably Fred and John Thompson, brothers who launched the *Lydia Thompson* at Port Angeles in 1892 and whose later steamship company served passengers and shipping out of Seattle for several years.[77]

Other construction opportunities beckoned. In December 1888, the colony contracted to build a school in Port Angeles, "the first important outside work ever undertaken by this company . . . a step in the direction this company should have taken long ago. . . ." The colony constructed homes for former colonists and newcomers in Port Angeles as well as the First Congregational Church, the Catholic Church, the first office building, and the Opera House. [78]

The colony claimed that the absence of a profit motive was an advantage in competitive bidding because profits were split among the workers; no employers were "pocketing the surplus." Actually, the incursion into commercial competition was prompted partly because the wage and labor system of the colony was becoming more, rather than less, like that in the outside business world. Colony founders cherished the belief that labor, not capital, was the foundation of the economy. As each worker assumed those tasks for which he was best fitted and as cooperation replaced competition, individual efforts and colony profits were expected to increase. Although capital was necessary, dividends were considered a form of wages, and it was agreed that "wages" for labor and for capital would be the first payments taken from the profits. Additional profits, not to exceed 50 percent, were for general expenses and colony improvements.[79]

All workers, including officers, were covered by a sliding wage scale based upon present outside costs and upon "quality, quantity, and consumption of human energy." Wages received for eight hours' work were divided into three categories—one scale from $3.25 to $4.25, the next from $2.25 to $3.25, and the lowest at $2.25. The foreman of each department would determine the scale for individual workers, with appeals taken to the board of trustees. Additional rewards could be granted by the board. Minors between sixteen and twenty received half pay, except that those "capable of performing the work of an adult" merited full salaries. The work day was eight hours for men and six for women, with extensions only for necessities or emergencies and at proportional overtime pay.[80]

Payment was made with "pay-checks or due-bills" within the colony and based upon specific units of value, coins being reserved for the necessary outside exchanges. Thus colony "scrip" was established. The steel-blue paper was about the size of United States currency, adorned with an eagle and other artistry, its value inscribed in yellow. Smaller denominations were similar to postage stamps. Scrip was actually a promissory note from the colony to pay the bearer on demand with merchandise at any department. When the economic situation of the colony worsened, scrip dropped in value until it was bartered for from ten to twenty cents on the dollar. At least one civil suit against the colony sought redemption of $120 of scrip which had been accepted by a neighbor. Defended by George V. Smith, who was no longer an officer, the colony was ordered to pay in United States coin. Several colonists who were disgruntled with the labor and wage system filed complaints in the local court.[81]

Demands for changes in labor and wage policies were central to colony disputes throughout 1888 and influenced the election of the new board that November. "THE WAGE SYSTEM MUST GO" headlined the colony paper, also under new direction. Secretary Thomas Maloney and two board members proposed to substitute for daily wages a plan based upon the principle "that the toiler is

entitled to a just proportion of his toil." "Every industry should
be based upon the true co-operative plan, of dividing the results at
the close of a quarter or a year among the workers in proportion to
the time of service. . . . If nothing is made in a year, nothing
should be expected. If something is made, it should go to those
who made it, as it properly belongs to them."[82]

Under the new plan, individual work time was reported in
hours, with the foreman allowed to adjust the scale according to
extra efforts or shirking. The foreman's wage scale was 10 percent
more than the service rendered, and the officers' earnings were
scaled by the foreman. Every three months colony earnings would
be divided by the total hours worked, with the quotient becoming
the hourly wage for that quarter. Maloney lauded this "according
to merit" plan as a worthy substitution for the former "dead
level" plan, for it gave each worker what he truly earned. The
secretary only incidentally noted that profits from real estate sales
and increases in land values would now go to the stockholders.
Significantly, Maloney was moving the colony toward real estate
speculation, and he now called for further sales of stock.[83]

But the new wage plan was abandoned before April. Its
flaws came not in theory, the editors claimed, but because man
was accustomed to weekly earnings, and he desired "to saddle the
responsibility of all loss upon the employer. . . ." Although colony
leaders honored the rhetoric of cooperation, they lapsed regularly
into phrases that distinguished worker from employer. The leaders
complained that "we had not been out of slavery long enough to
free ourselves from the old system of selling ourselves for so much
pay."[84]

Neither system spared the colony from litigation. In April
1890, Francis H. Godin demanded $127.10 for materials and labor
for plastering a building in Port Angeles. Other complainants also
sued to receive payment for labor.[85]

The Puget Sound Co-operative Colony had seen land development as an integral role of the colony and its membership. Lot
interests, however, could be sold only to members for their own
homes, were never to be mortgaged, and could be resold only to
colonists. As leadership changed, so did these attitudes. The
"business-like" element believed real estate activity would

strengthen the prosperity of the colony and its members. Lucrative opportunities seemed close by, for Port Angeles was experiencing a land boom accompanied by optimism and speculation common in the Pacific Northwest during the late 1800s.

As early as October 1887, the *Model Commonwealth* advertised 160 lots in the colony's "First Addition to Port Angeles," which straddled Ennis Creek on the high land south and west of the colony. Most lots were 50 by 140 feet; the streets were 70 feet wide and the alleys 20. Prices ranged from $40.00 to $75.00 per lot, with terms of 120 days available without interest and longer periods at 10 percent. Although this was the first real estate addition offered, it was the second one officially filed. Other blocks had been platted between the colony site and the West End settlement. [86]

The plats were probably drawn with the needs of the colony and its original members in mind, but circumstances surrounding the filing with the county auditor are curious. The second plat was notarized on 6 March and filed on 7 March 1888, over the names of President G. V. Smith and Secretary Thomas Maloney. At this time the first great leadership struggle was taking place; on 7 March Smith's opponents called for the paired resignations of the board which took place the next evening. The "First Addition," although advertised the previous October, was not formally filed until May, over the signatures of the new president, Fred R. Thompson, and Maloney, still the secretary. Real estate disputes were likely caught up in the upheavals over colony government and in the rise of leaders who wished to extend business operations. [87]

Real estate ventures increased rapidly. In July the "Puget Sound Cooperative Colony's Subdivision of the Townsite of Port Angeles" was platted on the bluff above the colony. The following January a fourth plat included over nineteen blocks a half mile inland and abutted the southern boundary of the still closed federal reservation. A year later, the *Model Commonwealth* advertised "Edgewood," comprising city lots and five-acre tracts. This was a corner portion of a timber tract owned by the colony a mile inland from the base of Ediz Hook. Clearly, colony leaders had forsaken colonization for full-scale land speculation.[88]

The extent of real estate involvement is suggested by two

financial reports. On 1 April 1889, the secretary listed total resources as $155,161.78, including $124,995 in real estate and $10,355.19 due on notes and mortgages. A year and a half later, the amounts had increased greatly. Total resources were $239,531.61, of which $201,600 was in real estate, with $12,686 due on notes and mortgages. Each report showed a substantial balance of resources above liabilities: $79,569.19 in 1889 and $163,233.90 in 1890. Although these valuations may well have been inflated, it stands that 80 percent of the resources were in real estate. The second report showed that land sales were greater than purchases, but land was an asset only if it could be sold readily when money was needed, or if it contained marketable resources such as timber, or if it could be held for speculation. A newly arrived observer of the colony's demise later noted, "although throughout the Puget Sound area at that time real estate was more or less legal tender in all transactions among the populace it could not buy more beefsteak—unless the much-sought real estate buyer was about when needed."[89]

Much of the 1,896 acres held in 1890 was timbered; the remainder was largely for land developments. Although all but one lot in the "First Addition" had been sold, 385 lots remained in other subdivisions. Standing timber proved difficult to sell, log, or transport before fire destroyed much of it, along with a newly built mill and tramway. The property became a liability. In 1894 the colony receiver found "a large amount of real estate, mostly vacant lands," heavily mortgaged and encumbered by liens.[90]

But in 1889 and 1890 mortgages and debts did not seem so large. Many colonists were enthusiastic about a possible land boom, although others questioned the new speculative activities. Norman R. Smith reappeared to "put in a hard winter of starvation with the members. They had run in debt and the trustees voted me a[s] general manager so that its failure would fall on my shoulders. Ben Mastick and I pulled it through the winter and spring by wiping out the wage lien. We did this by getting every one to take stock for his wage account. By that stroke we wiped out over forty thousand dollars of liabilities. Then we had no trouble getting all the credit we needed."[91]

Smith's pompous evaluation of his efforts was not universal. In February 1890, L. T. Haynes and an alleged majority of stockholders pointedly criticized Smith, Maloney, and Fred Thompson, and sued to dissolve the colony. The case was heard in King County because the local judge was Smith's partner in a sawmill. The complaint charged officials with giving stock to various colonists in return for their proxy votes which elected a new board that had altered the bylaws. The new trustees were accused of appropriating and selling real estate and timber from colony holdings, of leasing the colony store to Thompson for his personal benefit, and of failing to keep accurate public records. Denying these allegations, the defendants claimed that the Haynes group was trying to depreciate real estate values and prevent sales so as to obtain land cheaply for themselves. The defendants claimed to have reduced colony debts drastically in only six months, and they asserted that even Haynes had refused to sell his stock except at an inflated price. This first suit to seek dissolution and receivership was dismissed when the plaintiffs failed to pursue it.[92]

Friction led to factionalism and constant disputes over management of colony properties. Norman R. Smith resigned with presumed sadness and obvious bitterness. "I had no politics for the kind of politics that was rife in the colony." The Haynes faction called the experiment a failure, having "long since discerned that the innate selfishness of the human race, long since acknowledged, can neither be ameliorated or cured by an attempt of the Utopian policy of mutual and unselfish co-operation."[93]

The original ventures were also failing. As early as April 1889, the six colony cows had been sold at auction for $370.75; "a fair price," acknowledged the newspaper, "yet but little over their actual cost." In following weeks other assets, mostly land, were auctioned. Several times the sawmill was leased to private concerns and returned. The brickyard was also leased out, and by May 1892 it had stopped operating. In 1888 the *Model Commonwealth* was leased to colony members, who operated it privately but gave space to colony matters. This was not profitable, and at the end of 1889 the colony severed all connection. A. H. Howell acquired the plant, changed the name of the paper to the *Times*, and moved it to the West End. As important was the departure of colonists. Many moved to former homes or to new ones in the Pacific Northwest, often on property the colony had platted in Port

Angeles, where an interesting, unusual "land rush" was taking place. [94]

Victor Smith's dream of a model city had brought about a government reservation in the 1860s. A later generation viewed the 3,520 acres that remained closed to individual settlement as a hindrance to expansion and sought to occupy and develop the reservation. Prospective owners were urged to move onto surveyed lots as squatters, clear land, and build homes, thereby forcing the federal government to legalize the squatters' claims. Both of the two organizations formed to coordinate the movement and keep it orderly were headed by former colony men, George V. Smith and John Henson. On 4 July 1890, the first rush of people moved in. The scheme proved fruitful, for in eight months squatters officially received rights to their land, although they had to "prove up" their holdings in order to secure clear titles. Most purchased land at the minimum price; remaining lots were sold in a twenty-day auction held by the General Land Office in the Port Angeles Opera House. Amidst ceremony and prolonged excitement, the federal reserve disintegrated and Port Angeles headed toward further development. [95]

Soon Port Angeles became the seat of Clallam County. New land promotions followed, business and professional people arrived, and the city prospered. Then, in the midst of this growth, the Panic of 1893 hit, and many residents moved, leaving behind an expansive, desolate city of buildings and homes dotted amongst vacated properties. [96]

Even during such hardship, the West End was winning over the East End for control of the region, for the colony as such had ceased to exist. One account sets the last full meeting of colonists as early as a Fourth of July picnic in 1889 that was visited by a freak summer snow. Lingering on, the colony resembled a dying business struggling to extricate itself from financial muddles. Much of Maloney's time was spent mortgaging properties and leasing equipment. Occasionally he accepted stock in unstable corporations as collateral, but each attempt seemed to bring further disaster. [97]

Late in 1893, a second suit sought to force a receivership.

Dissatisfied stockholders challenged the machinations of Maloney and the operations of the colony store, now transferred to Port Angeles. Directors were accused of padding the value of merchandise in a mortgage obtained from a Seattle firm. Challenging the $7,079.06 mortgage, the plaintiffs claimed that actual indebtedness was no more than $1,026.29, although additional claims by four directors totaled $3,336.27. The seven thousand dollar mortgage possibly represented an attempt to satisfy the directors' claims. The defendants categorically denied mismanagement and replied that total indebtedness indeed exceeded the smaller amount. Two weeks later the complainants rushed back to court, charging that the inventory was at that very moment being loaded on a ship for Seattle. An injunction halted the action.

The complaint challenged a plan to allow Maloney control of $125,000 worth of unencumbered real estate and securities so that he could pay outstanding debts. For services and expenses Maloney would receive one hundred dollars a month salary. If the indebtedness was not paid by 1 January 1895, the trustees would receive the land for the benefit of creditors. The plaintiffs believed that the colony was insolvent "and that its assets, which under proper management would pay its liabilities and leave a handsome surplus, will be wasted and sacrificed; and that an emergency exists." The defendants replied that lawyers representing a group of unsecured creditors had proposed Maloney's appointment as trustee and would extend the deadline for payment of claims only if Maloney would sell colony property to raise the funds. On 12 January 1894, Judge James McClinton gave judgment for the defendants, citing insufficient facts, a lack of jurisdiction, and the failure of the plaintiffs to respond to the denials made. [98]

But this victory was only a reprieve for the colony. Within two weeks, a simpler complaint was filed by Peter F. Kiernan, a stockholder, who asserted that the colony had long since abandoned its original purpose. A year earlier, Kiernan had received a promissory note from the colony for $504.37, due with interest in thirty days. It had not been paid, and the colony lacked funds to pay except from the sale of real estate. Concurrently the leaders admitted insolvency and agreed to accept a receiver. Declaring the company indebted to about forty thousand dollars, with approximately six thousand dollars totally unsecured, Judge McClinton appointed as receiver R. C. Wilson, a local attorney and political figure recommended by both parties.

Wilson went about untangling finances and properties, and attempted to satisfy claims against the colony. There were eighty-four separate items of real estate, including various properties in the subdivisions. The office building in Port Angeles remained, and a part of the land was leased for a blacksmith shop. Frank McGill now owned the former colony store and leased its property, although he intended to remove the building when that lease expired the next spring. The colony still held the Opera House, its heavily mortgaged equipment, and the property at Ennis Creek, although the sawmill currently was under lease.

Remaining personal property included furniture, Opera House equipment, some construction equipment, and thirteen thousand feet of lumber. There was also the mundane, as a paragraph of the receiver's first inventory indicates: "Letter press, fountain brush, sloping top table; 1 box with doors (base box.); 1 case of books etc. no doors; 1 cabinet with panel doors, pigeon holes, drawers, etc.; 1 handing lamp; 1 glass stand lamp; 2 window shades; 1 axe; 1 dustpan; 1 waste paper basket; 1 gallon oil can; 1 blue print of townsite; 1 cloth map western Washington; 1 cloth map, Port Angeles; 2 paper hooks; 8 upright paper files and 1 Shannon letter file." [99]

Most of the 336 claims against the colony were for less than $100, many less than ten, but the seven over $1,000 included the store invoice ($8,366.64) and claims from once prominent colony figures. There were 196 separate notes and debts. All in all, the receiver estimated total assets at $93,239.91, total liabilities not including capital stock at $55,829.29, with an excess of assets over liabilities at $39,410.62. [100]

Wilson proceeded to sell or salvage what he could, to collect outstanding debts, and to disentangle accounts. During 1894 and for several years thereafter, numerous claims against the colony were filed in superior court. Hoping that land prices would rise, Wilson tried to dispose of land slowly to secure the greatest return, occasionally reporting on his successes. A full decade after his appointment, the receiver made a thirty-page final report, which recounted the final years of the colony and his own frustration.

The organization of the colony, its special purposes as indicated in its name, and its history, while exceedingly interesting, need not be recited in this report. The receiver found simply a corporation organized under the laws of this state, with a large amount of real estate, mostly vacant lands; nearly all encumbered by mortgage to an amount equal to its full value, and the remainder encumbered by liens of judgments. . . ; a lot of notes and securities held by creditors as collateral, a lot of odds and ends of personal property scarcely equal in value to the amount of personal property taxes due from the colony; office fixtures mortgaged to a creditor, and a lot of accounts scattered through five successive ledgers, left uncollected after vigorous efforts to that end under pressure of debts and in view of the winding up of the corporation.[101]

The sawmill, finally sold on foreclosure of the mortgage, had been destroyed by fire. Other properties had also been sold on foreclosure. Store goods had been removed by the mortgagee, and attempts to dispose profitably of large pieces of property proved unsuccessful. A group of Port Angeles citizens tried to raise money to buy the Opera House, but they failed and it was sold. Only then did the buyer learn that the colony lacked full title, and he was forced to buy a remaining half interest. A series of unpleasant incidents frustrated attempts to extract minerals or timber from other lands held:

Mr. Carrigan desired to prospect for coal near the lands of the Colony at Dry Creek, and this receiver, bu [*sic*] order of this Court, executed contracts covering said lands, to Mr. Carrigan. Mr. Carrigan did not find the coal.

The citizens of Port Angeles induced Loggio & Evans to extablish [*sic*] a shingle mill at Dry Creek, and to help the enterprise along the Court ordered the execution of contracts with said Loggio & Evans covering the cedar timber on said Dry Creek lands, the proceeds to be applied on taxes. . . . A small sum had been received when the mill burned down.

It was then proposed to rebuild the plant, using a saw mill that had been used in connection with the shingle mill. Before the plans could be carried out a forest fire burned that mill.

It was then suggested that the lands might be logged and the logs hauled out to the bay over a tram theretofore used by the Port Ageles [*sic*] Mill & Lumber Company. While plans for this scheme were under consideration the forest fire crept up on the tram road and burned that.

It only remains to be added that before the rain came and put out the fire it destroyed a considerable portion of the timber on the lands mentioned.[102]

The receiver's task was further complicated by the facts that securities in other unstable companies had been taken as collateral and there were unclear titles to some properties, including tidelands. A frame building went for taxes. Personal properties were sold or auctioned, with some proceeds going for tax payments. Wilson expressed disappointment that poor bookkeeping practices had led him to overestimate the amount of money that would accrue from accounts and notes. Most remaining assets were sold at an auction on 26 November 1900.

After all settlements had been made and the books closed, there remained $14,071.74 for the court to divide among claims of almost $10,000, and to pay the receiver. On 2 December 1904, Judge George C. Hatch discharged Wilson, and the Puget Sound Co-operative Colony ceased to exist.[103] The buildings at Ennis Creek were abandoned and fell into disrepair.

The Puget Sound Co-operative Colony was founded by theorists and idealists as a venture in communal living and economic production. During its short history, the purpose, direction, and leadership changed so radically that it became instead a handler of lands and properties, a joint-stock company seeking a profit for investors. From a society of workingmen who would better the lot of their class, the colony became a middle-class business corporation. In its final years, the dreams of the Seattle radicals were forgotten as directors, trustees, courts, and the receiver tried to salvage whatever money they could. The Puget Sound Co-operative Colony lacked leaders of sound management ability and strong spirit who joined a sense of the visionary with practical know-how. The colony leaders' philosophy was vague, their goals general, their expectations unrealistic, their acceptance of all comers too willing, and their leadership poor. The ultimate effect of the isolation was a competition with the neighboring settlement of Port Angeles to control the immediate region and its resources. If harbor and climate were suitable for a cooperative colony, they were also suitable for a competitive traditional town. There was always opportunity just outside the colony for the malcontents, the rebels, the disenchanted, the drifters, the personally ambitious, and for those physically crowded out. Cooperation in all aspects of life seemed less favorable when actually faced than when philosophers idealized it or propagandists eulogized it.

The ideal of a model society based upon cooperation quickly

gave way to a wholesome but conservative town of homeowners, industry, and culture. Had there never been a colony, there might well have been a Port Angeles on the harbor of Ediz Hook. But the colony contributed to the development of the city. It advertised the area and its potential. It platted and sold residential developments. It operated early industries, including the first sawmill in a town ever after associated with lumber. The *Model Commonwealth,* first newspaper in Clallam County, is the ancestor of the present Port Angeles *Evening News*. The colony constructed the first downtown office building, the first permanent elementary school, and the Opera House. Several Port Angeles churches derive their origins as congregations and as buildings from the colony.

But the façade of a city is little more than the reflection of its people. More than one colonist stayed to make vigorous, substantial contributions. George Venable Smith, lawyer, city official, and always a promoter, became a respected civic leader, but he was only one of a host of colonists who contributed extensively to the growth and development of the city. Second and third generations continued to lead. One such son, prominent in his own right, wrote that the colony "brought to Port Angeles a group of people who spearheaded every economic growth of the city over a long period of years. Calling the roll of the colonists is to recite the names of leaders of the community while they lived."[104] And a long-time leader never associated with the colony concurred: ". . . the Colony brought to Port Angeles people with the true pioneering spirit who remained and took part in community upbuilding long after their colonization dream was but a memory."[105]

The former radicals took diverse political paths as they left the colony. Ben and Nellie Mastick remained interested in communitarian ventures in the state; Albert E. Sanderson continued this interest briefly in California before returning to St. Louis and participation in various socialist movements. Paul Land served as Populist in the state legislature; Herman Culver worked in the Socialist party in the state. Others returned to established political parties. Dr. F. S. Lewis remained an active Democrat, and Thomas Maloney once served as state secretary for that party; he died a member of the Arizona State Legislature. George Venable Smith returned to the Republican party, although he found his radical past a hindrance when he sought appointment as a superior court judge. Port Angeles became neither a hotbed nor even a reservoir of radicalism, despite its past and the early philosophies of certain leaders. [106]

As the first major communitarian experiment of western Washington died, it helped give birth to a strong permanent city, one vastly different from the model commonwealth envisioned by the colony founders.

3. Equality Colony

THE PLAN TO SOCIALIZE A STATE

A decade after George Venable Smith moved his little band to Ennis Creek, another group of reformers was starting Equality Colony far across Puget Sound in Skagit County. Its socialist founders saw Equality as more than just another American utopia. To them, it was a first step toward converting the liberal young state to socialism, a forerunner of their goal for the nation. "We are the advance guard of a mighty host," exuded G. E. (Ed) Pelton from the farmhouse where the colony was begun in 1897.[1]

The two colonies were separated by more than time and water. Much had happened in ten years. The activity prompted by Laurence Grönlund, Edward Bellamy, Julius A. Wayland, Henry George, Grangers, Populists, labor unions, Socialists, Christian Socialists, and others had culminated in a brief massing of liberal efforts during the 1896 presidential campaign of William Jennings Bryan. But Bryan's defeat created confusion and disorganization. As reform elements struggled again to promote their several theories and programs, the Brotherhood of the Co-operative Commonwealth emerged with a plan to colonize a western state. During its brief lifetime, the BCC attracted a national following and the support of many prominent radicals.

The BCC sought to establish a socialist colony. This colony—a model cooperative commonwealth—would demonstrate the advan-

Parts of this chapter appeared as "Equality Colony: The Plan to Socialize Washington," *Pacific Northwest Quarterly* 59 (July 1968): 137-46.

tages of common production, distribution, and consumption of goods and a pure democratic government. Once secure, it could aid the establishment of similar colonies. If all were located in one sparsely populated state, the colonists could inaugurate a socialist government; when one state and its congressional delegation were captured, the Socialists would then convert the nation. Ambitious, radical, and yet naïve, the plan appealed to some idealists and to many who were seeking personal betterment. The movement offered a nonviolent alternative to conventional political methods.

The idea was conceived and developed by a small group of New Englanders. First among them was F. G. R. Gordon of Manchester, New Hampshire. In 1894 several eastern reformers proposed a chain of socialist colonies along the Atlantic seaboard. Gordon suggested that forces be concentrated rather in a single, carefully selected state—he mentioned Texas—and that they operate within the legal framework of that state. The idea evoked little enthusiasm. A similar scheme was proposed independently by W. Ruble of San Francisco in the *Coming Nation*. Gordon's own socialist evolution moved him from early membership in the Socialist Labor party through other factions. Eventually he became lobbyist for the National Association of Manufacturers and denied his parentage of the scheme.[2]

The real father of the BCC plan was another New Englander, Norman Wallace Lermond, of Warren, Maine, who had helped found the People's party in his state. In his middle thirties in 1897, he was of average height and build and wore a full dark beard. This son of a pioneer family had been bookstore employee, accountant, reporter, and farmer; he would later become known as an amateur natural scientist. The Gordon proposal attracted him. Perhaps spurred on by an employee, Ed Pelton, Lermond seized upon the plan to socialize a state. Pelton and Lermond launched a voluminous correspondence with leading reformers throughout the country.[3]

Earlier, Pelton had broached the idea to the prominent author Henry Demarest Lloyd. Discounting the current Populist movement, Pelton suggested another path toward the cooperative commonwealth:

That way is to make an organized effort and colonize some state or states, so as to have a majority therein of Socialists, then inaugurate [*sic*] Public

Ownership of all means of production and distribution as far as can be done within State lines.

Not only could we do this but we would have more influence in National affairs by having a solid congressional delegation, and also be in a better position to defend ourselves when Plutocracy forces the final inevitable conflict than if scattered and disorganized.[4]

Pelton recommended California.

However, it was Lermond whose fervor and pen created the BCC; on 18 October 1895, he and two Warren neighbors formed the first local union. That winter Pelton organized the second "L. U." at Damariscotta Mills, Maine, and a third appeared in San Francisco. In December, Lermond issued a "call" in the pages of the New York *Commonwealth* for more locals and for a national organization. By spring he was setting an organizational meeting of the "National Union of the Brotherhood of the Cooperative Commonwealth" for St. Louis on 24-26 July. The national Populist convention there would ensure the presence of like-minded persons at that time. A total of 143 "leading social reformers," including Lloyd, Frank Parsons, Eugene V. Debs, Eltweed Pomeroy, and the Reverend William D. P. Bliss, lent their names to the BCC call.[5]

In a lengthy letter to Lloyd, Lermond sharpened his proposals. He visualized a "National" or "Center" Union led by seven trustees and buttressed by local unions, which would provide funds, materials, and incentive to the pioneer colonists. With the zeal of the classic reformer, Lermond called for support, moral and financial: "The people must be aroused from their present lethargy, indifference, and dispondency [sic]. The country must be stirred from centre to circumference. And the quickest and best way to do this is by colonizing a state such as Kas. was colonized prior to the Civil War. The example thus set would be contagious, and neighboring states would not be slow to follow in the same road."[6] Lloyd's interest allowed meager financial support but little more. Earlier he had warned that money interests of any state could extinguish such a venture with ease.[7]

The convention failed to materialize. At St. Louis the Populists became embroiled over the nomination of Bryan, and activities of other organizations were greatly curtailed. With Lermond, a Populist delegate from Maine, held at the political convention, the formative session of the BCC was reduced to an announcement that candidates and a constitution would be voted upon by mail. The *Coming Nation* allotted space each week for news of the group, lists of new locals and members, comments and suggestions, and, most important, the facilities to direct the "national referendum." On 19 September 1896, a constitution was thus adopted and officers were elected.[8]

The constitution followed the general pattern outlined by Lermond. A two-paragraph preamble deplored the "downward" trend of civilization and cited the need to "break the power of monopoly and give the people industrial as well as political freedom." Three specific objectives appeared in the body of the document: "(1) to educate the people in the principles of Socialism; (2) to unite all Socialists in one fraternal association; (3) to establish co-operative colonies and industries, and so far as possible, concentrate these colonies and industries in one State until said State is socialized."[9] The first goal assumed minor importance in the early days; the second would not be achieved. Colonization was the immediate concern of the founders, with industries incidental.

The organization sought persons "of good moral character" who would pledge to "do all in my power to aid in establishing the co-operative commonwealth" and pay monthly dues of ten cents. The national union was governed by an eight-member board of trustees, each of whom headed one department of the BCC. They would be elected annually each January.

The president would head the executive department and generally supervise activities. However, the constitution and practice both demonstrated that the real power rested with the secretary and the colonization department. This department was to "have charge of securing land, locating colonies, and assisting individual Socialists to emigrate and secure employment," as well as handling correspondence, keeping membership rolls and department reports, and receiving moneys.[10]

The treasurer headed the financial department. The dean, through the education department, distributed information about the BCC and socialism. The organizer and the organization department were to form local unions. Of prime importance was the publication department, under the editor, which would publish the official newspaper; meanwhile, the *Coming Nation* served this purpose. This department also printed propaganda materials. An industrial department under the master workman was to "build factories, mills and shops and establish industries of all kinds to give employment to the members. . . ." The storage and distribution of products were the responsibility of the exchange department.

The constitution also provided for annual general meetings, the arbitration of disputes, and an amendment process. Shortly bylaws were added to clarify procedures pertaining to colonies.[11]

Under an elaborate BCC letterhead, Lermond announced the elected officers. Henry Demarest Lloyd had been chosen president and Lermond secretary. B. Franklin Hunter of Philadelphia was the treasurer; Professor Frank Parsons, dean; Morrison I. Swift of Berkeley, California, organizer; A. S. Edwards of the *Coming Nation*, editor; and I. E. Dean of Ionesta, Pennsylvania, master workman. The question was, would they accept? Lermond did, of course. So did Edwards and Parsons, a Boston University economics instructor, prolific writer, and participant in many reform movements.

Lermond pleaded with the reluctant Lloyd. "This move is destined to lead us out of the Wilderness," he prophesied, but he underscored the rest of the sentence, *"if our strongest men will lead the way."* Recognizing Lloyd's displeasure with the Bryan nomination, Lermond closed with a plea to "push forward the good work and build the Co-op Com. here and now, and not wait for the Bryanites or Revolution to do it."[12]

But socialism's most prominent advocate was more interested in the cooperative stores and industries developing in Europe. He doubted the success of colonization, he lacked time to devote to the BCC and refused to be a mere "figurehead," and he was reluctant to confine his activities to a single mode of attack. Lloyd's refusal disheartened the founders. Parsons feared that the organization might disintegrate or the office of president be eliminated: ". . . the situation is *very* unfortunate since *all* were united upon you whereas any one else seems discordant somewhere along the line," he wrote. And Lermond probably reechoed his earlier lament, "What shall we do if all our prominent leaders decline to serve?" In January members did elect a new president, Myron W. Reed of Denver, a Congregationalist minister sympathetic to labor and reform and a former publishing associate of Bellamy. Reed's role was merely perfunctory until his death two years later.[13]

Nor was Lermond successful in securing the acceptance of others. The young BCC experienced a rapid turnover of officers. When Hunter declined, the treasurer's post went to Dr. C. F. Taylor, editor of a medical monthly and an advocate of direct legislation, and later to Helen E. Mason, a former teacher who became a devoted follower of Lermond. After the January 1897 election, Walter J. Smith became master workman, and W. W. White, storekeeper at Ruskin Colony, distributor. [14]

Early in 1897, Eugene V. Debs accepted the post as organizer. As president of the American Railway Union, Debs had gained a strong reputation. During his six months' imprisonment in 1895 for leading the Pullman strike, Debs became interested in socialism rather than mere unionism as the antidote to the workers' problems. While in jail, Debs reread Bellamy and Grönlund, sampled Karl Marx, and admired Karl Kautsky. He was also visited by several prominent Socialists. Lermond wrote him describing the BCC, and a subordinate's reply expressed Debs's interest and encouragement. Perhaps the defeat of Bryan, whom he had supported, caused Debs to renounce conventional political activity. By the spring of 1897, he was a convert to socialism, an advocate of colonization, and organizer of the BCC.[15]

Meanwhile, Debs had determined to form a new party, the Social Democracy of America, by amalgamating his ARU with the BCC, dissidents from the Socialist Labor party, and other groups. Colonization would be a major part of the program. The June convention of the ARU brought its dissolution and the formation of the SDA. Lermond, Parsons, and Edwards attended, and Reed was recognized as an associate. Through Debs's convention speeches and his flair for publicity, colonization drew increased attention and comment.

But Debs's conversion was more to the theory of colonization than to the BCC program. He did little as organizer, and the SDA came to resemble scarcely more than a modified ARU. Debs's concept of colonization differed from that of the BCC leadership. To Debs the hastening of the Co-operative Commonwealth was incidental to the work and relief benefits that a colony might provide to union members in case of depression or old age. Some BCC leaders had recognized this from the beginning; Frank Parsons had praised Debs but warned the SDA convention against adopting a narrow class base, and he had sought to modify the union leader's slogan, "Work for the Unemployed." [16]

Despite a façade of joint participation, the SDA and the BCC proceeded separately. Lermond confirmed that there would be no merger. When Equality Colony was established, founders emphasized that Debs was no longer associated; later the colony newspaper sought to make clear that Equality was not a "Debs Colony." Never was there an outright repudiation of Debs, although he was replaced as organizer by the Reverend George Candee of Toledo, Ohio. Always a hero to BCC socialists, Debs clearly was not one of them. When members of the SDA split on the issue of colonization, Debs abandoned both. In 1898 the remnants of the SDA founded another Puget Sound colony at Burley in Kitsap County.[17]

Thus, ostensibly backed by the SDA but actually on its own, the Lermond group during 1897 prepared to establish a colony. A prospectus demonstrated how a large number of "reserves," by contributing small amounts of money, could maintain cooperative industries strong enough to resist outside competition. Enthusiasm was built each week in the *Coming Nation*. The year had begun with pledges over $32,000, and the figures increased; by midsummer 130 local unions claimed almost 2,200 members. The search began for a site. Lermond went south to investigate Tennessee and Arkansas, but the already settled population, the Negro problem, and the influence of Debs shifted interest farther west. By the time of the June SDA convention, Washington was considered the most likely location, and in August, Lermond announced it to be the chosen state.[18]

The climate, growing conditions, and natural resources of the state were considered favorable, but social factors were equally significant. Its small, sparse population would make Washington easy to "capture." The liberal disposition of voters was demonstrated by recent Populist successes, and Governor John R. Rogers was rumored to be sympathetic to the BCC. Furthermore, local BCC unions were functioning in the state, most of them on Puget

Sound, and at least seven of these claimed to have sites available. Encouraged by such reports, BCC officers determined that "a special locating agent would have to be sent to the front in order to straighten out matters, secure a colony site and make preparation to receive the pioneers." The job fell to Lermond's early associate, Ed Pelton.[19]

On 1 September 1897, Pelton left for the Pacific Northwest. A few years earlier he had been wounded during a political argument in Minnesota in which his brother was killed. Pelton had married his brother's widow. In Maine he worked in the woods, but he occasionally left home to ride the rails throughout the country, particularly in the South. Now he was about to establish a community that would acknowledge him as its pioneer and leader until his death.[20]

Pelton first visited socialists in Seattle and Tacoma before proceeding to Buckley to meet E. L. Robinson, whose own colony plan had been published recently. Anticipating the selection of Buckley, Robinson had described plans and facilities, and he claimed some members. But this small community, thirty miles inland from Puget Sound and subject to "exploitation" by the railroad, seemed unsuitable, so Pelton looked elsewhere. On 17 September he arrived at Edison in Skagit County, where Carey E. Lewis showed him two attractive sites that unfortunately were owned by a man who was unwilling to exchange property for membership. At Sedro on the Skagit River, at Lummi Island, at Castle Rock and La Centre, and in Portland, Oregon, Pelton met continued obstacles. Meanwhile the national board had wired him five hundred dollars along with instructions to secure options on the land near Edison. [21]

Pelton arranged to buy 280 acres just east of Blanchard for ten dollars an acre from Mathias Decker, a wealthy Skagit farmer. Although socialists were opposed to contracting debts of any kind, the contract provided these terms: ". . . beginning October 15, 1897, paying $100.00 down, $100.00 November 2nd, and the balance on or before January 15, 1898, receiving a contract for deed and paying 10 per cent on the balance remaining due." Pelton admonished his associates to meet the terms punctually: "It is with a gold democrat that we are dealing," he cautioned melodramatically, "who will show us no mercy." By spring the final payment on this original parcel had been made. Pelton purchased the land under his own name to avert local opposition, but he transferred title to the BCC on 31 December 1899. [22]

An early settler rhetorically described the land as a "magnificent tract" in "the still primeval forests of the least developed state in the Union." The major site occupied a wooded hillside, down which a creek flowed the year around. Colonists built their first buildings on the lower slope; later, private homes were built farther up the hill. Parts of the tideflats had already been reclaimed by drainage and diking to produce rich farmland. A mile or so west was Samish Bay, picturesque, but accessible to boats only at high tides. South of the site, a house with four and a half acres planted in crops had been contributed by Mr. and Mrs. Carey Lewis. This provided space for the earliest arrivals.

The Lewis home became temporary headquarters and later was the "Hatchery" in which many prospective members lived before settling in the colony itself. Lewis, who had farmed in the Northwest for many years, was thereafter recognized as the original settler of Equality. Meanwhile, an option was obtained on an additional 160 acres a short distance southeast of Equality, and that land was acquired the following spring from Kenneth McKenzie in exchange for membership. The colony newspaper delighted in the assessor's estimate that the quarter section contained one million feet of good lumber. The holdings of the colony reached 600 acres by June 1898 with purchase of 160 acres adjoining Equality and 20 acres nearby. [23]

On 1 November 1897, fifteen persons gathered at the Lewis home to form the first BCC colony, named Equality after the new novel just published by Bellamy. In future years Equality commemorated this date with a great annual celebration. [24]

Throughout the winter of 1897-98 workers prepared for the influx of members expected the following spring. Crops were harvested and dikes repaired on the Lewis farm. On the larger site land was cleared, buildings constructed, and about thirty head of horses, cattle, and hogs were acquired. One pioneer later recounted the activity: ". . . during the winter . . . not a day was lost; men waded through mud in the rain before daylight and after dark to and from work. Machinists, tailors, engineers, carpenters, blacksmiths, school teachers and preachers all used the saw, axe and grubhoe to make a showing before spring when the national board was to come. . . ." [25]

The first building completed was named Fort Bellamy. Constructed of logs, it was built before February 1898, when George A. Savage, an upriver pioneer, brought his portable mill and provided finished lumber. By spring a small crew was turning out rough lumber to build a three-story "apartment" building, a barn, and several smaller structures. Pelton, Henry W. Halladay, a Kansan who remained on the site until his death in 1931, and others spent winter evenings writing distant members, describing their progress and appealing for support. In Maine, Lermond observed, "the pioneers write enthusiastically of the place." Neighboring communities were less enthusiastic. On 9 December 1897, the New Whatcom *Reveille* informed its readers: "The colony arrived in Washington in prairie schooners and came from many states, from Texas and Kansas and Nebraska and other prairie states mainly. They are not rich in worldly goods and have the rope harness and battered wagons and flea bitten nags of the camper who is eternally on the wing in the middle states." A week later the editor was more charitable. He refuted speculation that the colonists were free lovers and described them as "apparently good earnest, intelligent men. . . ." [26]

In early March the original settlers greeted members of the national board and the first major body of colonists. From Maine, a "special train" brought Lermond, Miss Mason, A. L. Young, Mrs. Pelton and her two daughters, and E. L. Irish, Mrs. Pelton's brother, and his family. The party moved by railroad through eastern Canada before it crossed back into the United States and worked west, picking up prospective colonists along the way. With the arrival of officials and more settlers, the formative phase of the BCC and Equality Colony ended. [27]

Throughout the spring and summer of 1898, most Americans were excited about the Spanish-American War and those in the Pacific Northwest about the Alaska-Yukon gold rush. But to the socialists of Equality Colony, these were of secondary importance. The war was laid to misdirected energy that threatened basic values while aiding the privileged classes; otherwise, it was ignored. The gold rush was more apparent to colonists. When they changed trains in Seattle or traveled to Bellingham, they encountered boats embarking for the North, newspaper advertisements for passage and equipment, and interviews with returned prospectors. Here was confirmation that money-grabbing ambitions were inevitable under capitalism. And so the members of Equality dismissed the thrill and delusion of war and fortune, smugly convinced that their way represented the future. They proposed a solution to that other condition of the 1890s, the lengthy depression that had afflicted both nation and region.[28]

During 1898 optimism seemed to prevail at Equality. "The TALKING stage of Socialism has passed. . . ," wrote a spokesman, "but now ACTION is the live word." A spirit of vitality was evident to visitors and newcomers. One wrote later: "My first impression of the colony land was a sense of action, of movement, of stirring about, rather than the leisurely going that used to characterize for me the common country life." Even persons who became disenchanted remembered the excitement and satisfactions of that first year. By the second summer the population was as large, the colony as strong, living conditions better, and activities stabilized, but disillusion, hardship, and conflict had set in.[29]

During 1898, Equality settled into practices that were to prevail for almost a decade. The bond was socialism, even though the faithful might dispute the finer points of definition or falter amid the harsh realities of living them. These colonists would not be sidetracked into fads or other distractions. There was no common religious tie; suggestions that Equality become vegetarian or adopt fraternal degrees and ritual were considered and rejected. Nor did the BCC establish an "anti-secret colony . . . for those who are opposed to secret societies; wherein also tobacco and intoxicants of all kinds should be excluded." Despite disputes and upheavals in leadership, the communal ideal survived almost as long as the colony. There always remained a small corps of individuals sincerely dedicated to making a reality of this ideal.[30]

For a year and a half, Norman W. Lermond directed the BCC from his home in Maine with little help. But early in 1898 he announced that "the National Secretary's office will be moved March 2 . . . to Edison, Wash., where the largest building in town has been leased for National headquarters." Edison was a small community about two miles southwest of Equality. Surrounded by farms and near logging camps, about twenty business houses catered to the needs of town and countryside. The BCC established headquarters in a building leased from the Independent Order of Odd Fellows. From their second floor offices, Miss Mason and Lermond looked across the flats to the snows of Mount Baker; the building also housed a print shop and other offices. Five of the eight board members settled in Edison. W. H. Kaufman, a Minnesota reformer who had been elected editor, arrived in April; Master Workman Charles H. Swigart, a civil engineer, arrived from Ohio in March; and E. F. Nolan, at Equality since November, was now distributor. President Reed, Frank Parsons, and the Reverend Candee were the only officers not in residence, and their roles subsequently diminished. [31]

The first weeks at Edison marked the high point of the BCC as a national organization. Money flowed in. Funds grew from twelve thousand dollars in May to over sixteen thousand by June, a sizable amount although far short of the seventy thousand reportedly pledged. Enrollment of BCC members passed the 3,000 mark in July to reach a peak of 3,558 in December. Scrip was being distributed, and *Industrial Freedom*, the official newspaper, began publication in May.

The organization department continued to bring in new members. At least eighteen state organizers and lecture bureaus operated in eastern cities, and local unions were active throughout the country. Those in Butte, Montana, and Dayton, Ohio, vied to be largest, the former with a campaign that secured a total of 107 active members. Through this department and through its paper, the BCC maintained a national character, but dissension quickly divided those who spoke for the national organization and the Equality colonists. [32]

There was little understanding or communication between the two groups. The officers viewed the BCC as a national body consisting of local units and individual members committed to advancing socialism by establishing numerous colonies, of which Equality was but one. To the colonists, such broad goals were secondary. As they saw it, the scattered national membership existed primarily to assist their pioneering efforts. The socialization of the entire state should await the colony's success, for the premature establishment of additional colonies would weaken the whole effort. [33]

Suspicion and resentment developed toward the Edison group, who controlled finances, propaganda channels, and scrip. Colonists complained that donations were providing salaries and living expenses for officers in town while they endured hardship at the crude unfinished colony. Some questioned the honesty of Lermond and his associates. Poor roads accentuated the short distance between the two groups, as members remained virtual strangers.

Considering themselves spokesmen for the entire BCC and its national program, officials viewed their talents as being in administration, finance, commercial transactions, and printing, functions which could be handled better from an established town than from the colony. "The board members and their associates could see no field of service for them as farmers or sawmill workers. . . ." They defensively claimed that no one received salaries except Organizer Candee, who got twenty-five dollars a month plus credit on his colony membership fee. Perhaps Candee, two thousand miles distant, was to be sacrificed. [34]

The dispute erupted during a joint meeting of the two groups on Good Friday, 1898. Lermond announced plans to establish a second colony at Edison centering on BCC officers and small industries. Pelton, once described by Lermond as "one of the brainiest men in our ranks (and to be heard from later) . . . ," denounced the Edison colony as "fantastic and premature and ruinous," and launched "a virulent personal attack on Lermond." Miss Mason, devoted to Lermond, was shocked: "Good Friday—yes, they also crucified Christ on Good Friday." The Equality members rejected the plan for a second colony and offered a building for BCC headquarters. Reconciliation was sought, but the rivalry between Equality and Edison mounted amidst discussions.

The issues smoldered through the summer, but the colonists, who were better organized than the amorphous national membership, held an advantage. They secured the board's support for a constitutional amendment to give the colony "complete autonomy," except that the BCC would hold all land titles and receive monthly dues, and only BCC members could join the colony. Otherwise, the resolution allowed Equality to control its own finance and membership while the BCC would direct national programs and establish new colonies. [35]

Equality leaders claimed that adoption would lessen discontent. "Men grown up in the forests and mines of this country are better qualified to run the business end of the colonies than others . . ."; yet, some national rule would continue, as in the federal government of the United States. National officers agreed that persons elected by colonists should rightfully govern a colony. Those "on the ground" accepted the need for change, said one Edison worker.[36]

Members not "on the ground" were less inclined to agree. Organizer Candee, miffed that the national board claimed unanimous agreement, called for further discussion and charged that collective ownership without collective operation would break both the BCC and Equality. A Michigan supporter threatened to stop financial contributions to "any colony which has withdrawn from the association or has taken upon its self [*sic*] 'Complete Autonomy.' " Another writer summarized objections. The amendment would nullify rules adopted by the majority in the national organization, it would reduce the powers of the board on landholding and dues collecting, it would make colonies "virtually independent and isolated," and it would alienate the reserves, "the very men who have made the movement a possibility." Obviously, "the right kind of people" were not at Equality.[37]

But opponents of the amendment, scattered and not directly affected by the change, scarcely had a chance. The proposal carried by a vote of 298 to 176. Equality was free to go its own way. Colonists, it was reported, now worked with "renewed ardor."[38]

A more startling event followed. Early in August 1898, Lermond abruptly resigned his position " 'after . . . five months of wrangling and discord, sick in mind and body,' " and left. "Stunned," his assistant, William McDevitt, informed the colonists. *Industrial Freedom* noted Lermond's departure briefly, and the *Coming Nation* buried the news beneath a smokescreen: "Secretary Lermond, to whom the movement and the development and the prosperity of the BCC are more indebted than they are to any other individual, has been compelled, it grieves us all exceedingly to state, to retire temporarily from the active duties of his office and to take a much needed relaxation from work, and the worry attendant upon such self-effacing and self-forgetting devotion to principle and to duty as has always characterized his invaluable labors in the field of reform." To Pelton, the departure was a shock. Despite their differences, he liked and believed in Lermond. Pelton considered leaving himself, held back only because he was needed now more than ever.[39]

Lermond returned to Maine, where his attention shifted to a new publication, *Harmony*, and to another grandiose scheme to socialize the nation. The Industrial Brotherhood would establish "great wheat farms in the Northwest; . . . cotton fields in the South; . . . sheep ranches in the central West; . . . iron, copper, and zinc mines; . . . great industrial plants for the manufacture of all the necessaries of life, and the Brotherhood would build model dwelling houses, theaters, libraries, art galleries, etc. By locating the central city on the Great Lakes or the Mississippi River transportation could be largely affected on the Brotherhood's own steamers."[40]

He was a candidate for governor of Maine in 1900, and he continued to distribute socialist tracts, often written by himself and financed by benevolent relatives. His activities extended to natural science; "the John Burroughs of Maine," a Boston newspaper called him. To Lermond socialism and nature went together. He converted his home into a park and arboretum where he hosted rallies and meetings. On 4 April 1944, the eighty-two-year-old Lermond died, "buried as he wished in a pine box in an unmarked grave, in the woods he loved." Like his dreams of a colony in Washington, the arboretum vanished; a scientific society he had formed cut down the trees and sold the land.[41]

Other board members soon left Equality. Miss Mason, although rumored to have accompanied Lermond to Maine, died in Seattle in January 1901. Distributor Nolan, Editor Kaufman, and Master Workman Swigart had departed by the end of 1898. Candee, still disputing, was replaced as organizer. William McDevitt succeeded to Lermond's position, then he also left. He remained in the Puget Sound area as shorthand teacher, typewriter salesman, and assistant registrar at the University of Washington before he moved to San Francisco. There he operated a bookstore that for forty years was both a connoisseur's delight and a meeting place for radicals. He died in 1959.[42]

Meanwhile, the Equality colonists set out to secure BCC

headquarters for Equality. They argued that the first and thus far only colony was the logical center for BCC activities, and its selection would ensure economy and restore unity. Opponents did not lack arguments and alternatives. "Don't isolate the National Committee in the backwoods as if we were ashamed of them," wrote one. Equality, summarized the Reverend Candee in one of his last letters, lacked room for expansion, had no good harbor, could never be more than an agricultural colony, and had already disappointed members who had left. Headquarters should not be located in any colony, which might thereby receive favored treatment, wrote a hopeful colonizer from southwestern Washington, reminding readers of the plan to socialize the whole state. Edison, Seattle, and nearby Anacortes were proposed as alternative locations for headquarters.

The result was never in doubt; Equality was selected by an undisclosed margin, and its residents were "jubilant" over the results. The transfer of headquarters was completed in February 1899. That January the slate of BCC candidates recommended by the colony, but including nonresidents, was elected. A Californian who complained that Equality had "practically withdrawn" from the BCC was wrong. Scarcely a year after its founding, Equality Colony *was* the BCC. [43]

"The victory was Dead sea fruit," recalled a member later. "Without the aggressive organization work of the old General Officers the outside organization languished and died." Income from membership dues dwindled, the circulation of the newspaper fell to two thousand, and, worst of all, he continued, new members stopped coming in. An Equality official admitted that the national membership "rapidly dropped from 3,500 to 250 or 300." The BCC, although it never incorporated, continued to own colony land, and its officials were elected by the remaining national members. A few reserves occasionally sent oft-requested help. But essentially the national organization that had flourished for two years was dead, the victim of its only colony. [44]

The twin goals of colonizing and socializing Washington were forgotten. In June 1898, the BCC still declared itself eager to find sites and assist groups to start new colonies. Land was said to be available "in almost every section of the state." Less than three months later, a Californian who proposed to start a Washington colony learned that no money was available. By April 1899, the goal of colonizing Washington received lip service in *Industrial Freedom*, but "experience" had shown the plan to be "a little premature," and methods had changed. Now the BCC would develop Equality rather than "scatter our forces to the four winds, in an attempt to establish several straggling, struggling communities simultaneously." After Equality had gained experience, had become self-supporting, and could afford additional land and machinery, "you'll hear of new colonies," the editor promised, "not before."[45]

Equality lent little assistance to the few colonies that did appear, as the disappointed founders of Harmony Colony quickly learned. In a farming region on the upper Cowlitz River, a small group of former Populists organized this cooperative experiment on the 220-acre hop farm of S. M. Dunn. They printed a brochure that outlined their plans, received approval from visiting BCC officials, and sent an occasional column about their progress to *Industrial Freedom*; in March 1899 they incorporated at five hundred thousand dollars. But they attracted only one outside recruit, and they received neither funds nor other support from the BCC. By summer's end Harmony was, as a nearby newspaper headline reported, "A BUSTED COLONY." During 1898, when members of the SDA Colonization Commission arrived to colonize at Burley, they were welcomed and publicized in the Equality paper, but the tone suggested that rivalry overshadowed brotherhood. [46]

Nor did plans to socialize the state progress. The founders had shown interest in state political issues. *Industrial Freedom* and its readers supported proportional representation and direct legislation as possible aids to further socialism. The BCC reiterated plans to carry the state by 1901. Socialists from elsewhere were invited to "concentrate their forces in Washington until this state is socialized, that is till the functions of the present state and local governments are so extended that they shall include all productive industries." No secret, the intentions were outlined in the Seattle *Post-Intelligencer*. Even during the confusion of September, the BCC compared its goal for Washington with that of the Kansas Free Soilers fifty years before. It supported legislation to facilitate the organizing of cooperative enterprises and proposed constitutional amendments on suffrage and tax reforms. *Industrial*

Freedom repeated the objective: "Sometime we hope to have socialist headquarters in the capital at Olympia. That is our aim." [47]

Such talk soon faded. Equality socialists made little impress politically. Notwithstanding their failure to capture the state for socialism, they failed in quests for county office and did not even play a significant role in Socialist party politics. In 1901, Equality President Henry W. Halladay recalled that the founders' major objects were "to organize the workers into cooperative colonies and by pooling their capital, labor and money, build homes for the other fellow." The grand plan for a network of colonies that would socialize the state and create the cooperative commonwealth was as forgotten as if it had never existed. [48]

Internal affairs demanded the principal attention at Equality. The colonists aimed to have a pure democracy in their government. The major governing bodies were the general assembly, colony officers, and the board of department supervisors. Department heads had charge of such specific functions as manufacturing, agriculture, cuisine, public works, education and recreation, transportation, exchange, and public health. The number of departments, their titles, and their respective responsibilities changed several times, but the principle of a division of work always remained. Superintendents were nominated by the workers of each department and voted upon by the entire colony membership, which had the power to select a person not nominated. Because terms were not specified, there were frequent elections during certain periods. Colony officers met at least once a week to make general decisions or deal with specific problems.

Decisions of the board were subject to reconsideration by the general assembly, which met on alternate weeks. The general assembly permitted all men and women over eighteen to participate in discussions and vote. This "freest and most democratic organization that has ever existed in the United States" experienced difficulties because a simple majority of those present could suspend the bylaws. Moreover, a minority could call a special meeting; at least once this enabled a small group to convene a midnight assembly and vote an unpopular action while the opposition slept. [49]

At the general assembly, questions were argued and settled, appointments made and revoked, decisions great and small transformed into policy. Discussions affected most aspects of life in the colony: "The General Assembly debated everything—from the question of whether Comrade Stiebritz was using too much charcoal gas with the bees, to how to nail boards on the new printery or whether the timbers in the new barn were large enough." Although decisions could be overruled by secret referendum votes of the entire membership, decisions of the general assembly were usually final. Especially in the later months of the colony, controversies heightened tempers and meetings became particularly hot. [50]

The colony president had few real duties other than to preside at meetings and ceremonial functions. Over several years the office was held periodically by Henry Halladay, whose early arrival gave him a certain prestige and who had an effective, direct manner.

But Ed Pelton, more than any other man, was the natural leader during the first two years. Although he was once BCC president, his role as founder, his ability to work fairly with men, and his devotion to principles created prestige and power that outweighed mere official title. A colonist wrote: " . . . in all that pertains to Equality and the BCC he occupies a commanding position. . . . He is considerable of a 'sky-scraper' is 'Ed,' but his feet are on solid ground and his sleeves rolled to his muscular elbows for any hard, disagreeable job for the benefit of the commonweal . . . in season and out of season he works with those who are trying to prove the practicability of cooperation and even those who differ from him respect him." Personal reasons prompted Pelton to move to Seattle in 1900, until members urged him back. He returned to Blanchard, just outside the colony, but he assisted with its affairs in the few weeks that remained before he was killed by a falling tree in February 1901.[51]

The lack of truly effective leaders was a hindrance. Pure democracy worked as long as members got along and cooperated, as long as their goals harmonized, as long as people were somewhat homogeneous, but in the hands of people disagreeing and disagreeable, democracy could be chaos. Thus the success of Equality depended in the long run upon the character of its membership.

Membership rules for the BCC were set by referendum in August of 1897. Members enrolled either in the local unions or by individually sending monthly dues to national headquarters. Those not at the colony were classed as "reserves," and they supported the experiment with money, gifts, and, often, freely given advice. Well-known reformers such as temperance leader Frances E. Willard, writer William Dean Howells, Professor John R. Commons, and Christian Socialist George D. Herron received honorary memberships. Their enrollment meant publicity and complimentary letters for publication, but no more.

The most significant BCC members were the colonists. The fee to join the colony was set at $160 for an individual or a family, following a vote that averaged $161.52. This could be paid in one sum, in regular installments, in property, or by work for the colony. Pelton was one who worked his fee out.

Membership applications asked for pertinent information about family members and included such questions as: "How much capital can you furnish?" "Have you any experience in cooperative colonies?" "What books have you read on Socialism?" "What papers are you taking?" "What do you consider the best incentive to effort?" Inquiries concerned diseases and infirmities, work preferences, and previous trades. Failure to answer all questions does not seem to have disqualified applicants.

A six-month probationary period and approval by two-thirds of the membership were required of new members. Those rejected or expelled, and there were both, were assured that money paid would be returned, but withdrawing members had no such guarantee. Several cried swindle when money or property was not returned. [52]

The population of the colony varied. Between March and July 1898, the number increased from 115 to 260 besides the several dozen at Edison, and in November, 300 persons were reported at Equality. By the summer of 1900 there were only 120 adult members, and 125 the following March. Then the decline was sharp. A visitor in December 1903 estimated a mere 38 persons. Clearly, total membership rose rapidly to between 250 and 300 during the ambitious summer months of 1898, fluctuated and declined during the ten years the colony existed. [53]

Despite the several families from Maine, many colonists came from the Middle West, with large numbers also from the South, the Pacific Coast, and nearby northwestern states. An early visitor noted members from Missouri, Massachusetts, Washington, D. C., Ohio, Kentucky, Michigan, Illinois, Wisconsin, Iowa, California, Nebraska, Kansas, Colorado, Oregon, Montana, Virginia, North Carolina, Alabama, and Louisiana. Many people had left very small towns, such as Newport, Kentucky; Bucyrus, Ohio; Faribault, Minnesota; Kelso, Oregon; Dolphos, Kansas; Sycamore, Illinois; Etiwanda, California; Blockhouse, Washington; and Dennison, Texas. National descent was mostly European; an observer who thought the members "cosmopolitan," noted only English, Scotch, German, Bohemian, Scandinavian, Irish, and Hebrew backgrounds. Occupations can only be guessed. Despite attempts to recruit persons with specific professional and craft skills, many of the members lacked specific training.

What motivated people to come to Equality?

> The Cleveland administration had left the country flat.
> And folks, in desperation were trying this and that.
> A group who came from Eastern states, by train and some by team —
> Began a self-supporting plan. It seemed a wondrous dream.
> My pa had tried out politics, and got a rotten deal —
> He said, "Let's try the colony. It promises a meal."[54]

Perhaps the young girl of the poem touched on common reasons for the colonists' coming. People who had seen conventional methods fail turned to communal life to seek relief from economic pressures. But if "pa" was desperate or merely curious, other colonists were motivated by idealism, utopian dreams, and dedication. At Equality they could help themselves and establish a better life for others.

Reasons for coming might not have been recognized by the colonists themselves. At the Smithsonian Institution, clerk William McDevitt picked a radical newspaper from a wastebasket and became intrigued with socialism and colonization, but probably the opportunities of a new area "hypnotized" the young bachelor to foresake the city of Washington for the state. A granddaughter suspected that Henry Halladay was simply "adventurous" and willing to try new things, and James B. Ault, ill for some time, probably joined to provide security for his large family.[55]

They arrived by various routes and means. Halladay came

months ahead of his family, traveling through the Southwest to spread word of socialism and the colony. His wife came with four of their children by train from Kansas to Seattle and by boat to Anacortes, where he met them. Halladay had suggested that colonists pool resources to charter a railroad car, and several groups including the Lermond party came in this manner. So did more than sixty persons from Dayton, Ohio, who had solicited funds and held a "box party" to raise expenses. The Ault family and several others arrived in April by train. Traveling tourist class from Kentucky to St. Paul and then by sleeper, the family cooked meals on a coal stove in one end of the car. At Seattle they transferred to another train for Belfast, where a colony wagon met them to carry the women, small children, and baggage over six miles of puncheon and mud road to Equality. The men walked, through thick "glossy green and healthy looking" foliage, and arrived just in time for dinner at Fort Bellamy.

J. A. Peek arrived the first autumn from Wilderville, Oregon, "with a good wagon and team, loaded with provisions. He takes with him 300 pounds of beans, 100 pounds dried apples, 50 pound sack dried corn, 75 or 80 quarts canned fruit or berries, 1,000 pounds of flour, and a quantity of garden seeds and an outfit of dishes." Not all were so well supplied. One family of eight traveled six months up the coast from southern California in a horse-drawn covered wagon, stopping to pick hops or to cut railroad wood. Only a few days away from the colony they had to sell stock and provisions when the wagon mired down in mud. [56]

Once arrived, newcomers met their fellow colonists. "A more cheerful, happy and contented class of people we had never met," commented one, while Annie Billingsley agreed they were "mostly kind and considerate to each other and . . . the outside world." One observer thought them "strong and vigorous . . . [with] intelligence above the average." "The place," said a schoolteacher, "is a great attraction for 'cranks' of all sorts, sizes, and shades of opinions. Here you will find the sensible 'crank' who really has ideas and you will find the erratic sort who thinks he has." But twenty years later a neighbor recalled the "motley collection of human beings." McDevitt viewed his fellows as the "seemingly solid, stalwart, rural or smalltown type—in short, they represented reasonably well the pioneer Western type among whom I was to live up and down the Pacific Coast most of my next 50 years."

As at Port Angeles, many arrived anticipating more conveniences and advantages than existed. The editors, denying responsibility, feared that people had an "alluring picture of us that our over-enthusiastic friends create in their own minds..." and warned against persons coming who were apt to be dissatisfied. They were not likely to become good colonizers; "as a rule the people who ride in here on the high tide of their own emotions are not long stayers, they can't stand the wreck of their air castles."[57]

Such persons were not "good socialists," an undefined phrase the colonists used frequently. "Many people come here who are not educated up to the standard of Equality, and not finding things as they had anticipated them, go away again. These people are all moderate socialists ... ," a member complained. ". . . a big part of the members didn't claim to be Socialists and surely didn't prove it," remembered one, who did not stay long himself. Leaders occasionally tried to limit membership, but they never established a sound method of selection. They circulated glorified accounts of colony life, realizing too late that the persons attracted were not necessarily the most valuable workers; needing money, the colony accepted some who had the required fee but were not strong contributors thereafter. [58]

And so people came—and they left, with reasons as varied as those for coming. Lermond and other original officers could not readjust to life in a colony which they did not control. Even Pelton went away, prompted by his wife's growing unhappiness with communal life and perhaps by disillusionment; William Lieseke and George Savage, their children recall, were too independent to take orders from the leaders. Surely improved economic conditions and job opportunities on the "outside" tempted many. Some left in groups. Several families gravitated to Freeland Colony on Whidbey Island, where they experienced greater individual freedom. The Dayton, Ohio, party felt the colony had been misrepresented, and they moved to Bellingham Bay and then scattered. Some went to other colonies in Washington or elsewhere.[59]

Several who left reappeared, "after," the paper maintained, "a short trial of wage slavery again." Such were the Odells, who had lived at Equality for about nine months before they left in

November 1898. Disillusioned, Amy Odell wrote back, "Yes, in the colony some of us at times got discouraged, dissatisfied, and even homesick. . . ." Yet who, in new surroundings, did not? Colonists are, after all, "human bein's." So the Odells returned, but not for long. Bothered by asthma problems and the damp climate, they left again for Kansas. [60]

Some colonists remained as long as Equality existed, always trying to practice the principles of cooperation that had attracted them. A teacher observed the personalities around him and wrote: "It is the cool, calculating, level-headed sort that is to come in on the home run, if there is going to be any home run. The leading spirits here seem to be made of that mettle, they never think of going away, judging by what they say nothing is further from their minds, and some of them are noble souls, too, wholly deserving of success."[61]

Despite politics and ideology, economic necessities made the greatest demands upon the colonists. They could not live on theory alone; nor did they expect to. The communitarian experiment was a practical application that involved providing a living for large numbers of persons and possibly realizing profit for the common benefit. The BCC originally envisioned a nationwide network of colonies, mills, and factories which would produce and trade goods free from restraints and competition. Washington had been selected partially because of the diversified economic potential. Thus, for itself and to fulfill the national objectives, the first BCC colony wrestled with problems of labor, agriculture, and industry. [62]

Equality, like the Port Angeles experiment, anticipated a built-in labor supply, with laborers and artisans working harmoniously at the jobs each preferred and knew best. The ideal was never realized. Workers with certain skills were always in short supply; some worked hard while others shirked; not all foremen enjoyed unanimous approval; and improving economic conditions drew workers away. Thus Equality, founded in part as a response to labor problems, was not free from them.

Early recruitment efforts abounded with optimism: "We need 100 pioneers at onces [sic], especially lumbermen, sawmill hands, carpenters and farmers; also a few machinists, mechanics, bricklayers, blacksmiths, bakers, engineers, ship carpenters, and cooks."

In response, the earliest "pioneers" journeyed to Equality the first autumn, creating within weeks such an apparent oversupply that Pelton announced, "No more pioneers will be admitted . . . without a passport from the National Secretary." [63]

Persons with skills were needed more than general workmen, and calls became specific: "The Colony Wants—a shoemaker, a tanner, a dentist, and a cook." "The colony is in need of a socialist tinner, blacksmith, shoe repairer, and a printer, or compositor." Warnings appeared the first summer: "Before coming to Washington it is wise to learn whether work such as you are willing to do is needed. . . ." After 15 August, no more persons were wanted, unless called for special service: " . . . colonists, like horses, are worth more in the spring than in the fall. . . ." Even skilled workers were warned that they must first be good socialists, although skills were still important. Now and then notices became especially frank: "WANTED! Men and women who are willing to work, and are not jealous for fear they will do more than their associates; who are willing to go ahead and set a good example, instead of waiting for the other fellow to do it; who believe thoroughly in co-operation whether they are working inside or outside of the Colony; who have bulldog tenacity. . . ." [64]

Despite the presumed choice of occupations, newcomers signed labor contracts agreeing to work where needed. When a particular job was required,

the foreman or department head of each branch of work made his call for volunteers and he chose his assistants from the ranks, usually well filled, of those volunteering workers. These calls were usually made either in the dining hall or the assembly; when the call could not wait, the colony bulletin board at the store or post office would be used. Some of the more enthusiastic members were signed up as permanent volunteers, or self-drafted, men or women of all or every service, provided of course they were not already engaged in a service of a similar or greater importance.

Assignments were not always voluntary, however, and members expecting one kind of work might receive a totally different task, sometimes accusing leaders of perversity or of trying to "break" the independence of newcomers. [65]

This question of "Voluntary Co-operation" versus "Business Methods" provided the basis for a lively debate the first summer. One viewpoint stressed individual freedom as a paramount objective of the colony, but another ridiculed "a colony where everyone works when he pleases and at what he pleases . . . [as being] about as feasible as . . . a regiment of brigadier generals."[66]

A census taken the first spring indicated the number and ratio of workers in the different departments. At this time, BCC headquarters were still located in Edison, where twenty people worked mainly at office jobs. Of the members on the colony site, twenty-two were engaged in agriculture, twenty in subsistence (food preparation, laundering, supplying fuel, and the like), ten in manufacturing, ten in logging and lumber, four each in transportation, education and recreation, public works, and fishing, and a total of six in health, publication, and public safety.[67]

Eight hours was the specified work day, but persons often worked as many as fourteen hours. *Industrial Freedom* described a fifty-five-hour work week with holidays on Saturday afternoons and Sundays. Men were paid five cents an hour in colony scrip or labor checks, and women received eight hours' pay for five hours' work. Otherwise, adults were paid equally. Neither officials nor workers with particularly disagreeable or arduous jobs received additional consideration; the latter group rejected a proposal to decrease their hours. Because colony benefits included housing, laundry work, mending and sewing, and medical and funeral expenses, only personal items and the two dollars a week board remained to be paid from these wages.[68]

As opportunities and wages improved outside the colony, it became difficult to keep workers at Equality. Even during the first month, Pelton worried about such competition. Younger men particularly were lured to nearby farms and lumber camps. Although they were expected to put money thus earned in the colony treasury, many refused. This created resentment from fellow colonists and brought ridicule from noncolonists: "It would seem that the competitive world is not so bad after all, eh, brothers?"[69]

Most communitarian settlements had an agricultural base. Besides providing essentials, farming also might yield a surplus to sell. Seemingly incompatible with socialist principles, this factor nevertheless led communities to search for marketable products. Most agricultural pursuits did not require highly specialized labor, and farming implied permanence. "In almost all of the communities studied," summarized a one-time community leader in the East, "farming was a unity pursuit. There were often small private kitchen gardens, even when it was against the 'principles' of the society or when it was quite unnecessary. But farming was a social function, and the farm and timber and orchard lands were practically always undivided."[70]

Equality was no exception. During the first winter, the pioneers rented scattered parcels of land to raise vegetables for spring. Meanwhile, the colony land was being prepared by clearing, burning and slashing, and draining and diking. The head of the industrial department boasted that, once drained, the marshland on the flats would "rival in productiveness the far famed valley of the Nile." By November the colony paper reported the accomplishments of the first year: "This department has cut over 1½ miles of ditch; have 'slashed and burned' about 100 acres of timber land, pulled the stumps on about 15 acres, which are about ready for the plow; will probably have 50 acres ready for a crop by planting time. . . ." Another fifty acres of burned-over bottom land was being prepared for pasture. [71]

The colonists were already farming other lands leased and owned. Potatoes and vegetables were planted, and ground made ready for oats. A short distance from the colony site colonists "planted over 3,500 trees, bushes, vines, etc., of many different varieties, [of fruit] including berries, cherries, apples, and many others." Occasional donations of seed and abundant advice flowed from the reserves; an agricultural college professor's recommendation that the colonists raise flax was ignored.

Men exchanged work with neighboring farmers for oats, hay, and fruit, and they cooperated in cutting and threshing grain. Their own efforts produced "40,000 head of cabbage, 50 tons of carrots, 1,500 to 2,000 bushels turnips and rutabagos [sic], 70 bushels potatoes, 50 bushels dried beans, 10 bushels English peas, 100 bushels onions." At least three orchards were planted and a root house was built that first season. [72]

By the second spring farming was well under way. Despite a "backward" season that frustrated the new Washingtonians, the planting was "up-to-date." Seven thousand strawberry plants were being set out; a ton of potatoes had been planted, and over three hundred cabbages and fifteen hundred cauliflowers, a quarter-acre of onions, as well as beets, rutabagas, and lettuce. Next season still more areas would be put in crops. The agricultural success of Equality seemed assured. [73]

Early efforts to sell produce outside the colony were not successful. A good cabbage crop and the highly praised sauerkraut made from it prompted an assault upon the Seattle market. But before the shipment reached Seattle, kraut was oozing from the poorly made barrels of green spruce and willow. "It was all shipped back to the colony and had to be eaten there. . . ." In later years fruits and vegetables were sold to nearby markets, mostly in Whatcom, and to railroad construction camps. By this time colonists also boasted of "a lot of fine new farm machinery," and of the abundant food supply for members. Its agricultural endeavors gave Equality an aura of prosperity. [74]

Certain colonists were especially valued for experience and knowledge. Charles Swigart, a trained engineer who directed the initial clearing and diking, later achieved distinction in irrigation and reclamation developments in the Yakima Valley. Of the others who guided the agricultural development, the most notable was Carey Lewis. He taught newcomers and novices how to cope with the vagaries of the Puget Sound climate and soil. Lewis seemed to be everywhere: "Down by the creek, over at The Hatchery; on the 160; at the Estes place [probably a leased area] —plowing, spading, hoeing, cultivating; and long after everyone else had quit for the day he could be seen plodding barefooted along the rows of cabbage plants with a five-gallon oil can hung at each end of a wooden yoke across his . . . shoulders, patiently splashing a little water on each thirsty plant." Less effective working with men than with plants and soil, and haughty in his new importance, Lewis could not maintain the workers' confidence. Other interests seemed peculiar; he talked of travel into space, and he joined the small group of Spiritualists. After several years, Carey and Grace Lewis moved from the settlement that recognized them as its earliest citizens to nearby Anacortes. [75]

The colony acquired livestock slowly. In 1898 there were sixteen horses, ten cows, and a number of hogs and chickens, some of them brought in by members. Stock-raising remained a goal but pasture land was cleared and planted in timothy. That summer a barn was built on the northern edge of the village just off the flats. Forty-two by one hundred feet and standing twenty-four feet high, it used lumber and shingles from the colony mill. The growing cattle and dairy herd was eventually judged by a neighbor, not usually sympathetic, as having " 'some of the best cows ever seen in this part of the country.' " The livestock experiment reached a disastrous end amidst burgeoning factional rivalries. A mysterious, perhaps incendiary, fire early in 1906 destroyed the barn along with the cattle herd, several horses, and hay and feed. This loss hastened the decline of the colony. [76]

Such industries as lumbering were given a priority. The colonists first acquired the portable sawmill and services of George Savage, who had come west from Iowa in the early 1870s and worked in a sawmill on Camano Island. Later he had settled up the Skagit River to farm and mill on an isolated homestead, but permanence was not for him. During the 1890s he set up his small, steam-operated mill at various places. Then in the winter of 1897-98 he heard "of a peculiar colony in the north end of the county . . . and in the end made a bargin [*sic*] to run the Portable Mill for the colony."

Savage headed a crew of about ten persons during his six-month stay. The property had abundant fir, cedar, and spruce, and in ten weeks the men furnished about eighty thousand feet of lumber and fifty thousand shingles. The colony hoped to retain the mill equipment as a part of Savage's membership fee or as a donation when he left. But he moved on, taking mill and equipment with him, to remain in Skagit County as mill operator, merchant, and surveyor until his death in 1920. [77]

Meanwhile, the BCC was raising money for a permanent mill. The fund quickly mounted to a thousand dollars beyond the expected cost. In August, C. B. Fisher traveled to Oregon to purchase the equipment, including a forty-five horsepower mill, for six hundred dollars plus shipping charges and a tract of donated land. Members were told that the price was but one-fourth of what the seller had paid because the mill had lain idle, unable to compete with the "colossal machinery of the trusts." When it arrived the first week in September, the mill was estimated to have a daily capacity of thirty-five thousand feet of lumber. Soon it was erected on the northern end of the Equality site.

With a portable thirty-five horsepower donkey engine, needed in the timber and to help remove stumps, plus additional borrowed machinery, the logging and mill facilities were fairly complete. Horsedrawn wagons brought logs down a skid road that sloped in front of the village. At the mill building constructed the second spring, lumber was cut, planed, and finished, and shingles were made. A visitor in 1903 praised the "good sized saw mill including dry kiln, shingle shed, donkey logging engine, machine shop, etc." [78]

The extent and length of the mill operations is unknown. Except for a few individual homes, construction at the colony was scant after the first two years, and it is doubtful that much lumber was sold outside. Northwest Washington, high in lumber output, frequently suffered from overproduction that forced mill closures. Equality could scarcely hope to compete under such conditions. As early as 1899 a neighboring outfit was permitted to log part of the colony land, a practice that was repeated. In 1903 the mill was leased to outsiders, and several successive agreements followed. While one such arrangement was in effect in 1904, the mill was destroyed and much of its equipment lost by fire. [79]

Attempts to exploit the fish resources of Puget Sound moved slowly. For $150 the colony purchased the sloop *Progress*; there were also a few smaller boats and a small marine engine. The nearest landing was at the Blanchard slough, nearly two miles away and usable only at high tides. Fishing parties the first spring brought in catches of herring variously estimated at twenty-five barrels and fifteen hundred pounds. The first catches were salted, but soon a smokehouse was built. In late July, crews went north to Birch Bay and Point Roberts for sockeye salmon. [80]

Industrial Freedom liked to poke fun at the "theoretical and amateur fishermen who do not know how to hang or handle a net." And it pleaded that "the colony needs a good sailor and a good practical fisherman." Resented by the sensitive crew, such comments reflected a general problem in this community of sincere but often inexperienced workers. Heading the fleet for awhile, however, was a young vegetarian with seafaring experience, "Captain" Neal Gunnison, reportedly a Danish sailor, blond and stubby, with a Vandyke beard.

In time the fishing program became better organized and

equipped. A gill net and a herring seine were purchased, and the men went after silver salmon, herring, and sockeye from the Samish River to Birch Bay. Colonists of all ages dug for clams on Samish Island. When the smokehouse burned, with a loss of 150 fish on the racks, a larger and better one was built. In later years some fish was sold to canneries. In the meantime, the *Progress* had been sold and the original landing destroyed by railroad construction. Also the socialists had turned conservationists, calling for government action against the "syndicates" to prevent extinction of the salmon.[81]

On a smaller scale were such industrial activities as "shoe making, tailoring, dress making, coopering, blacksmithing, wagon repairing, and furniture making. . . ." Furniture was manufactured with colony lumber. Metal work usually involved repairs rather than products. Nevertheless, Robert Barton, the blacksmith, reportedly could produce "anything out of iron or steel that any man can make," and a tinner made milk cans and pails. But the more routine jobs were described by Barton's successor:

A. comes in from the donkey [engine] and wants a hook for a block that will resist a strain ranging from 150 to 300 horsepower; B. wants a shoe put on a horse; C. wants to know if you can't draw his axe out a little and temper it, as it's too thick to grind. Mrs. D's tea pot has a hole in it to be soldered before dinner; and the lock on the bakery door is out of whack, and when can you fix it? One of the girls has broken a stick pin and wants it fixed before school; and one of the colony kids wants a nickle [*sic*] plated octagon burr for his bike; and most of this is to be done right away.[82]

A well-equipped sewing room kept a force of women and a male tailor busy making garments for members. From bolts of purchased cloth, colonists and outside customers could buy a coat or leave orders. "If any of our readers would like a supply of good flannel shirts and underwear, well made and at a price less than you would have to pay in an ordinary store, send us your measure and order, and satisfaction will be guaranteed."[83] Not all customers were satisfied. Girls complained of the dreary sameness of their clothes. When Kate Halladay was planning her bridal gown, she balked at the choice of fabrics, held out money from her salary as a teacher, and sent away for silk and lace. But colony-made clothes were low cost; years later, former members would rankle at the thought of persons who had remained long enough to stock up with inexpensive clothing and quickly move on. A shoeshop took local and outside orders and proudly noted a request for boots from a nearby logging camp. Doubling as harness maker, the shoemaker kept busy in the early years, but by 1900 his work had fallen off. Hopes to secure a colony tanner never materialized. [84]

Another manufactured product was cereal coffee, "a pure, wholesome, healthful, invigorating beverage, better than coffee and much cheaper" that was made from grains that were probably grown locally. This was sold outside the colony by mail order or by individuals. [85]

Except for these items, manufactures were few and usually confined to things needed by colonists. A feed and grist mill existed, but a proposed woolen mill and canneries for fish, vegetables, and fruit remained only plans. Perhaps if other BCC colonies had materialized, a network of factories, mills, and canneries would also have developed, but, alone, Equality never progressed beyond trying to meet its own needs. [86]

Isolation and the lack of adequate transportation facilities hindered industrial and commercial developments. Freighting goods was a responsibility of the transportation department with its teams and wagons. Because county roads were crude or nonexistent, the colonists sought to connect themselves with nearby farms. The poor landing made shipping by water unsatisfactory, despite the proximity to Puget Sound and regular steamer service in the area. In its early days, the colony hoped to build a steamboat with plans from a professional boat designer, and a steamboat fund was established. The boat could make regular runs to Seattle and other ports, thus reducing freight costs and giving the colony publicity as well as a share in the Puget Sound trade. A trial run of the *Progress* did indicate advantages, but donations only trickled in, attempts to improve landing facilities failed, and the steamboat plan died within a year. Nor did the coming of a railroad, later the main line of the Great Northern, improve transportation facilities for the colonists, although fees were received for the right of way through their land and products were sold to construction crews. Had Equality been a success, the transportation problems might have been solved; conversely, as the ambitions of the colony declined, transportation difficulties mattered less. [87]

Printing was an important activity. The BCC first used the *Coming Nation* of Ruskin Colony as its mouthpiece, and then established its own publications department. An editor was found almost immediately. W. H. Kaufman, a Faribault, Minnesota, newspaperman with a demonstrated interest in reform, promised to bring a press, type, and other printing equipment as soon as the site was acquired. In April 1898, hopeful and proud of his importance, he arrived at Equality.

Kaufman soon proved he was not the man for the job; his arrogant, contentious manner led members to petition for his removal, and his wife irritated the women. The press itself was not practical. Big, cumbersome, and requiring several men to operate, it was later described by a helper as "the most remarkable piece of printing machinery that I have ever seen in 30 years of experience as a printer." Kaufman, who also acted as minister, his wife, and his printing outfit departed in September for a farm in Whatcom County. [88]

Before he left, a Hoe double-cylinder press had been purchased from the Tacoma *Ledger* for twelve hundred dollars and installed at BCC headquarters in Edison. Preparations got under way to inaugurate the official newspaper on 1 May, the international workers' holiday. A week late, the first issue of *Industrial Freedom* appeared 7 May 1898. A four-page sheet published each Saturday, the paper contained articles on socialism and reform, official news and gossip about the BCC and its colony, and correspondence with socialists and radicals throughout the world. An elaborate masthead centered around the BCC emblem of sun bursting through clouds and encircled by broken chains, with sheaves of wheat, gears of industry, and books of learning interspersed.

Early issues carried discussions of radical topics, many of them reprints, by such well-known persons as Eugene V. Debs, Toledo Mayor Samuel M. Jones, Henry Demarest Lloyd, and Washington Governor John R. Rogers. The paper became a forum to discuss broad aspects of socialism as well as specific problems of the BCC.

The major tie with three thousand BCC members in the United States and Canada, *Industrial Freedom* solicited support for the colony and conducted elections and referenda. Although denying a need to emulate the competitive journalistic world, it carried some advertisements for reading matter related to socialism or colonization and for nearby stores and services. As the BCC diminished, the broader aspect of the newspaper narrowed to colony concerns. [89]

One worker called it "our house organ, our mouthpiece, or clarion or bugle call to the nation," and the son of the Freeland Colony editor remembered it as the "most noted of all colony newspapers," except the *Coming Nation*. At a subscription rate of one dollar a year, forty-seven hundred copies were being issued weekly by the end of 1898. The paper was not free from trouble, however. Refused acceptance as second-class matter at the post office, it once altered the name to *Freedom* and continued publication until a favorable decision was received from the government. [90]

The talent that produced *Industrial Freedom* included persons with past journalistic experience and others with potential. Editors included David Burgess, former editor of a farm weekly in Arkansas, and L. F. Austin, a journalist from Bellingham. Briefly a columnist the first summer was George E. Boomer who wrote under the pseudonym of "Uncle Sam" and had been with the *Appeal to Reason*. Boomer later edited radical papers in several Washington communities, became known as a lecturer, was Socialist candidate for governor, and died while publishing a Port Angeles socialist newspaper. Another columnist was Bige Eddy, a "well known and lucid reform writer," who came from his southwestern Washington home to write "Musings of a Mossback: Independent Comment on Current Conditions by a Dyed-in-the-Wool Calamity Howler." Two women writers known to socialist readers were Annie Billingsley and Sarah Ward Temple. Kaufman continued in Northwest reform journalism and became editor of the *Pacific Grange Bulletin*, the official Grange publication of Oregon and Washington. [91]

No one who worked on the paper achieved greater prominence than E. B. (Harry) Ault, who arrived as a teenager from Kentucky in April 1898, learned the newspaper and printing business on

Industrial Freedom, became its editor before he was eighteen, and moved on to work for the Seattle *Socialist.* In the late 1910s and 1920s, Ault was editor of the Seattle *Union Record,* published by the Central Labor Council, the only daily newspaper published by organized labor in the United States. In this post, Ault worked closely with labor leaders and was a power among them locally and nationally. He played a key role during the Seattle General Strike of February 1919. After the paper failed in 1928, its former editor became a deputy United States marshal in Tacoma for fifteen years. He died in retirement in 1961. [92]

At Equality, Ault's publishing activities had included a monthly magazine for children, *Young Socialist.* A Kansas librarian had been editing a "Children's Corner" each week for *Industrial Freedom,* but in April 1899, "Sister Helen" asked to be relieved, and fifteen-year-old Harry Ault suggested a children's publication at Equality. In a shed a few feet away from the main print shop, Ault and a friend set up their own press. From November 1899 to May 1902, Ault issued his magazine there almost single-handed.

At first the publication fulfilled its objective of "a paper of, by and for the young people. . . ." One representative issue contained a lead story about two self-centered little girls, a poem by James Russell Lowell, editorials on mother, on worry, and on kindness, a page of letters, a column of didactic anecdotes and quotations, and some notes about children at Equality. Copies of *Young Socialist* were mailed to many parts of the United States, although circulation was never much more than a hundred copies and contributions from readers were meager. As Ault grew older, he became more interested in adult publications and in amateur press associations. Long before he left the colony in the early summer of 1902, his magazine had lost its juvenile aspect. Sporadic issues came from Spokane and from Lewiston, Idaho, until the final copy appeared in February 1904.[93]

Meanwhile *Industrial Freedom* had also disappeared. When the colony sold its printing press, in April 1902, a Whatcom newspaper wrote that Equality itself had died, a conclusion vehemently denied by Ault. Later that year, however, *Industrial Freedom* ceased publication, and in December the *Whidby Islander,* published at Freeland Colony, began to carry official Equality statements. By this time the ambitions of the national organization—and the consequent need for a newspaper—had vanished. [94]

Some clues to the general failure of Equality Colony may be discerned in its industrial weaknesses. The potential for success in dairying, logging, and milling was there; others later carried on such activities in the same location. The colony needed sound managers and foremen with technical knowledge and skills, the ability to lead men, and a willingness to stay; it also needed a corps of dedicated, disciplined workers willing to exert themselves for the common benefit. Equality had neither. Ed Pelton, Charles Swigart, Carey Lewis, and others successfully inaugurated projects, but they were unable to maintain the effort. Able, willing, and practical workers were never present in enough proportion to outbalance the unproductive, the hangers-on, the dissidents, and the disgruntled. The ultimate values and goals were not in sight clearly enough to sustain an industrial effort. Furthermore, there was insufficient capital either initially or from sales. The colony was not located close enough to population centers or to effective transportation to compete with outside markets. These factors of industrial failure represent in capsule the total colony failure. At certain moments or in specific areas, matters went smoothly, but over the long run successes were too infrequent or too briefly maintained to endure.

In the early months colonists began to shape the social aspects of their lives. On the one hand, Equality was a western frontier town. Isolation joined with the rush of people during the first year to encourage cooperation. These needs were enhanced by the communitarian ideal of sharing and cooperating in daily experiences. Living communally in large apartment houses, preparing and eating meals together, meeting certain personal needs of members, providing for the young, and participating in meetings and recreation were both social necessities and acts of belief.

A first essential was housing. During the winter of 1897-98, the pioneers constructed dwellings for the several hundred settlers expected in the spring and summer. Five log cabins were built first. Fort Bellamy, the largest, was later converted into the dining room and kitchen, but the attic temporarily housed newcomers.

The other four cottages were strung close together near the foot of the hill. Fourteen by twenty feet in size, they were crude and primitive. Then with lumber from the Savage mill, colonists began the two apartment buildings that would survive throughout most of the communitarian existence.

Apartment House No. 1 was ready by April. Two stories high, it measured twenty-four by fifty-two feet and contained twelve rooms and an attic dormitory. Work was rushed on the second apartment house, ten feet wider and twice as long, for completion in May. The two floors could crowd thirty families into as many small rooms, and a long open attic sufficed for bachelors. Eventually families would receive two or more rooms. The self-sufficient colonists proudly noted that the second building used lumber and shingles cut on the site, with money paid out only for such things as hardware and windows.

A photograph taken just before Apartment House No. 2 was completed shows eight windows on each floor with an outside stairway leading to a small porch. Inside, long central corridors led to apartments with meager and plain furnishings. Beds, tables, and chairs were manufactured by the colony, and personal possessions were brought by some colonists. Some walls were plastered; one member who was a professional wallpaper hanger added this finished touch. But pictures of these buildings failed to satisfy the aesthetic taste of a Massachusetts correspondent. Houses of finished lumber lacked the charm of the log cabin, "which seems capable of endless variety and beauty," he wrote. [95]

Close living conditions hindered privacy and facilitated quarrels and the spread of disease. A teenage boy was exasperated by fleas. Fire was an ever threatening danger that could have brought disaster, but it was late autumn 1901 before chimneys replaced stovepipes that stuck through windows. To the dedicated, apartment living represented a major component of communal life, a test of sincerity and perseverance, but many had come expecting homes. Bitterly, one mother wrote, "I, with my son had one room (had there been ten of us we would have had the same) in an apartment that is not [as] well lighted, heated or ventilated as a stable would be." [96]

These rooms were essentially sleeping quarters; most activities were carried on elsewhere. Several hundred yards away a laundry room drew creek water for washing and bathing. A small force of men and women did laundering and ironing for everyone, boiling water over furnaces and struggling with troublesome equipment. By the second summer water was piped from the creek to the area near the buildings.

A few colonists lived at the "Hatchery,"and the first summer some BCC office workers remained at the small hotel or in rented rooms in Edison. Others in Edison and Equality lived in tents.[97]

These living conditions were considered only temporary. When pressures eased, a hillside town would arise with individual homes authorized, planned, constructed, and owned by the community. The promise of privately built homes was intimated, but this retreat from the communal ideal was rarely allowed until later days. During 1898 the projected townsite was surveyed. The general assembly determined the size and design of houses according to family size, economy, and the wish to avoid individual distinctions. The next spring the first foundations were laid, with allotments granted in the order of the colonists' arrival—lot 1, block A, went to the Carey Lewises. By midsummer houses were ready for the Ed Pelton and Ernest Marquart families, who professed to be "reluctant" to leave the apartments. Although builders contemplated finishing two houses a week, few were completed. A year later almost half of the now diminished population still lived in apartments. [98]

The colony produced most of its own food, although milk and meat were often in short supply. Colony livestock provided eggs, butter, and milk. Vegetables and fruits were stored for winter in a large bin. A bakery started early; and in a building "fitted with brick furnace and copper-bottomed pan," the ladies canned fruit, apple butter, and pickles. That first July, however, these local supplies had to be supplemented by wagonloads of groceries from Whatcom. [99]

In the cuisine department, as many as eight women worked in three shifts to prepare meals. During the first summer, Fort Bellamy was adapted for preparing and eating meals. The kitchen, pans and utensils hanging on log walls, had a great wood stove and oven at one side, with cupboards and work areas opposite. A long sturdy table, used to prepare and serve meals, separated kitchen from dining area.

Three times daily the colonists gathered to eat and socialize. On arrival, each person parted with one of the twenty-one meal tickets issued weekly. At times, perhaps when the population was the largest and facilities most crowded, colonists ate in shifts, first the men in from work, then women, and finally children. During another period, family groups had assigned tables. "Watching our people come to breakfast," wrote a participant, was "like a circus." Most waited until they heard the second bell. "At that signal the stairs rattle and rumble like a hundrnd [*sic*] mules on a barn door . . . , and if the ground is covered with snow a percentage of them will be seized with an uncontrollable desire to stand on their heads for which eccentricity another percentage will charge upon them with snowballs. Scuffling, joshing, some laughing and others grumbling, they all get to the table in less time than it takes to write it."[100] This for the adults; better conduct was expected of the young. "One of the most pleasing sights," that one witness observed, "was about forty neatly dressed children, ranging in ages from five to ten years . . . ," marching in true soldier style to their dinner.

A colonist later recalled the food being "meager fare of sauerkraut and beans." But contemporary description appraised it as "very simple, but good and substantial, consisting chiefly of bread, beans, and corn and oatmeal mush, boiled and fried; for butter an excellent substitute is furnished in the shape of gravy, made of milk, flour, and cottolene. Sugar is given once a day, pie and coffee cake once a week. Fresh meat I have not seen since here. Sometimes we get a relish in a bit of bacon and fruit. Cereal coffee is used and much relished. . . . At the tables you may occasionally hear a jocose remark about beefsteak, mutton chops, quail on toast, and prairie Chicken, etc., etc., but rarely a complaint about the fare." Food, then, was plain but adequate; mealtime a highlight. [101]

The second summer a store in the printery building offered items for personal needs. One fall *Industrial Freedom* noted receipt of a "big case full of dry goods and furnishings. . . . Hats and caps, blankets and underclothes." Besides merchandise from the outside, the store sold clothes and other products manufactured at the colony. The means of exchange was BCC scrip. Members received allowances each week, originally at fifty "fractions" to persons over eighteen years of age, with correspondingly smaller amounts for those younger.[102]

A post office occupied one corner of the store. The small Edison office had been unable to handle the increased volume of mail created by BCC headquarters and *Industrial Freedom*. Service to Equality was poor, and after considerable effort Equality was granted a fourth-class post office in February 1899, with Mrs. Carey Lewis as postmaster. She was succeeded by James B. Ault, who served until his death in 1901. That year the post office was moved to nearby Bow.[103]

A newcomer the first spring was alarmed by the large number of children and feared crowded accommodations, a need for activities to interest the young, and conflict among families, although he confessed surprise that this "was not much keener than it turned out to be." The "Colony kids," wrote one of them, "are of all ages and sizes from the boy of 17 who has just begun to shave and is anxiously waiting the arrival of his mustasche, and the girl of the same age who is looking around for a beau, to the baby of three weeks who thinks of little or nothing." [104]

A department of education and recreation was formed in 1898, with the Reverend C. E. Walker as superintendent. Three women, one of them Kate Halladay, still in her teens but with teaching experience, took charge of the young children; a few older ones went to Edison for schooling. District No. 68 was later established and maintained with county and state funds and certified teachers. The department aimed "to teach subjects rather than books and dead authors. The outline system is used as far as practicable, making the use of a variety of textbooks possible, and indeed, broadening the interest thereby." Here was as clear a statement of educational philosophy as ever emerged. Despite talk of teaching "socialistic principles," the colony professed unorthodox theories of neither process nor materials. Former students later scoffed at rumors that they had been indoctrinated in the theories of Karl Marx. [105]

Summer allowed time to prepare for the fall opening. "We need readers, arithmetics, grammars, geographies, histories, etc.," continued the department report. "Send prepaid, if you have any to donate to us." Such requests for teaching supplies frequently went to reserves. During July and early August the colonists built a two-story schoolhouse that would also serve general community functions, and they manufactured desks and other furnishings.[106]

On Monday, 19 September 1898, school opened with David Burgess as principal and Kate Halladay as teacher. Attendance was small; many older children were still working in the fields. By October, however, Burgess contemplated needing one part-time and four full-time teachers. Expectations were overly optimistic; in November there were seventy students, in January fifty. Usually two teachers handled eight grades in two rooms. Most instructors remained but a single year, although some were regular colony residents. Instruction was enlivened with occasional field trips along the Chuckanut shore, and one teacher took pride in the innovation of industrial training for boys. The quality of education must remain unknown, but at least two students found that when they self-consciously transferred to "city schools," they were up with or ahead of their peers academically. Students beyond grade eight could go to a nearby town; by 1905, District No. 68 and five neighboring districts had united to form a high school at Edison. In 1914, seven years after the colony ended, District No. 68 was dissolved. [107]

The youngest children received care while parents worked. Mrs. Ida Jolly met with thirty-one charges, aged three to six, from eight until four, with breaks for lunch and snacks.

But life was not all schooling for Equality children. "My childhood up there was about the happiest childhood that any child could ever want. . . . Friendly! . . . You knew everybody and everybody knew you . . . the entertainments . . . masquerade balls and basket parties." Water and wooded areas afforded swimming, fishing, and hiking. Children played around a big rock, its appeal enhanced by the discovery there of a skeleton, probably of some animal, but clearly adaptable to more romantic origins. Pets were few, except for Bounce, a much-loved dog left by a former member. More urban pleasures were attested to by an advertisement for a bicycle outgrown by its owner: "King's Own Scorcher, weighs 19 pounds, '95 model, in good order, with new Morgan & Wright tires, $15, F.o.b. Edison or Belfast." Older children participated in adult and group entertainments, dances, and picnics.[108]

A few adults were especially popular with the children. Barton the blacksmith fixed "spears" or made toys and told humorous stories, and kitchen workers would occasionally slip goodies to the children. But other adults seemed harsh, strict, or impatient when bothered by the young. The young people were not always responsive. A boy recalled lectures on the steps of the "Hatchery": "On clear summer evenings the Lady Editor would dilate on the wonders of astronomy to the group of youngsters who, having nothing else to do, would listen more or less politely and calmly let her words of wisdom pass into one ear and out the other."[109]

Several teen-agers organized the "Iriquois [*sic*] Literary Society," a debating and literary club: ". . . you ought to see the red fire and hear the fireworks go off" as members heard a report on the personality of Admiral Dewey. The topic for the next meeting? "Resolved—That it is better to work outside than go to school." Other organized activities included an "industrial school," which was a subterfuge to recruit clearing and roadwork from the younger boys, drilling practice, and a Junior BCC. First attempted in the spring of 1898, this was reinstituted later by Harry Ault, who offered his *Young Socialist* to coordinate a nationwide junior brotherhood. It functioned briefly if at all. [110]

The boys were expected to help with clearing and field work, the girls with cleaning and food serving. A moralistic appeal appeared in the *Young Socialist*: "There is quite a number of boys and girls in Equality. Some of them try to be useful, and some, we are sorry to say, do not, but would rather play and go fishing all the time. There are a great many ways that boys and girls could be useful here if they wish. Some of the girls who are old enough wait on tables, wash dishes and sweep floors; some of the boys saw wood, help dig out stumps, or work around the barn . . . . he [a worker] will be much wiser than the boys who waste their time playing and getting into mischief." When young Harry Ault made a similar comment, he added with candor, "it applies to the older folks as well."[111]

Adults did not lack recreation. Evenings were free, and work ceased for the week at Saturday noon. "The cultural aspects of the colony were not slighted," Ault recalled. "The dance was, of course, the most popular with the younger folk, but the amateur dramatics, the discussion lyceums, and mass or choral singing all drew capacity houses." Saturday evening dances were held on the bottom floor of the schoolhouse. Colony members looked forward to them, and they attracted guests from nearby farms and communities, such visits occasionally being returned. One printed program listed eighteen dances from the "Grand March" to "Home Sweet Home" that included quadrilles, waltzes, a schottische, and a two-step. Music that evening was provided by the "Colony Orchestra—Profs. Young and Potts and Smith Family." James Potts, a "splendidly artistic concertina player," was always in the center of things musical, as was A. L. Young, noted for his clarinet playing, his strong singing voice, and a repertoire of humorous songs. Other musicians included violinists, "with a 'fiddler or two,' " a baritone, a piccolo player, and performers on the mouth organ.[112]

Plans to organize a brass band faltered for lack of instruments. A "Thursday evening singing school" was an excuse for group singing. The director was " 'Hallelujah' or 'High Pressure' Young"; after he left, the singing sessions deteriorated, but for a time they were grand affairs. Along with traditional favorites, songs included Populist or radical lyrics set to familiar tunes, and newer socialist songs. One girl particularly remembers "We Are All Merry Socialists." But the singing mattered more than the songs, and especially for the children, the louder the better.[113]

Group singing was supplemented with a mixed quartet. Young was the tenor, but the mainstay was "the little Welsh Baker," probably W. C. Davis, barely four feet tall, with a full beard and a deep bass voice: " . . . it was excruciating to the kids to see him rise on his tiptoes at each explosion of 'trinke' in the drinking song, and to hear the deep notes of 'Simon the Collarer' from such a diminutive body." Potts, his concertina in hand, sang an occasional baritone, and the soprano was "a little woman with a big mouth full of teeth." Their repertoire varied, but the "sure-fire bid for applause" came when, wearing red bandanas, the quartet offered, "We All Have a Very Bad Cold." [114]

Plays and skits were popular. The original organizer was Mrs. Ida Jolly. A "Grand Entertainment & Ball" for the day after Christmas 1898 was announced by the Equality Dramatic Company. There would be music, a grand march, a tableau, and two plays, "Persecuted Dutchman," a one-act farce, and "The Fortune Hunter." In February the "Jolly Dramatic Co." prepared to present a drama in Edison. Probably the play was "Kathleen Mavourneen," which would have toured nearby communities but for a veto by mothers of some of the younger thespians. [115]

Few outside speakers came to Equality, but some with special appeal spoke in nearby towns. When William Jennings Bryan visited Whatcom during his 1900 presidential campaign, several young men made an overnight journey to hear him, and others probably saw him in Mount Vernon later that day. At least one Equality resident was among the two hundred persons that heard Eugene V. Debs in Whatcom in 1899. The active socialist organization of that city drew such other speakers as the feminist Charlotte Perkins Gilman, former mayors John C. Chase of Haverhill, Massachusetts, and J. Stitt Wilson of Berkeley, California, and the Seattle editor, Dr. Hermon Titus. Colonists quite likely traveled north to hear them. [116]

Intellectually inclined colonists engaged in ever present talk; many were well read and versed in current issues of socialism and reform. The general assembly, *Industrial Freedom,* and weekly lyceums offered forums. One young listener recalled "wonderful debates on aspects of the radical movement that would leave the listeners all at sea and the debaters physically exhausted." Once, when a lecturer on "Health" failed to appear, the colonists substituted a lively discussion on the "tramp question." A small library included books donated by distant BCC members. One frequent contributor was Charles D. Raymer, a Minneapolis bookseller interested in the communitarian movement, whose later bookstores in Tacoma and Seattle became gathering places for radicals. [117]

The area offered recreational activities. Adults and children enjoyed clam digging, boating, walking, hiking, and picnicking, with fishing and hunting both necessities and pleasures. Especially diverting were sails to Samish or Eliza islands on one of the two colony boats. The *Progress* could handle at least twenty persons on an overnight jaunt, and the *Dora,* a four-oared, single-masted skiff, could carry ten. Not all members shared in such fun. Some chafed at those who played, for there was always work to do. But relief from chores was generally considered necessary, and "recreation itself became almost an industry." [118]

Special events called for celebrations. Each first of November commemorated the founding of Equality Colony. The 1899 celebration was probably representative:

November 1st, day of the second anniversary of Equality Colony, dawned bright and clear, an ideal day for a celebration, and so Bros. Pelton and Lewis spent a day on the ditch, the sawmill ran all day, the donkey engine worked and the women were busy preparing the goodies for the midnight lunch. The ball was started rolling at 7 p.m. sharp, and was kept rolling until 10 p.m. Then the orchestra struck up a march and the dance was on, and it stayed on until 4 a.m. At midnight the lunch was served and everybody enjoyed themselves and the pie immensely.

An address by colony president Halladay was followed by recitations, group singing, instrumental and vocal offerings, and plays. At least one celebration of May Day was held, although the long-planned program was postponed because of the accidental death of a child. [119]

No event was more notable than the first colony wedding, that of Kate Halladay, teacher and daughter of the colony president, to Bert Savage, whose father had operated the first sawmill. The ceremony took place on the morning of 28 November 1898. Ferns, fir boughs, and wild grape tied with white ribbons adorned the schoolhouse, and an organ was borrowed for the occasion. In the best society column tradition the colony paper reported the bride's ensemble as "cream Henrietta silk, lace and watered silk sash, moss roses and buds in her hair, carrying in her hand, a bouquet of maiden hair ferns tied with cream ribbon." [120]

Not all occasions were happy. Funerals were memorable and many. One child never forgot the somber black procession of mourners singing "Our Circle Is Broken" as they wound over the creek and through the orchard to the tiny cemetery atop a knoll. Her father, colony founder Ed Pelton, was buried there, as were Postmaster Ault and others. In the middle 1920s "Daddy" W. R. Giles, a white-whiskered Englishman who remained long after the colony died, was last to be placed in the small plot.

Death sometimes visited in particularly sad and shocking ways. Ault's illness had been long and Pelton's death was sudden. A bachelor broke his neck in a fall when a railing collapsed on the upper porch of an apartment house. Leonard Hoehn was thrown from his wagon while driving a team home from Edison; his four orphaned children were cared for by the colony. An eighteen-

year-old was killed in a logjam. Even sadder were the deaths of
small children. Jimmy Mooney's drowning in the creek postponed
the May Day celebration, and seven-year-old Rochill Gifford was
playing near a brush fire when he fell into a burning log. Several
premature babies died in infancy. [121]

General health was good, but ordinary childhood diseases could
reach dreaded epidemic proportions in the apartment houses.
When isolation was necessary, patients were removed to a
fenced-in "sick tent," where the only advantage was special food
allotments. After frequent references to mumps, measles, and
whooping cough, the colony paper finally appealed, "Equality
needs a physician." Previously there had been at least one doctor,
and several women acted as nurses. A new doctor arrived in
response to the request, but he soon moved on.[122]

Formal religion had a small part in the colonists' lives.
"Mutualism or the Kingdom of Heaven Here and Now" proclaimed the letterhead on some of Lermond's early BCC correspondence, but this bow toward the Christian Socialist movement
was soon forgotten. Some Christian Socialists lent their names to
the circular calling for the BCC, and a few religious leaders—
notably BCC President Myron W. Reed—participated. But neither
Equality Colony nor its parent organization stemmed from solid
religious foundations.[123]

The first issue of *Industrial Freedom* outlined the practice:

The colony has no religion; . . . Some of the members of Equality Colony
have a denominational religion, and others have not; but the colony as such
does not deal in denominations, the fullest freedom in matters of dogma and
creed being left to every individual. Whenever any of the individual members
wish to follow any form of religious worship, they are at liberty, as
individuals and in the same manner as citizens of the United States
throughout the country to follow their own private convictions in their own
private affairs. We have no religious question here, any more than we have a
dress question or a diet question.[124]

Later comments reiterated the unwillingness to obstruct individual
liberty. Organized religion was seen as a form of hypocrisy
unnecessary to living the good life:

If you entertain the belief that no person can be religious unless he believes in the doctrine of man's total depravity brought about by the fall of
Adam and Eve; their salvation through faith in the vicious atonement of Jesus

Christ, and endless punishment, if that atonement is not accepted and trusted in before death, then . . . a large majority of the colonists are not religious, for they have no belief in any such doctrine. But if you mean by religion a manifest desire to bring to the individual and others the consciousness of a present sense of good, to live according to the golden rule, to be honest, sober, faithful to duty, mutually tolerant on all subjects of belief, industrious almost to a fault, . . . then I think they will compare most favorably with any religious community in this or any other country.

A visitor who rhapsodized about Christianity consciously being put into daily practice simply misunderstood what she observed.[125]

But if religion was not prescribed, neither was it proscribed. Buildings and meeting rooms were available for services, and the first meetings held at the schoolhouse were to organize a "Sabbath School." The Reverend C. E. Walker, whose Presbyterian theology had taken a liberal turn during his ministry in the Middle West, inaugurated a Sunday School and church services but they drew only a few colonists. Walker, discouraged and having personal problems, did not remain long, but others carried on. Nondenominational services were held, and there were evening prayer meetings twice a week. The Halladay wedding was a religious service. Most regular religious observances, however, attracted only a devout minority.

There were a few minor sects. Several early members formed a Theosophical Society, and later a small Spiritualist circle centered around the adult daughter of an Illinois family. There were few or no Roman Catholics; a presumably Jewish group arrived later, but they observed few religious practices. "Most of us," summarized a colony official in 1901, "might be described by the term of agnostic." [126]

In social aspects, Equality Colony was the most fully developed communitarian experiment in the Pacific Northwest. The early rush of population and frontier exigencies combined with founders' beliefs to ensure certain cooperative practices in daily life. Despite crowding, a lack of certain foods, inadequate help in some areas, and occasional personal antagonisms, communitarian life was carried on with some success at Equality. The ultimate failure was as much a flaw of the theory as of the practice: a basic unwillingness of persons to sacrifice individuality permanently for communal practices and regimentation.

In the long run, then, Equality failed not only to achieve its broad goal, but also to continue its very existence. As population fell and goals narrowed, a decline set in that culminated with the final dissolution of the colony in 1907. Events moving toward that end spanned several years.

In November 1901, Equality observed its fourth anniversary with a special edition of *Industrial Freedom*. The colonists presented a picture of strength. Several departments were working and producing; there were many activities for members to engage in; old family names remained among new ones. But that edition revealed different ideals and goals and substantially different communities than did early issues. The settlers no longer dreamed of starting other colonies, of capturing Washington for socialism, or of creating a better world. They had, rather, an implicit hope that the future would merely continue and stabilize the present direction. Yet unfinished, Equality was a proud, self-contained community of persons trying to make a living and gain a small profit. The special edition might have been describing any one of a hundred or a thousand small, rural, isolated communities in the western United States. Editor Harry Ault noted that the colony was emerging from "pioneer life into . . . that of the ordinarily well-to-do proletarian." Here was a fading echo of the old radicalism.

Progress during these four years had been slower than some hoped, but the value of colony property had increased from an initial outlay of thirty-five thousand dollars to forty-five thousand dollars' worth of land, improvements, and equipment. Ault added that despite past quarrels and problems, "we have lived and prospered." By 1901, living and prospering seemed to be enough for the hundred persons that remained.[127]

The next spring, the *Reveille* mentioned the colony for the first time in months, noting: "Equality colony has failed." Once shared poverty had held the experiment together, the paper averred, but the best workers were gone, leaving behind only the indolent. Ault jumped to answer. True, the printing press had just been sold and many persons had left, but Equality was not dead nor were the defectors the most valuable workers. *Industrial Freedom* would continue, and "skilled artisans" remained. Equality was "in a more prosperous condition than at any previous period in its history. . . ." But Ault, too, would soon leave, and a generation later he would recall that, "Those who were left were the die-hards who would not give up. . . ." Then he wrote the word "drifter," but crossed it out in favor of "incompetents who could not make as good a living anywhere else, and a few self-seekers who hoped to profit in the final breakup by getting control of the colony property." [128]

Industrial Freedom suspended publication and the population declined further, but when Rochdale organizer Alonzo A. Wardall visited in 1903, he wrote encouragingly, "The Colony here is in fine shape. Have 620 acres of land and out of debt, except $800 on the shingle mill, which they can pay any time. Have 100 acres in fine crops—oats, hay, fruit and vegetables; new 80-ton silo, which they are filling with green oats, clover, and corn; 50 cattle, 35 hogs, 300 hens, 9 horses and 80 swarms of bees. They have thirty houses, saw and shingle mill, feed and graham flour mill, dairy and cheese factory, laundry, bakery, etc. They have 38 people on the ground now, but I believe will gain from now on." A 1904 letterhead suggested that small-town businessmen had replaced starry-eyed utopians: "Manufacturers of Lumber and Shingles," and "Cereal Coffee; Canned Fruits, Farm Products." However pleasant and productive, this assuredly was not the Equality of the founders' dreams. [129]

This calm was shattered by a flurry of activity reminiscent of the first spring but with ominous overtones. In 1905 a small band of newcomers appeared, led by Alexander Horr, a New York anarchist who sought to invigorate Equality along his own lines of thought. Under his influence, the constitution was altered and members were reorganized into small competitive groups. The colony name was changed to Freeland, borrowed from a utopian novel by Theodor Hertzka. [130]

Hertzka, an Austrian economist, had progressed from orthodoxy toward radical thought. His major influence came in 1891 with the publication of *Freiland*. In a preface Hertzka considered why workers' rewards were not commensurate with their efforts and why poverty existed despite man's ability to produce wealth.

His answer lay in the failure of capitalism to consume surplus produce and in the inequal interest system. Capital must be available for production without limitations being put on individual freedom or justice: " . . . *if interest can be dispensed with without introducing communistic control in its stead, then there no longer stands any positive obstacle in the way of the establishment of the free social order* [italics in the London edition]." In *Freiland* this was achieved.[131]

The novel was both travelogue and love story set in a colony in an isolated valley of Kenya. Twenty-five years produced a sound nation based upon peace, equality, public participation, individual freedom, and cultural attainments evenly spread amidst beauty and convenience. Europeans became impressed by this superior African state. In a debate between spokesmen for differing nations, the Freeland representative converted both rightist and leftist to his views.

Hertzka proposed a colony scheme, suggesting a constitution and "model statutes." Admission was open to all persons equally, with each member having a claim upon colony land and means of production. The highest governmental body was a general meeting, but association business would be managed by an elected board of directors. Wages were based upon the number of hours worked by each individual and by seniority, association profits being divided annually among workers. Women, children, and those unable to work were guaranteed maintenance proportionate to the general wealth, and each person was allowed maximum freedom, so long as he did not infringe upon the rights of others.[132]

In Europe, Hertzka's ideals inspired programs similar to those of the Bellamy movement in the United States, with the publication of journals, the translation of the book into several languages, the formation of *Freiland vereines* in large cities, and the appearance of related articles. The British government allegedly halted one attempt to establish a Freeland colony. By the late 1890s, the movement had spread to the United States, with headquarters in Philadelphia. When the BCC was formed, congratulations arrived from this group, and two Freeland officials became BCC members.[133]

The Freeland movement had attracted Alexander Horr. Born in Hungary and raised an orthodox Jew, Horr worked his way to the

United States, where he encountered the writings of Marx and Herbert Spencer. Becoming known among New York radicals, he was a friend of Emma Goldman and helped publish an anarchist journal. Horr became involved in a newly organized Freeland Central Association and was their delegate to a cooperative league. When the Freeland Printing and Publishing Company issued the American edition of Hertzka's book, Horr wrote the introduction and invited inquiries. [134]

In the autumn of 1904, Horr, thirty-three years old, arrived at Equality to become a member, identifying himself as a book dealer and, incidentally, offering the colony 160 copies of *Freeland*. A friend later described him as a "little man, redheaded, quick in his movements," like "mercury," and fond of arguing radical issues. The colony quickly became divided between Horr's followers and opponents. Before the end of the year, Equality Colony had been renamed. Horr returned briefly to New York to speak at a BCC-sponsored meeting in the interests of "Freeland Colony, Bow, Washington." He returned with his wife, an Austrian with experience "in the book business." [135]

Now Horr's work began in earnest. He was an able publicist and, it would seem, a practiced lecturer. News items about the colony reappeared in Mount Vernon, where the *Argus* headlined that "Equality is Rejuvenated" and described energetic plans centering around Horr. As colony secretary, Horr prepared a series of meetings on principles of economy, politics, and social life, and set out to organize a Mount Vernon local of the BCC. With holdings estimated at fifty thousand dollars, Equality reorganized its labor arrangement and made industrial changes, including construction of a fruit and vegetable cannery that Horr predicted would operate at a capacity of two thousand cans a day the following season. Recruits were arriving from the East, and the colony population increased by 30 percent. [136]

That summer the constitution of the BCC was fundamentally revised. The objective of colonizing a state was formally replaced by the goal of working and aiding "the establishment of cooperative colonies, a central warehouse and a central clearing house by accumulating land and capital for the benefit of all co-operators and libertarians." Instead of uniting "all socialists in one fraternal organization," the BCC would "unite all libertarians in a compact and flexible weapon with which to constructively undermine the basis of monopoly and invasion," the term "libertarian" being suggestive of anarchistic rhetoric. Old departments were abolished. The individual functions of the eight-man board of trustees were well defined; collectively they had wide control over money and lands. With a single stated exception, lands were not to be sold, encumbered, or mortgaged as long as three cooperators remained. Recall of officers and constitutional amendments were made difficult. Local unions had greater autonomy than previously. Freeland Colony became the new Local Union No. 1, and had thirty members that year; Local No. 2 was established in New York with thirty-four members; five other locals were created in the vicinity of the colony.[137]

Colonists divided themselves into voluntary groups with specific production goals. Seven groups were organized, responsible for dairy, orchard, clearing and agriculture, cereal coffee, apiary and baking, poultry, and building. Funds advanced from the general holdings enabled the groups to operate independently, but wages and profits within each were divided as its members saw fit, usually according to the hours worked. Thus the Freeland experiment went into operation with equipment, buildings, personnel, and over six hundred acres of land. The Equality ideal of cooperation was replaced by a plan stressing competition among small groups of individuals.[138]

Horr and his followers blended idealism and opportunism. The idealist saw in Equality the productive potential and a nucleus of people that could develop a program based on the Hertzka philosophy. The opportunist saw a stagnant experiment composed of tired, possibly disillusioned colonists whose lands and properties were plums to be picked. Horr converted enough old members and brought in sufficient new ones to alter the colony. But he aroused an energetic opposition. Controversies greater than the colony had ever known erupted into factional quarrels, agreements made and broken, threats, violence, and legal actions that left a reservoir of bitterness. The dispute evolved from personal antagonisms and from quarrels over control of colony property. The old colonists had developed a life that was settled, relatively calm and comfortable; they considered themselves to have prior rights to colony properties. Now their accomplishments seemed threatened by latecomers with different backgrounds and ideals. When Horr's opponents mustered force and strength to challenge him, factionalism became an emotional, personal struggle.

Its critics viewed the Horr crowd as politically extremist and morally loose: " . . . so-called socialists, who claim not only to be anarchists but free lovers, living in lewd, open, and notorious adultery, to such an extent that the decent element . . . are unable to relieve themselves of such obnoxious and unlawful practices. . . ." A Bellingham paper later reported in boldface type that Horr's walls were covered with "the pictures of many famous anarchists . . . including the likeness of the man who assassinated President William McKinley."[139]

The struggle for leadership teeter-tottered between one group and the other. In midsummer Horr and George K. Salvage, a new member, were replaced as secretary and treasurer respectively by I. H. Nosovitch and W. B. Boyd of the other faction. Yet by September the Horr partisans, calling themselves the "Hertzka Colony," had sufficient strength on the board of trustees to lease to themselves 160 acres of colony land and other properties including the store and print shop. Rental was $160 a year for 99 years. When opponents attacked the lease at a general assembly meeting, someone blew out the lights and a free-for-all erupted in the darkness. An attempt to oust Horr that evening failed; his opponents sued to have the lease voided, but greater dissension was in store.[140]

Colonists violated precept and constitution by mortgaging properties, in fact, by obtaining separate mortgages on the same property from two different sources. The general assembly, under control of the anti-Horr faction, authorized a mortgage of colony property to raise funds for legal services. Subsequently, they obtained a five-hundred-dollar chattel mortgage from M. P. Hurd and Willard Brickey, Mount Vernon law partners, using livestock, eighty tons of hay, and various equipment as collateral. Later A. K. Hanson, as colony secretary, obtained a similar four-hundred-dollar mortgage from two other Mount Vernon attorneys. The contest between the two mortgages ended in superior court when the judge allowed the Hurd and Brickey claim and ordered the property sold.

At the same time Horr's opponents sought to break his

ninety-nine-year lease. Arthur B. Ellis, Jr., brought as arbitrator from the Co-operative Brotherhood at Burley, recommended dividing the property and reorganizing the colony through amendments and reincorporation. His suggestions were unacceptable to the anti-Horr majority. During this discussion "the brute Hart"—Charles F. Hart—physically attacked Horr, the fourth such incident, according to the victim. Hart pleaded guilty of assault and battery and was fined five dollars. [141]

Meanwhile, Ontario-born Kingsmill Commander had moved from Burley to become a central figure in colony affairs. As national secretary of the BCC, Commander joined Hart and Hanson in their fight against Horr. They turned up a former New York associate of Horr's who seemed eager to make damaging accusations against him, then balked at testifying in court and failed to come. [142]

During the final week of 1905 the suit was heard by Judge George S. Joiner. He disallowed the lease because two defendants were not BCC trustees when they made it, but he also refused to enjoin Horr from participating in colony matters. Judge Joiner denied the request for a receiver to wind up colony affairs, although he hinted that he might reconsider under different circumstances. [143]

The decision brought little relief from the tense chaotic situation. Colonists met frequently to attempt to dispose of property, divide possessions, and settle accounts, but tempers flared so constantly that the disputants could not even handle elementary matters. Delinquent tax assessments mounted because neither faction would pay for fear of losing the property. Outsiders attempted to acquire the land by paying the taxes.

On 1 February, a motion was offered that a receiver be sought to sell or dispose of the property. Hart proposed that all indebtedness be paid and that land be divided among members according to seniority, adding that his side would fight to the end. Horr admitted the fairness of Hart's proposals but argued that the land had been purchased with BCC money and members who had not lived there should also be consulted. True to his Freeland scheme, he suggested that the land be divided either by groups or individually and according to valuation rather than acreage. Halladay and Hart expressed concern about the expense of a receivership. A committee of three men who represented both factions tried for a week to devise a settlement, but could not agree. [144]

Between these two meetings a major catastrophe had wrought further frustration and heightened tempers. On the evening of Tuesday, 6 February, the barn, pride of the colony when completed in 1898, was suddenly in flames. All was well when "Daddy" Giles, who had charge of the dairy, had left it at seven-thirty, but by eight o'clock the structure was afire. Flames shot across a pathway to destroy the root house and threaten other buildings. Except for three horses and a few sacks of potatoes, everything in the building was lost: " . . . twenty head of milch cows, five calves, all the hay, being about 100 tons, and all of the products of the labor of said association including potatoes, roots and vegetables; two work horses, four sets of harness and tools necessary to carry on the operation of the farm, and the silo. . . ." The loss estimated at between eight and ten thousand dollars, and uninsured, left the colony "almost destitute." [145]

The cause of the fire remained unknown, but each faction accused the other of incendiarism. A few years later an unnamed former Equality member wrote an inquirer that " 'we burned the barn.' " Upon requesting more specific information, the correspondent heard "from a younger relative that the old colonist has become irresponsible in his old age and there was no truth in his assertion." If arson, the fire was a tragic, direct attack upon the welfare of members and a cruel treatment of helpless animals. But the loss of barn, root house, equipment, livestock, and winter food supply had even greater implications: it was a death knell to whatever willingness lingered among colonists to cooperate or live together peaccably. Suspicion, fear, and hatred engulfed the colony. [146]

Now it seemed inevitable that the colony would be dissolved, the only question concerning the apportionment of land and whatever funds remained. On 19 February, W. C. Davis, colony secretary, presented the following resolution:

We the assembled people of Freeland Colony recognizing the fact that irreconcilable differences having arisen among the members of the colony, several of whom have declared their intention to leave the colony and are now preparing so to do owing [here half a line, containing the word "fear" has been crossed out] to incendiarism, and violence and fearing further incendiarism, violence, assault, and perhaps murder, and having already been assaulted by certain members of the colony with deadly weapons, and plainly seeing the impossibility of further harmony, confidence, friendly relations or intercourse between the warring factions now existing in the colony, declare it to be the sense of the assembled people that the honourable court of Skagit Co., Washington be asked to appoint a receiver to wind up the affairs of the colony and dispose of the remaining property. . . .

The resolution carried and the action got under way. It did not, however, quiet matters in the general assembly, where a new proposal by Horr to lease lands prompted denunciations of the Freeland system as a failure and a fraud.[147]

The petition requesting a receiver reviewed the founding of the BCC and its colony, listed the remaining assets, and estimated the personal property, including buildings, at fifteen thousand dollars. The application graphically launched into the crux of the problem. Since 1905 when the new group had come in, the colony had been rent with "discord and violent dissension." Particularly since the burning of the barn, there existed a "reign of terror" that caused people to flee or live in fear. Appeals to county officials for protection had brought no help. Conditions prevailed "as should not be tolerated in any civilized or law abiding community." The objects of the BCC could no longer be carried out because the members could not live and cooperate together. Accompanying the receivership application were four shorter, identical supporting affidavits signed by colony members. The Horr faction denied the most sensational statements and protested the request, asserting that the property did not belong to the colonists alone and doubting that an equitable division was possible.[148]

Judge Joiner accepted the allegations of the petitioners and denounced the minority: "It is clearly shown . . . that these people cannot as a whole get along together." He ordered dissolution of the colony and of the BCC. The property was to be sold to pay indebtedness, with any remaining money divided individually among claimants. Members were ordered to cease cooperating even in small groups, and E. W. Ferris of Mount Vernon was appointed receiver. "Socialism as it is sometimes practiced came to an inglorious end Wednesday . . . ," the Mount Vernon *Argus* confirmed.[149]

A former court stenographer long active in county politics, Ferris set about untangling colony affairs. Confusion existed as to who constituted the legitimate membership. Numerous former members widely scattered had to be sought; many contacted Ferris. This search, along with litigation and the filing of claims, continued for over a year. Judge Joiner meanwhile permitted the lease of some land and the sale of other lands and property.

In his final report, Ferris listed four schedules of claims and properties. Some persons, mostly remaining colony members, wanted to purchase lots, some including buildings or houses. Others had claims, usually equal to the $160 membership fee, which the receiver favored paying in full, and there were still more claims which Ferris would only partially allow. Claims he could not verify were listed without recommendation.

The remaining four hundred acres were sold at auction on the afternoon of 1 June 1907 on the steps of the courthouse in Mount Vernon. As the high bidder John Peth, a well-to-do Skagit County farmer who was in many respects the antithesis of the colony founders, secured the lands for $12,400 plus payment of approximately $760 in delinquent and due taxes. In total, the properties brought in a little over seventeen thousand dollars. On 17 June, the sales were confirmed by Judge Joiner, and the history of the BCC and Equality Colony was closed. [150]

Controversy did not end. Dissatisfied former colonists challenged the proceedings, and the Peths sued to quiet title to their property. A lawsuit involving an Edison lumberman who had tried to secure the land by paying delinquent taxes was carried to the state supreme court, which in 1911 confirmed the claims of the Peth family. Meanwhile the new owners, sensitive to tales of violence that marked latter colony days, experienced additional irritations. When a bridge broke, dropping a loaded wagon into the creek, a son found that the runners beneath the structure had been cut; another time saw filings appeared in the hay. [151]

Several colonists, including the Halladays, W. R. Giles, Charles Herz, and Charles Hart, remained at the colony site on small plots of land now their own. Most others had long since scattered. Alexander Horr, the last of the major colony figures, moved on. Within a few weeks he was in San Francisco and in frequent trouble with authorities over activities, demonstrations, and protests. He continued to publicize Freeland ideas through pamphlets and magazine. Briefly he was partner in the bookstore of William McDevitt, but the two men who had been prominent during different critical times at Equality rarely compared their experiences. By 1922 Horr had retreated from his most extreme views and was the Socialist candidate for governor of California. Twenty-five years later, living "in a half-sunken shack between the hills" south of San Francisco with his second wife and a houseful of cats, and nursing dreams of a "steel city," bomb-proof, earthquake-proof, and available to the poor without profit, he died.[152]

Of the three objectives stated in the BCC constitution, two had clearly failed. Far from uniting "all socialists in one fraternal organization," the BCC merely added to the maze of socialist organizations in the 1890s. By the time the Socialist party was founded in 1901, the BCC was to most a dim memory. The great objective of socializing Washington through cooperative colonies and industries failed, and the BCC socialists made no great impression even within the socialist movement of the state.

The first stated objective to educate people in socialism may have had a modicum of success. At least thirty-five hundred families came into contact with the organization and perhaps five hundred directly with Equality. *Industrial Freedom* had possible influence through its national circulation, the continuing work of former staff members, and articles republished in other radical sheets. Some former Equality members continued to lecture and write, to publicize radical and reform doctrines, and to engage in politics. Most of these men would probably have carried on such activities had there never been an Equality Colony or if they had never lived in it. Yet Equality had drawn them west.

Equality directly touched the lives of more people than any other communitarian experiment in western Washington. No community of three hundred persons in a frontier state should be dismissed lightly, and Equality drew many who remained in the Pacific Northwest. Liberal in outlook before they arrived, the former colonists may well have made Washington more receptive to the radical and progressive ideas that soon flooded the state. That Washington never became the cooperative commonwealth of the socialists' dreams is not to say that it remained untouched by their efforts.

Equality Colony passed out of existence ten years after its founding at the Lewis farmhouse. Among the secular communitarian experiments of the nineteenth century, such a life span was creditable. Yet the heyday had lasted little more than a year, and in the final months disorder had been so great as to belie any real community spirit. Had they been willing, disciples of Edward Bellamy might have noted an apt obituary in his own *Equality*, published the year of the colony's birth. From the vantage point of the year 2000, the character Dr. Leete commented upon the communitarian efforts of the 1890s: "Economically weak, held together by a sentimental motive, generally composed of eccentric though worthy persons, and surrounded by a hostile environment . . . . it was scarcely possible that such enterprises should come to anything practical unless under exceptional leadership or circumstances."153 It was almost as if he had known Equality Colony.

4. Freeland

THE ROCHDALE TOWN

The Brotherhood of the Co-operative Commonwealth had intended to secure Washington for socialism by planting a series of colonies within the state. Equality, as the first colony in this scheme, was expected to help found others. In its most ambitious days, the BCC proffered assistance, and *Industrial Freedom* regularly called upon socialists elsewhere to establish local colonies. "Don't be backward, brethren, about soliciting our assistance," they promised. "We are at your service." The role Equality might have played can only be surmised, for the problems of maintaining her own existence left neither the ability nor the disposition to assist sister colonies, as the founders of Harmony learned. [1]

There was always some dissatisfaction at Equality. Several of the dissidents wished to leave Equality without abandoning their dreams of a socialist utopia that offered cooperative benefits. Some who left during 1900 and 1901 joined to create a less formally organized experiment on Whidbey Island at a place they named Freeland. Their efforts were inadvertently assisted by the Fidelity Trust Company, a Seattle land speculation firm soon to go bankrupt, for Freeland was partially a real estate promotion. [2]

The Seattle entrepreneur behind the Freeland movement was Irish-born James P. Gleason. In 1888 Gleason settled in Seattle to become active in real estate, investments, a law practice, and government service. In the early 1890s, as an officer of the Fidelity Trust Company, Gleason began to acquire real estate along Holmes Harbor, the long bay on the eastern shore of Whidbey Island. He was prepared to dispose of large tracts of land just when the disenchanted Equality socialists were seeking to relocate. [3]

As his agent among these socialists, Gleason enlisted George Washington Daniels. A man with an imposing name and a flowing white beard, Daniels had long been interested in socialism and had belonged to the Owens community at Topolobampo. Interested early in the BCC, he moved to Equality, but by 1899 he wanted to leave. On behalf of Gleason and his company, Daniels helped organize his fellow dissidents and to sell them land on Whidbey Island. [4]

Late in 1899, Daniels, Henry L. Stevens, originally from Burley Colony, and Henry A. White organized the Free Land Association, which incorporated in Island County on 12 January 1900. In addition to buying and selling, owning, and generally trading in lands, personal property, and stocks, the association was authorized

To engage, generally, in and to carry on . . . the business of merchandising and all kinds of business incidental thereto and which may be found convenient and advantageous in the furtherance thereof. To bond, mortgage, lease or otherwise acquire and to construct, own, manage and operate sawmills, shingle mills and other timber manufacturing plants, railways, toll roads, wharves, depots, sheds, store houses, bridges and other structures, means and appliances convenient, useful and necessary in the carrying on of said corporate business, together with the business of printing and the publication of newspapers, periodicals, books and means of advertising. To carry on farming, dairying, stock raising, and the building of houses for rent or sale and all other business incidental thereto. [5]

The charter was to run for fifty years, with headquarters at Newell, the post office nearest Freeland. Capital stock was set at ten thousand dollars but could be increased to one hundred thousand dollars by the trustees at any time, though shares were always to be ten dollars each. Trustees could pool all or part of the stock, and they could limit the holdings of one person to twenty shares. Regardless of the extent of his holdings, each stockholder was limited to a single vote. The incorporators were among the first five trustees chosen to serve until 2 April 1900. Elected annually thereafter, the trustees would serve as president, vice president, secretary, treasurer, and auditor. They had to be stockholders; they were bonded; and they were subject to recall. Monthly meetings of the trustees and two annual meetings of the entire membership were required. [6]

Originally stock could be pooled by the trustees in any manner which seemed in the best interests of the corporation; but this provision was revised, and the general fund was divided into an association store fund and a machinery fund. Now nonresidents might buy stock in the mercantile department at ten dollars a share and receive rebates on purchases from the store. Interest was 8 percent, and stock could be transferred only to the corporation or to other members. The machinery fund offered regular dividends. A member could purchase land with a 20-percent-cash down payment and pay the balance with dividends from the store or other association industries. Thus the founders considered the land to be free; hence, the name, "Free Land." Once land payments were complete, profits went to the individual, although the association kept 5 percent for future expansion. A full membership in the association cost fifty dollars, including ten for a share in the store, ten for the purchase of land, and thirty for an interest in other industries. These adjustments created dissension, and the early withdrawal of several founders suggests an internal struggle. *Industrial Freedom*, perhaps smarting from the defection of Equality colonists, labeled Freeland a "partial failure." [7]

The Freeland experiment early abridged its grandiose communitarian ideals to limited objectives. Freelanders proudly pointed out their differences from other colonies, particularly from the parent and rival, Equality:

A writer in Industrial Freedom gives the people warning that the Freeland association on this island is a profit sharing, interest paying outfit, all of which is a fact. . . . Freeland is not a communistic organization, the founders believing that communism on a small scale is a failure. The Freeland scheme is bound to be a success, and those coming from the communistic colonies are no evidence that communism is not the ideal, but it simply shows that they are not ready for it. Though Freeland is a profit sharing institution it may do as much for the advancement of radicalism as some of the more radical colonies.

At Freeland, cooperation was reduced almost entirely to the operation of the store, which followed the Rochdale plan. [8]

One of the earliest cooperative proposals, the Rochdale plan had an enduring vitality. Despite ultimate objectives that were far-reaching, the first step was limited but adaptable; it concentrated on the cooperative ownership of a single store. The prototype had been organized by weavers in the town of Rochdale, England, in 1855, and the example had interested reformers throughout Europe and the United States. Proposals for Rochdale stores were discussed in most of the Puget Sound communitarian experiments, often encouraged by professional organizers. The Freeland store, on the other hand, appears to have developed from within the community itself.

As explained in the local paper, a Rochdale store could be established by selling shares for about 10 percent down plus a small entrance fee, with the remaining cost of the shares coming from dividends. Interest was to be paid on all paid up shares. Part of the profits went into a reserve fund, stock depreciation, and an educational fund, but the remainder was credited to customers as dividends proportionate to their purchases. Thus, a shareholder profited from patronizing the store as well as from holding stock. Ideally, the store would expand its activities to selling real estate, starting industries, providing employment, and building new communities. Because the number of shares allowed an individual was limited, so was his potential for control. The plan was open to all races, creeds, and parties of society. Although the Rochdale plan was basically economic, its ultimate goals resounded to the uplift of man: "It is a united effort to improve their domestic, social and industrial condition."[9]

Freeland became "a Rochdale town." Shares in the store were sold to local members, to other island residents, and to persons more distant. A ledger for the early years includes sixty names. Daniels was the original manager; other individuals managed the store until it was acquired by the Blair family, nonmembers of the association, in later years.[10]

Although the store was "The Mercantile Department" of a "Co-operative Company organized on the famous Rochdale Plan," its advertising suggested a typical rural general store:

Rare Bargains

For eye-openers on prices; read this: Late Style, Boy's overcoats, large enough for small man; regular retail price $6; our price $3.50. These coats are good cloth and are excellent bargains.

One Dress Suit for 16 year old boy, regular $7.50; our price $4.50.

Boys' Suits, 4 to 9 years, at $1.50 and $2 per suit. These are bargains. See them.

Girls's Shoes, 12 to 2, only a few pairs left, were up to $2.50; our price to close, 50 cents to $1.

Good corn 10 cents per can; tomatoes two for 25. Lemons, 20 cents per dozen.[11]

The ownership of a small steamboat also gave Freeland a cooperative aspect. The island location made a craft necessary for transportation, shipping, and fishing. Uncertain and unreliable commercial water service was a constant frustration; Everett, although "within nine miles of us might as well be across the continent so far as steamer connection is concerned." Occasional ships stopped at nearby Langley; but Freeland, located at the head of a long bay and subject to extremely low tides, was an unlikely place for regular service. [12]

A succession of boats, most of them undependable, gave hope that Freeland would either be included on a regular island-to-mainland run or would possess her own boat. The *Bessie B.,* known as "the association sloop" but usually privately owned, was frequently pressed into service, as were other small boats belonging to Freeland colonists. Disappointments followed, as the example of the *Pilot* shows: "Capt. Peterson has brought the steamer Pilot to Freeland for headquarters. Her run has not yet been definitely arranged; but it is the intention to run her between Freeland and Everett if it can possibly be made to pay expenses. We sincerely hope it can be arranged so as to make daily trips. There will be no charge for wharfage at Freeland and quite a freight business may be worked up. The Captain is moving his father and mother into Mr. Lovejoy's house near the store. Success to the Pilot." Success was to elude the *Pilot.* Two months later she "was taken to Everett to be turned over to her creditors. The old tub isn't good for much but it seems a shame to lose her machinery for the little which was against her."[13]

Water transportation problems ended with the arrival at Freeland of the man who would provide continuing service to the south end of the island. John H. Prather was the son-in-law of

Daniels, and a socialist financially interested in Freeland since 1900. The Iowa-born son of a Dunkard minister, Prather had engaged in ranching, business, and lumbering in the West before coming to Freeland. In 1904 or 1905 he leased a twenty-eight-foot passenger boat which he named the *Freeland* and operated alone until he could acquire a second and then other large boats. With his brother, Enoch P. Prather, he developed an extensive freight and passenger service between south Whidbey Island and Everett and by 1910 was a leading businessman of the area. [14]

Although Freelanders spoke of developing additional industries and selling products on the outside market, they remained far from the goals of their incorporation papers. In 1902, they still dreamed of having a sawmill. Occasionally they would load a ship or a scow with lumber or bark, with poultry or produce, to sell in Everett, but Freeland and its people were basically isolated and self-reliant. The community consisted of men like John Prather, who professed socialist beliefs but who conducted their lives and business as private individuals. [15]

Many of the settlers had come from Equality Colony. Along with Daniels, the S. S. Longs and the William Gearharts were among the earliest, and a few months later others followed. Several had been officers at Equality, including Mr. and Mrs. Oliver P. Darr and A. K. Hanson. "Quite a number of discontented Equalityites are now trying Freeland," admitted the Equality paper in June 1901, publicly wishing them well. Several groups came to Freeland from other towns, including Lowell, the milltown just outside Everett, and Edgemont, South Dakota, which provided twenty-five persons in a single contingent. But from wherever they had come, they remained individuals, for this was not strictly a communal experiment. [16]

Except for the Free Land Association, the store, and the ship, the cooperation that existed was like that found in many new settlements where neighbors helped one another to clear lands, burn brush, plant or harvest crops, and build homes. In 1900 the original townsite was platted by Daniels into five-acre tracts with wide streets. Two years later he platted a second addition, and in 1904 a Tacoma development company added a third. Plats stretched back from the tidelands, up the hill and west. In March

1901, the colonists boasted of having "One of the most beautiful locations in the world. Each member owns and lives on his own farm—usually five acres. You are your own boss and your success depends upon yourself. No labor wasted." Many settlers built large, sturdy houses, but means of making a living were meager. Residents farmed and fished to provide family needs—Freelanders initiated no commercial fishing—worked in mills or logging camps, on neighboring farms or in construction. [17]

The Freelanders recognized that their vision must remain limited. By 1902 the *Whidby Islander,* unofficial spokesman for the colony, was admitting that the early land-financing schemes had not worked; now they wanted simply to prove "that co-operation is a success": "One noble object of the organization was to settle families on small tracts of land under a plan which would make their land practically free of cost. On account of disappointments in real estate matters this plan had to be abandoned for the present at least. So new settlers coming in now will simply have to buy land as in other places." And the editors chided an Everett newspaper for remarking that Freeland was "proving to the world that Altruism is not an empty dream." Although Freeland might like to be proving this, it was no socialist colony, but "simply a settlement of socialists co-operating on semi-capitalistic principles."[18]

In a social sense, Freeland resembled other communitarian settlements. There were clubs and literary and lecture groups, and the newspaper. Discussions frequently centered on socialism and occasionally on religion, although this was not a religious community. One New Year's Eve, said the *Whidby Islander,* "there was an animated discussion in the store on religious and other topics between some of our Freelanders and the Reverend Mr. Shephard of Seattle, at which time some hard hits were made on both sides, in a friendly spirit, but no converts made. Come again, Bro. Shephard, it was amusing as well as instructive."[19] The Reverend Mr. Shephard did return for visits, although his success at making conversions never improved. Yet he must have touched some strain of thought on the place of religion in communitarian societies, for after his first visit, the editor criticized those colony papers which led readers to believe that socialist colonies were invariably atheistic. "It looks to outsiders as if you were either denying God and His Christ or laying upon them the blame for existing conditions," he wrote, "which any sane man knows have been brought about through the ignorance and selfishness of the people." If the statement suggests that some socialists were reluctant to abandon religious convictions, it also indicates a conflict both in the socialist movement and in the church as to the proper role of each in molding a better society. [20]

During 1902 and 1903 some Freelanders turned to Spiritualism. In December, a class in mental science was organized and the next spring the Reverend B. O. Foster held Spiritualist meetings. Accepted by only a few, Spiritualism was derided by the skeptical as a hoax and a fake. [21]

The earliest and most enduring club was the First Thursday Club, organized by the women in May 1902. Photographs show several generations of women with small children in tow as they met at members' homes. Demonstrating an interest in the role of their sex, they discussed such topics as women's rights and the life of Elizabeth Cady Stanton. The First Thursday Club remained a prominent organization in the Freeland vicinity, its success capped about 1950 with the organization of a men's auxiliary. [22]

Not unlike settlers in other small isolated towns, those at Freeland met frustration in dealing with local officials. In 1902 they struggled to obtain a school, despite strong opposition from neighboring towns. Freeland children walked three miles across the island to Useless Bay, but that building became crowded and the Freelanders were forced out in February 1903. It was many years before Freeland obtained its own school; in the interim, local residents helped construct a building at Mutiny Bay to serve the south end of the island. [23]

The lack of roads posed continuing problems. A single road west across the island allowed mail deliveries in 1902, and a trail wound east to Langley. But Freelanders complained plaintively of isolation: "The roads around Freeland are getting no better fast. We would be just about as well off if the old Roman walls were around us, with gates locked and keys lost. The road to Bush Point has an almost impassible [*sic*] mud hole; the road to Useless Bay has a very bad place in the dike which it crosses; the road to Mutiny Bay has been fenced here so that there is no chance for a team to get near the store. How long, O Lord, how long must we put up with this?" Except for minor improvements, county officials left the basic problems unsolved. [24]

Freeland also had difficulty securing adequate postal services. In November 1901, triweekly service was promised, but the next September citizens were still petitioning for a carrier on the Freeland route, and late that month a post office was granted. Although usually a part of the store, the office moved frequently, as did the store management. In December 1902, Postmaster Martin Davison sought permission to house the office at his private residence. Two months later, *Islander* editors jocularly discussed the state of local postal services:

The Freeland postoffice is on the move these days. On the morning of the 17th Mr. Davison boxed it up and moved it up to G. W. Daniels' residence. Ten days of that proved enough so on the morning of the 27th he packed it up again and took it home with him. That is just as unsatisfactory to the patrons as it was to Daniels. Many of the patrons are having their mail changed to come to Austin and Newell. It has been remarked that the postmaster should have a little steam wheelbarrow to put the office on so he might blow the whistle occasionally so the people could keep track of it.

In June, Davison was replaced as postmaster, and a year later the Freeland post office was discontinued.[25]

More serious difficulties with postal authorities confronted the publishers of the *Whidby Islander*. Not officially a colony paper, this was the voice of its editors rather than of any other persons or group. Yet the *Whidby Islander* tended to emphasize socialism as the dominant philosophy of the community. The paper was the creation of DeForest and Ethel Brooke Sanford. Born in Pennsylvania in 1871, Sanford followed his father's occupations of carpenter and sawmill operator, but he also developed an interest in printing, "an early love . . . he soon became proficient in all branches of the trade, working as a compositor, pressman, linotyper, stereotyper, commercial printer." He worked for or published papers in several states. Concern for problems of miners and railroad workers brought him into contact with such groups as the Knights of Labor and the Populist party, for both of which he edited papers, and the American Railway Union. He observed the developing socialist factions in the late 1890s and determined to start his own socialist paper in the Far West. Traveling part of the way by "covered wagon," he landed first at Langley and began publication.[26]

In 1900 Langley had few homes and a single general store, but, in contrast with Freeland, it was an established community. The first edition of the *Whidby Islander* appeared in October 1900 and consisted of eight pages, ten by twelve inches. Under the heading, "Good Morning," the editors stated goals and purposes:

The WHIDBY ISLANDER enters the field of journalism realizing that there are many literary periodicals of various titles, aims and objects, and it comes not to fill a "long felt want." Politically we believe the forms of government in general use today have been weighed in the balance and found wanting. We shall endeavor to deal with all matters in a fair and impartial manner. We believe the laborer and producer is [*sic*] unjustly rewarded.

Upon labor depends the progress of the world, and an unjust distribution of the products tends to devastate mankind physically, morally and socially. An equal distribution of labor's product would equalize dignity and bring mankind to a higher stage generally. In every avenue of life labor is the foundation of progress. It has paved the way through despotic regions for civilization; it has placed the foot of progress on both land and sea, and has so linked together the various sections of the globe that it has made men who were once strangers comparatively neighbors; it has so bridled and harnessed the elements to the use of man as to enable him to communicate intelligence to a far distance in the twinkling of an eye.

Someone has truthfully said that the laborer builds railroads and travels on foot; he builds houses with mosaic walls and marble floor, and when his work is done he picks up his tools and walks away and never comes back any more. With the introduction of "labor-saving" machinery the condition of the laborer seems to grow more critical. We believe that in the installation of the Co-operative Commonwealth lies the only hope for the producer, and if we can assist the common people in locating on [*sic*] pleasant homes and advance some ideas that will assist in bringing about the Co-operative Commonwealth our labors will not have been in vain.[27]

Centered in the article was a picture of Christ holding the "Banner of Civilization" emblazoned with the words, "Equality, Justice, Love."

The simple masthead in early editions carried only the name of the paper. Later the editors added "Peace on Earth, Good Will to Men," and similar slogans. Soon, as the "Editorial Platform," they published each week the poem by James Russell Lowell beginning:

> We will speak out, we will be heard,
>   Though all earth's systems crack;
> We will not bate a single word,
>   Nor take a letter back.

The first edition indicated a general socialist tenor inclined toward farming and rural America. Two items on Debs accompanied a reprint endorsing his presidential candidacy. Other socialist features were an article by H. N. Casson, a quotation from the *Appeal to Reason*, and a poem by Ella Wheeler Wilcox. Reprinting articles from other publications, the newspaper would eventually boast that its writers included Francis [*sic*] Willard and Kate Richards O'Hare; in mid-1902 the editors announced a series by the former editors of the *Coming Nation,* Casson and Lydia Kingsmill Commander.[28]

During its year at Langley, the paper showed attitudes close to the Freelanders. It carried advertisements for the Free Land Association and a regular column of Freeland gossip by writers who identified themselves with initials or such sobriquets as "the Association Crank" and "the Devil Himself." [29]

The paper began to acquire a minor reputation on Puget Sound. The Home Colony editor, not always kind to rivals, called the *Whidby Islander* "a bright little Socialist paper," and one of his fellow anarchists wrote effusively: "Brother, Sister: Such articles as I find in the ISLANDER brings the angel side of human nature to the surface, reversing the current of emotion, surging, when shrinking from the voluminous vituperations hurled upon a class of people who are mentally, morally and spiritually the peers of the class or classes that malign them." The same issue carried a less flattering letter from Jacob Anthes, the leading Langley merchant, canceling his advertising. Anthes was thought to be disturbed about the paper's attitude toward the recent slaying of President William McKinley and the ensuing mass arrests of anarchists. [30]

The assassination of the President by a self-proclaimed anarchist wrought general consternation among American radicals. The *Whidby Islander* condemned the act but remained critical of the slain President's policies. The view typified that of other such papers, which regretted the killing but considered that people who were "not satisfied with the condition of this country, politically . . . [should] vote for something better. . . . While we hold that it is no worse to shoot a man dead than to kill him by degrees, that is no excuse for shooting." Political differences aside, "the whole nation mourns that he lost his life in this dastardly manner." A reprint of another socialist editorial called for a study of the spirit that would permit such crimes while denouncing "the hysterical capitalistic press and pulpit crying out for lynch law and vigilence [*sic*] committee." The Sanfords described most anarchists as being "peaceable, liberty-loving people, believing that mankind can be educated to the high moral standard where there will be no need of written law for government." [31]

Such statements "brought some condemnation from republicans and slopovers," but editor Sanford doubted that it had prompted Mr. Anthes to remove support; rather, he had probably canceled because the paper was about to move to Freeland. That autumn, the Sanfords, their pedal-operated press, and their newspaper moved to the new home from which the 1 November 1901 edition emerged. [32]

In December the *Whidby Islander* confronted another problem when the Post Office Department withdrew its second-class mailing privileges. This "Christmas Gift" accused Sanford of using the privileges to promote his real estate sideline, but Sanford viewed the action as part of a sustained national effort to discourage and silence the radical press. Decrying the supposed persecution, Sanford quietly withdrew his personal advertising and continued to publish until second-class privileges were restored in March. As the price of continuing, Sanford promised to comply with the government—at least for awhile. By spring he was inserting such items as: "The Postal Department knocked my real estate business into a 'cocked hat' last fall; but for all that, I have for sale some of the very best land on Whidby Island. $400 takes a forty that there is no discount on. One of the best tens on the Sound, very easy clearing, $200. A splendid ten for $150. Will locate none but families." And a column contained at least two other references to real estate bargains. [33]

For another year the paper presented local news, agitated for socialism, and helped sell real estate. Then in April 1903 came an advertisement for the *Whidby Islander* itself. The editors lacked "necessary time to do it justice." Two weeks later Sanford reported that he had resigned from Freeland and that the future of the paper was uncertain. Perhaps he would move his press to Everett; possibly the *Coming Nation* would take over his subscription list; he was not sure. "But you will hear from us again from somewhere, so we will not say goodbye." [34]

The family may have remained at Freeland for awhile; they kept their shares in the Free Land Association until August 1904. Mrs. Sanford's health required a warmer and drier climate, and so, recalled their son, "Oceano, California became our new home, whence the family was drawn by attraction of the Theosophical colony at Halcyon, and an attractive farming opportunity." Thereafter they lived at various places throughout California and the Southwest before Ethel Sanford died in 1931 at the age of fifty-four. Ever fascinated by communitarian experiments, DeForest Sanford spent several years at Newllano, Louisiana, and at other cooperative communities before his death in California on 30 November 1956.[35]

The Sanfords and their newspaper probably sharpened the Freelanders' socialist image of themselves and helped build a local philosophy and identity. Although founders and early settlers were inclined toward socialist beliefs, none of their founding documents used the word "socialism" or its derivatives. Nor did the article about Freeland that Equality Colony published in 1901, although it freely used such phrases as "cooperative commonwealth," "cooperator," and "Rochedale [*sic*] profit-sharing." Yet Freelanders thought of themselves as socialists and retained socialist attitudes and party activities for years to come.[36]

In 1900 and 1901 the *Whidby Islander* noted local visits by socialist speakers and organizers such as William Hogan, the 1900 congressional candidate, and David Burgess, a former Equality editor who visited Freeland occasionally and wrote for the paper. In 1901 the Sanfords feuded with their socialist colleagues, arguing that smaller papers in the Northwest were as sound in their doctrine as the dominant Seattle *Socialist*. They suggested that it would be "very sensible and practical" for the colony papers to consolidate.[37]

The next year, the paper was printing a statement of:

WHAT SOCIALISTS WANT

Every human being to be well housed, clothed, fed, and educated.

The adoption of a social and industrial system that will put an end to profit, interest, rent, and all forms of usury.

Land, water, machinery, all the means of production and distribution, and all the available forces of nature to be owned and operated for the benefit of the whole people.

The gradual elimination and finally the abolition of all useless and unproductive toil.

Every person of suitable age, and physical and mental ability, must work or starve. "He that will not work shall not eat!"

At the same time, there began a series of articles and a running debate with Burgess on the class struggle and class consciousness. [38]

The Socialist party of the United States was born in 1901, and the following May a local organization was formed at Freeland. By September this local was progressing and adding members. In that election year, members participated in the first county Socialist convention—"One of the most harmonious [conventions] one ever saw." Eight of the eleven county candidates were members of the Free Land Association.[39]

"On the beautiful shores of Holmes Harbor, in the quiet little village of Freeland the members of the Socialist Party of Island County" met two years later to select another set of candidates. This time seven of the twelve were Freeland residents. And the *Island County Times* of Coupeville acknowledged that "while the members thereof knew full well that the ticket placed in the field would go down to sure defeat, they are laboring for the maintenance of the principles of their party."

The Freeland local remained active. In 1913 regular meetings were held at Crest House, the F. J. Pierson home at the head of the bay. A. K. Hanson was still secretary. In 1915 and 1916, William Lieseke was paying local dues, attending socialist gatherings around the island, writing letters to *Appeal to Reason*, and generally concerning himself with socialist matters. As the Freeland socialists maintained political and local activities, they kept up with recent literature. When the library of the association was acquired by the University of Washington in 1968, it included thirty-three titles, most of which dealt with socialism.[40]

There is no clear conclusion to the story of Freeland. It never was a colony, although its founders had aspired to many and varied economic activities. More correctly, Freeland was a gathering of like-minded radicals who sought to retain a socialist entity outside the confines of a regimented communal existence.

Freeland quickly evolved into a Rochdale community and then gradually into a permanent settlement of socialists on an isolated arm of Puget Sound. Ironically, Freeland retained its socialist character more fully and longer than those colonies which endeavored emphatically to create the cooperative commonwealth.

5. Burley Colony

BROTHERHOOD ON HENDERSON BAY

The desire of eastern socialists to found the cooperative commonwealth in a western state resulted in the establishment of Equality Colony and of Burley Colony on the southern reaches of Puget Sound.

The marriage of the Brotherhood of the Co-operative Commonwealth and the Social Democracy of America was never fully consummated, and the two organizations followed separate but parallel paths. Whereas the BCC emphasized colonization to change the social order, the SDA included political action to obtain "the capture and 'possession of the public power.'"[1] While the BCC moved to establish Equality, the SDA debated its course.

But that organization was divided by its diverse membership and by its dual goals. Along with BCC officials, the nucleus of its founders came from Eugene V. Debs's American Railway Union. The *Railway Times* of the ARU became the *Social Democrat* of the SDA. Other radicals also joined in this attempt to create one large socialist body. Dissidents from the doctrinaire Socialist Labor party included Victor Berger from Milwaukee and Jewish socialists from New York City. Representatives from smaller socialist bodies attended the founding convention in June 1897, along with former Populists and other reformers. Anarchist leader Johann Most lent support, and Lucy Parsons, widow of one of the Haymarket Square martyrs, attended. Among other labor leaders, "Mother" Mary Harris Jones was present.[2]

This wide representation did not impress one New York

reporter, who claimed a "natural sympathy with men who cannot find work," but observed sadly that "there was not a substantial-looking person in the hall, and by that I mean that I did not see a person who looked as if he had ability to be the foreman of an ordinary workshop. There were abstract Anarchists present. Single Taxers, Communists, new-fledged and illiterate Socialists, men of all ages and all conditions of shabbiness but the average face was either dull and unintelligent or was plainly fanatical." And though he spoke well of Debs's character, this observer was unimpressed by the leader's major address.[3]

Debs explained the plan to send colonizers to a state—he specifically mentioned Washington— in order to "secure control of the politics of the State and start the co-operative common-wealth." Socialist pressure would force the legislature to revise the state constitution and alter the tax structure. The state would become a gigantic trust, and socialist programs would be inaugurated. Anticipating a counterreaction, Debs intended to consult "good lawyers and learn just what the rights of the colonists were. 'We want to know our rights,' he said, 'and make them [the government officials] the rebels. If they send the militia to invade our rights, then there will be an army of 300,000 patriots on the State line to meet them on that issue.'" The SDA adopted a Declaration of Principles and a constitution, and established headquarters in Chicago, with plans for local and state organizations.[4]

Even during the period of organization, a schism developed over colonization versus political action. Proponents of political action tried to dissuade Debs from the utopian colonization scheme and decried the emphasis placed on it. Victor Berger belittled the plan as "only a side issue" exaggerated in the press.[5]

Nevertheless, the SDA constitution outlined a colonization department headed by three persons with "sound business judgment and unquestioned integrity." The colonization commission was empowered to choose a state for settlement, to arrange for the establishment of a colony, and to seek transportation for the unemployed who would come. After Henry Demarest Lloyd and Laurence Grönlund declined to serve, the commission was announced on 2 August as consisting of Richard J. Hinton, chairman, Cyrus Field Willard, secretary, and Wilfred P.

Borland, treasurer. Although these three men lacked the luster of Lloyd and Grönlund, their careers spanned many years and diverse interests in the realm of reform; all had journalistic backgrounds.[6]

Hinton, of Washington, D.C., was introduced as a mining engineer "peculiarly well adapted for the very important position" of chairman. Described by Willard as a "short peppery Englishman," Hinton was born in London in 1830, the son of a trade unionist, and emigrated as a young man to the United States, where he pursued separate careers in topographical engineering and journalism. In the middle 1850s a Boston newspaper sent him to troubled Kansas armed, he said, with Sharps' rifles donated by Theodore Parker and Dr. W. H. Channing. There he met John Brown. After wartime service in the Union Army, Hinton worked for several large city newspapers. During these years he became aware of the problems of wage earners and began intense socialist activities. In the 1880s he was corresponding secretary of the Washington, D.C., section of the International Workingman's Association, and he belonged to the Socialist Labor party until his expulsion in 1893. In difficult financial straits, Hinton exploited his earlier experiences to write a romantic, sometimes inaccurate, and always self-glorifying account of his days with John Brown. His selection as chairman of the SDA colonization commission opened a new phase in the varied career of the sixty-six-year-old socialist. [7]

The commission secretary was the scion "of an old, aristocratic Boston family, [but Cyrus Willard] had alienated his people by his sympathy with labor and by his non-aristocratic interests." Interest in reform was not entirely new to the family, though, for Frances Willard, founder of the Women's Christian Temperance Union and a versatile reformer, was a second cousin. "I had a pile of correspondence with her four inches tall," Willard reminisced, "and converted her to the proposition that poverty caused as much intemperance as intemperance caused poverty." A career in industry and journalism occupied him professionally, but his nonprofessional interests better define the man.

A wide reader on social topics, Willard had corresponded with William Morris, Sidney Webb, and Peter Kropotkin. He had enjoyed arguments and discussions with a Boston newspaper colleague, the anarchist Benjamin R. Tucker. An ability to speak German enabled him to converse easily at Marxist socialist gatherings in Boston. But Willard's esoteric interests mingled with the economic. He was a Theosophist from the day in 1884 when he discovered *Isis Unveiled,* the exposition of that Spiritualist movement by its high priestess, Mme. H. P. Blavatsky. Upon reading the book, he wrote the author that he desired to become a follower. After joining the Boston Lodge of the Theosophical Society in 1887, he studied at Mme. Blavatsky's London school and began a lifelong association with the sect and its leaders. About the same time, he was moved by Edward Bellamy's *Looking Backward.* With the author's endorsement, Willard and a fellow enthusiast organized a Bellamy Club in Boston. Although this group died shortly, its remains merged with a similar venture to become the First Nationalist Club of Boston in 1888, with Willard as secretary. This was the forerunner of a nationwide league of Bellamy clubs. Willard worked on the *Nationalist* magazine until struggles within the movement prompted his withdrawal.[8]

His personal relationship with Bellamy was not severed, for in 1897 he asked the author to write an article that might help put "into practical operation the ideas of industrial co-operation as exemplified in 'Looking Backward.' . . . Even in the most enthusiastic days of the Nationalist movement, there was nothing like the present move of the Social Democracy." The colonization scheme seemed to represent the culmination of Willard's various ideals: " . . . as I still regarded Socialism the instrument to bring about the Universal Brotherhood on the material plane, I was enthusiastic." Thus Willard began his work in the SDA, helping to edit the *Social Democrat* and always fitting these new activities into a constant round of theosophical meetings. Self-conscious among laborers, the aristocrat sought their approval: "They thought I was a good fellow and harmless, but a little cracked on Theosophy."[9]

The treasurer of the commission came directly from the ranks of labor. Two years younger than Willard, the thirty-seven-year-old Borland was a railway fireman until a train accident in 1889 crippled him and he turned permanently to his previous avocation of writing. A member of the Brotherhood of Locomotive Firemen since 1884, he wrote for labor periodicals, including Debs's *Firemen's Magazine* and the *Railway Times.* Borland was a "practical man, capable with the pen. . . . " He viewed the commission job as an opportunity to improve his personal finances, and he added the editorship of the *Social Democrat* to his duties. [10]

SDA officials now set about their work. Debs traveled to address enthusiastic audiences, but his tours were interrupted by labor crises and bouts with illness, and he never exercised strong leadership. Other board members found interest in various parts of the country; the *Social Democrat* reported support from reform leaders and a growth in local unions. Locals were organized in New York, Buffalo, Philadelphia, Minneapolis, St. Louis, and San Francisco, and in such smaller towns as Trinidad, Colorado; Moline, Illinois; Evansville, Indiana, and Palouse, Washington. In Cleveland and Milwaukee, German-language newspapers became official organs of the SDA. [11]

Expansion and enthusiasm did not necessarily bring money, however, and the leaders sought individual donations, occasionally reminding potential donors of BCC needs as well. Critics later recalled that the "utopian and fantastic" colony idea "drew support from gullible people from all classes and no trouble was experienced in getting contributions for it." But results were insufficient. In September the board tried to assess each local branch twenty dollars for the colonization fund. The final report published in June 1898 listed only $2,430.87. Rumors circulated that unfriendly officials were withholding money intended for colonization. [12]

Meanwhile, commission members searched out possible colony locations. Although they were charged to investigate several states, including Utah and Texas, Washington appeared to be favored. Nevertheless, the first visit was in the South. In October, Hinton and Willard visited Ruskin Colony in Tennessee along with "Mother" Jones. They recommended colonization as "an object lesson for the entire South." They also proposed that the SDA build a seventy-five-mile railroad connection to be turned over to the city of Nashville as a first step toward government ownership of railroads. The SDA board authorized further negotiations, but the venture fell through the following May. That spring Willard became interested in a Cripple Creek, Colorado, mining venture. A contract was drawn up for 560 acres which held "a gold mine of 'the deeper you go, the richer the ore' variety."

Willard proposed paying five thousand dollars over a ninety-day period, plus ninety-five thousand dollars in 5 percent bonds to be financed by a two hundred thousand dollar bond issue. After this scheme had collapsed, opponents within the SDA mimicked the commission's report: " 'Then if we sold the entire amount of bonds,' said the commission, 'we would have $100,000 after paying for the property, and could use, say $25,000, to develop the mine, and the balance to establish the colony. Who will get bond No. 1?'(!)"

Although such proposals contrasted with the professed objective of colonizing a state, commission members had also investigated possible sites in Colorado, Idaho, and Washington. During Christmas week 1897, Hinton reported to the SDA executive board and received encouragement to proceed. [13]

As the investigations became prolonged and diverted, opposition mounted from those within the SDA who preferred direct political action. Hinton was made personally aware of dissatisfaction during a New York visit with Charles H. Sotheran, a disillusioned compatriot of his Socialist Labor party days. Hinton recounted the dreams of the commission to Sotheran and his wife, but their "countenances fell" as they listened. The host especially regretted that the plan involved isolated groups of people. Sotheran argued that socialism should be carried to the mines, milltowns, and cities where workers lived and that the ballot was the most effective tool. Hinton had no greater success with other New Yorkers; he left the city "a keenly disappointed man." The political activists strengthened their wing with municipal election successes in Wisconsin. Even the former ARU leaders close to Debs were splitting into factions, while their acknowledged leader remained aloof. [14]

When the second national convention of the Social Democracy of America convened on Tuesday, 7 June 1898, in Ulrich's Hall in Chicago, the colonizationists demonstrated initial superiority over their opponents. But each faction was dickering for control, and the seventy delegates got into an immediate hassle over admitting representatives from eight Chicago "branches on paper" formed by the colonizationists. A bitter floor debate ended when the national board, dominated by colonizationists, chartered the branches and allowed the disputed delegates, including anarchist Emma Goldman, to be seated. The political activists accused their opponents of prolonging the convention so as to force delegates from distant points to return home. Thursday a quarrel erupted on the floor when Treasurer James Hogan, a colonizationist, charged the secretary and former treasurer, Sylvester Keliher, a political activist, with mishandling funds. After an argument over Willard's recommendation to purchase the Colorado mining property, the political activists caucused and vowed to "fight colonization uncompromisingly."[15]

Friday afternoon a showdown became inevitable when the three-man platform committee offered two conflicting reports. A majority report called for political action and the abandonment of colonization, while John F. Lloyd's minority report recommended both tactics. The debate ended at 2:30 A.M. on Saturday, after a two-hour defense by Lloyd. A roll-call vote showed fifty-three delegates for the minority report and thirty-seven against. The colonizationists were jubilant. But the exultation ended abruptly when Isaac Hourwich, a consistent opponent of colonization, climbed upon a chair to call an immediate meeting of the minority at the Revere House across the street. One by one the dissidents walked out. In the early hours of 11 June, they created the Social Democratic Party of America, appointed themselves as its national committee, adopted the majority report from the convention they had just left, and prepared an address to the SDA membership before adjourning at 4:00 A.M. The temporary chairman of the SDPA was Frederic Heath and secretary was the politically ubiquitous F. G. R. Gordon, one of the earliest proponents of colonization. [16]

The man who might have united these warring factions remained cautiously enigmatic. During the spring, Eugene V. Debs had seemed sympathetic to the political activists and he favored them in the SDA credentials fight, but his convention address was a call to colonize. As the dispute grew into crisis, Debs was confined with a recurring headache, but he finally sent a message of support to the rebels. In short order Debs would become an official of the SDPA and lead it into the Socialist party in 1901. The colonizationists avoided public refutation of socialism's most dynamic figure, but they felt betrayed. Willard cherished a lifelong bitterness over "the way Poor Hinton and Myself were treated by Debs . . . [who] deserted us."[17]

The SDA learned that victory could be an illusion. On Saturday, they elected a new board and adopted a constitution that encompassed both political action and colonization. Hogan became president and Borland secretary-treasurer. The former colonization commission became an economic committee, and educational and political committees were established. Under Willard's direction, the *Social Democrat* appeared three more times; financial disputes and litigation, "together with silence and apathy," caused suspension while the fourth issue was in type. Willard's final attacks upon his opponents portrayed the SDA as an American party opposed to the European class-struggle thesis. A nativist tendency was evident as the obviously Jewish names of certain bolters were listed.[18]

Conscious of weakness after the defection, the new SDA leaders grappled to salvage party and program. Briefly they courted Laurence Grönlund who had attended some Chicago meetings and had condemned the bolters, and the author wrote an article intended for the *Social Democrat*. Although cautious in his enthusiasm, he welcomed colonization as one way to "bring a State to the threshold of Socialism." If the SDA made overtures to the Chicago anarchists, there were no results; their inclusion would hardly have been compatible with the well-expressed nativism of the colonizers.[19]

Bereft of prominent leaders and lacking a press, the SDA gambled to save itself by proceeding at once with colonization. "This would revive the lagging interest, build up the organization to its former strength and power and even increase its membership and efficiency." Accordingly, the national council sent Willard to locate a colony, giving him the "full power to do what in his judgment appeared the best thing to do." Cyrus Field Willard thus became the dominant figure of the movement.[20]

Willard journeyed west, accompanied by J. S. Ingalls, a young Minnesota lawyer. They first conferred with SDA members in Denver and in the small mining town of Iris, Colorado. This settlement in the Gunnison country had experienced four years of apparent boom before times had turned bad. Here Jerome C. DeArmond, "a tall husky giant with a straw-colored mustache," had assumed the leadership of disillusioned miners. A supporter of colonization at the recent SDA convention, DeArmond promised to bring men into the scheme. Although property was available, Colorado socialists opposed colonization in their state, and the commission rejected an interior location where they would be "the slave of a railroad corporation." The two men continued to Seattle and a meeting with J. B. Fowler, an SDA member with whom Willard had corresponded. [21]

Fowler's home became headquarters for Willard and Ingalls. After conferring with Seattle socialists, Willard proceeded to Grays Harbor in search of available homestead land but found it all taken up. A chance remark that "we ought to get somewhere where we would not be at the mercy of the railroads, by being on tide-water, and near some harbor," reminded Fowler of the myriad peninsulas and inlets on southern Puget Sound.

Willard and Fowler took a small steamboat to Olalla, where they inquired of lands that might be purchased at "any price." The postmaster and store proprietor recommended the region between Olalla and Henderson Bay to the west, and he named several settlers of the area. One of these was Henry W. Stein, whom Fowler recognized as a man sympathetic to socialism. Hitching up his team of horses, the postmaster "drove us back from the Sound through glorious tall fir trees in a splendidly wooded country which promised much in the way of timber and forest products, which would afford labor to the many men we could bring in to utilize their labor in creating wealth for which the state of Washington was already becoming famous. In about an hour or so we got to Stein's house where we had a warm welcome." [22]

Here the men found a friend and listener. A local political and community leader with liberal inclinations, Stein wrote a Seattle newspaper column promoting the single tax. Willard was further pleased to find that Mrs. Stein was a Theosophist. Stein had recently become executor of the estate of a deceased surveyor who had owned a tract of fertile bottom land through which Burley Creek flowed into the head of the bay. Part of this land was for sale. [23]

Back in Seattle, local SDA members unanimously voted support. The persuasive powers of Ingalls and others were reinforced by generally improving financial conditions as wealth from the Klondike poured into the city. "Much enthusiasm was aroused," Willard later recalled, "and many new members obtained." An office was set up in the Pioneer Building, close to Seattle political activity. With Fowler doing most of the negotiating, the men on 18 October 1898 purchased approximately 260 acres of land for $5,917.40, on time. The buyers envisioned this as the first step toward acquiring at least a thousand acres more. [24]

Meanwhile the founders had taken necessary organizational steps. Since April, the colonization commission of the SDA had been incorporated in Kansas as the Co-operative Commonwealth Company. The charter listed among the directors the three commission members, SDA officials including Eugene and Theodore Debs, Kansas Populist Annie L. Diggs, and Ingalls. The objects and purposes were to acquire and own land for colonies in several states, to provide settlers with the necessities of life, and to develop the agricultural and industrial potential. Quite likely the organization had been created to enable the Colorado mining-lands purchase.[25] Willard now determined to reincorporate and transfer headquarters to Washington. The name was changed to avoid confusion with the Social Democratic Party of America. Hence, the Co-operative Brotherhood was formed in September 1898, its articles of incorporation being filed in Seattle.

The Co-operative Brotherhood was incorporated for a fifty-year period with five thousand dollars of capital stock divided into five hundred shares of ten dollars each. The stated purposes were expanded to include the collective ownership and cooperative production and distribution of goods. It planned to engage in "all kinds of production, mining, manufacturing, buying, holding or selling of real estate or personal property and establishing, owning and operating lines of transportation and communication, and generally to engage in any species of trade or business necessary or requisite to carry out the principal objects herein set forth." Seattle was designated as the principal place of business, and the "several states" clause was omitted. Only Willard and Ingalls remained from the predecessor as trustees; the other ten members gave Seattle as their principal address. [26]

Willard was enthusiastic about the prospects of the colony: "The combination of land in abundance, of unsurpassed richness, with ample water power for years to come, and situated on tide water, where we can be independent of the exactions of transportation corporations, is something which realizes my fondest hopes. It is a combination hard to beat. We expect now to bring in thousands of honest and industrious American citizens from the East to build up happy and contented homes for themselves and to increase the wealth and population of this great Empire State of the Northwest." Vastly exaggerating the potentials of a shallow bay, Willard planned to dredge a harbor and build a wharf that would draw local and world trade. He also expected tiny Burley Creek to provide ample water power for mills and factories. Willard anticipated purchasing two thousand additional acres and leasing timbered school lands.[27]

The first settlers of the Burley area had come quite recently. In the late 1880s, homesteaders had scattered homes and farms over the low land. But recurrent bank crises and hard times had driven many away. Stein and his neighbor, Justice of the Peace Robert Gibson, assured Willard that no one would object if the colonists occupied some of the abandoned log houses while they cleared their own lands and built houses.[28]

The initial settlers, including DeArmond and his Colorado followers and several men selected by the Seattle local, moved to Burley on 20 October 1898. Willard temporarily remained in Seattle. This separation of duties would lead to a schism among the "pioneers." Willard came to deprecate the DeArmond crowd as crude and unreliable, while they challenged the leadership of persons who did no physical work. But in the fall of 1898 both groups cooperated. Within a month there were sixteen persons at the site, eleven men, one woman, a twelve-year-old boy, and "three young ladies." A spokesman reported, "The boys in the colony are feeling good, and as one of them remarked, when he pulled off his coat to go to work, 'I feel like a free man, I never felt so relieved in all my life.' "[29]

In addition to clearing and logging, other activities were initiated in those first ambitious months. By December the Henry L. Stevens family offered meals and lodging at their home, "Hotel Commonwealth," for sixty cents a day. The colonists considered the prospects of fishing and of salting or smoking the catch, and investigated oyster beds. A cigar-making industry was born. There was a tramway under construction, with a car to facilitate clearing timber and selling cordwood. Later a sawmill would be erected. Publicists spoke vaguely of developing small manufacturing plants that would enable calling fifty or seventy-five men from different trades.[30]

The expectations and needs always outdistanced reality: "We want ten wood choppers and carpenters, a shoemaker, a blacksmith with complete outfit of blacksmith tools, a team of horses, wagon and teamster, several cows and chickens, pigs, turkeys, geese and ducks. We are now prepared to accept donations of all sorts. Anything intended for Colony use should be shipped freight prepaid in every case, marked 'Co-operative Brotherhood, Ollala [sic], Wash.'" Some donations did come, including a horse and light wagon from William Burns, a former ARU official and current SDA officer; the horse, named Billy Burns in his honor, remained a steadfast worker for several years. Less useful to men clearing a forest was a packet of "shade tree seeds from one of the fine parks of Chicago."[31]

As the physical work progressed, so did the organizing and planning. The original colony name of Brotherhood became a forgotten anachronism, as "Burley" came into general use. Willard, who moved to the site in late November, devised a system of paper scrip "based on time checks and being of the denomination of $1 for a day's work of 8 hours and fractional parts called minims for the number of minutes worked over or less than 6 hours."[32]

Propaganda occupied the office workers. At Equality, *Industrial Freedom* reported on the colonization commission and the establishment of Burley Colony. A supplement honoring the first anniversary of Equality added detailed accounts about Burley, and a column of "Co-operative Brotherhood Colony Notes," usually edited by Fowler, appeared frequently. Such publicity aided the cause, which had lost its only public voice with the demise of the *Social Democrat*. Fowler excitedly reported a day's mail that brought thirty-eight letters to an office bustling with activity. The new colony sought assistance from the older one and named three Equality members to its board of trustees, hoping to benefit from their experience. This "favor" mystified the already busy Equality colonists and was spurned.[33]

But sustained propaganda and the prominence of journalists in the leadership assured Burley of its own press and paper. Armed with subscription lists of the *Social Democrat,* Willard planned to start his own newspaper. A small press was set up in the kitchen of an abandoned house, with type cases in the bedroom; Willard found an "editorial sanctum in another house nearby where I could keep warm." Aided by one-eyed "Gib" Crofut, a Colorado miner and former printer, he published in December the first issue of the *Co-operator*, originally a four-page sheet. Copies were mailed to former *Social Democrat* subscribers. "The effect," effused the editor a generation later, "was an electric shock." Orders for subscriptions of a dollar a year and requests for membership applications "came piling in. . . ."[34] An Equality columnist called the new venture "bright and breezy" and pictured the editor as one who had walked the streets of Chicago hungry. The newspaper would continue with different formats and several editors for eight years, longer than any other single journal in the western Washington colonies. Its establishment aided the transitional phase of the Co-operative Brotherhood from its origins in the SDA to the establishment of Burley Colony. At last, the Brotherhood, its colony, and its official organ had a clear identity, separate from both the old Debs organization and the BCC. [35]

The first Christmas celebration was another milestone, although physically Burley was far from complete. A homemade card of eight pages decorated with dried leaves was signed by twenty-seven "pioneers," including wives and children. Fifteen of the signers were men, most of them single. Those with families were DeArmond, Stevens, and Myron J. Willard, who was from Colorado and not related to Cyrus Field Willard. Christmas Day brought the colonists and a dozen neighbors to the Stein residence for a tree and a visit from colonist W. H. Packer, "a jolly Civil War veteran with a white beard [who] entered the second story of the house by a ladder and came downstairs to be Santa." The holiday season helped to create a sense of community in the colony and also in the larger neighborhood. [36]

But this spirit was not to endure, for Burley Colony was already developing internal stresses. As at Equality six months earlier, the men who considered themselves the directors and those engaged in physical work began to challenge one another. Not the least of the problem was the overbearing personality of Cyrus Field Willard, who saw himself as the founder and legitimate leader of the colony. His principal adversary was DeArmond, who had brought the nucleus of the settlers. Only after the arrival of the "Colorado crowd" did Willard, the urbane, utopian Theosophist, discover that the miners were "Communistic anarchists of the William Morris type" who wanted all colony funds placed in a common treasury. Willard "laughed them out of the idea . . . [and] laid down the law" that this was a socialist, not a communist, colony. He won the initial joust, but he was to lose the battle, for his enemies increased. [37]

Opposition came not from the Colorado miners alone. Although Willard considered himself entitled to the first completed colony house, he patronizingly passed it on to Fowler and suffered in a single room above the store, noisy each evening from a gathering crowd. His personal life was to complicate matters. Divorced, Willard was engaged to a Chicago Theosophist who suddenly announced that she was coming to join him. Willard met his fiancée in Portland, Oregon, where they were married in January 1899. Upon his return to Burley, Willard found that others had taken new houses, leaving him "a log house that was a deserted ranch house on the outskirts of the colony in which my delicately nurtured wife from a steam-heated flat in Chicago had to come." Furthermore, his bride had had furniture shipped west and delivered to the crude cabin. Other colony women became envious of Bessie Willard, her fine belongings, and her cultured demeanor. Mrs. DeArmond suggested that Mrs. Willard work in the colony kitchen, and this "tall red-faced ignorant woman . . . prejudiced Bessie against the colony so much, she never became a member of the organization and never did accept socialism."

While the women made colony life unpleasant for the genteel bride, the men plotted against her husband. A friendly neighbor warned Willard that they met nightly and discussed ways to depose him. Willard began to take personal affront at each hint of opposition. When he learned that Crofut the printer was among his opponents, he prepared to bring a replacement at any sign of insubordination. One day the printer slightly revised some copy, and Willard made his threat. Aside from this incident and a minor work stoppage, there was no direct struggle. Willard felt secure in his ability to maintain discipline and believed that DeArmond grudgingly respected him.[38]

But mutual resentment set in. Willard rationalized that socialism required each man to do the job for which he was best fit, and "I would make a poor risk out felling trees." The workers scoffed at his theoretical talk and dictatorial manner. As they plotted against control "from the office," the laborers queried how "cooperation" could permit one man to boss another. Four summers later, a colony editor recalled this first year:

The Directors? They held their meetings, at first in private. Establish order? Why, they first had to see that nothing stopped advance. Get to work on the land? What, slash and grub like the helpless mortgaged rancher? Cut cordwood? They were there to found the new era, to lay aside forever the galling load of toil. . . . Had all the residents had faith in the plans adopted, and had the officers invited confidence, resistance to the administration would never have grown strong. But from the earliest times were those, who believed that industrial justice was to be secured by first making all individuals equal, and that, to protect the people, the thing to do with authority that asserted itself was to crush it.[39]

Willard felt that the distress stemmed from improved financial conditions due to entrance fees, cigar sales, and *Co-operator* subscriptions. Success weakened the dependence upon a leader which Willard coveted. He became disillusioned over "graft" that was as widespread inside the colony as outside and frustrated in attempts to elevate the unappreciative workers. Refinements of life and the fine points of Theosophy seemed lost on his companions. Willard considered Burley a failure, a "Frankenstein" that would create a slavery worse than capitalism. Yet he believed that a communal venture centered upon religion might succeed. A visit to a Theosophy convention and the budding Theosophical settlement on Point Loma north of San Diego Bay strengthened Willard's fascination for that sect. He determined to go south, "entirely cured of socialism":

After Bessie and I talked matters over I wrote out my resignation on the official letter-head and signed it and then tossed it on [his assistant, Wilfred P.] Borland's desk saying, "There Borland is my resignation. You have long wanted my position, there it is." "What's the matter," he asked in surprise, "have I done anything wrong?" "No," I replied, "Mrs. Willard and I want a climate where there is not so much rain and we are going to Southern

California." So we went quietly and without any fuss. Many of the neighbors came to say "Good-bye."[40]

Although the Willards lived at Point Loma for only three years, they continued to reside in San Diego, and he remained a steadfast Theosophist and a Freemason. Two years before his death in 1942 at the age of eighty-three, the Theosophical University of Point Loma conferred an Honorary Doctor of Letters upon him. Mrs. Willard had died ten years before. Despite the coolness at his departure, Willard was visited in later years by several former Burley colonists. DeArmond and Stevens even sought his help in founding colonies in Mexico and Cuba. [41]

Richard J. Hinton, Cyrus Field Willard, and Wilfred P. Borland had been charged by the SDA to found a communal colony and two of them had helped to convert their commission into the Co-operative Brotherhood. Hinton never visited Burley, although he wrote occasionally for the *Co-operator* and praised its progress. He died on 20 December 1901, in the city of his birth, London, England. With the departure of Willard, Borland was the last of the three founders who remained directly involved. Borland had come west as Willard's assistant in 1899. Soon Willard came to despise his colleague as "narrow in head and brain," weak and subject to flattery and domination by others. He heard afterward that Borland had gambled away colony funds in California. Whatever the circumstances, Borland left the colony about a year after Willard. Later he held a minor government position in Washington, D.C. With his departure, the triumvirate of founders was gone. [42]

Members of the Co-operative Brotherhood were both resident and nonresident. The latter had only to subscribe to the bylaws and to pay a one-dollar entrance fee and the first month's dues; dues were one dollar a month with penalties for delinquency that ranged to a complete forfeiture. When a nonresident's payments reached one hundred twenty dollars, he and his family were eligible to become resident members. He might join earlier under certain conditions, including a "call" from the colony, payment of three hundred dollars or more, or in order to receive certain insurance benefits. Resident members fulfilled their obligations through service and did not pay dues. [43]

The increase of membership was "solid and substantial tho not as rapid as some hoped," reaching one thousand members in June 1900. Over a period of twenty-one months, the colony had averaged forty-eight new members a month, including persons from twenty-six states and all the Canadian provinces. Inquiries had come from even farther afield, from Britain, Germany, Australia, New Zealand, the Philippine Islands, and South Africa. The editors contemplated 2,000 members by the end of 1900, but that year ended and the next, and the membership was still not above 1,227. Long before this, half the people on the rolls were delinquent and a third considered totally lost. [44]

Members were called when the colony needed specific skills and had the means to sustain new residents, but many came without being called. Each head of a family was required to sign a contract agreeing to accept work assignments, to obey rules and regulations, and to help provide services as needed. Although there were no stated qualifications for membership, the leaders argued whether to deny elderly or infirm persons or large families. Early in 1900 the colonists faced a challenge of their willingness to evaluate members when a "colored applicant" sought admission. After a series of meetings the board decided to neither admit nor reject such persons, but to establish a separate colony for them. Apparently the applicant did not pursue his request, and no other Negroes applied. [45]

By the first summer there were seventy-six men, women, and children in residence. Two years later the colony, recognizing that the high ratio of nonproducers to the working force had been a weakness at similar experiments, boasted that its resident membership had never "been as effective as at the present time." Of 105 members, 35.3 percent were men, 23.9 percent were women, 18 percent were children over fourteen engaged "a certain number of hours each day in some productive industry when not attending school." Only 22.8 percent were under fourteen and thus "subject to maintenance . . . and we believe no colony can make a better showing than this when making comparisons." [46]

The population climbed a bit more before it dropped drastically. The previous summer Borland had reported about 145 residents, and a Seattle newspaper elevated the population to nearly 200. But by the end of 1901 the count remained fairly stable at 115. This included 45 men, 25 women, 29 boys, and 16 girls. Discrepancies over the inclusion of families and nonmember neighbors confuse each count, but the colony population apparently remained close to 120 for several years. [47]

A feature that tended to weight the population toward the elderly was an "extraordinary insurance provision," according to Borland, "the most humane and far-reaching ever devised by a corporation or fraternal association." Any paid-up member who became "totally and permanently incapacitated either by sickness or accident for his usual vocation" would be allowed to come and bring his family. Should he die, his family would be received. Assuming that service from family members would compensate for their expenses, the originators used insurance statistics and programs of fraternal organizations to defend its practicality. This was "one of the best kinds of life and accident insurance, because a home and employment is more valuable than a lump sum of money, which may be stolen or wasted." Yet the plan was also criticized as inefficient and impracticable. [48]

By 1903 only one person had taken advantage of the insurance provision, but elderly or sick residents did come and this augured poorly for success. Several were suffering from injuries or infirmities. For instance, Emile Tennant arrived from Colorado while recovering from mining accident injuries, and a later arrival from Chicago had only one leg and was recovering from a stroke. Several colony members, including leaders, were elderly and died either at Burley or soon after leaving, occasionally in rest homes. The colony paper noted frequent illnesses and injuries, sometimes of a chronic or serious nature, and at least one diarist recounted the number of "more or less maimed" residents. Adequate medical facilities or personnel were not available. [49]

The governing powers of the Co-operative Brotherhood were granted to a twelve-man board of trustees and a board of directors, each with different purposes and functions. Each December a mail vote of the entire membership elected three trustees to four-year overlapping terms. These officials collectively held the capital stock of the company, except for a few personal shares retained by each director, and they handled general financial affairs, making certain that stock never be disposed of or encumbered. Dividends were not paid; rather, newly created capital was to be reinvested in the corporation. Regular company business was

G. E. (Ed) Pelton (Photo courtesy
of Florence Pelton Clark)

George Venable Smith
(Photo courtesy of Bert Kellogg)

Jay Fox, *ca.* 1919
(Photo courtesy of University of
Washington Libraries)

James F. Morton, Jr.
(Photo courtesy of Radium LaVene)

Puget Sound Co-operative Colony buildings from the bay, *ca.* 1892, with hotel and sawmill (Photo courtesy of Bert Kellogg)

Log-cabin home of George V. Smith (seated) and Ione Tomlinson, his future wife, Puget Sound Co-operative Colony (Photo courtesy of Bert Kellogg)

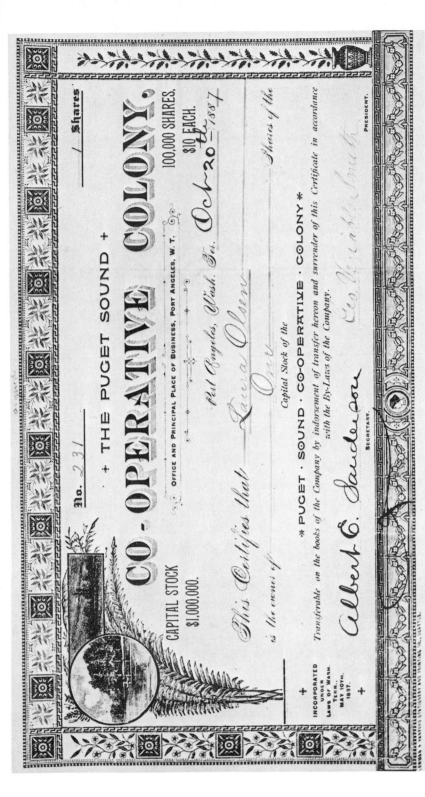

Stock certificate, Puget Sound Co-operative Colony (Photo courtesy of Bert Kellogg)

Five-dollar scrip, Puget Sound Co-operative Colony (Photo courtesy of Bert Kellogg)

Sawmill, Puget Sound Co-operative Colony (Photo courtesy of Bert Kellogg)

First kindergarten and school at Puget Sound Co-operative Colony, Ione Tomlinson, teacher (Photo courtesy of Bert Kellogg)

Equality Colony, 1900, looking southeast from garden, showing shingle house, sawmill, and other buildings and shops (Photo

Equality colonists before original log cabins and apartment house no. 2 (Photo courtesy of University of Washington Libraries)

Equality apartment building no. 2 while still unfinished (Photo courtesy of University of Washington Libraries)

Norman W. Lermond at his home in Maine, 1897, with Helen Mason (third from left), Mrs. Ed Pelton (fourth from left), Mrs. Pelton's two daughters, and an unidentified relative (Photo courtesy of Florence Pelton Clark)

The "Hatchery," former Carey Lewis home, at Equality Colony (Photo courtesy of University of Washington Libraries)

Interior of the kitchen, Equality Colony (Photo courtesy of Seattle Historical Society)

Equality Colony dining room (Photo courtesy of University of Washington Libraries)

Masthead of *Industrial Freedom* (Photo courtesy of University of Washington Libraries)

Composing room in printery, Equality Colony (Photo courtesy of University of Washington Libraries)

Freeland Colony store, with the *Bessie B.* alongshore (Photo courtesy of University of Washington Libraries)

Members of the First Thursday Club beside Blair Store, Freeland, *ca.* 1909

Burley Lagoon from colony townsite, showing the blacksmith shop with the boiler for the mill in the background, 1898 (Photo courtesy of Kitsap County Historical Society)

J. S. Ingalls on third floor of Burley Hotel, 1898 (Photo courtesy of Kitsap County Historical Society)

Home Colony, showing fenced plots of land and members' houses (Photo courtesy of University of Washington Libraries)

Home Colony members in Liberty Hall, *ca.* 1910, including George Allen, Grace Allen, J. W. Adams, Jay Fox, Esther Fox, Mattie Penhallow, and Gertie Vose (Photo courtesy of University of Washington Libraries)

conducted at monthly meetings of the twelve directors, who were selected each January by the trustees from a list nominated by resident members. Such shared authority was designed to avoid a schism between resident and nonresident members. Each director submitted his resignation when taking office, to become effective immediately upon acceptance by three-fourths of the trustees, thus ensuring "efficiency and faithfulness of service." Local affairs were normally handled by the directors, although some decisions were made at general meetings. In February 1901, the work of the colony was divided into departments, the heads of which organized themselves into an additional body called a board of management that agreed to meet each Saturday evening. [50]

Members almost constantly considered reorganizing the government of both the brotherhood and the colony, often in the context of a struggle between autocrat and democrat. In the spring of 1901, newly elected leaders prepared bylaws amendments to allow individuals to retain some profits from their efforts. Although criticized as a return to "wage slavery" competition, the plan was adopted. This reorganization coincided with a spirited but fruitless debate over the establishment of new colonies or industrial unions in other states. [51]

Two years later members wrestled with other problems, including the relationship between the parent organization and its colony. The colony was ultimately given greater autonomy. Financial difficulties prompted a decision to lease the physical facilities. Although an outside lessor was sought, a one-year agreement was finally made with Arthur B. Ellis, Jr., a colonist with private financial resources. [52]

The arrangement gave colonists an extra year to consider permanent reorganization. It coincided with the first appearance at the colony of Alonzo A. Wardall. A Civil War veteran and midwestern farmer, Wardall had long been involved in agrarian protest movements, and had represented an aid association affiliated with the Farmers' Alliance. Attending a cooperative congress in England in 1901, he was impressed with the Rochdale Cooperatives, and he became a Rochdale organizer in midwestern and other states; the "Father of Cooperation," a Wisconsin newspaper called him. In this capacity, he toured the Pacific Northwest in 1903. That September, Wardall and his wife visited

Burley, where their two sons, law students from Seattle, had spent the summer vacation doing farm work. For several days, Wardall preached the Rochdale plan as the solution to the difficulties that Burley was facing, and on his last evening he addressed "a good Audience of 50 in the schoolhouse."

After outlining the history and advantages of the plan, Wardall made specific proposals for Burley. The company should recapitalize at its present value, determining the value of shares according to the number of members, and sell shares to new members at 8 percent interest. Plants, houses, the mill, and similar properties should be maintained by the association but kept as separate accounts. He further proposed dividing net profits annually among members according to the hours worked and appointing an experienced general manager empowered to hire outside help at standard wages. As a gesture of good faith, Wardall promised to subscribe a share himself. [53]

Wardall, who moved to Seattle the next spring, visited Burley often, always promoting the Rochdale plan. In December 1904 reorganization began under his direction. "All seem glad to see me," he noted the first day. "In eve had meeting with Directors & it was voted to change their Store over to an equally owned # 100. [sic] share Rochdale store—I am to do the work." The Burley Mercantile Rochdale Association was formed, with twenty-three members subscribing twenty-six hundred dollars. Three months later the incorporation papers of the Co-operative Brotherhood were amended so as to facilitate landholding, production, trade, and business in the manner of a joint-stock company. These phases of reorganization altered the original communal concept, although the Co-operative Brotherhood survived for several years to come. [54]

Throughout these changes, Burley developed the character of a unique, small, rural community. In 1903, a national magazine described the town that visitors would encounter after a boat trip from Tacoma to Gig Harbor and a six-mile wagon ride through "glorious woods" to Henderson Bay:

Near the entrance gate is to be seen the mill, where logs are made into lumber, shingles and boxes, these being the branches of manufacturing in which the colony is now engaged. Driving through the grounds the visitor sees on the left a blacksmith shop, a two-story building used for a printery, carpenter's shop and general offices, a cluster of houses known to the colonists as Circle City, and straight ahead another two-story building, in which is the post office, store, dining room, kitchen and rooms for single men. Clustered around the hotel are a cigar factory, milk house, laundry, root house, shoe shop and several cottages. All these buildings are plain, mostly covered, both roof and sides, with shingles.[55]

As in other colonies, the logging operation and sawmill were essential. At Burley, the production of lumber, shingles, and shakes was a corollary to land clearing. The first logs were used for houses, including the earliest major structure, Hotel Commonwealth, and for cordwood. During the first winter, Willard heard of a mill for sale in Bellingham, and he went north to investigate. Under the direction of DeArmond and Stevens, a "first class carpenter and all around mechanic from Maine," the mill was rafted down sound to Burley. At the end of the year the mill was in operation. The editor romanticized over the "busy clipping of our shingle machine, as it converts the blocks of cedar into roofing material," and a lumberyard owner from northern California inquired about contracting for the entire output. But the inexperienced mill operators had difficulties. Shingles were so poorly cut that thousands had to be destroyed before an outsider came from Tacoma to refile saws and set things aright. Early improvements included a table edger and a sawdust conductor. The colonists soon boasted of their "first-class saw and shingle mill. . . . The former is used mainly to manufacture such lumber as the company itself needs in its building operations. A planer is part of the outfit, and both rough and dressed lumber are turned out as needed. The shingle mill is already a source of considerable revenue to the company, as besides turning out what shingles are needed in the local building operations, from five to six hundred thousand first-quality shingles are marketed monthly in the Tacoma market."[56]

Logs came both from colony lands and from camps in the area. By 1902 these operations far eclipsed the other activities of the colony, and improvements were being rushed. That fall a second story was added to the mill, and an acetylene gas plant enabled evening work. A lumberyard was constructed and systematized as the outside demand for colony lumber increased. The Tacoma Mill Company and the Willamette Casket Company were among the major outside customers. [57]

Acting Superintendent of Industry Francis Ficke reported that in September 1902 a logging crew at a camp near Gig Harbor cut eighty-one thousand feet of logs, scale measure, which were towed to Burley and cut into lumber. More than three-fourths of this was sold, and some was used by the colony. More than one hundred thousand shingles had also been sold, and Ficke anticipated a daily output of thirty thousand shingles with a kneebolter recently put into operation. Tacoma and nearby towns were the major markets. By March the demand was greater than the cooperators could handle alone, and they discussed the "burning question" of outside help, finally deciding to restrict work to members. [58]

New equipment, replacements, and procedures improved the operation. By fall fifteen men directed by a veteran of thirty years' milling experience could cut thirty thousand feet and plane ten thousand feet of lumber a day. In a virtually rebuilt shingle mill, one man could produce a thousand shingles an hour. Log booms now came from various places around the sound. [59]

In 1906 the Co-operative Brotherhood leased its mill, along with equipment and adjacent property, to the Allen Shingle Company. The rent varied with production but averaged about thirty-five dollars a month. This company maintained the mill for more than a year before financial difficulties led the colony to take successful legal action against it. [60]

In addition to the lumber operation, the founders envisioned starting small industries. Few materialized. Colonists talked of brickmaking; one correspondent proposed a foundry, machine shop, and blacksmith shop; a broomhandle factory was inaugurated; a member bottled perfumes; and "Burley Home Made Jams" were made and shipped out. [61] But the most flourishing small industry was cigarmaking.

Soon after Burley Colony began, *Industrial Freedom* advertised its cigars. Although J. B. Fowler was the first of several cigarmakers, the job passed to Mike Marine, a popular Creole. Often working alone, the cigarmaker developed a market for his product in nearby communities as well as larger cities on Puget Sound.

Prices post paid ranged from a dollar and a half for fifty "Coquetas" to three dollars for fifty "Elegantes" or "Matinee Stars." Although the colony attempted to raise tobacco leaf, it was necessary to buy from a Chicago firm. Marine left the colony in April 1903, but even after cigar manufacturing had ceased, profits came in from stock on hand. [62]

The colony depended upon agriculture, but found problems of land clearing greater than her sister colonies: "The conversion of the virgin Washington forest into arable land is a work of years that none but those who know can realize." A particular problem at Burley was the presence of "watery bogs. So while one party of land reclaimers is hewing and hauling and burning another is ditching and draining, and tapping the numerous springs that well up from under the hillsides. Wielded by men clad in jeans and hip boots, the spade draws off the superfluous water, converting gradually the home of the willow and skunk cabbage into land that will furnish luscious celery, new potatoes, asparagus, onions and cauliflower, and almost any of the temperate zone vegetables." But the spade was not enough, for the axe and the crosscut were also needed to "hew and cut through the submerged trunks beneath the soil." The first plowing was done with a "jumper, a kind of plow that declines to become caught and hung up by importunate roots, but takes a flying leap over them to dig its iron nose into the softer ground beyond, to be dragged round and round the patch. . . ."[63]

Potatoes were usually planted between the stumps, although corn needed for forage was sometimes the first crop. In time the vicarious tourist could survey the results:

West and northwest . . . lie the colony lands, of which there are 294 acres of rich land, known to settlers in Washington as beaver bottom. Of this land some 70 acres have been logged, 15 acres cleared and planted, 40 acres under fence and partially cleared. . . . On the side hill facing east will be the orchard and beds of small fruits, all of which can be irrigated from abundant springs, which latter will also give a plentiful supply for the town. Last spring on a third of an acre poorly cultivated from lack of needed help, a ton and a half of strawberries were picked. So plentiful and fine are the wild berries, including raspberry, red and black, huckleberry, blackberry, salmon berry, salol [*sic*] berry and mountain raspberry, that the Indians called the neighborhood Olalla or berry.[64]

Among the assets of Burley was the printing plant. The

makeshift kitchen shop where Willard had initiated the *Co-oper-ator* gave way to a permanent shop in the two-story office building. The paper had several editors after Willard, including Borland, the Reverend William E. Copeland, and Kingsmill Commander, a frequenter of several Washington colonies with a flair for journalism and poetry. "Gib" Crofut continued as printer throughout most of the seven years the paper existed. In 1902 the format was changed from a tabloid-size weekly, usually with eight pages, to a thirty-two page monthly magazine produced on quality paper with several printing refinements. [65]

The periodical maintained a relatively high journalistic quality, combining discussions of socialism and other reform movements, official news and debates of the Co-operative Brotherhood, and Burley news. Like similar ventures, the *Co-operator* used reprinted articles, and it showed a greater interest in other communitarian experiments than did sister publications. Curiosity about the Doukhobors was evident, and Francis Ficke described a visit to Oneida Community in New York and a conversation with William A. Hinds, who was gathering information for a book on American communities. A series on life at Burley was thorough and interesting, sympathetic but not maudlin. From Freeland, the Sanfords welcomed the magazine format as "a typographical beauty . . . [with] an abundance of cooperative news," and an Oregon socialist called it "indispensable." Praise came from no less a personage than Henry Demarest Lloyd.[66]

But the *Co-operator* could not meet expenses. In October 1903, the editors reluctantly halved the magazine to sixteen pages and resorted to a thin, cheap cover paper. Subscriptions were canceled on their expiration date. During this time of colony reorganization and property leasing, the printery remained the "only portion of the plant reserved by the C. B." Three years later the paper lingered as a last means of communication with the 150 remaining members of the brotherhood. The editor considered expansion inadvisable without a full-time, skilled writer. In 1916 the old printing equipment was among items disposed of to the Alaska Junk Company for a total of two hundred dollars.[67]

The *Co-operator* was not the only product of the printing office. In addition to colony scrip, necessary materials, and job printing, the shop produced *Soundview*, a "Magazinelet Devoted to the Obstetrics of Thought and the Philosophy of Existence." At a dollar a year, *Soundview* was a monthly publication usually running thirty-six small pages. Although a local judge was a co-owner, it was principally the child of L. E. Rader, Olalla resident, journalist, former Populist member of the state legislature, and occasional official of the Co-operative Brotherhood. Rader's interests were many. Frankly patterning himself after Elbert Hubbard of Aurora, New York, and his magazine after Hubbard's *Philistine*, Rader assembled brief articles, short homilies, anecdotes, comment, and book reviews. Most concerned radical or esoteric subjects, and they demonstrated advanced social, political, and economic views. The double meaning of *Soundview* derived from the local geography as well as from the "sound views" of editor and readers. Rader envisioned it as the organ of a new society of men and women called "Evergreens," "whose prime object in life is to learn to think and think to learn, with a view to securing the greatest amount of truth, enjoying the greatest amount of happiness and doing the greatest good for the greatest number, for the greatest length of time possible." In its earliest issues, *Soundview* frequently mentioned Burley and nearby Home community. Later they were virtually ignored, although the general tenor and format changed little otherwise. [68]

The Co-operative Brotherhood and Burley gained publicity through scattered local units sometimes called Temples of the Knights of Brotherhood. It is unlikely that many functions attained the frenzy of the Second Annual Basket Picnic of a Chicago local: "After the noon repast, J. H. Copeland, who acted as master of ceremonies, and the band headed for a procession which went to 'Mother Kleiminger's reservation.' Here the presentation of a very pretty red bannerett took place. On one side it contains the words 'Co-operative Brotherhood' and on the other 'Burley' in large white letters. It is the work of Mother Kleminger's [sic] own hands and is therefore the more highly appreciated. J. H. Copeland made the speech of acceptance and then called for three cheers and a tiger, which were enthusiastically given." Activities such as this and the sale of colony photographs and products served to advertise the colony and raise funds. [69]

The colony on Burley Lagoon was occasionally publicized in conventional publications. A full-page Sunday feature article with photographs romanticized the social life of colonists in the Seattle *Post-Intelligencer*. Articles by the Reverend Copeland appeared in *The Independent*, an old Congregationalist journal now spreading interests in reform, and in the *Arena*, a leading reform spokesman, and Borland outlined goals and plans in *The Pacific Monthly*.

True to his conversation with Francis Ficke, William A. Hinds included six pages about Burley in the 1902 edition of *American Communities*. Charles E. Buell, a minor American diplomat, wrote a pamphlet which proposed Burley as a model for labor colonies that the United States might establish in its newly acquired overseas possessions. [70]

The normal flow of guests included local tourists as well as friends and relatives of colonists. Burley also attracted European travelers, including Roland Eugene Muirhead, a Scottish reformer; P. A. Braams Scheuer, a "student of social problems from Amsterdam, Holland, who is making the rounds of all the colonies he is able to reach"; and Professor Andre E. Sayons, of the University of Paris, who also was studying social conditions in the United States. [71]

If such students found problems at Burley, they also encountered a populace that was basically content with the life they were attempting to follow. The character of Burley stemmed from the intent of its founders, from the philosophy that supported their enterprise, and from the quality of the people who followed. It was not, assured one spokesman, a communist colony: "We do not in Burley hold all things in common, we only hold some things in common. What we can do by co-operation to make life easier to live and to increase our general comfort we do. We may dine together, have various matters done in common, but we are alloted our own houses and land, to be ours as long as we live in the houses and improve the land." [72]

Home and the family were sacred. Communal living existed only in the apartments or dormitory for bachelors; the goal of most was a house of their own. Thus, Circle City was begun near the water, a cluster of homes around a looped road. Here colonists, some coming from outlying deserted ranch houses, took private homes on land leased from the brotherhood. The hotel was intended to remain just that, a place for visitors and for single men. Its quarters, conceded Copeland, were "rough, but better than are found in the logging camps." [73]

Meals were usually taken together in the cooperative dining room at the hotel. Here a staff of women, sometimes headed by a man, cared for the kitchen and prepared and served meals; the younger girls waited tables. Meals were pleasant functions where people could meet, talk, and relax at the conclusion or an intermission of the day's work. The room had the refinement of "clean white table cloths," but benches substituted for chairs.

Despite demands of economy, "We live on good, wholesome food. . . . The following bill of fare is a fair example of the provision for dinner: Soup, nearly always purely vegetable, but tasty and nutritious, peas, beans or lentils, providing the flesh forming constituent. Beans, potatoes, fried parsnips, made gravy, home-made tomato catsup, home-made pickles, pies with crust that does not offend the most delicate of digestive apparatus, two or three sorts of bread; washed down with tea, coffee or wheat cereal." Meat appeared infrequently, more often a relish than the main course, although fish was sometimes served. There was rarely a sufficient supply of eggs and dairy products. [74]

To most, the absence of meat was regrettable. To others it was by choice, for a contingent of vegetarians had their own table "just inside the door to the left," although the general shortage of meat made their fare almost indistinguishable from the others. These practices were subjected to "joshing" and badinage: "The meat eaters look upon the vegetarians as very good fellows suffering from a harmless kind of monomania; while the vegetarians think the rest are equally good fellows but not yet sufficiently enlightened on certain aspects of the food question." [75] But ridicule had little effect upon such a man as Duncan Pearce. His vegetable diet and his single meal a day did not diminish this blacksmith's "magnificent strength"; a twelve-day fast failed to reduce his weight, but "plainly improved his general health." Three miles away, a separate group of vegetarians were rumored to be starting a community of their own.

There was, however, greater unanimity regarding other forms of abstinence. "There are no grog shops in Burley, no low dance hall nor gambling dens to corrupt the morals of our youth. We have no prohibition law, nor do we need one. There is no demand for liquor, and there is no profit system to support its sale. The inhabitants of Burley lead healthy, natural lives, and do not crave the excitement which comes from stimulants." Some questioned the morality of manufacturing cigars, and the *Whidby Islander* taunted that Freeland had "no saloons or cigar factories."[76]

Other pleasures and entertainments were frequent. Informal dances were held most evenings at the schoolhouse, colonists attending in work jumpers and overalls and dancing to the music of a harmonica. Most "formal" dances were on Saturday evenings, with music provided by colony young people or neighbors. The Finfrock family, neighbors who participated in many colony activities, comprised virtually an orchestra of their own with guitar, violin, and cello. Calls were provided by W. H. Packer and occasionally by the Olalla storekeeper.[77]

Music played an important role in colony life. Usually it was informal, with songs and instruments present even on a Sunday cruise to Horsehead Bay. Early on that morning there appeared to board the colony launch "Fred Corpron and Kate Finfrock with violin and guitar, and Sammy Finfrock carrying his big 'cello lovingly in his arms, carefully wrapped in a mackintosh to preserve it from the dampness." That afternoon, on the beach of their destination, "the musicians at intervals, play as they feel in the mood."[78]

Musical instruction was more formal during the several months in 1900 that H. M. Draper of Calumet, Michigan, lived at Burley. Draper arrived early in May, bringing with him two horns. Using additional instruments sent from his home, borrowed, and rented, he soon organized a band of about twenty-three children between eight and eighteen. The first photograph published in the *Co-operator* showed the young musicians, instruments in hand, grouped with their leader. The editor credited this "genius" at working with children with having a "better faculty of gaining their confidence and respect than any person we ever met." Welcomed by oldsters, the band presented a unique way to publicize Burley and solicit funds. During the summer, members took excursions to play for gatherings in Tacoma and Seattle, and in the fall, they undertook a longer tour to Oregon. Despite favorable comments, the expenses of this trip outdistanced funds and receipts. Furthermore, Draper, according to plan, continued east alone. He intended to return but never did, and the band died without its leader, as did the adult choir he had organized. "Daddy" Draper did eventually return to Washington, where his band at a Des Moines orphanage gained renown. Later he joined a communal venture in Nevada and again formed a children's band.[79]

A mandolin and guitar club of young adults also played engagements away from home. Its leader was Dalmiro Brocchi, an Italian who was said to have jumped the man-of-war to which he had been consigned in New York and headed for a socialist colony.[80]

Literary and musical entertainments were held regularly on Tuesday or Wednesday evenings in the schoolhouse. Occasionally lecturers came from the outside, sometimes from the nearby community of Home. But most speakers were colonists or neighbors. Although their topics varied, reform and radical topics were favored.

Notwithstanding their radicalism, the Burley colonists were patriotic, loyal citizens; even neighbors did not consider them otherwise. Their socialist grounding was in the American rather than the European tradition, and their founders had berated the supposed alien sentiments of SDA rivals. A newly arrived member, who misinterpreted local attitudes and spoke disparagingly of the United States at an entertainment, was "gently rebuked" when one of the young ladies rose and sang "My United States." Any holiday provided an excuse to celebrate, and the patriotic ones were no exceptions. Thanksgiving meant a traditional dinner, although centered around seafood; the colonists likened their own experiment to that of the Pilgrims. Washington's birthday brought a larger crowd than usual to a Sunday evening service at which the flag was displayed, patriotic songs were sung, and the ministers gave addresses. The Fourth of July was celebrated with games, a dinner, speeches, songs, and readings—including the Declaration of Independence. The children's band played in a Tacoma parade one year, and at another celebration "eight little girls clothed in white dresses and red, white and blue ribbons" performed a Maypole dance. With "foaming bumpers of good lemonade" the colonists

of 1900 offered toasts which reflected their mingled attitudes
toward country and reform:

"The United States—may it become a land of equal privileges
for all its people.

"The Co-operative Brotherhood—leader of the greatest revolution of the age.

"Our Pioneers."[81]

The religious base was firmer than in other Puget Sound
colonies. An early broadside stressed religious freedom as "one of
our cardinal principles." The bylaws restricted interference "with
the free exercise of individual preferences, convictions or desires in
religious, political or domestic affairs." But religious references
were not merely negative. The Buell pamphlet compared the
Burley spirit "to that which inspired the primitive Christian
organization," and included an address which the colony had
distributed. This writer placed the Co-operative Brotherhood in
the tradition of the Apostles who administered to material needs
of people while satisfying their spiritual hungers. "The Master is
thus our teacher also, and we desire to be imbued with His Spirit
and go about doing good as we have means and opportunity."[82]

Willard failed to imbue others with his Theosophical sentiments. A few years after his departure, however, a new group of
members formed a Theosophical Club. Regular meetings continued for at least a year. But the religious inclinations varied.
Some preferred no religion, "some are Spiritualists and others
Materialists; some are orthodox, others heterodox or interested in
some form of New Thought."

Protestant services were held Sunday evenings. The Reverend
Copeland considered the attendance small, but another writer
claimed that most of the colonists and several neighbors came. The
simple traditional services included hymns and prayers, with
sermons delivered alternately by two resident ministers, William E.
Copeland and Arthur B. Ellis, Jr. Both Unitarians, these men
delivered sermons elsewhere on occasion, and other colonists
occasionally substituted for them. After Copeland's death, his
mother-in-law, "Grandma" Townsend, conducted services for a
time.[83]

The two ministers personify the role of the social gospel and of Christian Socialism in the communitarian movement of the 1890s, and at Burley in particular. According to these men, Christians had a particular responsibility to help create a better life and environment for their fellow man, a task that called for cooperation and brotherhood. Boston born, Copeland graduated from Harvard University in 1860 and became an infantry private during the Civil War. When poor health forced him to leave the army, he entered Harvard Divinity School. Upon graduating in 1866, he became pastor of the Unitarian Church in Brunswick, Maine, seat of Bowdoin College. He remained in New England for several years before migrating to Omaha, where he held a pastorate for twelve years, and then to Tacoma, Washington, Stockton, California, and Salem, Oregon. Throughout his ministry, Copeland extended his interests to social work and welfare. Experiences among the poorer working class of Boston during his student days aroused his insight into the social and economic needs of the laborer. He also found that Theosophy supplemented his doctrinal beliefs, and he joined the Bellamy Nationalist movement; he was a Scottish Rite Mason and a Knight of Pythias.

Possibly because of similar interests, Copeland became acquainted with Willard, whose marriage he performed in 1899. It was well after Willard's departure, however, that Copeland, a man of sixty-two, came to Burley. At first he and his son occupied a tent while Mrs. Copeland remained at Gig Harbor, dreading life in the "hastily built, unceiled shacks set close together" that she eventually came to appreciate. The home they later built was one of the largest and most modern in the community. Immediately upon his arrival, the minister was drawn into colony affairs. He became editor of the *Co-operator*, president of the colony, and one of its most eloquent advocates. Those who attended his church services were impressed with his kindliness, his desire to uplift people, and his fine speaking voice. Copeland died suddenly of a stroke while gardening one March afternoon in 1904. The funeral service at the schoolhouse was attended by most of the colonists and a large gathering of visitors: "A few hymns were sung and Brother Ellis made a brief address after which the procession wound its way up the hill to our beautiful cemetery, where a few final words were spoken and the remains tenderly consigned to their last resting place, under 'the murmuring pines and the hemlocks' which Brother Copeland loved so well."[84]

Arthur B. Ellis, Jr. was also a Unitarian with a Massachusetts heritage and a Harvard education. Reserved and quiet, he was well read and intellectual. The visionary Ellis lacked the practical bent that might have made him a greater asset to the colony, but he was well-meaning and abundantly generous. A man with private resources, he once bought a fifty-foot launch for colony use, and he personally provided money to lease colony property in a time of severe financial need, earning the deep respect of the community. Ellis remained at Burley for many years, and he owned property there when he died. His final months were spent in a Steilacoom boarding house. By hearse and by ferry, his body was removed to the Burley cemetery for burial. The two ministers illustrate an affinity at Burley between religion and economic betterment, and they demonstrate the desire of some churchmen to create a better society in the physical world.[85]

Such a desire also led to the recognition of the need for an educational system for the young. Education at Burley began when Willard imported a Seattle teacher to instill refinements in the Colorado miners and their children. The teacher lived in one tent and used another for her school, but instant and loud complaints came from the DeArmond crowd about "such high-falutin nonsense." Willard warned that if the colony did not act, the state would "force us to build a school house and a school teacher would be sent for us to support by taxes who cared less for socialism. . . ." His bluster quieted the men, but the attempt to raise their cultural level had clearly failed.[86]

Willard's statement, however, was realistic. When the colony arrived, local children were attending the Big Bottom School, a long walk to the north, but the increased school population necessitated additional facilities. On 1 June 1899, the district served forty-two children between the ages of five and twenty-one from sixteen families, few of them colony members. A year later the census revealed fifty-eight children, including nine new families, mostly from the colony. In subsequent years the number of children remained about the same, with the Burley area providing about two-thirds. These needs led the colony to construct a schoolhouse for lease to the district. The "small building of vertical, hand made, cedar slabs, roofed and shakes [sic] . . . was made by hand except for windows and nails and hinges." It doubled as the community center.[87]

The teaching was without apparent socialist bias, most of the teachers coming from the outside, although several colonists were school board members and teachers included Ellis and a noncolony neighbor, Nellie Gibson. The board was less concerned with curriculum than with fuel wood and teacher contracts.

Securing teachers was a problem, especially during the confused 1900-1901 school year. That fall the board reconsidered an earlier decision against having a school at Burley and hired Miss Carrie Lowe, who, however, "was suddenly called home to Kansas City." A few weeks later a highly recommended teacher signed a three-month contract at twenty dollars a month, and the *Co-operator* rejoiced that, despite the delay, "we will now have at least six months of school." The brotherhood intended "to have better educational facilities than any village of the same size in the state, . . . [as] fast as circumstances permit." But in two months the board called a special meeting to consider "the conduct" of their teacher, and Burley seems to have been without a school until Miss Gibson was hired in April at forty dollars a month. Meanwhile, county officials criticized the board's annual report as incomplete and inaccurate. Teachers rarely stayed more than a year. In 1903 school opened under C. B. Simmons of Seattle, "a gentleman . . . highly recommended." In due time, Simmons proposed manual-training classes, the boys to remodel a shed and make furniture and the smaller children to garden. Assured that no extra costs would accrue, the board granted permission.[88]

Despite its cooperative aspects, the social atmosphere of Burley resembled any small community. This the colonists came to recognize. They regularly described themselves by saying: "We are not a 'peculiar people,' gathered here at Burley but about the same as you will find in any western community."

Yet if there is one thing that distinguishes Burley from similar experiments, including those which were larger or more sensational or more doctrinaire, that characteristic is the quality of its people. Although the effete easterner that was Cyrus Field Willard and the rough-hewn Colorado miners were poles apart in background and manner of living, later Burleyites exemplified a more homogeneous middle ground. They were idealists with much in common; simple, intelligent, and well-meaning, they could disagree heartily and yet maintain mutual respect. Copeland, less a romantic than Willard, called them a "collection of choice souls." Early in his stay he wrote, "I have never found a village of the size of Burley which would begin to compare with it for intellectual vigor and moral attainment." A neighbor who befriended them recalled that "they did very well—they made no money, but they all were happy. All were on an equal footing, all friendly." Long after the dream of socializing Washington had faded beyond memory, they went quietly about their lives, trying to build a solid, contented community based upon brotherhood. Their ripple in the world was negligible, but it was there. [89]

Although the aspiration "to make Burley . . . the social and intellectual center of a considerable district" sounded pretentious, it had some substance. Meetings, church services, dances, and holiday parties drew neighbors and colonists into a single bond. Nonmember families were as vital a part of colony life as many bonafide members. The lines of distinction between member and nonmember became blurred. Yet the lines existed, and Henry Stein recalled with some sadness: "The people who lived in the country around the colony took advantage of the opportunities it offered for entertainment and recreation, but told wild tales about 'those dreadful socialists.' The colonists were very nice people, but they were always under suspicion from the other residents in the county. There was trouble with the county commissioners, who did all they could to hamper the colonists." [90]

Nor was the Burley settlement aloof from the larger world. Its membership and philosophy reflected the progressive ferment of the times. The founders were participants in the struggle within labor, reform, and radicalism to respond to the challenge of industrialism. Willard's interests always transcended the colony as he continued his involvement with the Bellamy movement, Theosophy, and Freemasonry. Borland remained a labor journalist. Copeland and Ellis personified the Christian Socialist ideal, and Copeland retained interests in some of the same movements that had engrossed Willard. The activities of neighbor Stein spanned reforms from the single tax to the New Deal. L. E. Rader was a link with populism and with a multitude of eccentric causes. Charles Buell promoted Burley as a model to civilize the newly acquired dominions of the United States. Alonzo A. Wardall, a frequent visitor, kept the colony in touch with the cooperative movement. And one of his sons linked Burley to a dramatic incident of municipal reform in the Pacific Northwest.

Max and Ray Wardall came to Burley in June of 1903 to help with farm work during their summer vacation. Athletic and clean cut, these long-distance bicycle riders had seen much of the United States and had journeyed around the world; in Australia and New Zealand they had perfected a stamp photograph device that created an instant sensation and financial profit. After leaving Burley and finishing school, they formed a Seattle law partnership and developed a substantial practice. In 1908 Max became a member of the city council; a colleague remembered him as "a young lawyer of broad humanitarian outlook and of lively intelligence." In 1909, while acting mayor, Max Wardall initiated the sensational vice investigations that would send the police chief to prison and recall Mayor Hiram Gill from office. A Theosophist while at the colony, Max Wardall eventually moved to Point Loma, where he remained active in the movement.[91]

Thus its people gave Burley a distinctive character. "We are over four years old," they confessed in 1903, "but we don't profess to know it all yet. We are learning something everyday, and some things we learned yesterday we are unlearning today. We will bear watching. We may not succeed in reforming the world, but if we succeed in making one little spot better we have done a world of good. . . . As said before, 'We will bear watching.'"[92] But even such cautious optimism was to prove disappointing.

As the size and goals were reduced, Burley made constant attempts to reorganize its structure and assets so as to make the holdings secure. The colony never truly failed financially, but it drifted toward stagnation. A monthly report in 1906 was a tired document that apologized for its presence by admitting that "the C. B. has ceased to conduct any industries at all. . . . Still there is a certain amount of business done, from month to month, in which the C. B. is either directly or indirectly concerned." Cash returns were being used to reduce indebtedness that now surpassed twenty-five hundred dollars. The condition of the land was good, with orchards bearing fruit and the soil improving. Several families had established themselves on home lots and were engaging in home industries. The writer reminded readers that this "was one of the objects which was sought in the original plan." Unintentionally revealing decline was the lead article in a late *Co-operator*, a nostalgic reminiscence of Wednesday evening entertainments in days when activity and optimism prevailed. Two years later the colony claimed "substantial progress," with 150 members still in the brotherhood, although only seventeen of them lived at Burley. Property values were estimated at between thirty and forty thousand dollars; the county assessor's official valuation was only seventy-five hundred dollars. [93]

By 1912 the trustees, sensing widespread desire to dissolve, called a stockholders' meeting to wind up affairs. Although their proposal was well received by most of those present, it lacked the required two-thirds vote. This failure, the trustees claimed, stemmed less from a desire to continue than from suspicion and jealousy that a few members felt toward officers. These few initiated the court action that finally dissolved the colony. Yet the overtones of bitterness during the final hearings were faint compared with other colonies. [94]

M. F. Bruce, Francis Ficke, S. H. Bohlman, and J. C. Davis filed suit in December 1912, asking that the colony be dissolved and a receiver appointed. The plaintiffs, who claimed to be stockholders and fully paid-up members, asserted that the colony was fraught with "dissention [*sic*], jealousy, discontent and trouble," but their legal justification reached back seven years to the reorganization of 1905. Before this time the company had been "an eleemosynary corporation, a corporation not for profit, but for the development and promotion of Co-operative Brotherhood theories and ideals." The economic base was to rest on collectively owned means of production and the distribution of the products from cooperative industries, while family life was to be encouraged and ennobled. But the 1905 reorganization placing properties and stocks in the hands of the twelve directors had been inaugurated illegally, the suit charged, and it had "changed the entire character and objects and purposes . . . to a corporation organized for profit." Moreover, the plaintiffs objected to the increase in capital stock from five thousand to fifty thousand dollars, an amount never subscribed. They challenged a recent decision by the directors to issue new notes to lessees and to enable forfeiture of leases for nonpayment or for disobeying certain rulings. Land titles had allegedly become entangled, and the corporation was nearly insolvent. Bohlman specifically complained that he had been refused payment of $450 due from checks and due bills of credit. The complaint characterized the goals of the brotherhood as "visionary, impractical, and impossible of being carried out, unbusinesslike and theoretical, a vain and impossible attempt to develope [*sic*] into realities, impossible theories and ideals." The colony had become a "hot-bed of discontent, a menace to law abiding and orderly citizenship . . . an obstruction to the progress and prosperity of community and public at large." [95]

The defendants denied most of the allegations, including Bohlman's personal complaints, and they stressed the orderliness of the 1905 reorganization. They labeled the plaintiffs troublemakers who were causing a long and expensive court proceeding instead of an orderly dissolution and property settlement. But attempts to block action were only half-hearted. On 10 January 1913, Judge John B. Young ordered the Co-operative Brotherhood to be dissolved and appointed Joseph Pitt as receiver. Pitt, an early rancher in the area and a frequent political officeholder, would take twelve years to complete his task. [96]

He reported annually to the court. An early petition to sell personal property indicated how little remained: " . . . a printing press, blacksmith tools, a small boiler, two small engines, a wood turning lathe, a few articles of office furniture, some wire fencing and gates, four barrels of mineral paint, and some other small articles which will not increase in value but are likely to deteriorate." He praised the 290 acres of "good agricultural land . . . suitable . . . for truck gardening and small farming and poultry raising," and he recommended disposing of it slowly over a period of time to enhance its value. Much of the land had been leased to colony members with options to buy at stated prices. Pitt's efforts involved the disposition of landholdings either to the lessees or to purchasers.

When the receiver presented his final report on 29 October 1924, he listed receipts and disbursements that both totaled $32,147.72. The greatest amount—$23,616.80—came from the sales of land, with other receipts from rents, loans and auctions, collections of old accounts, interest, sales of personal property—a scant $475.58—and cash paid on stock subscriptions. Land purchasers included colony members and neighbors. A little more than eleven hundred dollars remained on hand. The largest share of disbursements—$14,517.72—went to stockholders. [97]

The report brought a legal conclusion to an experiment that had in fact ceased years before. Many of the colonists and their neighbors lived on at Burley, but if they spoke of the old colony, others forgot or ignored it. When a nearby chamber of commerce labeled Burley "progressive," it spoke in the hometown "boomer" sense rather than of social or political theories. Favored by soil, slope, and climate to produce berries and poultry, Burley became famous locally for an annual agricultural fair, "the best small fair in the state," and for an active, well-organized citizenry. Historians of south Kitsap County who mentioned Burley did not tell of the colony, although one made reference to Circle City. But there were some who remembered. [98]

In 1925 a new highway linking Gig Harbor with Port Orchard was opened, and the governor and other state officials mingled with residents at Burley, where a ladies club provided luncheon. For the occasion, Henry Stein reminded readers of a Tacoma newspaper that the new highway touched "Historic Ground." He described the colony and the dreams and the work that had gone into it:

There is no record left today of the hundreds of happy days these people spent in Burley. But what these people did, their material developments, is yet visible. There remains the school (now used as a library and community hall), the old hotel, the store and a dozen or more homes covered with vines and comfortably located among trees and fertile fields. Whatever developments may have been made in Burley, including the building of roads, is very largely the work of the Co-operative Brotherhood. They found a wilderness and left homes and fertile fields.[99]

6. Home

NEST OF ANARCHY
OR HAVEN OF INDIVIDUALISM?

Occasionally on a Sunday, the people of Burley sailed south on the colony launch through Purdy Channel to Joe's Bay and the community of Home. Here they visited the freest and most famous of the Puget Sound communitarian experiments. Less auspicious in origins or intentions than the Puget Sound Co-operative Colony, Equality, or Burley, Home flourished with a unique character that lasted for almost two decades. In its own time, the reputation for anarchism, the liberal Home press, and stories about free love and nude bathing made Home anathema to nearby conservatives. The individualism of local residents and famous visitors helped give the community a flavor that fascinated later journalists and historians. [1]

Home developed from the failure of an earlier, tightly structured experiment inspired by the Bellamy nationalist movement. The Glennis Cooperative Industrial Company had been located seventeen miles south of Tacoma on the Eatonville road. Oliver A. Verity, a carpenter and occasional politician, had acquired 160 acres of homestead land near Clear Lake in April 1894, and this became the colony site. Although it once had nearly thirty members, a school, a dairy, a blacksmith shop, a cigar factory, and a post office, Glennis deteriorated rapidly. Verity recalled, "The desire of the many at Glennis to make by-laws restricting others from doing things that in reality were

Parts of this chapter appeared as "The Anarchist Colony at Home, Washington, 1901-1902," *Arizona and the West* 14 (Summer 1972):155-68.

private matters, causing so many meetings which were noisy and bred inharmony from the diversified views of what should be done, not only made us lose interest in the meetings, but finally disgusted us at the wrangles and disputes over petty matters." [2] Lack of confidence in the leaders and an unwillingness of some to do their share sapped the strength of the colony. Yet the stated ten-hour work day was not enforced because the colonists did not believe in force. Many members left, and those who remained became doubters. The last seven decided to dissolve the colony, but three of the men, united by economic necessity and hopeful of finding a workable panacea, determined to start anew. [3]

Thus Verity, George H. Allen, and B. F. Odell built a boat and toured southern Puget Sound in search of a location. Personal losses and demands of withdrawing members upon the Glennis treasury left only twenty dollars between them for the land purchase. After several spots were rejected, the trio successfully arranged to buy twenty-six acres fronting Von Geldern Cove. Twenty dollars was the first down payment, with a like amount due every sixty days until the full $182 was paid. Allen secured a teaching position near Tacoma to raise expenses, and Verity and Odell established themselves on the site cutting and selling cordwood. Captain Ed Lorenz, owner of the steamer *Typhoon*, accepted cordwood as delayed payment for passage and freight. [4]

The spot had a serene beauty that befit its formal name of Von Geldern Cove. But the commonly used name was Joe's Bay, probably after Joe Faulkner, the first permanent settler who had arrived in the early 1870s, or possibly for a drunken fisherman remembered only as Joe who fell from his boat to drown in waters derisively called by his name thereafter. The small bay, about a mile long and almost as wide at one point, was an indentation off Carr Inlet. At high tide, the water was a deep blue, enhanced by the sloping woods that framed it; low tide revealed a vast mud flat abounding in clams and other shellfish. A few families lived and logged near the bay before the three colonists arrived. [5]

The Odell and Verity families debarked on the north shore on 10 February 1896, the Allens settling after the school term finished. The three pioneers had quite different backgrounds. Odell, a blacksmith by trade, was a tall, dark, moustached man, with a stout and pleasant wife in her late thirties and a son and daughter. He remained for a shorter time and his influence was less than that of his colleagues, although he kept in touch with the colony. Verity, an Oberlin College graduate, was probably the most practical of the three, a "close reasoner" of wide experience whose advice was valued. "He is the kind of head," wrote Allen, "necessary at the beginning of an experiment such as this." This clean-shaven man with prominent facial features and deep-set eyes had the appearance of strength and stability. He and his wife also had an adolescent son and daughter. Later the Veritys separated, and he moved to California, retaining contacts and occasionally returning to visit colony members.[6]

George Allen lived at Home for the nearly half century that remained of his life. Well educated and the most theoretical of the three, he was born in New York State and attended college in Canada. There he met his wife, and the couple came west to homestead near Tacoma. He lost much of his money in the Glennis experiment. A joiner, talker, and organizer, Allen was more fascinated by ideas and arguments than by the necessities of making a living, although he was the Home schoolteacher for many years. He viewed his education and his mechanical talents as assets to the experiment. Despite a touch of the impractical romantic about him, Allen considered himself "not a man to be carried away by an unreasonable or dream-like ideas but . . . a thoughtful American citizen." His wife Sylvia was the intelligent, strong-minded mainstay of their family. Not enjoying colony life nor sharing all of her husband's ideas, she remained the dutiful partner and mother. Their four daughters were all under ten when the Allens came to Home; the youngest was named Glennis after her birthplace.[7]

Each of the three men took two acres near the waterfront and began to clear brush, trees, and stumps. With lumber purchased on credit, they built the original houses of the colony. The first was a one-story house of shakes occupied by the Verity family. After his arrival, George Allen helped to construct "Welcome Cottage" for the Odells, and then the Allen home was built. The two-acre apportionment was based on a desire to divide land equally. Using figures allegedly from the Department of Agriculture, the men divided the total acreage under cultivation in the United States by the population and got an answer of one and three-quarter acres, which they rounded off to two. According to a contemporary scientist who challenged their accuracy, "they decided to make the maximum holding in the colony two acres, since if one acre carefully managed would suffice, two would provide an affluence."[8]

Meanwhile, the founders worked out fundamental principles for a community that emphasized tolerance and independence. "We had heard and read many isms," recalled Allen, "and had tried some of them with varying success. We wished to give each ism a chance to prove its usefulness to humanity." Verity viewed their ideals as "the personal liberty to follow their own line of action no matter how much it may differ from the custom of the past or present, without censure or ostracism from their neighbor," and "the placing of every individual on his or her own merits, thereby making them independent." The first objective could be attained by publicizing the ideals of the community, thus attracting similarly inclined persons while discouraging the narrow-minded. The second could be "made easy by the absence of all laws, rules or regulations" with which willful persons might force ideas upon others. Each family was expected to build and maintain its own home without promises of future benefits. The indolent were shunned for their tendency to destroy individualism and weaken the economy. Hence, the Home founders, remembering Glennis and critical of the communitarian ideal, emphasized that this was to be a community of individuals, rather than a cooperative colony.[9]

Considering rules and laws an interference and distrusting government generally, the founders avoided formal organization for almost two years. But practical needs prevailed, and the Mutual Home Association was effected in January 1898. The charter, drawn up by a Tacoma lawyer who was not a member, defined simply a landholding organization with no provisions for other economic ventures. The only stated purpose of the association was to assist "members in obtaining and building homes for themselves and to aid in establishing better social and moral conditions." Members were entitled to secure between one and two acres of land from the association by paying the cost of the land, one dollar for a membership certificate, and taxes assessed against their particular tract. The association could use money thus received only to purchase more land. Houses and other improvements were considered personal property that could be sold or bequeathed, but the land itself was retained by the association and could never be sold, mortgaged, or disposed of. Membership certificates, including land rights, could be willed to a remaining spouse, children, or other beneficiary. [10]

An elected board of trustees governed the association. The original seventeen subscribers elected the first officers; E. C. Miles was president, Verity was secretary, and the trustees were Allen, H. B. Wren, and H. E. Thomson. The five officers were afterward elected each January at an annual meeting of the membership. Little else seems to have been considered at such meetings, and one might conjecture that the usual business of the trustees was mostly routine. [11]

Its landholding scheme gave Home the aspect of economic communitarianism. The founders expected future comers to follow their examples and select one acre near the water for their homesite and the second farther back to farm, possibly as a cooperative. But some newcomers took two front acres and additional plots in the names of wives and children. Their abhorrence for laws apparently restrained association leaders from limiting or controlling such abuses. Verity rationalized that these circumstances possibly prevented a land rush and kept out opportunists. He noted further that "the majority of avowed free lovers and anarchists have built their houses and made their improvements upon the acres chosen by wives and mothers, while the majority of these believing in government have built and improved on the acres of the husband." Possibly this was coincidence; yet, he suspected that the more liberty-loving individual tended toward "a strong sense of justice." Occasionally members had to be reminded to pay their tax equivalents to the association. One year individual assessments were apportioned on the "single tax plan," presumably an equal distribution of the association's tax burden. [12]

Verity recognized early that success would depend upon

publicizing the founders' views. A few days after his arrival, he invited correspondence from readers of the *Coming Nation* "wishing to establish a cooperative colony." In June 1897, he issued the first newspaper from Home. *New Era*, printed on a used, hand-operated job press that covered only a half a page at a time, was freely distributed throughout radical circles. It described the community, its liberal spirit and freedom from laws, as well as the beauties of Puget Sound. [13]

Perhaps it was this paper that attracted Martin V. Dadisman, whose material wealth assisted with further land acquisition. About forty, Dadisman had left his comfortable West Virginia farm because he "could not get Peace to live as his opinions were different from those around him." He had rebelled against a strict upbringing and drifted toward free thought and anarchistic beliefs. Coming west alone, Dadisman first lived at Equality Colony, but he was annoyed by the laziness of some members and impractical orders of foremen. He and a son by his first marriage arrived at Home in the fall of 1898. When his wife and their two children anchored in the bay on 12 June 1899, Dadisman's small house with its garden was one of only five along the shore. [14]

Dadisman immediately began to purchase land along the waterfront and in the vicinity; some he sold to the association, other pieces were made available for settlement. In October 1898, he paid four hundred dollars for forty acres plus additional properties, soon afterward deeding sixty-four acres to the association at ten dollars an acre. A year later he purchased eighty-nine acres a short distance to the south, and the following summer he bought nineteen acres at Home. This provided additional lots for newcomers and gave the colony "a complete line of waterfront from the point to the head of the bay." Land held by members of the Verity family, probably constituting the original purchase and some later ones, also accrued to the association. In 1901, when the Mutual Home Association as sole owner platted Home, it contained 217 acres that stretched along the northwest shore of the bay and back over the hill. In the meantime, persons associating themselves with the colony had purchased or leased other properties across the bay and just west in a draw known as Happy Valley. [15]

Home had few other communitarian aspects. The founders would have professed that individualism and the emphasis on personal liberties and freedom were a rejection of communal life. Nevertheless, Home tended to attract individuals united by their very differences and their receptiveness to new ideas. Additional residents were drawn by the burgeoning reputation of Home as a place where freedom and tolerance prevailed.

One who stayed was a wandering printer, Charles L. Govan, a "small, slender man, middle aged, his hair commencing to gray, looking . . . like a Catholic priest of French stock from New Orleans," his native city. He had not lived a priestly life; his experiences, he said, were those of a dissipated man. Reading Verity's *New Era* in a San Francisco saloon, he was attracted to Home by the sinner's desire for reform and the printer's wish to practice his trade. By the time he arrived, the *New Era* had died, and Govan, Verity, and a few others inaugurated a new paper, with a larger press and additional type.[16]

Discontent: Mother of Progress, a tabloid-size, four-page publication, first appeared on 11 May 1898. The weekly publication issued from a small print shop constructed with ten dollars' worth of materials. For several years the paper was printed there, then in the large living room of the J. E. Larkin home, until a two-story print shop was built and fitted with a newer press and type. Neither *Discontent* nor its successors purported to be the official organ of Home or of the Mutual Home Association. They were published by individuals or, as in the case of *Discontent*, by a group who considered themselves anarchists. Yet the writings of the most vocal residents tended to sharpen the thinking of the whole community and to reinforce its reputation elsewhere. In its first "Greetings," *Discontent* pledged to "first of all, be an Anarchist paper, and . . . battle for the freedom of the human race from tyranny and superstition of all kinds and sorts. It will advocate communism as the ultimate ideal, as we believe mankind must have an ideal to strive for if they are to progress, and we can conceive of no higher ideal of existence than that to be secured by the consolidated efforts of a band of brothers striving for the full freedom of all to enjoy life untrammeled by statutory enactments and deep-rooted prejudices fossilized by time."[17] The union of anarchy with communism would allow each individual to pursue personal rights and desires freely while promoting a stronger productive effort through association than an individual could achieve alone.

Discontent was also an open forum for liberal views. Politics, economics, religion, world affairs, sex, and differing trends of liberal thought were among topics discussed by Home residents, by correspondents, and through reprints by noted radicals. *Discontent* emphasized theory more than bread-and-butter issues or specific, immediate reforms, and it aspired to be more than the house organ of a community. As *Discontent* aroused interest and attracted persons to the community that had subsisted quietly for several years, the unique character and reputation of Home became solidified.

Among early controversial figures to come were Henry Addis and Abner J. Pope, who had helped publish *Firebrand*, an anarchist newspaper in Portland, Oregon. In September 1897, the paper was closed and three participants arrested for sending through the mail an allegedly obscene poem by Walt Whitman. Denouncing bail as a concession to government, the seventy-four-year-old Pope was imprisoned for eight months before and after his trial. He found opportunity in adversity by offering his photograph and an account of the case for small donations. The third man involved, Abe Isaak, moved to San Francisco to publish *Free Society*, which briefly became a major anarchist journal, but Addis and Pope turned their efforts to *Discontent*. [18]

Meanwhile, Home received its first famous visitor. Emma Goldman was the most noted woman anarchist in the nation. Once a factory worker, she had become imbued with anarcho-communism and radical causes; she was the helpmate of Alexander Berkman in his attempt to kill steel magnate Henry Clay Frick. Yet this feminine symbol of violence had a pleasant matronly air that surprised those who met her.

Emma Goldman had acquaintances at Home, and when speaking arrangements in Seattle and Tacoma collapsed during her first western tour in 1898, she came to Home. For three successive evenings she lectured on "The Woman Question," "Authority vs. Liberty," and "Patriotism," and she proved herself "as radical as anyone in the West" to small but enthusiastic audiences. Coolly received at first, she won the colonists' friendship as a "jolly comrade, a good looking, sensible girl, who is even not averse to a little flirtation, and a sympathetic woman with a heart so large that it embraces the whole world." The following year she stayed a weekend and delivered a Saturday night speech, returning in later years to visit friends or to lecture. To her, these were brief interludes in a full life, and she was said to have belittled this community where the people seemed more interested in vegetables and chickens than in propaganda. She called Home "the anarchist graveyard." To people at Home, the visits were memorable, a confirmation of their status in the anarchist world; conservative neighbors took them as nettling reminders of rampant anarchism in their midst. [19]

Another person who aspired to national reputation arrived at Home about this time. James Ferdinand Morton, Jr., was born in 1870, the son of a Baptist minister and grandson of the author of the song "America." He graduated with honors from Harvard University, where he received A. B. and A. M. degrees in 1892. Besides his study of languages and the classics, Morton organized and presided over an intercollegiate debating society and became interested in sociological research. At Harvard he became acquainted with the Negro leader, Dr. William E. B. DuBois. In the late 1890s Morton visited Europe and then moved to San Francisco to work on *Free Society*. There he heard of Home, possibly from Govan. [20]

When *Free Society* moved to Chicago, Morton prepared to lecture en route. He first visited Home in April 1900, arriving in time for the weekly Wednesday night "paper folding." The following evening most of the residents turned out for a reception, and on Saturday they filled the schoolhouse to hear their guest discuss "Growth of Liberty." On Sunday almost two dozen members accompanied their guest aboard the Dadisman launch to Tacoma for his speech before the Theosophical Society, in which he demonstrated a unity of purpose between Theosophy and anarchy. All in all, it was "one of the pleasantest events in the history of Home community." Morton spent several more days with recitations and a lecture before departing from Home. [21]

Roland Eugene Muirhead, the visiting Scotsman who left Home on the same boat, was less overwhelmed. Muirhead counted only twenty or thirty persons in the Tacoma audience, which he believed was a meeting of a local temple of the Co-operative Brotherhood of Burley. "Morton gave a lecture of the brotherhood of man, finishing up by exposition of Anarchism. he defined it as 'government by none.' he is quite a good speaker but did not impress me deeply. uses many big words. Though he gave a good scientific resume of evolutionary theory, he did not claim that Anarchism was the only way to improve, but that different minds had different methods of reform, but claimed A. as the ultimate goal." [22]

If the residents of Home enjoyed Morton's voice, it was fortunate, for they would hear it many times again. A year later, he came to Home to live and to edit the newspaper. Briefly the colony teacher, Morton lacked, however, "a teacher's first requisite the ability to impart his knowledge to young charges," and he failed to secure the respect of his students. Perhaps his mind was on greater things, for he had editorials to write, lectures to prepare, crusades to fight, interpretations of Home to make to a curious world, challenges to deliver to conservatives, and contacts with fellow radicals to maintain. For several years Morton was the intellectual spirit of Home. [23]

Although Home was acquiring a minor reputation among radicals, it was only slightly known to its nearest neighbors before 1901. Early that year the colony received notoriety when printer Govan was fined for distributing a *Discontent* article judged to be obscene. In August a colony excursion to nearby Anderson Island prompted the Tacoma *Evening News* to denounce an apple orchard lecture on anarchy made there and to harangue about colony launches that sailed under red flags. Tacomans were told that Home was a free-love colony, that its leaders were "vicious," and that two residents drew government pensions, thus placing the taxpayer in the position of supporting anarchy. When colonists wrote to the paper to defend Home, a brief printed debate enlivened its pages. But this exchange had subsided before the assassination of President William McKinley triggered a more sustained attack from the press, certain civic leaders, and veterans' groups of Tacoma. [24]

On 6 September 1901, President McKinley was shot while attending the Pan-American Exposition in Buffalo, New York. Eight days later he was dead. Police, press, and public soon learned much about the easily captured assassin. His name was Leon Czolgosz. He was a twenty-eight-year-old Polish immigrant, an unemployed mechanic, and a self-proclaimed anarchist who considered it his destiny to eliminate the President. If Czolgosz was influenced more by mental and emotional imbalance than by philosophical beliefs, that possibility was ignored in the days just after the shooting. National grief was accompanied by a wave of antianarchist sentiment and a round of reprisals against anarchists throughout the country. During more than a decade of disturbances and assassinations in Europe and such occurrences as the Haymarket Square riot, the Pullman and Homestead strikes, and the attempted assassination of Henry Clay Frick in the United States, Americans had become increasingly alarmed by the menace of anarchism. This latest outrage strengthened the belief that anarchists were a violent lot who would destroy law and government by any means. Public attention focused on the arrests of certain well-known leaders and on such acknowledged strongholds as Chicago and Paterson, New Jersey. Imprisoned were Abe Isaak, the Portland associate of Addis and Pope and a brief acquaintance of Czolgosz; Jay Fox, a Haymarket veteran and future Home editor; Emma Goldman; and the anarchist leader Johann Most. Suddenly, conservatives in the Pacific Northwest recalled the tiny anarchist community in their own midst. [25]

Immediately after the McKinley shooting, both Tacoma papers attacked anarchy and individuals of suspect loyalty. On 7 September, the Tacoma *Daily Ledger* issued a fire-eating call to "Exterminate the Anarchist." "Freedom of Speech has run mad," shouted the paper. "Each anarchist should be killed as a wild beast, a mad dog . . . eliminated, tooth and branch." Sunday sermons reflected grief while denouncing anarchism. A Presbyterian minister berated the "filthy dreamers of every land [who] flock to our shores," and a Roman Catholic priest declared that "religion must work with the lawmakers of the nation to wipe out anarchism." The *Ledger* informed Tacomans that an anarchist was "a type of pervert. He has degenerated to a point at which conscience, the perception of right and wrong has vanished. He does not enter into the economy of affairs. He is alien, supremely selfish, unspeakably brutal; apart from the decency around him. He is sullen and vicious. He has no faculty of reason. His course is directly the evil prompting of a nature foul and cruel. He has his own literature, such as it is; his own speakers, such as they are."[26]

The *Ledger* was excitable, but the rival Tacoma *Evening News* was the first to remember Home. On 11 September a banner across the front page cried: "SHALL ANARCHY AND FREE LOVE LIVE IN PIERCE COUNTY?" An article on "damnable" anarchists twisted a defense by editor Morton, who pictured anarchists as peaceful people and blamed suffering and discontent for breeding assassins. Professing its willingness to hear both viewpoints, the *News* promised readers further information. A reporter visited Home and talked with acknowledged anarchists and practicing free lovers.

The next edition brought pictures of a launch flying its red flag and a group of anarchists, including schoolteacher Kate Cheyse. Items were excerpted from *Discontent*. The *News* congratulated itself for arousing the people of Pierce County "almost to a pitch of desperation" by its "sensational expose." Editions recounting the President's final moments carried angry denunciations of anarchists generally, and especially of those at Home. Correspondents joined the outcry with letters, and Tacomans pledged themselves to "wipe out" the people of Home. [27]

The *Ledger* did not point directly to Home until 14 September, when its black-bordered edition announced the President's death. "Close to Tacoma is the settlement of Home," an editorial began. The residents were "a collection of outlaws" who defied the decencies of life, flouted virtue, railed at government, and sympathized with the assassin. "What is to be done about it?" the paper asked. "Is this a nest of vipers, this unclean den of infamy, to remain undisturbed?" It demanded that Morton "and his kind must be driven forth." Although it foreswore violence and claimed to be vindicating democracy, the *Ledger* asserted that if the federal government did not act against Home, local officials would. Extralegal means were justified on grounds that anarchists who despised the country and its laws had "thrust themselves outside the pale of the constitution." Such persons were not even citizens "but execrences [sic], and in the effort to purify itself Pierce county must drive them away."[28]

Tacoma papers were joined in their attacks by others on Puget Sound and some as far distant as Bellingham and eastern

Washington. In Seattle, Jacob Blumer recalled hearing San Francisco anarchists, including a man living at Home in 1901, plotting to destroy the government and to kill its leaders. [29]

The anarchist community greeted news of the President's death with considerable apprehension. While admitting opposition to McKinley's policies, editor Morton mourned the killing as "wanton and useless" and denied that anarchists would be sympathetic. "It is a pitiable fact that the unthinking many will look on this deed as a logical outcome of Anarchist teaching," he wrote, "and will inaugurate an era of persecution against all who are unsatisfied with existing conditions." Now it seemed that one act by a "criminal mad man" might discredit the whole search for a higher individuality. He called upon anarchists to "prove to our calumniators the magnitude of their error." Morton wrote the *Ledger* that Czolgosz was no true anarchist, and he pleaded for justice. The paper refused to print his letter. A second unpublished letter was answered with vituperation. The legend that the people of Home rejoiced with a great celebration when McKinley died was repeated in a wartime government document seventeen years later. [30]

The frenzy worked up by the Tacoma papers brought about more overt action. On the evening of the President's death, some eighty-five excited members of the Grand Army of the Republic met at Custer Post Hall to form the GAR Loyal League. Their aim was "the extermination of anarchy in all its various forms, by legal means, if possible, and if not by other means which will be equally as effective." A half-dozen or more speakers recounted what they knew or had heard about Home and other local anarchists; the gathering then enthusiastically resolved that they who had saved the nation during the Civil War would answer the call again. They would help to suppress "this latest phase of treason, which has not only robbed our country of one of the greatest of all executive heads the world has ever known, but is at all times a menace to humanity." They pledged to punish anarchists "by banishment or burial." A committee was appointed to further the league's plans. [31]

Two mornings later the group took more formal steps to organize effectively. Designating themselves the Loyal League of North America, they expanded their mission "to accomplish the utter annihilation of anarchists and anarchistic teachings within the borders of North America, and to prevent disloyalty to the existing form of government." Despite a disclaimer of violence, the members swore to obey their officers. Local newspapers frankly called the league a vigilance committee. The league considered sending an "investigating committee" to Home, then rejected the idea on the grounds that legal steps to end free-love practices probably would break up the colony. Force was not then considered necessary. In an enlistment campaign, the league added several hundred new members locally and solicited every GAR post in the nation for support.[32]

Although Pierce County had a few other scattered radicals, Home became the prime target of the league's activities. The colonists rallied under verbal attacks and the threat of a raid, which they believed imminent. In *Discontent*, Morton again argued that the true anarchist did not preach violence, but rather absolute nonresistance. He condemned persecution of dissidents as both futile and unjust: "Will governments never learn that their security is not to be promoted by stifling the voice of discontent, but by removing its cause?" he asked. Government should fear instead a "silent hatred," for "a happy and prosperous people will breed no malcontents or assassins." It was a quiet and reasoned response lost in a paper with little circulation or popular credibility.[33]

Colony leaders invited league members to visit Home and talk with residents. Tacoma judge Thomas Mattison, an officer of the league, replied that no visit would be considered until they hauled down the red flag and hoisted the "stars and stripes" above the colony. One colonist who was a Confederate veteran traveled to Tacoma to dissuade members from taking action. Some attention was directed to Captain Lorenz, a nonresident whom many regarded as the savior of Home. His boats regularly carried passengers and freight between Home and Tacoma. By refusing to charter a boat to the league and by defending Home as a community of good and peaceable people, Lorenz may have prevented a raid. In the meantime, the colonists agreed in open meeting that if the feared raiding party came, it would be received with a handshake.[34]

Although Home leaders begged critics "to come out here any day, and see us exactly as we are . . . ," few accepted. The most valued visitor was the Reverend John F. Doescher, pastor of the Evangelical Lutheran Church. Doescher was welcomed as the only Tacoma clergyman who investigated Home before condemning it. He spent two days talking with colonists and gave a lecture on Christian views which were inimical to most of his audience but won their respect. He could not accept their attitudes toward religion and government nor their free-love theories. But the minister found that most of the people were industrious, intelligent, and willing to hear divergent views, and that neighboring settlements found little fault with them. The *Ledger* printed Doescher's report and his advice not to "become anarchists ourselves in our zeal against anarchism." Specifically addressing the religious community, he added, "It is certainly not becoming for Christians and Christian ministers to cry out and say, 'Exterminate these vipers; send them back to the dust from which they came.'" The Christian duty was to love anarchists, "as well as others who are in error; to pray for them, and to seek their conversion and salvation."[35]

After a week of denunciations, the vigilante threat subsided, and opponents of Home turned to legal action against the colony through its newspapers. Throughout the country the radical press was reeling under federal postal restrictions, and several journals lost mailing privileges or found their editors jailed when they expressed unpopular views. The device frequently used to prosecute was the so-called Comstock Act of 1873, which broadened definitions of obscenity and prohibited the mailing of lewd and obscene matter. The law was a useful tool to suppress radical or unpopular views, including those attributed to Home.[36]

On 24 September federal officials arrived at Home to arrest Charles L. Govan, James W. Adams, and James E. Larkin for mailing obscene literature. To their surprise, the deputies were hospitably received and given lunch at colonists' homes before leaving to take the prisoners to Spokane, where the federal district court was sitting. After the cases were remanded to a later session in Tacoma and each man was released on one thousand dollars bail, they spoke freely to the press. Despite an "enthusiastic" defense of free love, the interview centered largely on anarchism and on the McKinley assassination, rather than on their indictment. The men condemned the murder and violent methods. The *Ledger* rejoiced that the arrests should surely finish the colony and scatter its "anarchists, freelovers and other moral mongrels." That the action was leveled more against anarchy than against obscenity was recognized at Home and elsewhere.[37]

The principal complaint centered on a defense of free love by Adams that had appeared in the January issue of *Discontent*. Tall and white-haired with a flowing beard, Adams looked every bit the Spiritualist and philosophical anarchist that he was; but his seventy years and his approaching fiftieth wedding anniversary made advocacy of free love seem incongruous. Much of his article merely quoted a familiar tract that denounced formal, monogamous marriage as hypocritical. Larkin was named as editor at the time of publication, but the charge against Govan, the printer, was dropped.[38]

The case was heard on 11 March in Tacoma before Judge C. H. Hanford. Although prodded on by Postal Inspector C. L. Wayland, the district attorney by noon had established only that *Discontent* was the paper cited in the indictment and that it had been mailed from Home. The defense sought to undermine Wayland's testimony by challenging his motives. The crucial moment occurred, however, during the noon recess when Judge Hanford perused the article. After lunch the judge calmly remarked that he did not consider it obscene. The announcement elicited a sudden defense motion to acquit and the most exciting exchange of the day between the two attorneys. Quietly Judge Hanford stated that although the views expressed were radical, they did not lead to licentious conduct. He directed a verdict of not guilty. Despite his decision, the Tacoma *Evening News* warned that the "anarchists and free lovers at Home should publish no more such rot." In retort, the smaller Tacoma *Sun-Democrat* lambasted the *News* for "doing its utmost to hound down" the people of Home.[39]

But the colonists' victory was bittersweet. A grand jury had returned similar indictments against two colony women, Lois Waisbrooker and Mattie D. Penhallow. Mrs. Waisbrooker had arrived from California early in 1901 and published a small monthly journal, *Clothed with the Sun*. For over thirty years, she had written articles and books, most of them concerned with sex, marriage, and the emancipation of women, and she had experienced persecution for her views before. Seventy-five years old, frail, and in declining health, her fervid convictions aroused her to an intense energy. Mrs. Penhallow was postmistress at Home.

The indictment concerned an article, "The Awful Fate of Fallen Women," from Mrs. Waisbrooker's magazine, which the postmistress was accused of mailing. "The editor argues that there can be no sin nor crime in a mutual sex relation," explained the *Ledger*. "The editorial proclaims its [free love's] many advantages and condemns the present conditions which restrain it." In court in July, Lois Waisbrooker accepted responsibility for the article but denied that it was obscene. The jury disagreed. After four and a half hours of deliberation, it acquitted Mrs. Penhallow but judged the author guilty. The next morning, visiting judge John J. DeHaven, who personally disagreed with the verdict, levied the minimum penalty, a fine of one hundred dollars. The second trial concluded, "the little band of colonists went back across the water to their work." [40]

Official harrassment also interfered with the mailing of *Discontent*. During the winter, when subscribers complained that issues were not arriving, investigation showed that stamped packets had been withheld at the Tacoma post office. Only after Morton's inquiry were they released and mailed on, but there was neither official acknowledgment nor explanation. Meanwhile, *Discontent* accused Tacoma police of persecuting a distributor of that paper and other radical sheets.[41]

Federal authorities were completing an even more direct assault upon Home. The same federal grand jury which had returned the Adams indictment, submitted a special report concerning the Home post office. On the day that Govan, Larkin, and Adams were arrested, Postal Inspector Wayland had also questioned Postmistress Penhallow. The *Ledger* speculated that a person more friendly to the government would soon replace her. Local residents heard that Mrs. Penhallow had introduced herself as an anarchist to Wayland, thus becoming vulnerable to dismissal or other action.

On Wayland's recommendation, the grand jury agreed that the post office be closed. The jurors' statement labeled Home "a settlement of avowed anarchists and free lovers, the members of which society on numerous instances, with the apparent sanction of the entire community, have abused the privileges of the postoffice establishment and department." For more than two years and with the full knowledge and compliance of the postmistress, residents of Home had mailed "non-mailable matter and matter calculated to corrupt and injure the members of the body politic." Despite indictments for such conduct, the residents had remained "defiant" and unwilling to cease their activities. The jury's statement concluded that "the postoffice at Home [should] be abolished, and the privilege which the members of this society have so long abused be taken from them." Judge Hanford forwarded the recommendation to postal authorities in Washington, D. C.[42]

The *Ledger*, notwithstanding its inflammatory words a few months before, praised Tacomans and the grand jury for using the law to cope with a "lawless" aggregation. Morton and J. W. Gaskine, a participant in several communitarian experiments and an occasional visitor to Home, criticized the jury for overstepping its powers and issuing a conclusion instead of merely preferring charges. Gaskine particularly criticized Judge Hanford for sending on the report. A post office is a "right" and not a privilege, he contended, and its abolition would punish a whole community for the actions of a few. Late in April the postmaster general closed the Home post office, effective at the end of that month. Attempts to secure reinstatement were not successful. Mail came through Lakebay, and Home residents took turns walking to pick up local mail, which the Penhallows then distributed.[43]

To Home residents, the post office decision was the final blow of a tumultuous year. *Discontent* suspended publication, reappearing almost a year later as the *Demonstrator* and issued along with other mail from the post office at nearby Lakebay. The fight for a free press became a new topic for speeches and writings. To radicals elsewhere the incidents at Home constituted minor additional evidence of persecution by the government, and the story was repeated in various publications. Local conservatives reveled in their victory, but efforts to stem anarchism in the state did not end. The next session of the Washington legislature in 1903 overwhelmingly passed one of the strongest antianarchism statutes in any state. Reported out of committee by a Pierce County representative, it defined criminal anarchy as "the doctrine that organized government should be overthrown by force or violence, or by assassination of the executive officials of government, or by any unlawful means." The law made it a felony to teach or spread the doctrines of criminal anarchy, to publish or edit printed matter containing such material, and to assemble to advocate or teach such doctrines. Later the Home community and its publication would encounter a revised form of this law. [44]

In some respects, these events had little effect on life at Home. Certainly they did not deter residents from acting as they wished. On the other hand, life at the community could never afterward be described as quietly "idyllic." Residents became more conscious of the face they presented to the world and began to feel persecuted. The attention drew visitors, the illustrious and the nondescript, the sincere and the curious. Before the McKinley assassination Home was quietly becoming a distinctive community. After that event, growth continued in the public eye. [45]

The public, the press, and many persons directly associated, thought of Home as an anarchist colony, a communal experiment, or a free-love colony. Strictly speaking, it was none of these, despite elements of each. Founder George H. Allen expressed the frustration that it was "impossible to make one at a distance fully understand the conditions here. What one will understand another will but perceive from the same words." The many self-defined anarchists viewed the very idea of a community with laws, regulations, and officials as distasteful. Home was intended to be a place where individuals with differing views, especially those unacceptable in conventional society, could thrive in peace and freedom. "This little handful of people, or at least most of them," wrote one resident, "come here in order to live as near their ideals as is possible. . . ." [46]

This kind of freedom was what some residents meant when they spoke of anarchy. *Discontent* introduced itself as "an Anarchist paper," and colony founders called themselves anarchists, although the term was not used in formal documents. *The Independent* magazine, which was turning away from its Congregationalist past to take a broader view of reform movements, suggested that an "anarchist experiment station" be set up, and considered Home the "most thorough-going" such experiment known to it. Visitors described Home as an "anarchist colony," "the so-called Anarchist colony," "a Tolstoi Colony," and "An Experiment in Anarchy." One early visitor noted faithfully in his diary which of the persons he met were professed anarchists, and *Discontent* observed that "none but Anarchists would find it congenial here." [47]

Home anarchists were mostly of the individualist school. Considering individual rights and powers supreme, they sought to remove themselves from restrictions erected by government, institutions, and society in general. "I (an Anarchist)," Allen described himself, "do not object to organization of any kind; I simply object to being forced into any organization against my will." Any value or merits the organization might have did not matter, for Allen simply denied "the right of such organization to force me to contribute to their scheme." Later he defined anarchy as "the supreme right of the individual to be, to say or to act just as seems to him best." To Morton, anarchy envisioned "an orderly society, based on individual liberty and reliance on self-govern-ment." Although these men did not propose abolishing government, they would weaken its hold on the individual. They regarded voting as an act by which the majority controlled the minority. Man's problems could better be lessened by reducing dependence upon institutions, laws, or public pressures. "The watchword of this place," wrote Charles Penhallow, "is 'Mind Your Own Business,' which is equivalent to saying: 'Do unto others as ye would that others should do unto you.' " Residents perhaps described themselves more precisely when they substi-tuted "individualist" for "anarchist." Notwithstanding quarrels and personal antagonisms, Home allowed a marked tolerance for the person to act as he chose without interference. What one did on or with his own property was his private concern as long as it hurt no one else. [48]

Most residents disclaimed the stereotype of the violent anar-chist who fomented strikes, threw bombs, or plotted assassin-ations. They opposed physical force and violence, and maintained a peaceful community. Home anarchists enjoyed retelling how they could not find anyone who knew how to make dynamite so as to blast stumps. Other anarchist friends were no more knowledgeable, and they eventually got the information from a scientific journal. Government authorities who came to Home, including those with arrest warrants, were greeted peaceably. Nonviolent attitudes were not unanimous, however. A short-term publisher of the *Demonstrator*, although generally opposed to violence, stressed that government exercised it, and he advocated resisting in kind when necessary. [49]

The community honored radical heroes and martyrs. Portraits of Karl Marx, Ferdinand Lassalle, Peter Kropotkin, and Michael Bakunin reportedly hung on schoolroom walls. Residents contributed funds for current causes, including free-speech fights, the Russian revolutionists of 1905, and the defense in the Steunenberg murder case in Idaho. Each anniversary of the execution of the Haymarket rioters, memorial services were observed, including occasionally an eye-witness recollection of the events. Conventional holidays inspired ridicule. "Today is our banner bamboozling day," wrote Gertie Vose one Fourth of July. "Today the nation is plunged in a sickly patriotism." One Christmas entertainment included "a mockery of the institutions of the people who call him God." A mock preacher, police force, jail, and court made merriment of thievery and of "marrying and divorcing." Surely anarchism, as it was understood at Home, was the prevalent attitude of the colony. [50]

Home residents were frequently called free lovers, a charge no one denied, although they considered the term misleading. "Companions" not formally married had mutual living arrangements, and Muirhead faithfully noted in his diary which persons believed in "variety," who did not, and who accepted the theory but did not practice. [51]

A contemporary encyclopedia of reform placed free love in the context most residents shared. It was based on the belief that neither state nor church had a right to control the family or sexual relations. Those who practice free love "would make love supreme . . . , unfettered by any law whatsoever. They argue that compulsory love is not love; that all marriage save from love is sin; that when love ends marriage ends." Each person should be free to support himself without depending on another individual. Thus, "the purest and highest, the most enduring love" was realized "when a woman gave herself in love . . . not . . . for reason of family, or position, or custom, or support, or help in any way, but simply because she loved." Parents would raise their children because they wished to, not because they were forced to.[52]

Free love implied neither irresponsibility nor licentiousness, but rather the right of couples to love as they chose and to separate when love died. Conventional marriage vows were denounced as hypocritical, for they placed a burden upon women, and they encouraged widespread prostitution. The people of Home would have been amused to know that when a visitor who had stayed two weeks in their alleged free-love colony stepped back into the conventional world, his first act was to visit a Tacoma "house of ill fame."[53]

Ironically, the two most vocal defenders of free love at Home—James W. Adams and Lois Waisbrooker—were in their seventies. Neither was silenced by legal pressures. In 1903, Mrs. Waisbrooker issued two pamphlets, *Women's Sense of Power* and *My Century Plant*. L. E. Rader called the latter a "perfect encyclopedia on the sex question," but he warned persons who "do not know how to take plain, unvarnished statements along this line" not to order the book. "To the pure it will seem purity itself." In May 1904, her magazine discontinued, the seventy-eight-year-old author left for Denver, where she reissued an earlier pamphlet and continued a wide correspondence. In constant poor health, she moved about frequently. She died, probably in Antioch, California, on 3 October 1909. From Denver she had written, "What I want most is the power TO DO, TO DO."[54]

Some outsiders believed Home to be vegetarian, "from the belief that it is wrong to kill for personal gratification of appetite. . . ." "The ducks know it, for the cove is filled with them, floating within easy gunshot of the shore." Although some residents were vegetarian, the community was not. The lack of meat was more the result of economic factors than of principle, for there were occasional food shortages. Seafood was abundant, and poultry raising became a major activity; yet, Philip Clayton Van Buskirk observed that the chicken he was served one Sunday was the first "flesh of any kind" he had eaten since arriving ten days before.[55]

Van Buskirk, a retired naval officer of worldly habits, was bored in his surroundings: "In the afternoon trudge over to Lake Bay to get a handful of cigars; two friendly loungers are in the store whom I join in a round of beers. In the Home Community no tobacco nor intoxicants of any kind are to be had." He made the pilgrimage at least once each day. *The Independent* confirmed that "there are no users of intoxicants, and there is not a drink of liquor to be had on the bay." All but two or three smokers had given up tobacco, "not because any one protests against it, but because they do not wish to do anything to discomfort their fellows." One resident, however, made wine. [56]

Home was no religious colony. "We have neither church spires that point to an imaginary heaven, nor dispensaries of that which inflames the passions of men. We hold that 'the kingdom of heaven is within,' " wrote Charles Penhallow. The absence of a church was a source of pride, and one anarchist criticized citizens who dressed up on Sunday as if it were a special day. Christmas celebrations stressed "giving," but had no religious significance. Yet religious speakers were allowed to use the Home podium, one prominent family was recognized as Christian, and at least one woman practiced Christian Science.[57]

The many Jews who settled at Home appeared to have forsaken their religious training. Spiritualism was widespread. A Spiritualist circle held seances at various homes, and one visiting reporter dramatized a campfire as a religious rite. Spiritualists and Theosophists sometimes spoke to larger groups in the community hall. Octogenarian Olivia Freelove Shepherd edited a monthly paper called *Spirit Mothers*; another woman considered donating ten acres of adjoining property for a Spiritualist campground. There was interest in the mystical Koreshanity sect. Born in Chicago and based in a Florida communitarian settlement after 1903, this sect combined elements of reincarnation, alchemy, and astrology, and maintained that the earth was the interior of a hollow sphere. Perhaps the fascination for several religious practices, some exotic, and the general acceptance of none, illustrates that Home was less a community of a particular united group than of unique, curious individuals.[58]

Indeed, there was little to justify calling Home a "colony" at all, although the term was convenient for residents and their contemporaries, both friends and opponents. From the beginning the individualists of Home proudly stressed the differences from communitarian experiments. The Mutual Home Association continued to be the basis for community organization, but *Discontent* regularly emphasized that this was "simply a land-holding institution, and can take no part in the starting of an industry." Replying to a questionnaire, George H. Allen scribbled along the side, "You say *co-operative* colonies. *This was not one.* "[59]

Yet there were a few other cooperative practices. Cooperative stores were formed. The first store appears to have been private, maintained "simply for the good of the colony" rather than for profit by Martin Dadisman and later by Fannie Miner. Open two days a week, the store secured stock from a Tacoma cooperative and quoted Tacoma prices. Work, eggs, or produce were accepted as barter. Late in 1902, a cooperative store opened. Quarters were cramped and the store was open only one hour on particular afternoons, but the shareholders considered expansion when monthly receipts climbed above four hundred dollars. Subscriptions were sold and by fall a new enlarged store was "wide open for the best part of three afternoons of each week and . . . averaging $100 worth of business per week." The Home Grocery Company continued for several years, being converted to the Rochdale plan in 1907, with occasional disputes among shareholders. In 1911, the directors fired the clerk and manager, Oscar Engvall, charging that his poor handling of records had lost members. Although the new manager claimed to be putting things in order, recovery was short-lived; in September, Engvall sued for over a thousand dollars owed in bills and loans. Others began to press claims, and on 26 July 1913, the Pierce County superior court ordered the company dissolved and its store sold. Conveniently not believing in court decisions, some shareholders failed altogether to pay judgments. At least one other cooperative store and a competitive store were operated at Home. [60]

Other cooperation was voluntary. When Home needed a school and general building, a two-story structure was built by community effort. The floating dock of the original settlers drifted away after several years' use, and a second one was later replaced by a long wharf, all built through cooperative efforts. Volunteers also built roads in and near the community, a pedestrian bridge at the head of the bay, and a picnic ground and waterfront park on land donated by Martin Dadisman.

Voluntary cooperation extended beyond public needs, as neighbors helped one another to construct houses, sheds, and fences. Thus, the elderly Lois Waisbrooker had a small house constructed for her, and the whole community turned out to build a home for a newly arrived couple expecting a child. Individuals frequently allowed items they owned to be used by all. The colony as such owned no boat, but those belonging to individual members were regularly pressed into general service. In the spring of 1901 someone counted "a fleet of two launches, three sailboats and fifteen small rowboats with a carrying capacity of about 150 people."[61]

Daily life did not resemble a communal colony. "We live in separate homes," Oliver Verity replied to an inquiry, "and each family is supposed to build their own home. We are NOT LIVING COMMUNISTIC. . . ." Although Verity added that many believed in communism, he doubted that all had the "natures agreeable to one another" to make a success of it. Plans for a communal house never materialized. In the early days, two families lived together, but that was a rare exception.[62]

The earliest houses were small and crude, usually built with lumber off the property or from a mill at Lakebay. A Minnesota widow had the first painted house, and the community came to have a finished air. One correspondent wrote that "on the whole, the colony makes a good impression . . . on account of the neatness and thrift apparent in the homes and the kindness and hospitality of the people." By contrast, he added, the communal settlements at Burley and Equality presented an "appearance of squalor." That some substantial homes were built was demonstrated by a 1911 advertisement for "a two-story frame house of seven rooms, bathroom, pantry and cellar, with two acres of land, partially cleared. Well situated, commanding an excellent view of bay and mountains. . . ." About this time, Home reminded a traveler of "a quiet, English fishing village."[63]

Residents provided their basic needs by living off their land with garden, poultry, and a cow or two. Several children later estimated that their families had no more than ten dollars to subsist through a winter. Some recalled this bitterly; one remembered that poverty shared was less evident. Little work for pay was available in the community, although a prevailing wage scale of fifteen cents an hour was being raised to twenty cents for carpenters. Some families lived at Home only part of each year, or the men worked in Tacoma and came home on weekends. Families or individuals might take jobs elsewhere and return when possible; one group set out for Alaska and later returned. [64]

The colony grew steadily, and by the spring of 1899 it included eleven families totaling fifty-four persons. Even during the attacks by Tacoma papers, the population grew from eighty-five in May 1901 to ninety-four the following April, when a tally recorded twenty-eight men, twenty-five women, and forty-one children. After the ten months' interval between papers, the population had reached one hundred. In 1905 there were 120 residents, and five years later the paper indicated 213 persons, including 75 children, living in the 68 homes. During World War I, a United States Bureau of Immigration report stated that the population had recently approached five hundred, although the otherwise inaccurate account may well have exaggerated. [65]

Specific figures are disputable. The boundaries of Home were not definitely fixed. Persons sympathetic to the attitudes of the community had spread outside of the original settlement into nearby areas; not all were members of the Mutual Home Association. On the other hand, not all residents of the area professed the liberal persuasion the community represented. More significant than actual numbers is the reliably steady growth over approximately twenty years, during which the community often experienced turmoil and notoriety. Home continued to attract settlers for at least twice as long as the life span of any other experimental community on Puget Sound. While others rapidly declined in population, Home grew.

Very possibly more persons were attracted by the publicity and criticism than were repelled. During 1903 a register indicated 241 overnight visitors. Colony papers aroused interest. The generally curious Philip C. Van Buskirk found *Discontent* in the Seattle Public Library and began the correspondence with George Allen which resulted in his coming. There were some attempts to proselytize, especially in the later years. Excursions and balls in nearby cities drew attention and support. One young married woman with liberal views was gazing into a Seattle store window when a stranger realized her loneliness and invited her to a picnic the following Sunday. With her less enthusiastic husband, she showed up at the Colman Dock and embarked with a boatload bound for Home. She enjoyed the day, made friends, and maintained contact for several years before the couple moved to the community in 1916. Others learned of the community by word of mouth or by letters from friends who preceded them. They were attracted, one resident thought, by the promise of living as individuals and by the abundant natural foods available in bay and woods. Comparatively low living costs probably had some influence. An early resident grew ecstatic discussing how ideals attracted people:

> They come here to live normal lives, away from the maddening crowd's ignoble strife; away from the dictatorship of church and state, away from the study of duties they impose upon their subjects, their obligations, restrictions, persecutions, etc. They come to live lives far above the average lives, lives of protest against corrupt institutions made and sustained by society. They are here because they wish to avoid the depraved and enforced idleness of our competitive system, the harmfulness of buying and selling human flesh where a price is put upon every virtue.[66]

Many, like the three founders, had tried more formal communal experiments and were seeking greater freedom, yet in compatible surroundings. Of the earliest arrivals, James E. Larkin had also lived at Glennis, Martin Dadisman at Equality, and Charles Govan at Ruskin Colony in Tennessee; several more came from Burley or Equality. The Ben Mastick family had lived at the Puget Sound Co-operative Colony. C. H. Cheyse was from Topolobampo Colony in Mexico, and Nathan and Bessie Levin had stayed briefly at a colony en route from the eastern states. Richard Bowle came to Home from Elbert Hubbard's Roycroft Community at East Aurora, New York. Home acquired a cosmopolitan air as European exiles arrived to mingle with native American radicals. In 1907, several Frenchmen settled near the point across the bay, and others followed. Seeking escape from government regulation and military conscription in Europe, they had lived first in eastern cities before learning of the liberal atmosphere of Home. The region northwest of the original settlement attracted Jewish families, some of Russian origin fleeing persecution, all seeking greater political and social freedom and economic opportunity. [67]

A few individuals had habits of living that were unique even at Home. Laura Woods kept house in an Indian wigwam in the woods. One of the most delightful homes in the community belonged to Joe Koppelle and Franz Erkelens—the stump of a giant maple with large shoots encasing it. A transvestite who occasionally donned women's clothes to walk the sea wall was accepted by the community. The aura of a European aristocrat who spoke of Leo Tolstoy as a friend surrounded a "Lady of Mystery" who was never identified and quietly disappeared. Along with the exotic there arrived one day a man refreshingly described as "John Newman, a wanderer." [68]

The Home press warned newcomers against expecting too much. Living conditions were unfinished, and each individual had to provide his own home and employment. But there was always room for "resolute-hearted, self-supporting comrades. . . ." One who was "in practice as well as in theory, a thorough believer in liberty," could expect "a cordial welcome, and . . . congenial companionship. . . ." [69]

Some did not get along. While other men were building a house for one recent arrival, the recipient amused himself by making a child's toy and directing peevish instructions to workers. He was soon deserted and his house left unfinished. Van Buskirk, the cantankerous seadog, succumbed to boredom, deprivations, and a tendency to have "spats" with the anarchists, and he left after two weeks. More permanent strains developed. A nationally published letter conceded that "we are trying here to live up to the ideals of anarchy and free love; but theory is one thing, practice is another." Members did lose tempers, and jealousy was present in free love. But Home never professed to be a community of saints, and an early editor had warned that "those who are inclined to boss, or to insist on conformity to their ideas, had best stay away, as they will find no congeniality here." [70]

More than a few residents fancied themselves intellectuals; so, indeed, did some of their visitors. Emma Rader of Olalla wrote "in all candor" that she had "never met, in a body of like number, so high an average of intelligence, refinement and liberality." Colonists would have been pleased to know that forty years later a journalist-historian would refer to Home as a western Brook Farm.

Surely many liked to talk, write, discuss, and argue, although not, thought one of their daughters, to listen. They developed a library, organized lyceums and reading circles, and even proposed a university. Residents gathered frequently for lectures and discussions, originally at a small grove set aside for Sunday afternoon discussions. This was soon replaced by the schoolhouse.[71]

In 1900 the Scottish visitor Roland Muirhead noted that the schoolroom being used for a dance was about twenty by forty feet. A platform at one end had in big letters the word "LIBERTY & other mottoes decorated with fresh flowers and blue draping." A bookshelf was at the other end, with chairs and wooden benches lining the walls. After this building burned, a major effort went to construct a new schoolhouse and a community center. The structure contained two schoolrooms and a print shop on the ground floor. The room upstairs quickly became known as Liberty Hall. It was "well ceiled," and had "a large stage at one end, and a fine hardwood floor. . . ." After a month of constant use, residents wondered "how we managed to exist without it." The opening of the hall on 23 January 1903 was cause for a celebration that attracted neighbors and a delegation from Burley. Liberty Hall was used regularly for Sunday evening lectures and discussions, dances, Wednesday socials, and a singing class. Dramatic entertainments were anticipated.[72]

The weekly lectures and entertainments were often well attended. Self-assured in their beliefs but curious to hear others, colonists bundled up their small children and headed for the hall. There was, of course, little other entertainment available. Usually local residents lectured or led discussions. Lois Waisbrooker spoke on women and sex. When Mattie Penhallow one evening posed the question, "Does Suffering Strengthen Character?" she received mostly affirmative replies, causing a cynic to note that most preferred to suffer "by proxy." Gertie Vose centered a discussion on definitions of anarchy, free love, and the benefits of each. Too much for one evening, the series was carried over to the following week. During the trial of Bill Haywood, Charles Moyer, and George Pettibone for murdering former Idaho governor, Frank Steunenberg, A. Kleminic evoked tears from his listeners with an "eyewitness" account of miners' lives.

Other speakers included advocates of particular viewpoints or sects. Theosophy was an occasional topic, as was Spiritualism. One discussion concerned diet, and a lecture by Linda Burfield Hazzard, operator of an Olalla sanitarium and advocate of fasting, prompted several Home residents to practice her theories. L. E. Rader also came from Olalla to speak. [73]

But no one spoke with greater frequency or diversity than James F. Morton, Jr. His activities and interests spread far beyond the paper he edited or the school in which he taught. Soon after Liberty Hall opened, he addressed his comrades on "The Relation of Art to Life." A series of lectures included "Evolution," "Primitive Man," "Rome and Its Influences on Modern Civilization," and "The Middle Ages." Nor were his contributions confined to formal lectures. Informal readings in homes had taken place before, but after he came, Morton dominated the intimate gatherings, perhaps with less success than he admitted. When Van Buskirk arrived at the Penhallows' one evening to hear Mr. Morton read from Shelley, he found only three ladies besides himself. A week later, mistaking the night, he went at dusk to call on Mr. Penhallow, one of the few souls he found congenial, "only to be trapped into listening to another reading of the Poets (this time Wordsworth) by Mr. Morton. Audience same as before, with the addition of Mr. Penhallow, who, however, needing rest from the labors of the day, soon fell asleep." [74]

Morton was the chief spokesman for Home at picnics, celebrations, excursions to other communities, or whenever a speaker was needed. He occasionally lectured in Tacoma, and once he followed a prepared itinerary around Puget Sound. A tour to the eastern United States was extended to nine months because of financial difficulties; listeners seemed interested in his message but failed to realize "that a propaganda lecturer has other needs than those of the birds in the air." [75]

In 1905 Morton left Home permanently. He had begun to grate on some of the comrades. One complained that his earlier idealism had turned to pessimism and bristling epithets. Increasingly bored with the isolation of Home, perhaps he truly desired "to carry out other plans which have long been maturing in my mind." He served on the staff of the *Truth Seeker* in New York and later joined a law firm for which he won a decision in a celebrated censorship case involving the George Bernard Shaw play, *Mrs.*

Warren's Profession. In 1906 he wrote a polemic, *The Curse of Race Prejudice*, indicting race prejudice as a national rather than strictly a southern problem. He was active in the single-tax campaign, the National Association for the Advancement of Colored People, the woman suffrage movement, an Esperanto league, and other organizations and causes. He served as curator of the Paterson, New Jersey, City Museum from 1925 until October 1941, when he was killed by a speeding car while, appropriately, on his way to deliver a lecture. His association at Home was an interlude in a varied and busy career; perhaps this phase of his life served to germinate the ideas and philosophies of this many-faceted minor reformer. [76]

Many speakers visited Home from elsewhere. A Tacoma woman used stereoptican slides to complement her lecture on astrology, phrenology, and palmistry. A Seattle herb doctor spoke, and Nathan Ward Fitzgerald described the "new holy city" of Acca, where he claimed to have communed with God. When he was converting Equality Colony to the Freeland concept, Alexander Horr visited several times and gained adherents. An IWW organizer came to debate socialism with a local anarchist, and an English labor reformer lectured. [77]

Emma Goldman was not the only nationally known radical to come. Others came to lecture, to visit friends, or, like the Rubensteins, to stay. The Chicago home of Mike and Ida Rubenstein had been a favorite anarchist gathering place where traditional Jewish foods offset less orthodox guests, stories, and songs. Asenath Macdonald was the elderly mother of two sons who for many decades edited the *Truth Seeker*, a leading free-thought periodical in New York. This Civil War widow and nurse had been raised as a Quaker, and she frequently wrote in a philosophical vein for colony publications. Kate Sadler was a prominent speaker and agitator for labor and socialism before World War I who was imprisoned during the wartime roundup of radicals. She came to Home with her husband, Charles Greenhalgh, and spent her final years there. Elizabeth Gurley Flynn, whose career began as a girl soapbox orator during free-speech fights in Spokane and elsewhere, and who became one of the great ladies of the socialist movement, was said to have visited. "Big Bill" Haywood, nurtured in the mining camps of the West, where he became a power in the IWW, stayed during his days of wandering. He later became a leading American communist. Dr. Ben L. Reitman, who entertained with ghost stories at a campfire one evening, and Alexander Berkman, the would-be assassin of Henry Clay Frick, visited in the company of Emma Goldman. Walker C. Smith, one of the better-known IWW writers, recuperated from an illness at Home. Harry Kemp also visited. Known as the "hobo poet," he fictionalized life at several communal societies in autobiographical novels, but none is clearly recognizable as Home. Lucy Robins Lang and her first husband Bob Robins, both with extensive careers and acquaintances in radical circles, lived at Home for several less than pleasant weeks. Moses Harman, who suffered persecution by federal authorities for his anarchist journal, *Lucifer*, reportedly visited. And Roland Eugene Muirhead, the young Scot who stayed during the spring of 1900, was on the threshold of a long career in his country as reformer. He would become "the grand old man" of Scottish nationalism. Home was one of "the most attractive" places he visited in a year of rambling through the United States; the trip convinced Muirhead that his nation could progress only after ties with England were severed, and he began his life's work. In later days many contacts with the radical world centered around Jay Fox, who came as editor in 1910 and remained most of his life. Fox counted among his closest associates William Z. Foster, who moved through IWW activity to become the principal communist leader in the United States. Foster was a frequent visitor to Home.[78]

No visitor save Emma Goldman attracted greater attention than Elbert Hubbard, founder of the Roycroft Community and prolific author of biographies and essays, including the famous, "A Message to Garcia." Although his message preached duty and conventional morality, this exponent of a simple, straightforward philosophy offered a peculiar attraction to these individuals. His Roycroft Shop promoted craftsmanship in printing and publishing, and workers owned shares in the company. Morton fancied that there was "probably more in common between Home and the Roycroft community . . . than between either of the other two and any other settlement in the world." [79]

Upon learning of Hubbard's intended visit to the Pacific Northwest during the spring of 1904, Morton and Rader separately sought to attract him across Puget Sound to visit and lecture. After hearing Hubbard's address in Tacoma, the two men accompanied him to Home, where he stayed with the Allen family. A gentle but magnetic man, "free from all showiness and all bombast," he spoke in Liberty Hall as if aware that he was "talking to comrades in intelligent sympathy with his ideas." He described the Roycroft spirit, and he espoused the need to bring beauty into the world by doing for others. Although Morton professed that the people of Home "are not hero-worshippers—anything but that," the guest captivated the editor. For his part, Hubbard praised his "day with the most peculiar community I ever saw—Anarchists." Yet they were peaceful anarchists; even the ducks on the shore were tame, knowing that these people would not harm or kill. "In this town of over a hundred people," he saw "neither a church, a preacher, a lawyer, a doctor, a pauper, a gambler, a prostitute, a drunkard, a justice of the peace nor a constable." Hubbard had never seen a "more intelligent lot of men and women...." A year later Morton visited Roycroft and so impressed its inhabitants that Hubbard was said to be considering setting up a shop at Home. [80]

The intellectuals of Home organized other activities for themselves and their children. "Besides providing for the education of the young we still keep putting knowledge into our more hardened heads." A library began in 1899 with books and furnishings largely donated, and the following year a library association was formed. Initial meetings of a junior literary society were well attended. Classes and clubs appeared in abundance, despite limited membership and brief existence. A mental science class was formed in the early days, to be followed by classes in German, Oriental philosophy and Hatha-Yoga, Oriental ideas of body care, and physical culture. There was a Eugenics Society. Several times groups formed to study the proposed international language, Esperanto. [81]

Summer art classes for children were offered by Miss Lucile A.

Mint, who was greeted as the "founder and director of the National Liberal Art and Science League . . . [and] an enthusiastic advocate of universal education in the principles and practice of drawing." While touring the Pacific Northwest in the spring of 1904, she conducted a week of sessions at Home for about twenty pupils. In later summers she returned to a little cabin on the point to teach water coloring, although the classes soon became "merely excuses for social afternoons."[82]

Some individuals had musical interests and talents. Kate Cheyse brought the first piano to Home in 1900, to be followed by the Allens and the Dadismans. In April 1904, an informal inventory revealed "3 pianos, 8 organs, 8 violins, 6 guitars, 2 mandolins, 2 cornets, 1 flute and about a half dozen harmonicas. . . ." Bands were started several times. Nor was the physical life forgotten. When the Home baseball team competed along the peninsula, ideological differences gave way to typical hometown rivalries. [83]

Theories of education were probably more distinct at Home than in the other communitarian experiments on Puget Sound. Several teachers living at Home believed that their radical views had cost them previous jobs. One of these was a Mrs. Kelly, a widow and the sister of founder Odell. "She believes in teaching through love and never using corporal punishment," wrote Muirhead, "and if scholars won't behave, blames herself & says something must be amiss with herself & searches herself accordingly (anarchist)." Most teachers, were also members of the community, including George and Sylvia Allen and their daughter Grace, Morton, and Kate Cheyse.[84]

Educational processes were debated in print and from the lectern. Many colonists expressed liberal educational theories. The birthday of Friedrich W. A. Froebel, the German educator and innovator, was cause for celebration and commemorative addresses. The anarchist belief in a weak government extended to classroom practice, at least theoretically. George Allen argued against placing a lot of "foolish restrictions" on children and praised the "liberty of thought and action allowed in our school." One father argued that children needed to make decisions, and he criticized adults who were too demanding of the young. Although the school was conducted according to state laws and was much like other rural schools, "the pupils are taught that rules destroy character, and, while they should feel that no restrictions are placed upon them during the hours of study, they owe good behavior to their parents and their teacher."

The ideal did not always exist. Even Allen placed limitations on children's freedom, and the hot-tempered Morton lacked respect and control of students. An observer probably had Morton in mind when he wrote that "one of our best declaimers on the right of free speech, has been known to command children in his care to 'shut up' and to enforce such commands by superior strength."[85]

The first school was a small wooden structure near the water. The 1898-99 school year ended with only nineteen students, but by the end of another year an increase required two teachers. After the building burned in the spring of 1902, classes were held in the Cheyse home. The completion of Liberty Hall provided two rooms for the school. These also became crowded, and in 1910 a new school building was built farther up the hill. A typical frame school of the time, it had "two large, well lighted, well ventilated rooms. . . . The workmanship is good; and the architectural outline is very pleasing to the sense of beauty."[86]

Residents hoped that as their children grew older they would "be the best possible advertisements of Anarchist principles and methods of training." The prediction was in some sense fulfilled, although probably not in the manner intended. Many of the young tended to become more conservative in politics and demeanor than their parents, although they retained a liberal and tolerant attitude. A noteworthy rebel against parent and community was Donald Vose, who informed on two anarchist fugitives and thus gained the opprobrium of his mother's friends. But Vose acted more from personal pique than from philosophical disagreement, and many of the second generation speak with fond approval of their parents. They became or married business and professional people to become solid middle-class citizens in conventional society; some attained distinction, but not as rebels.

Many, including the four Allen daughters, attended college. Ernest Falkoff entered the University of Washington at thirteen, graduated with honors, and practiced law. The daughter of colonist parents received a Ph.D. in bacteriology from the University of Washington to become a noted hematologist. Another girl became a leader and innovator as a photographer. If the young people from Home did not follow exactly in parental footsteps, many were prepared to achieve success in the world outside their community.[87]

For a decade after the loss of the post office, Home remained relatively secure from outside interference. Upon renewing a newspaper in March 1903, Morton noted that the Tacoma papers had "ceased their bitter attacks, and show a much fairer spirit, and that friendly articles had appeared in Seattle and San Francisco." New troubles were comparatively minor. When postal authorities challenged the authenticity of the *Demonstrator* subscription list, the problem was quietly resolved. A reported row between the colony and a neighbor proved to involve Burley rather than Home. Indeed, the once great notoriety diminished so much, and so little was heard of Home, that metropolitan dailies reported its demise in 1907, an event the *Demonstrator* hastily denied. [88]

By 1910 the United States was again becoming apprehensive of anarchism and violence. During labor disturbances late that year, an explosion at the Los Angeles *Times* plant killed twenty-one persons. Joseph J. McNamara, a union official, and his brother were arrested, and they confessed to the crime during their trial. Meanwhile, a search for two accomplices led the Burns Detective Agency to Home and to a local boy, who became their agent.

The fugitives were Matthew A. Schmidt and David Caplan. Caplan was thought to have lived at Home once and to have married a girl from there. In October 1911, Burns agents, thinly disguised as surveyors and booksellers, arrived in search of the men. William J. Burns directed operations from Tacoma, occasionally visiting the colony himself, while his men gathered information and observed the movements of selected individuals. Convinced that Jay Fox, the colony editor, was either involved in the bombing or knew the whereabouts of the fugitives, they concentrated on his house, noting each mail delivery. The trail of barber Lewis Haiman led his pursuer no farther than the Tacoma shop where he was employed. Detectives watched strangers that ventured into town and pumped a talkative storekeeper for information. As reprinted in Burns's autobiography, the reports enveloped minute details of very ordinary actions with cloak-and-dagger mystery. [89]

The barber's wife never forgot Burns's visit: "'He came to the door one day,' says Mrs. Haiman, 'and he had a book under one arm and another in his hand. I knew him at once. He made a sweeping gesture and a low bow, but he was only trying to see behind me into my house, to determine if there were anyone else about the place. And all the time he was talking to me, posing as a book agent, he was trying to look over my shoulder.'" [90] Detectives learned that Fox had recently returned from San Francisco without his wife, looking "very much worried; eyes blood-shot; . . . as though he had been under great strain." They found little else. Admitting that "we did not get close enough to Caplan or Schmidt to either rope them [gain information by securing their confidence] or arrest them, the surveillance was discontinued." [91]

Perhaps the detectives just missed their quarry. Years later Jay Fox hinted vaguely that Caplan was not at Home, but was hiding on Bainbridge Island. A later government report insisted that he had been at Home part of the time, and the house where he had hidden was pointed out to a woman reporter. Mrs. Caplan was soon located elsewhere. [92]

The Burns detectives derived one gain from their visit—an undercover agent, Donald Vose. Vose's parents had been among the early and sturdiest settlers at Home. His mother was a close friend of Emma Goldman and other anarchists, and the son was his mother's pride. But her friends later recalled that they had never liked the child. William Foster remembered him as "a gangling youth . . . a dull-wit, a sneak and as generally unreliable . . . who grew up in the midst of radical teachings but remained impervious to them." Catching Donald Vose in an act of petty theft, the Burns men played upon weaknesses and enlisted him. Through his contacts with radicals, they hoped he would lead them to Schmidt and Caplan and possibly to other fugitives. [93]

Before long, Vose reported that David Caplan was employed as a barber near Seattle, where he was kept under surveillance. Attention turned to locating Schmidt. Vose sought out Emma Goldman in New York, saying that he wanted work while awaiting money so he could return to Home. She loaned him her apartment temporarily. Vose casually remarked that he had a letter for Schmidt, who by chance appeared one afternoon. The men met, and Schmidt forgot the incident. Vose lingered several weeks at an upstate farm used by Miss Goldman, coming into the city occasionally for mail; when Miss Goldman later returned from a tour, she was surprised to find him still in New York. Noting his shabby appearance, she was further concerned by gossip that he was spending large amounts of money, mostly on drink. Suspicious, she inquired at Home and elsewhere to learn that no one in Washington was aiding or supporting Vose. Thus, when he appeared one day to announce that funds had arrived and he was returning west, Miss Goldman felt relieved and "a little ashamed" of her distrust.

A week later Schmidt and Caplan were arrested. Burns had ordered Vose back to the Caplan hideout, and when the arresting officers arrived, Vose was nursing his prey for an infected tooth. Immediately Emma Goldman realized that her recent houseguest, "the child of Gertie Vose," had turned "Judas Iscariot." She prepared an article for her magazine denouncing Vose and defending her well-intentioned innocence, but she delayed publishing it at the request of the arrested men. Vose, still believing himself undetected, went to San Francisco and sought out other anarchists he had known at Home. "Shifty-eyed and jittery," he was nevertheless given a room by friends. While he was out one day, his hosts opened his suitcase, which contained revolvers, Pullman tickets, hotel bills, notebooks with names and addresses, and coded messages that his anarchist hosts immediately attributed to Burns. Donald Vose departed as soon as he realized that he had been exposed. [94]

Vose testified at the Caplan-Schmidt trial, while his late anarchist friends watched with detestation. Returning to Home, he was despised and treated as an outcast. Then, wrote William Foster, the "rat Voss [*sic*] his treachery completed, disappeared somewhere into the dregs of the underworld and was seen no more around his usual haunts." Finally Emma Goldman was able to print her denunciation: "Donald Vose, you are a liar, traitor, spy. You have lied away the liberty and life of our comrades. Yet not they but you will suffer the penalty. You will roam the earth accursed, shunned and hated; a burden unto yourself, with the shadow of M. A. Schmidt and David Caplan ever at your heels unto the last." But her heart went out to her old friend Gertie.

What should the mother do, asked Goldman. "Will you save the people from your traitor son? Be Brave Gertie Vose, be brave!"[95]

Other troubles were mounting for Home. As before, some of these centered around the newspapers. Control of the *Demonstrator* changed several times after Morton left in November 1905. Morton had expected his paper to be carried on "under far more favorable conditions" by Jay Fox, a Chicago anarchist "of ability and character." Since his report on the founding convention of the Industrial Workers of the World the previous July, Fox had become a regular contributor, concentrating on IWW affairs. This association coincided with a serious discussion among Chicago anarchists about their future. *Free Society* had ceased publication, and the *Demonstrator* was the only viable anarchist journal appearing in English. Thinking to start a paper in Chicago, anarchists there polled subscribers of the defunct *Free Society*, but found little encouragement. In his reply, Morton suggested that they take over the *Demonstrator*; they could double its size and fulfill their needs at half the city publication costs. When the recommendation was discussed in a Chicago meeting, it was supported by about half those present. Others doubted the value of a "backwoods" paper, and no firm decision was reached. Fox thought that the persons most experienced with publishing "American" (that is, English language) propaganda favored adopting the *Demonstrator*.

The argument continued. Lucy Parsons, who held to the idea of a Chicago paper, demanded that Fox turn over to them money already raised for the *Demonstrator*, but he refused. Meanwhile, Fox claimed to have promises of money and material, and he determined to move to Home. Delayed that fall, he spoke of arriving by spring. In May 1906, an eye injury detained him and he did not know when he could leave for Home.[96]

When Fox finally arrived in 1910, the *Demonstrator* had long been dead. After Morton left, the paper became less the Home journal than one reflecting international problems and the views of labor. In February 1906, an IWW department was initiated on the front page. By June, when the size of the paper was reduced, it almost ignored Home, concentrating on foreign news and Chicago events and meetings. No official notice was made of such changes, however, and publication was still at Home, "by the Demonstrator Group." 97

A year later the *Demonstrator* was merged with the *Emancipator*, and Lawrence Cass, its editor, took charge. Retaining the name *Demonstrator* and staying at Home, Cass wrote on 3 July 1907 that the new publishers would offer "a paper of broader agitation in behalf of the emancipation of the working class, which we consider will benefit the whole of humanity, continuing the propaganda started in THE EMANCIPATOR." The editors called themselves free thinkers and atheists, anarchist communists who advocated industrial unionism. Although welcoming divergent views and "free discussion," Cass intended to refute utterances and theories opposing his own. He appealed to English-speaking anarchists in other countries for support and reminded readers that this was "the only Anarchist Communist paper in the English language published in America." William D. P. Bliss's *The New Encyclopedia of Social Reform* called the *Demonstrator* the "principal organ in English" sympathetic to communo-anarchism, noting with irony that Home was "founded upon individualistic principles, and probably a majority of the colonists are individualists."98

Apparently this contradiction was also noted at Home, for six months after he began publication, Cass confessed that he had not fully understood the colony. He promised to pay more attention to local interests and to promote solidarity and harmony. At the same time, eleven colonists joined Cass in forming the Demonstrator Publishing Group, which secured ownership of the press and plant. Members hoped to enlarge the paper and to print pamphlets and other radical literature. Although disagreeing with Cass's personal views, the others expressed confidence in his management, and they left him responsible for what was published. The paper also noted that Charles Govan was no longer associated, which left Govan out of Home publishing for the first time since he started *Discontent* almost ten years before.

Desiring to expand, the publishers sent Nathan Levin east in a fruitless effort to solicit funds. Perhaps he received a cold reception from the Chicago anarchists. In any case, the plans did not materialize, for two months later, on 19 February 1908, the final issue of the *Demonstrator* appeared. Once again Home was without a newspaper. The void would be filled by Jay Fox, but not until 1910. [99]

Fox was widely known among labor leaders and anarchists. Born 20 August 1870, he had been wounded during the Haymarket riot and had marched in the funeral train of the martyrs. At one time he had collaborated with Henry Addis of the *Firebrand* in writing a widely distributed pamphlet. His Russian-born wife, the former Esther Abramowitz, was a factory worker turned revolutionary. Both Jay and Esther Fox became active in the IWW, and he attended its founding convention. Only forty when he came to Home, the tall, slim, gray-haired editor appeared to be a much older man, soft-spoken and scholarly.[100]

The first issue of his paper, the *Agitator*, was dated 15 November 1910, although its editor gloried that it came out on 11 November, the twenty-fifth [*sic*] anniversary of the execution of the convicted Haymarket rioters. (The execution had occurred on 1 November 1887.) The four-page issue contained material on other social issues, but it was dominated by pictures, articles, a poem, letters, and speeches about these martyrs. One brief item described Home, and another praised it as the ideal place for a revolutionary paper. The paper issued from Fox's house up the hill from the bay on a press used fifty years before by Ezra Haywood, an anarchist whose fight against imprisonment for his writings was a cause célèbre in the late 1870s.[101]

Appearing twice a month, the *Agitator* defined itself as an "advocate of the Modern School, Industrial Unionism, Individual Freedom." Fox declared that it would "stand for freedom, first, last and all the time," and would promote the right of every person to express his opinions. He hoped to popularize knowledge so that common toilers as well as "the rich and privileged class" should be uplifted to philosophy and science. Fox foresaw a "great struggle for mastery" between combined capital and organized labor. The *Agitator* would promote the industrial unionism of the IWW in opposition to the slower and divisive trade-union practices of the American Federation of Labor. Yet the purpose was not to attack any workers but to advise, to appeal to reason and experience, and to "help create that unity of effort and solidarity among the workers necessary to their own emancipation." The *Agitator* would try in plain and simple language to be a "live issue" that would arouse and unify all workers. Well-written and widely publicized, the *Agitator* received encouragement from many persons who hoped it would fill a gap long vacant, including such influential radicals as A. L. Ballou, member of a prominent anarchist family, and author Jack London, who commended its "free, open fair spirit." [102]

Although the paper reprinted articles by such notables as Clarence Darrow, Joseph Labadie, and Bernarr McFadden, it bore the strong mark of its editor. A regular first-page feature, "The Passing Show," contained short articles and comment on a range of current topics: "Strikes and High Wages," "Free Speech in San Diego," "The Autocracy of Our Corporation Judges," the death of Mary Baker Eddy, "The Mexican Revolution," and "Polygamy and the Rights of Others." The paper supported the IWW generally and in specific causes, and it was read in IWW reading rooms. It was on bookstands in England, Australia, and New Zealand, as well as the United States. Even subscription blanks became propaganda devices addressed to "Fellow Slaves." Despite its role as an English-language paper, there were appeals for foreign born subscribers. And at least one contributor testified that the *Agitator* did indeed agitate: "When I slipped a copy of THE AGITATOR where the eye of my employer would strike it, I little thot what a commotion it would stir in the 'capcous [*sic*] brain' of that great man. THE AGITATOR was surely true to its name. It flurried his egotistic brain and made him explode his bombastic tirade against the men and women who make his bread and feed him." Another writer noted a "scoop" in which an article denouncing the Mexican revolutionary Francisco Madero as a traitor to his cause was copied prominently by a metropolitan daily, as if it were a dispatch from its own sources. [103]

But the paper could not survive on enthusiasm. During the first three months of publication it received a mere $226.25 in subscriptions. Over the first half-year, there was financial progress; total receipts of $422.05 outdistanced expenses to leave a balance of $115.52. But the next six months saw a thirty-one-dollar deficit. Subscriptions and sales during that period would indicate that no more than 292 new subscriptions had been obtained, some of these perhaps renewals. Jay Fox held out a salary of ten dollars a week, and the linotype machine was an expense. Finances were only part of Fox's difficulties. He described the first year of the

Agitator as "stormy. . . . It has had to struggle against the indifference of a large part of the radical element, that should have been its main support." [104]

During 1912, William Z. Foster played an increasingly important part in the *Agitator*. A close friend and possibly a disciple of Fox, Foster had risen in the IWW movement and had become a leading exponent of syndicalism. In April 1912, he began a series of articles on "Revolutionary Tactics," which was followed by three accounts of French syndicalism. Foster was in the process of splitting away from the IWW to form his Syndicalist League of North America with headquarters in Chicago. A tour of French and German labor movements, he said, had awakened him to the error of dual unionism, and the Syndicalist League was modeled after the French Confederation of Labor. It soon boasted a dozen branches in the western United States.[105]

Foster's need for an organ coincided with the increasing financial and legal problems of the *Agitator* and its editor. Foster induced Fox to move his enterprise to Chicago at a time propitious for both. The last issue of the *Agitator* was dated 1 November 1912; it reappeared in January as *The Syndicalist*. For several editions the mailing address remained Home, but a masthead named the publisher as the Syndicalist Publishing Association of Chicago. "On changing the place of publication," Fox announced, "we have changed the name of THE AGITATOR to THE SYNDICALIST, the latter being a more representative title."

A lengthy editorial rationalized that the move signified not failure but success for the *Agitator*. The paper had endured for two years despite skeptics and a lack of wholehearted support. It had long been argued that the paper should move to "an industrial center, preferably Chicago, where it would come into closer touch with the toiling masses, whose cause it champions." The first paper to publicize syndicalism in America, it expected to expand and become a weekly, "the liveliest and best Syndicalist paper in the English language." Early that spring Jay Fox was en route to Chicago. For the fourth and final time since Oliver Verity had begun the *New Era*, Home was without a newspaper.[106]

In Chicago, Foster and syndicalism became the overriding features of the paper. Items increasingly were geared to workers and the labor movement, and opposition to both the IWW and to moderate sectors of organized labor became harsh and frequent. Management shifted between Fox and Foster. Yet, despite its new location, cause, and format, the paper did not endure half as long as the *Agitator* of Home. Although the issue of 15 September 1913 contained no mention of suspension, the *Syndicalist* did not appear again. [107]

Fox returned to Home to live. Foster, who had first been to Home in 1912, visited occasionally over the years. To a mutual friend, the two men seemed to resemble one another, "about the same height, both slim and lithe, and both imperturbable." A poem about the IWW factionalism of 1912 in one of Foster's autobiographies makes clear reference to the two comrades:

> "The proper way," said Jay the Fox,
> "To start the revolution
> Is just to bore a hole or two
> In existing institutions. "
>
> "Agreed," cried Mr. Foster,
> "I have my gimlet ready,
> My arm is long, my hand is strong,
> My nerves are cool and steady."[108]

In 1912 Foster married his friend's recently divorced wife, but the three remained good friends. The Fosters moved toward communism, and he rose in party activities in the United States—was three times its presidential candidate—and in the international communist movement.

In September 1961, William Z. Foster died in Moscow, six months after the death of his friend at Home. The communist leader's body lay in state while Premier Nikita Khrushchev and other Soviet dignitaries formed an honor guard. After a state funeral in Red Square, the ashes were temporarily placed in the Kremlin Wall before removal to the United States and a massive memorial service at Carnegie Hall. At his side when he died was his wife, Esther, once of Home Colony. [109]

As his newspaper was undergoing change, Jay Fox had become the central figure in turmoil, factionalism, and legal action involving morality and free speech. In 1911, Home became caught up in controversies over nude bathing. Certain residents had bathed nude in Joe's Bay for years without interference, usually in secluded coves or by rowing out into the bay and disrobing before the plunge. Perhaps newcomers increased or accentuated the practice. In any case, nude bathing was not antithetical to an isolated community which stressed individual freedom. [110]

But a conservative faction challenged the practice. In the early summer, four Home residents, three of them women, were arrested for swimming in the nude, found guilty, and jailed. Additional charges of indecent exposure were later filed against four women and two men. Adrian Wilbers, whose case was probably typical, was charged by Mrs. Della Geithman, a colonist, with "indecent exposure of his person" at Home on 5 July. Pleading not guilty, Wilbers was released on bond, with the trial set for 21 July at nearby Longbranch. [111]

The cases attracted considerable attention, and Deputy Prosecuting Attorney Grover C. Nolte came from Tacoma to try them. The first trial, that of Mrs. Stella Thorndale, lasted from 1:30 P.M. until after 8:00. A witness testified that he had seen the defendant and a small girl bathing "without artificial covering of any sort." Defense Attorney Roger Meakins, brought from Seattle, accused prosecution witnesses of spying and of seeking to be shocked. His warning that "persons possessed of an enormous amount of virtue who did not like the community had better get out of it," drew applause. Insisting that she bathed for her rheumatism, Mrs. Thorndale was nevertheless convicted and fined sixty-five dollars. When an unfriendly spectator shouted that it should have been one hundred dollars, a "lively free-for-all fight" ensued. A second defendant was released after testimony that she had remained at home that particular day, but the other two women were convicted and fined. After midnight the men's cases were transferred at their request to a Tacoma justice court. Anton Zoncanelli was tried by jury in August. Conflicting evidence revolved about the basic question of whether "Zoncanelli wore a pair of white trunks or breeches, made of a flour sack instead of a more perpetual garb donated by nature." When the jury failed to agree, a second trial was set. [112]

But the crucial case involved Adrian Wilbers, and it started the following day without a jury. Justice Frank Graham concluded that although the defendant may well have had on the "little much-abbreviated trunks he testified he wore, they did not amply supply the needs for which they should have been intended." The judge fined the defendant one hundred dollars plus costs, or sixty-four days in jail.

The Wilbers case moved on appeal into superior court, to be heard by a jury before Judge W. O. Chapman. The complainant testified that she had watched from two hundred feet away as the defendant swam nude. Her fourteen-year-old daughter estimated the distance as only half that, and a younger son volunteered that the trio had climbed a small mound for a better view. Other witnesses came from Home to testify. Notwithstanding the supposed sensational nature of the case, a Tacoma paper admitted that it was "dragging along." After deliberating for twenty-four hours, the jurors failed to agree and were dismissed. Rumors said that the jurors had been evenly divided on whether to convict. The Tacoma *Times* noted that the prosecution had not yet won a case before a jury and reported that the unlikelihood of obtaining a conviction coupled with increasing trial expenses, would result in dropping actions against Wilbers and the four convicted colonists, all of whom had appealed. [113]

Despite the publicity they gave the case, Tacoma papers demonstrated a vastly changed attitude over a decade before. The *Times* appeared sympathetic to the colonists, and the *Ledger*, although occasionally reaching for language reminiscent of earlier harangues, was usually calm. It even mustered sufficient humor to quip that Home was "being well advertised as a community in which people frequently take baths." Likewise, the *News* conceded "that between bathing in the nude and wearing a tight skirt we are inclined to believe the former more modest." The papers toyed with a rumor that Wilbers was a former husband of Emma Goldman, forcing his reply that he "never lived with her as her husband and our relations were merely friendly." The anarchist editor of the *Agitator* assumed the role of the miffed taxpayer, citing trial costs and transportation and lodging expenses for witnesses, including children. The trials had created, Jay Fox punned, "An Infant Industry at Home."[114]

The most serious effect of the cases occurred within the colony, where divisions and struggles reached a peak inconceivable in former days. Most colonists supported the defendants and prepared to testify or to raise money for their expenses. But the residents were split; Jay Fox labeled them nudes and prudes, although one faction was graphically called the skunks. Perhaps the disputes represented a latent antagonism between the high idealism of some and the narrower practical disposition of others. Oliver Verity sadly wrote a friend to describe what had happened: "Well the short story of it all they got to boycotting each other with the result that many animosities were aroused and depredations of a forceful nature were done by the prudes such as a night attack on Geo. Allen, and the cutting down of young orchards of Allen, [Paul] Roestel . . . , and others until the growth of Home stopped until at least such a time as the war between them could end." [115] These incidents shocked people who had always left alone the affairs of others. [116]

Antagonism centered around particular individuals, such as the camera carrier who hoped to photograph nude adults or bribed children to pose naked for pictures he might sell to metropolitan newspapers. Neighbors ridiculed the colonist who testified that she had used powerful field glasses to view the swimmers. Stores refused to trade with the prudes, now largely isolated from normal social contacts. Disputes continued to involve children. A parent whose daughter had received an obscene note from a schoolmate demanded the resignation of teacher George Allen and filed charges against the boy. L. H. Hicklin claimed that his thirteen-year-old son was being threatened at school and that the teacher encouraged such lawlessness. Target of particular bitterness was J. M. Tillman, a colonist who as deputy sheriff made the local arrests and whose son testified against Wilbers. A party of colonists sought to replace him with a member of their own faction. Although the request was denied, the sheriff did dismiss the deputy. Angry and vengeful, Tillman rejoiced to have more time to gather evidence against the nudes. [117]

The most celebrated aspect of the nude-bathing cases involved the *Agitator* and Jay Fox. After the first trial, Fox printed an editorial which he called "The Nude and the Prudes." "Clothing was made to protect the body, not to hide it," he began, and he criticized the local justice court. Home had always been "a community of free spirits, who came out into the woods to escape the poluted [*sic*] atmosphere of priest-ridden conventional society. One of the liberties enjoyed by Homeites was the privilege to bathe in evening dress, or with merely the clothes nature gave them, just as they chose. No one went rubbernecking to see which suit a person wore, who sought the purifying waters of the bay. Surely it was nobody's business." [118] But "prudes" had come into the community, attempting to suppress freedom, and lines were drawn. There had developed, and Fox thought rightfully so, a situation in which each individual had to choose his side. Fox defended the right of persons to be or to swim in the nude. Impurity is something seen by the eye, and nudity is impure only to the "coarse, half civilized barbarian, steeped in a mixture of superstition and sensualism," who thinks only animal thoughts when he sees a nude body. "The vulgar mind sees its own reflection in everything it views. Polution [*sic*] cannot escape from polution [*sic*], and the poluted [*sic*] mind that sees its own reflection in the nude body of a fellow being, and arises in the early morning to enjoy the vulgar feast, and then calls on the law to punish the innocent victims whose clean bodies aroused the savage instincts, is not fit company for civilized people, and should be avoided." [119]

Seven weeks after this publication, Fox was arrested. The information quoted the editorial in full. The law allegedly violated held that it was a misdemeanor "to encourage or advocate disrespect for law or for any court or courts of justice." In an earlier form, this law had been enacted during the furor over anarchism following the McKinley assassination.[120]

The delay between publication and arrest suggested that the prosecutor was uncertain of his ground, but he moved quickly after hearing rumors that Fox might leave to avoid arrest. Thus, a special deputy was sent to arrest the editor, returning with him at one o'clock one August morning. Held until dawn in a Tacoma hotel, Fox was taken to the sheriff's office. A state senator's offer to post the one-thousand-dollar bail was denied on a technicality, and Fox, exhibiting "not a tremor," was jailed in "the hardened tank where desperate criminals are held." Fox remained in jail for two days before bond was accepted. The prosecuting attorney promised a quick trial and hinted that the character of the Home community was at issue.[121]

Radicals came to Fox's defense. On the day of his arrest, the IWW of Tacoma held an impromptu protest meeting; following his release, Fox addressed another large meeting in their hall and received pledges of support. His Home comrades organized a Pierce County Free Speech League to solicit funds. In New York, James F. Morton, Jr., veteran of earlier newspaper persecution at Home, wrote a lengthy history of colony troubles for the *Truth Seeker*; and the secretary of the National Free Speech League, Theodore Schroeder, discussed appealing to the United States Supreme Court. Meanwhile, Fox heard that the Pierce County prosecutor had sent evidence to the Los Angeles district attorney supposedly linking Fox to the McNamara bombing, but the Californians attached no importance to it. Attempts to secure a demurrer or a dismissal were overruled. [122]

The trial took place in the courtroom of Judge Chapman on 10 January 1912, with two colorful attorneys pleading their respective cases. Deputy Prosecutor Grover C. Nolte handled the prosecution, and Colonel James J. Anderson, who had come to Tacoma fifteen years before with a government commission to sell Indian lands and had remained to participate in the 1896 Bryan presidential campaign, defended Fox. The selection of a jury brought the first debate. Prosecutor Nolte asked each prospective member whether he believed in anarchy, a question to which Anderson objected without avail. All accepted jurors swore they did not.

Several Home residents came to testify. The case pivoted on whether "The Nude and the Prudes" tended to create disrespect for law and to encourage further law-breaking. An increase in nude bathing after the editorial appeared was credited to warm weather rather than to any words. Two ladies from Home challenged the character of a star prosecution witness, who was believed to have served time in King County for murder. Judge Chapman directed that Fox's beliefs were not at issue but rather the content of the article and its possible effect upon law enforcement. "It doesn't make so much difference what is in a man's mind, it is what comes out of his mind that counts," he was quoted as saying. [123]

As the trial neared conclusion on the second afternoon, Fox addressed the jury, pleading for free speech and a free press. "It is only by agitation that the laws of the land are made better," a

Tacoma paper quoted him: "It is only by agitation that reforms have been brought about in the world. If the water of the bay were not agitated, it would become a poluted [*sic*] pool and would kill us all. Show me the country where there is the most tyranny and I will show you the country where there is no free speech." [124] Colonel Anderson's closing remarks called for action against other papers which freely criticized laws and courts. An outburst of applause brought a warning from the bench and a taunt from Prosecutor Nolte to produce such a paper. With this, Anderson flourished a copy of the Seattle *Post-Intelligencer*, which contained a recent address by a Bellingham judge criticizing a Supreme Court ruling. In his closing statement, the prosecutor refuted colonists' arguments that they had settled at Home seeking liberty: "It is no time for them to come in here and cry that we have encroached upon their liberty. The state of Washington was organized long before Home colony was. The laws were fixed here long before Home colony was founded. They knew that this state was an organized society at this time and if they didn't like it, why did they come here? They didn't want that liberty which is the liberty that means freedom under law and order; they just wanted that kind of liberty that gives them the right to do as they damn please." Rebuked for his "damn," Nolte promised to avoid such language in court again. [125]

Twice Judge Chapman gave instructions to the jury. The issue was not whether Fox believed in anarchy or whether he advocated nude bathing, unless that involved indecent exposure. The judge iterated the guarantees of free speech, writing, and publication, but he noted that such freedom did not allow the press to be used as "the lawful vehicle of malicious defamation or as an engine for evil and designing men to cherish for malicious purposes, sedition, irreligion and impurity." The judge further defined that "disrespect for law" as used in the statute, did not refer to a specific act but to law in general or law as the basis of government. Even if the editorial advocated disrespect for a particular law, that did not justify finding its author guilty. [126]

The case went to the jury at four in the afternoon and by ten there was no verdict. Rumors placed the jurors at nine to three for acquittal. Another full day of deliberation prompted reports of a "hung jury"; then at five o'clock, twenty-five hours after receiving the case, the jury returned. The foreman, one of two women in the panel, pronounced the defendant guilty, but recommended leniency. Fox, otherwise without emotion, smiled when his attorney sought to question jurors leaving the room. Attorney Anderson immediately gave verbal notice of appeal. The prosecution insisted that the verdict indicated a public desire to have the colony abolished. The Zoncanelli and Wilbers cases, due to be heard the next week, were pledged full attention. [127]

Anderson's request for a new trial was denied, and a date was set for sentencing. On 6 February, Fox, liable for a thousand-dollar fine, a year in jail, or both, was sentenced to two months in jail. Appealing once more, he was released on bond. "Two Months in the Tank" was the way the editor described his fate in a blistering argument in his own newspaper. The judge, he said, was "an eminently fair minded man, but a very conservative, old-fashioned moralist," who did not consider the editorial dangerous but agreed that it inspired disrespect for the law. A dangerous precedent was set, he said, for the verdict ensured that the rich would have their laws and that the poor could only be subservient. [128]

Supporters of Fox continued efforts during three years of legal maneuvering, although the local chapter of the Free Speech League had only $210.89 when the last issue of the *Agitator* carried the final statement in November. Fox had stated that "the *Agitator* is not in a financial condition to stand much persecution," and that if he could get a thousand new subscribers he would "go to jail with joy in my heart." Newspaper and court expenses and legal troubles prompted his decision to move his paper. On the train to Chicago, Fox reviewed Alexander Berkman's *Prison Memoirs of an Anarchist* and wryly recognized the resemblance to himself. A series of articles entitled "The Agitator in History," which he said were written for the Tacoma *Daily Ledger* but rejected, compared the Home persecution to earlier historical incidents. [129]

On 10 February 1913, the state supreme court denied a rehearing of the case, and the appeal was continued to the United States Supreme Court, possibly under the auspices of the National Free Speech League, forerunner of the American Civil Liberties Union, and its lawyer, Theodore Schroeder. On 13 May 1915, the state court learned that the federal bench had upheld its decision.

Defense Attorney Anderson, in company with J. G. Brown, an International Union of Timber Workers official, unsuccessfully sought an immediate interview with Governor Ernest C. Lister to request executive clemency. Anderson finally wrote him a three-page letter contending that Fox had meant to break no laws but had been persecuted for the reputation of the community where he lived. The *Agitator*, which had little circulation, had long been defunct, public feeling against Home had diminished, and Fox was living quietly on a few acres. A jail sentence could accomplish no positive result. On an enclosed copy of the editorial, Fox penned that he had recommended no more than a boycott and that the conviction had been secured "only through working upon the prejudices of the jury." [130]

Both Judge Chapman and former Deputy Prosecutor A. O. Burmeister assured the governor that they would not object to a pardon, although Chapman defended the sentence as light. Privately, Burmeister recommended that a full pardon would be inexpedient and politically unwise, since the governor could expect no political support from Fox and his associates. The two men affirmed that while neither had personal objections to Fox—a "rather quiet, inoffensive man" the judge recalled him—the actions had been taken to "curb" the anarchists. The citizens of Home, wrote Burmeister, had given "us much trouble in the way of law violations," and Fox was their leader and spokesman. The governor refused clemency and ordered Fox to serve at least a part of the sentence, a decision which the new Pierce County prosecutor applauded as tending to "discourage the anarchistic tendencies of Home Colony." [131]

Fox, who had returned from his short stay in Chicago, was regarded as a martyr at Home as he prepared to serve his sentence. He received three rousing cheers at the weekly dance, and a crowd gathered at dockside when a deputy sheriff took him to Tacoma. The sheriff commented incidentally to reporters that nude bathing had not subsided in the community. While Fox served the sentence, Anderson and Brown continued to seek his release. The attorney reminded Governor Lister of his hint that Fox need not complete the full sentence, reiterating that the family needed his support. A pardon was finally granted on 11 September, only twelve days before the sentence would have ended. Late that evening, Fox, described as a "model prisoner" by his jailers, was released. Smiling broadly, he quietly left for Home. "The release of the Home Colony Scribe," concluded the *Ledger*, "brings an end to a case that was fought from the superior court of Pierce County to the supreme court of the United States, the state proving victorious in each count." [132]

For the remainder of his life, Fox lived at Home with his family, including his second wife Cora, an artist. Contacts with national and international radicals continued, but public writings and agitation diminished. He never published another paper of his own, although he did write for the Seattle *Union Record*, and he wrote at least one pamphlet for the Trade Union Educational League founded by Foster. In the early 1920s the young American Communist party split into two factions, with an American-based group, largely made up of former socialists and trade unionists led by Foster, opposing a European group of theorists. Foster cited Fox as one who followed him into his faction in the party, a conversion that alienated some of his one-time anarchist friends. The Foxes moved across Joe's Bay into a house with a hammer and sickle outlined on the doorstep, and they remained the best-known among Home citizens. He began to write his memoirs. Jay Fox died there on 8 March 1961. [133]

The nude-bathing incidents were but surface evidence of ruptures that had been deepening over several years. The arrival of new groups, which on occasion included persons of similar ethnic background who lived somewhat to themselves, had altered the nature of the settlement. An early result was the transfer of ownership and then the demise of the *Demonstrator* in 1907-8. The next year fundamental changes in the Mutual Home Association laid the groundwork for its later dissolution. In 1911 the Home Grocery Association had collapsed amidst a bitter lawsuit; late in 1912 the *Agitator* had ceased publication; and in 1915 one resident denounced his fellows in a bitingly sarcastic diatribe. To the IWW publication *Solidarity*, J. C. Harrison ridiculed Home as a dilapidated community where cooperation had failed. A "motley assembly" of residents with greatly differing beliefs were divided into radicals and conservatives, who had "constant quarrels and bickerings, which at times amount to general warfare, but generally ends in court." He derided the professed anarchists, who denounced courts and the law but used them to their own advantage with legal wire-pulling, "parliamentary juggling," and real estate promotions. [134]

The anarchists had indeed discovered the courts. The Mutual Home Association, which was the foundation of the community, floundered amidst internecine warfare, with two panels of officers both posing as the legitimate leaders. Early in 1917, members had met in Liberty Hall to elect a slate of officers headed by Thomas J. Mullen. A month later, at the Lewis Haiman home, Jay Fox was elected president by another group, which included members of the Allen family and others who had been ousted from association membership by court order two days previously. The Mullen faction now sued for control, but a reconciliation was effected, and the action was dismissed the next February. The detente was only an interval amidst growing dissension. On 19 November 1918, twelve plaintiffs swore a complaint against fifteen defendants, who they claimed had usurped the organization, and they requested dissolution and a court-appointed receiver. Forty more persons appeared as interveners sympathetic to the plaintiffs. As Judge Ernest M. Card heard complaints, answers, and conflicting testimony, the recent history of Home Colony emerged. [135]

The dispute had its basis in 1909, when Home was platted and a change was made in the articles of incorporation of the Mutual Home Association. The original document had stipulated that the association was incorporated for benevolent purposes and not as a money-making organization; its real property was never to be sold, mortgaged, or disposed of. The 1909 amendment enabled officers to convey by deed to association members the fee-simple title to their land. Such a reversion to private ownership and individual deeds came as "a jar" to some of the founders. Some members acquired land and then sold it, clearly violating the original precepts. Tidelands were rented to Joe's Bay Trading Company, which by 1917 was verging on bankruptcy and failing to pay rental. These practices depleted association holdings and ended the promise of available land for incoming members. Commonly owned property—Liberty Hall, the sea wall, the sidewalks, and a cemetery—had fallen into disrepair. Only an amendment to the bylaws could allow the association to raise funds for repairs, and that was practically impossible to obtain.

Judge Card agreed that for nine years the association had been "wholly impotent" to perform the charter purposes, including finding homes and bettering social and moral conditions, and that these purposes were impractical and had been abandoned. Divisions and hostility among members in recent months made it unlikely that they could reconcile conditions themselves. The judge agreed that the defendants had usurped control of association affairs and had used lands and funds to their own advantage while denying objections or participation from others. Five years of disputes had "been barren of results . . . [and] intensified the bitter and irreconcilable hostility and . . . left no hope for the amicable settlement of the differences existing between them." Thus, on 10 September 1919, Judge Card ordered the Mutual Home Association dissolved and appointed Charles W. Johnson to be permanent receiver. Soon after, a group of defendants, including George Allen, were found in contempt of court for continuing to act as officers of the association against direct orders, and they were fined and disqualified as association members.

When receiver Johnson made his final report to the court, he listed assets of $2,314.65, mostly receipts from the sale of real estate. Property was sold to private individuals, usually to members, and the cemetery was bought by the Home Grange. Liberty Hall, condemned three years before the receiver took over, was sold for lumber, only to be destroyed by fire before the sale was confirmed. On 4 May 1921, the Mutual Home Association ended its existence when Judge Card accepted the final report and discharged the receiver. [136]

Thus the demise of the Mutual Home Association combined with other incidents to end what Home had been. Perhaps the greatest disruption of all was the psychological change, which probably passed unnoticed before the colonists. With population increases, the singleness of community spirit had been lost. Meanwhile, young colonists had grown up, and many grew away physically and philosophically. If they shared some ideals with their elders, they did not remain steadfast to promote them. And the older generation grew older. World War I helped distinguish

Home of the old days from the rural community it was becoming. War brought repression, demands for conformity, and internal struggles to radical groups throughout the United States, and Home was no exception. The war effort demanded expressions of patriotism and acceptance of common beliefs and values, especially from those persons suspect for views once held. George Allen, for one, became increasingly conservative and sought to prove his patriotism by purchasing Liberty Bond after Liberty Bond. [137]

Federal authorities did not ignore Home during the war or the wave of antialien sentiment that followed. The basis for investigation shifted from obscenity laws and the use of mailing privileges to alien and immigration violations. In August 1918, an investigator from the Bureau of Immigration visited Home and filed a report reminiscent of the lurid style Tacoma newspapers had abandoned fifteen years earlier. Noting a hostility toward government, law, and morality, the report contended that:

Typical, radical obsessions prevail throughout the colony. . . . Few of the characters residing there are openly active against the Government or war. But the colony forms a background for radicals of every breed. A rendezvous and general "get-away" for people of that type. There should be every reason to expect good citizenship and loyalty from the colony, considering their prosperity, the State and county expenditures . . . , etc., but, notwithstanding that, only one volunteer soldier from that colony so far. Their public school is used for every brand of radical propaganda, including a celebration which they held at the time President McKinley was assassinated. They are a quarrelsome people, always taking each other into court, and at the same time opposing the law. They will lie, cheat, steal, practice sabotage, and promote disloyalty if the opportunity presents.

In probable exaggeration, the report stated that the population had recently reached nearly five hundred, but that many persons had left, scattering to work in shipyards and elsewhere. Of the present 250 to 300, most were said to be foreign-born, and few had obtained final citizenship papers. A list of names and information gathered over a period of several years was appended. [138]

A particular objection was that Home residents had paid frequent visits to prominent anarchists imprisoned at the federal penitentiary on nearby McNeil Island, including the Mexican revolutionary Enrique Flores Magon, his brother, and a General Alexander Zen Zogg. These men were said to have distributed anarchist propaganda and encouraged draft evasion in the United States. [139]

The interception of a letter to a supposed Mexican anarchist led investigators to three Seattle men previously linked with Home. A member of the French community across the bay admitted his anarchist beliefs and his authorship of the letter, and he named several other anarchists. That night at the immigration station he hanged himself with a towel. His arrest led authorities to Leon Morel, who had presumably hidden David Caplan years before and who was sent to Ellis Island for deportation. A third person, at whose home Morel had been arrested, was Alex Snellenberg, an unnaturalized Hollander who had spent some time at Home and whose wife, also an active radical, summered there with their children. Proceedings were initiated against Snellenberg, and radical literature was confiscated from his home. But after fervent appeals from Snellenberg, his attorney, and a Seattle city official attesting to his long residence, work, and excellent reputation, his warrant was canceled. Despite these three individuals and a small clamor raised against the Home anarchists, little real action took place. Of the large number of persons, mostly IWW members, who were arrested and held for deportation at Seattle, no others were associated with Home Colony. [140]

After the war, life at Home was not what it had been before. Some of the same families stayed on, and a few of the radical heroes came to visit, but Home was becoming a conventional rural community. Ben Alt built a large hotel across the bay as a resort for summer visitors, largely Jewish. Local residents turned to raising poultry, until the Great Depression caused many to lose their homes. During a second world war, the persecution of the first was not repeated; there was no need in the 1940s for government action against Home. It remained in peaceful isolation until bridges and highways and recreational real estate developments nearby began to change even that. In the postwar years, Home became a community in which old and new residents mingled, a summer community for some, with a touch of suburbia about it. [141]

Outsiders' alarms about subversion, radicalism, anarchy, and morality at Home turned to infrequent curiosity. Each journalist who returned over the years in search of human-interest stories for metropolitan readers found successively fewer of the old anarchists alive. The Tacoma reporter who covered the otherwise forgotten seventieth anniversary of the founding of Home had to content himself with a comparative latecomer and with the daughter of George Allen, who had been only six when her family arrived. [142]

Situated in a remote corner of a nation that was only emerging from frontier conditions at the turn of the century, Home was isolated even within that region. Yet it became known in the radical world, and it excited curiosity, comment, and controversy. It attracted a remarkable group of permanent residents with varying beliefs and practices that differed from one another but were mutually tolerated. It drew visitors from throughout the radical world. A large number of celebrated persons, mostly nonconformists of one shade or another, came to this small backwater community, several more than once. Home was a strong little magnet in the remote Northwest.

Whatever effect Home may have had on the world is impossible to measure. The newspapers and correspondence that went out from Joe's Bay may have generated thought or created influence, yet they represented a tiny fraction of all the writings that circulated among radicals. The young who grew up at Home may, as at least one proudly believes, have been instilled with a liberal and tolerant outlook from their experience. One cannot fairly assess the impact of the community and its people on their visitors, even those like Bill Haywood, Elizabeth Gurley Flynn, or William Z. Foster, who came early in careers that were to be long and stormy. If some of the more permanent Home residents—such as editors Morton and Fox—deserve a place in the lower firmament of radicals of this century, the influence of Home may have been felt through them.

It is difficult to assess the effect of Home, but it is more possible to define what it was. First of all, it was a remarkable place to live, peopled with fascinating, colorful, provocative, and often highly intelligent individuals. More significant, Home was a place where ideas and practices were in ferment. The community was the open forum that Oliver Verity and George Allen hoped it would become. Its residents talked and read and wrote about topics and ideas that conventional society preferred to leave unchallenged. These people considered aspects of religion, economics, land-holding, taxation, sex, race relations, women's role in society, obscenity, nudity, free press, and whatever might occur to any among them. It is trite to suggest that the people of Home or other contemporary radicals were ahead of their time. By definition the radical must be ahead of his time. But when Lois Waisbrooker called for the emancipation of women from sexual enslavement; when *Discontent* debated the causes and effects of violence; when James Morton described race relations to be a northern as well as a southern problem; when Jay Fox pleaded for an honest assessment of attitudes toward nudity and prudery; when dissenters accepted jail to protest laws they considered unjust infringements upon their personal freedom; when men sought privacy; when the people of Home encouraged and tolerated those who lived and acted as they chose, then the individualists of Home were addressing themselves to issues that society later would be forced to confront.

That is the significance of Home.

7. Conclusion

UTOPIA ABANDONED

Three more Washington communitarian experiments were loosely connected with the others, one in time, the other by ideology. About the time of the Jay Fox trial, a small religious community appeared in the San Juan Islands. The Reverend Thomas Gourley had preached a fundamentalist doctrine from his Ballard pulpit and had attracted followers from afar, but his sect was repulsed by the fleshpots of society. To the literal-minded Gourley, the Bible offered an injunction that man must divorce from the world and commune with God among the elect, certain that God would always meet his needs.

In 1912, Pastor Gourley and 175 followers left Ballard for Lopez Island in a scow piled high with belongings and towed by a launch. For a few months they made headquarters at Mud Bay, but the poor location bred disease, and they moved across a point to Hunter Bay. Many lived in tents until lumber was obtained for more permanent structures. Then, sometimes using beach logs, they built private houses, a barn, a tent-house school, a bake house, a dock, other buildings, and a tabernacle. The colony had its own power plant and considerable machinery and equipment, and a launch made regular runs on Puget Sound. A laundry room held a commercial washer and dryer; kitchen facilities and farming and building equipment were operated. All things were owned communally.

This devout group made little attempt to proselytize or to recruit members. Their purpose was not to expand and develop but to provide a good, cloistered, God-like life for the believers. Smoking, dancing, and drinking were prohibited; marriages were performed and funeral services conducted by the pastor, with burials in a tiny cemetery. Several young men registered as conscientious objectors during World War I. Although families lived in their own homes, food was prepared and eaten communally. Meat was scarce; the colony was not strictly vegetarian, but scruples against killing prevented butchering, hunting, fishing, or even gathering clams along the beach. Although they would eat or preserve meat provided by others, they would not kill.

The colony subsisted on belongings members had brought, on sales of wood to a mill on Blakely Island, and from the earnings of a few men who worked on Lopez. Wages were often paid in barter and went into the common fund. Social life centered around religion and frequent meetings; neighbors from around the island came to Sunday services and sometimes lingered for dinner. A nonaccredited school was taught by colony members. Pastor Gourley and his flock looked after people in need as well as their own, caring for the sick and taking in widows, orphans, and others.

The religious colony existed thus for several years under the patriarchal benevolence of Gourley. But his failure to meet certain needs and rumors about misappropriated funds split the congregation, and an emotional general meeting forced Gourley's departure in 1916. He eventually moved to Georgia and another communal venture; later he was killed in a train wreck. The colony lasted a few years longer and then disintegrated. Under the leadership of elder Alva Green, remaining members sold their common belongings and divided proceeds that averaged about $175 a family. Looters, poultry-raisers, and a Prohibition-era bootlegger found their own peculiar uses for the vacant buildings until the property was divided and sold. The "Come-outers" of Lopez Island, as the sect was sometimes called, were similar to other Washington communitarian experiments only in having some communal arrangements and in point of time. They were really akin to the isolated sectarian colonies of an earlier period. [1]

A different kind of community interested residents of western Washington who were stirred by the 1917 Bolshevik Revolution and organized migrations to establish communal settlements in

Russia. IWW members were among those most frequently attracted. "Big Bill" Haywood and about two hundred American citizens, including some from the Northwest, founded the Kuzbas Colony in 1924, with Soviet sponsorship and American funds. The experiment was scarcely under way before differences erupted with the Soviet government; Haywood was ousted and many Americans withdrew. [2]

More successful was the Seattle Commune, Russianized to "Seyatel," which was established in 1922 in the north Caucasus. Eighty-seven Seattle residents contributed equipment, personal supplies, and initial donations of five hundred dollars each upon joining. This became one of the largest and most successful Soviet communes, partially because it was highly mechanized. In the 1930s, it was reorganized as a collective farm, and in 1961 the name was changed to that of a Communist Party Congress. Fifty years after the revolution that inspired it, the former Seyatel Commune was a relatively modern farm community of 1,460 residents, five of whom were among the original Seattle founders. [3]

But a religious sect and a Soviet commune represented schemes different from the secular experiments of western Washington that shared many common characteristics. All practiced some form of economic cooperation, from the nearly communistic Equality to the less structured Freeland and Home. Land was commonly owned, although leased out at Home and sold at Freeland. Each colony had a cooperative store, and farming, lumbering and milling, or minor industries were often conducted on a cooperative basis. Each scheme aspired to become an ideal society, but no plan was ever so final that it did not require alterations. Reorganizing usually tended toward greater individuality or separate returns for work. Even at the individualistic community of Home, the changes of 1909 sought to permit greater personal freedom.

Relative isolation tended to lessen interference and conflict from outside sources as well as distractions, ridicule, or harmful influences. If the socialists and anarchists in the secular colonies were less monastic than the "Come-outers" of Lopez Island, it was mostly a matter of degree. Critics sometimes noted that colonists sought to escape the problems of the day instead of recognizing and meeting them.

The communitarian ideal required some self-sufficiency if a "working model" were to ensure a better quality of life than that in conventional society. Paradoxically, colonists sometimes sought to enter the competitive economy they deplored. Thus, communities sold lumber, shakes, and farm products on the open market. The Puget Sound Co-operative Colony moved into real estate and land development, Equality and the Puget Sound Co-operative Colony planned steamboat runs of Puget Sound, and Burley considered bringing in outside laborers and managers. Home residents were regularly employed in Tacoma or elsewhere. And critics who chided Home anarchists for their use of the lawyers and courts they opposed on principle had a valid point. Even as colonists spoke of their isolated superiority and boasted of self-sufficiency, they employed methods of the outside world when necessary or expedient.

People who joined colonies were motivated by a blend of idealism and opportunism. The promises of colony promoters were like beacons to men tired of the economic frustrations and seeming inequities of the 1890s. Although the colonies fell short of fulfilling the material offerings promised, they suggested the opportunity of change to a new and promising life, a brotherhood of well-meaning men working together, and eventual security. Perhaps in each man there is something of the dreamer, the wanderer who would pull up stakes and start life afresh. It was less true of their mates. More than one skeptical wife, her children compliant and in tow, followed her husband to a new life less from choice than because of loyalty and duty.

Few who came were destitute, but some were poor. Membership fees and the backgrounds of known colonists do not indicate that they were impoverished. A contemporary Georgia colony leader who surveyed other colonies, suggested that communitarianism "was a movement of middle class idealists." Although complete data are lacking, it would appear that many members were single men, possibly just passing the prime of life, or parents in their middle years with adolescent or slightly younger children. Some were laborers, many had trades, and most seem to have come from small towns. All attracted some local followers, but every part of the United States was represented, with an apparent preponderance from the Middle West. Some were European born, but very few, even at cosmopolitan Home, came directly from Europe. Most had lived somewhere in the United States before hearing about the Washington colonies and moving west. [4]

Many colonists had experienced suspicion or ridicule from neighbors for their radical inclinations, the publications they read, and the meetings they attended. A daughter of Home colonists recalls earlier socialist picnics in their Seattle backyard and waving red flags at a parade, and a son from Equality remembered the socialist circles his father had joined in Ohio. Martin Dadisman realized that his views set him apart from his neighbors. To a degree they were outcasts, looking for similarly minded persons among whom they could live in peace and congeniality. [5]

Every colony had people who liked to talk and to argue. They fancied themselves thinkers, more enlightened than the great majority of their fellows. Lyceums, general meetings, newspapers, and stores provided forums where every man could be a philosopher or an innovator. Many a worker came in from mill or field to write articles and letters setting forth his views on whatever topic might occur. And some could debate fine technicalities with the seriousness of medieval theologians. Not every colonist aspired to be the universal man that James F. Morton, Jr., would emulate, but many cherished favorite issues, ideas, and crusades.

All the colonies had newspapers that blended local and organizational news with other radical views and reprints. Several sought to speak for a larger movement: *Industrial Freedom* would unite all socialists, *Soundview* would be the western counterpart of Elbert Hubbard's *Philistine*, and the Home papers, especially the *Agitator*, would embrace all American anarchists. None succeeded in its larger purpose. Several Washington colony journals achieved a journalistic quality at least as high as contemporary small-town papers, but remoteness from large population centers, lack of financial backing, and the over-abundance of small radical journals in the nation worked against their success. None emerged to win a true national following.

Most colony papers experienced difficulties from postal authorities. Perhaps such martyrdom was coveted, for not to have encountered interference in the days of "Maddenism" or "Comstockianism" would have implied that a paper was insignificant.

Sometimes trifling post office rulings were inflated into alleged persecutions. Yet there was some genuine harrassment. It is difficult to view the attitudes toward *Discontent* after the McKinley assassination and the later imprisonment of Jay Fox as less than attacks upon Home and its anarchist doctrines.

Each colony had distinct characteristics. Life at Burley was neither as frenetic as at Home nor as intense as at Equality. Yet, the colonists recognized similarities that might have drawn them together. More than one suggestion was made for a union or a confederation of colonies or the combining of newspapers. But ideological differences, local preferences and loyalties, and general provincialism kept them separate. Instead, they engaged in occasional backbiting and hurled innuendoes at one another. Even as *Industrial Freedom* extended outward friendliness to newborn Burley and stillborn Harmony, Equality leaders spurned overtures from Burley and turned their backs on Harmony. Home editors enjoyed sniping at socialists who refused to renounce government and at the poor living conditions and strict regulations in the communal ventures. The demise of another colony was likely to elicit from the colony press statements of regret, pity, a "there but for the grace of God" recognition, and a smug satisfaction that longevity was proof of superiority.

Sometimes colonies united for special functions. Alonzo A. Wardall organized a league of colonies and cooperative stores in Washington. Social functions and special excursions were held between colonies, especially Burley and nearby Home. Visits between individual members were commonplace. One summer the teenaged Harry Ault and Frank Hoehn of Equality visited all the existing Puget Sound colonies by boat. [6]

Some individuals migrated from one colony to another. The tendency was to move from one of the communal, regimented colonies to one allowing greater individual freedom. Thus, many left Equality to live at Freeland, or they departed Equality or Burley for Home. Alexander Horr's proposals to revitalize Equality attracted converts from both Burley and Home. Some persons were particularly ubiquitous. Kingsmill Commander, for instance, lived and assumed leadership at Equality, Burley, and Home, and possibly at Freeland, and A. K. Hanson lived at Equality, Freeland, and Home.

Such movement of people between colonies was not peculiar to the Northwest. Settlers had come from such experiments as the Topolobampo community in Mexico, the Union Colony in Colorado, Ruskin in Tennessee, and others. Likewise, many who left Washington communitarian settlements moved to colonies in other parts of the country. Such movement was characteristic of a certain type of colonist, who continually sought something different within the communal context.

The communitarian experiments of western Washington failed not only to achieve their grandest aspirations but also to maintain their very existence. Harmony was never really launched, and the Puget Sound Co-operative Colony was in full operation for little more than two years. However, both Equality and Burley endured for a decade. The less highly organized Freeland and Home lasted longer but evolved away from communal practices. Frederick A. Bushee noted that the life span of most nineteenth-century secular experiments was shorter. Thirty-nine of the sixty-two colonies which he studied lasted less than three years; those influenced by the economic and political theories of the late 1800s averaged about four years. A later student who was able to fix the closing dates of 236 communities found that 25 percent of all colonies, and 30 percent of the nonreligious ones, failed during the first year; 45 percent of all did not survive more than five years. Yet, a recent sociologist denotes twenty-five years—one generation—as the mark of success. Despite relative longevity, the Washington experiments, like those elsewhere, failed to endure.[7]

Many reasons can be suggested for these failures. Most settled on good land, although it sometimes had to be cleared or diked. At all colonies soil was productive enough for most needs. Each colony expected to do logging and lumbering, and all except Freeland did. Few had good access to water transportation. The Port Angeles group probably selected best in this regard, and they built a wharf into the Strait of Juan de Fuca. Others learned that water in sight was not necessarily accessible; some located on bays that boats could use only at high tides. Perhaps the locations were inadequate only to the extent that the goals were too great or surrounding markets had not yet developed. Later mills were erected on virtually the same spots as the Puget Sound Co-operative Colony mill and the Equality mill. Small, specialized farming succeeded at Burley, Home, and Freeland.

It was convenient to blame failure on hostile outside forces. Except at Home, however, the colonies encountered ignorance, skepticism, and ridicule rather than enmity. Immediate neighbors frequently shared in colony dances, picnics, lectures, and general fellowship. Even at Home during the furor after the McKinley assassination, the Reverend Doescher reported that residents of the neighborhood did not object to their anarchist neighbors.[8] Newspapers in towns somewhat distant, such as Tacoma or Bellingham, occasionally voiced hostility, but only Home experienced overt attempts to disrupt and end the colony, and these stemmed largely from national issues for which Home residents were not responsible. Moreover, these actions were confined to legal harrassment through courts and postal rulings and to newspaper harangues; there were no mass actions of people. Regardless of how persecuted colonists might choose to feel, external pressures neither slowed their activities nor killed their experiments. Indeed, it might be suggested that when outside opposition did occur, it tended to unify colonists. Home, which suffered most from outside interference, survived longest and most vigorously, and its growth increased rather than declined during the periods of greatest difficulty.

Return of general prosperity may have hurt the colonies. The rise of communitarianism in the 1890s was in part a response to the severe depression. As conditions improved, the appeal of colonies seems to have decreased. The Puget Sound Co-operative Colony abandoned its communal objectives when a local land boom attracted the more enterprising or speculative members. With improved economic conditions nationally and Yukon gold pouring into the Puget Sound area, construction and commercial opportunities increased. Some of the younger, more enterprising colonists found ample work in surrounding areas. "Equality as a cure for the depression," William McDevitt later concluded, "found itself in the midst of a surrounding territory of already cured depression; the demand for local labor was so intense that it drew out of the colony its most efficient workers. The doctor was turned away because his patient regarded himself as cured before the medico's [*sic*] arrived." [9]

McDevitt might also have concluded that the doctor was turned away because he had brought the wrong medicine. Despite its frequent recurrence and a supply of adherents perennially available, the communitarian ideal has remained outside the mainstream of American reform movements. Religious colonies with clearly stated doctrine, inner discipline based on moral sanctions, and usually a strong leader tend to endure longer than secular colonies. Communitarianism in the 1890s was but a detour on the path of reform. Successful reformers had to address themselves to problems of industrialization, urbanization, and unequal distribution of wealth rather than escape from them. Socialism and labor movements had to meet their capitalist counterparts in their own strongholds, through politics in industrial centers, and not in small remote settlements. Even Edward Bellamy doubted the efficacy of the communitarian ideal he inadvertently promoted, and Eugene V. Debs quickly turned to political participation. As the strength and unity of socialists increased, they created the Socialist party in 1901 and abandoned communitarianism. Likewise, many anarcho-communists tolerated the individualists at Home as harmless and ineffective. Critics who labeled the communitarian movement of the 1890s futile because it was visionary and utopian erred; rather, it was futile because it was an anachronism from an earlier and presumably simpler time.[10]

The communitarian movement failed, not alone because its theories were naïve and impractical, for seemingly naïve and impractical ideas have not always failed. There was something else that the communitarian plans lacked. Too often the communitarian experiments of western Washington consisted of paper plans. But these were only as effective as the men who would put them into operation, and none of the founders had adequate managerial skill, nor did most leaders understand human nature and psychology. Written plans tended to be elaborate and detailed while goals were broad. Governments were minutely organized, but often so inflexible that minor adjustments caused major upheavals. Schemes to reorganize and modify once fixed patterns were often advanced as more practical, workable, or "business-like." But new ways proved no better than the old. Cleavages developed between leaders and followers. Thus Port Angeles witnessed numerous contests for control of the colony, as did

Equality, Burley, and Home. Colonies that boasted of a general assembly learned that this body could easily be swayed by leaders of the moment, could become bogged down in petty matters, and could sometimes provide a theater for uproar and confusion.

Colony leaders tended to oversell their panaceas and attract more recruits than they could accommodate. Not unlike the society they protested, promoters sought people with technical knowledge and skills and willingness to work, even while they publicized colonies as havens for those who had found no place in conventional society. They thereby tended to attract the very persons least needed, while persons who had the desired skills were those least likely to seek sanctuary in a colony. Many colonists lacked essential knowledge and experience. Equality settlers were inept at fishing, and the Burley mill operators wasted time and lumber with mistakes. More than one settler complained of department foremen who knew less than the men in their charge.

Some individuals argued with possible justification that their talents lay in specific fields and would be wasted in common labor. This was true not only of such managers as George Venable Smith, Norman W. Lermond, and Cyrus Field Willard, but of some with skills or trades. Others simply balked at monotonous, unproductive, personal chores. Some settlers were doubtless lazy or indolent; others were elderly, infirm, or too young to work. Yet all these required colony support. And diligent workers complained of those who did not carry a full share of the burden.

The most effective colony leader would be an intelligent manager who combined a sound philosophical basis, businesslike practicality, and the earned confidence of his followers, or he might be an authoritarian who commanded sufficient respect to maintain order and progress. No leader of Washington colonies measured up. Possibly Ed Pelton came the closest, but his departure and early death cut short his contributions. Smith, Lermond, and Willard aspired to play the authoritarian but were not equal to it. Thomas Maloney and his circle rushed into financial involvements that proved harmful. Horr was divisive. Ellis had leadership thrust upon him and was personally well liked, but he was not the practical business head that Burley required. Freeland and Home had arrangements that did not require individual leaders, although George W. Daniels and James W.

Adams were their patriarchs. Home had spokesmen in Allen, Morton, and Fox; each of these men tended to be impractical, and Morton was sometimes an irritant. Dadisman had some prestige because of his financial position but was not a colony leader. Thus, the immediate reasons for colony failure often revolved around the quality of the founders and their plans, and of the membership, including the leaders.

There was also a failure in the basic commitment of the members to their communities. Rosabeth Moss Kanter explored this phenomenon in a recent sociological study of other early utopian experiments in the United States. Comparing nine "successful" or long-lived and twenty-one "unsuccessful" colonies, she concluded that the former were those which most strongly developed a sense of commitment among their members. This was the key, for successful utopias are "held together by commitment rather than coercion, . . . what people do is the same as what they have to do." The "core" of the communal relationship, according to Kanter, rests in a "reciprocal relationship, in which both what is given to the groups and what is received from it are seen by the person as accepting his true nature and as supporting his concept of self." She thus offers six commitment mechanisms as a tool that can measure the success of communes other than those she directly studied.

Each of the colonies in Washington sought to build a sense of *communion* among its people, a feeling that many functions and most facets of life could best be handled and experienced together in group efforts. *Renunciation* of the outside world was practiced to a limited degree, largely because of relatively isolated locations. There were no distinctions of dress or language, or other enforced barriers with the outside world. Despite some free-love practices and rumors of licentiousness, there was little attempt at sexual regulation or the disruption of family ties, which were, if anything, encouraged at all colonies. Hardships existed in the way of life and in starting new experiments, but *sacrifice* was nowhere a basic tenet either upon entrance or in later practices. Likewise, little *investment* was expected beyond the initiation fee. Equality quarreled over the ease with which members were allowed to leave; all colonies permitted nonresident members whose investment and commitment were scant. Nowhere was *mortification* practiced, the process in which a person was forced to reduce his sense of self so as to become more a part of the community. And despite a desire to create a feeling of *transcendence* in most colonies none developed the charismatic leadership, the "institutionalized awe," or the clear-cut ideology that might have lifted members beyond their own concerns to serve the greater purpose of community. Nevertheless, local traditions were built, and many individuals were self-motivated to a high level of community dedication. Over-all, measured in terms of Kanter's study, the western Washington colonies were among those that failed to create the sense of commitment that might have spelled greater success or endurance. [11]

Although the colonies failed, they were not without influence. Contributions of specific colonies to later communities have been noted. If Washington was not socialized by the Brotherhood of the Co-operative Commonwealth or the Co-operative Brotherhood, the colony experience may have influenced later socialist activity in the state. In 1912, only three states gave Socialist presidential candidate Eugene V. Debs a higher percentage than the 12.4 percent of all votes cast in Washington, while his national vote was but 5.9 percent. During the following decade, the Washington Socialist party vote was consistently above the party vote nationally. Several Washington towns elected Socialist officials. Socialist locals continued in the Freeland and Equality areas and even at Home, but few former colonists were prominent in larger political organizations. John Cloak was a Socialist councilman and mayoralty candidate in Bellingham, Herman Culver and David Burgess were leaders in the Socialist party of Washington, and Burgess was also active in the Socialist Labor party. Most Equality socialists who had run for offices during colony days disappeared from active participation. Party activities in western Washington centered around Dr. Hermon Titus of Seattle and Emil Herman of Everett, neither of whom was directly associated with the colonies. Several former Washington colonists became active in socialist politics elsewhere: Sanderson in St. Louis, Lermond in Maine, and Horr in California. McDevitt twice ran for mayor of San Francisco before his expulsion from the Socialist party for accepting a position from the victor. [12]

However, as a recent historian of socialism in the United States has pointed out, party politics do not tell the whole story, for the influence of socialist doctrines was often manifest in other movements and activities. Some influence of the socialist colonies may be found in journalism, the IWW movement, labor, and other reform movements in Washington. The colony press had disappeared long before these influences became apparent; the Home papers continued until 1913, but the Burley *Co-operator*, latest of the others, succumbed in 1906. At times, the *Agitator* of Home promoted IWW activities and William Foster's syndicalism, but most IWW journalism was located in Seattle, Spokane, and other cities. Likewise, ten socialist papers were appearing in the state between 1911 and 1918, most of which had been founded in that decade. The colony press pioneered radical journalism in the Northwest, but there were few direct relationships with later endeavors. [13]

Of those individuals from the colony press who remained active as journalists, the most notable was labor editor Harry Ault. More ubiquitous was George E. Boomer; Equality drew him west, but he left early to edit radical papers in various Washington cities. His quarrels were many and his opinions and press lively. W. H. Kaufman wrote letters and columns promoting direct legislation and he edited the *Pacific Grange Bulletin* for several years. David Burgess, an Arkansas editor before he came west, also turned to writing letters and columns during the 1920s. Kingsmill Commander wrote for Tacoma papers, published a book of poetry extolling flight, and was for many years a proofreader on a Tacoma daily. Jay Fox became a staff member of the Seattle *Union Record*. Yet in the "Checklist of Radical Papers in the State of Washington (1898–1920)" appended to Harvey O'Connor's account of Pacific Northwest radicalism, Boomer, Ault, Fox, and Burgess are the only former colony writers cited among many editors and major contributors of later radical papers. Ethel and DeForest Sanford and William McDevitt continued their writing in the Southwest. [14]

Others maintained interests in various reforms. When he denounced American participation in World War I and Liberty Bond sales in a 1917 Olympia speech, Kaufman was sentenced to five years in prison; the conviction was later reversed. Women from Home, as well as Laura Hall Peters, participated in state campaigns for woman suffrage, and Morton carried on similar efforts in New York City. Max Wardall was widely engaged in municipal reform in Seattle. In education, Anna Falkoff from Home conducted a Seattle school based upon the liberal ideas of Francisco Ferrer, a Spanish reformer.[15]

The small part that former colonists played in the labor movement was dominated by Harry Ault and Jay Fox. Aside from Fox, few colonists became interested in IWW activities; Alexander Horr became an active, sometimes obstreperous labor leader in San Francisco. Although some former colonists were active in radical journalism, in reform movements, in labor, and in politics, they tended to be the same men and women in a few overlapping roles. Moreover, they were active alongside those who came to such interests by routes unrelated to communitarian experiments. Most of their fellows had returned to the larger political parties or to the voiceless majority.[16]

The colonies recruited to the state many persons who became residents and raised families. Liberally inclined in thought, reading habits, and associations before they arrived, they may well have helped give Washington an atmosphere that was hospitable to radical views and activities. If the former colonists did not exercise formidable leadership, they at least allowed others to do so.

A half-century passed, and Washington all but ignored its communitarian past. Those who preached radical doctrines during these years knew or cared little about their predecessors from the turn of the century. Cooperation took the form of farm-marketing practices or joint ownership in such things as lumbering operations. Occasionally a neighborhood formed a partnership to share certain benefits and enhance the quality of life. But the old communitarianism had no place in an industrialized, urban society.

And then in the 1960s, the nation experienced another resurgence of the communitarian ideal. Radicals of the New Left, reformers, the disenchanted, and very often the young sought escape from a culture that seemed complex, alien, bewildering, and stifling. Many flocked to recently established communes in search of a new life style. At the end of 1970, the *New York*

Times estimated conservatively that nearly two thousand communes existed in thirty-four states, some of them along the shores and in the valleys of the Pacific Northwest. The new communitarians doubtless knew little of the people who had come before, even though the "underground" newspaper at the University of Washington inaugurated a series of articles on regional radicalism by describing Equality and Home. [17]

Differences from the cooperative communities of the past were striking, but so were the similarities. The return to a simple life, the isolation and removal from society, the sharing of goods and work, the desire for brotherhood and a meaning of life, the curiosity about exotic sects and beliefs, and above all the self-assurance that this was a better life, perhaps a path to the future—all such characteristics were reminiscent of the earlier colonies. Nor were the problems of group living new. Dissensions occurred in the new utopias, and more than one divided when members quarreled. Occasionally the same suspicion existed between leaders and workers, the same lack of practical skills, and despite pronouncements of freedom and individualism, there was concern that some members could not fit in even here. Former communitarians had worried about the influx of shirkers; a latter-day community pondered how to handle a recluse who "doesn't appear to relate to the work program."[18]

But differences went deeper than terminology. Whereas the earlier communal experiments were based upon what one student calls "politico-economic critiques" of society, those of the 1960s had varied origins but tended to stem from the "psychosocial critique," which "holds that modern society has put people out of touch with others and with their own fundamental nature." Thus, the new communitarians seek "liberating situations that are conducive to intimacy and psychological health." In the 1890s many of those who came to communities were disillusioned because they had tried to work within the system and had felt rebuffed and defeated. Often they were small-town laborers and artisans who had been stung by inequality and deprivation in an economic society that even then was huge and impersonal. The 1960 communities tended to attract persons who had not known economic or social deprivation, and some who had obtained marked success in competitive society. Often they had sensed or observed hardship rather than experiencing it. Where many former enthusiasts were family men, the new ones tended to be young, rootless or rejecting family ties. A Berkeley sociologist expressed alarm that their culture consisted largely of a single age bracket. Most of the new communes had small memberships, and many were located in urban centers and near college campuses. Whereas the interest in obscure sects and poetry had a counterpart in the communities of the past, the drug culture had none. Nor was there a parallel in the concern for international causes, which the earlier colonists tended to ignore. Widely publicized and visible, the communitarians of the 1960s probably encountered greater hostility than their predecessors.[19]

Those who looked to the future from their communes in the 1960s and 1970s could hardly be expected to acknowledge roots from an earlier generation. The old experiments along Puget Sound had passed from existence and were virtually beyond memory. A throwback to earlier days, out of step with the mainstream of radicalism in their own time, of uncertain influence in the later radicalism of Washington, they nevertheless contained in their search for a better society a germ of relevance to all time.

Notes

CHAPTER 1

1. On reform movements and radicalism in the Pacific Northwest, see Dorothy O. Johansen and Charles M. Gates, *Empire of the Columbia*, pp. 344-68, 447-90, 506-12; Harvey O'Connor, *Revolution in Seattle*; John Dos Passos, *Nineteen Nineteen*, in *U.S.A.*, pp. 321-85, 398-402. The story of the Farley toast appears in varying contexts in many writings about Washington politics and radical movements. The earliest reference this writer has found is in Richard L. Neuberger, *Our Promised ,Land*, p. 277. Neuberger, then a highly regarded Oregon journalist and later United States senator, stated that Farley was "supposed to have" used the phrase. O'Connor (p. 1) notes the irony of the remark in relation to the goal of the earlier communitarian efforts in Washington.

2. Arthur E. Bestor, *Backwoods Utopias*, pp. vii-viii, 1-19; Arthur E. Bestor, "Patent Office Models of the Good Society"; Alexander Kent, "Cooperative Communities in the United States," pp. 563-64.

3. Bestor, *Backwoods Utopias*, pp. 20-39, 58-59; Alice Felt Tyler, *Freedom's Ferment*, p. 109.

4. Numerous books have been concerned with these experiments. J. H. Noyes, *History of American Socialisms*, is the pioneer study written by a participant; Charles Nordhoff, *The Communistic Societies of the United States*, is based on visits to many of the colonies discussed; Bestor, *Backwoods Utopias*, deals primarily with New Harmony but provides a thorough narrative and analysis of its predecessors; Tyler, *Freedom's Ferment*, pp. 46-224, offers an intelligent, entertaining discussion of the major groups; Everett Webber, *Escape to Utopia*, is an adequate general account written in a popular vein.

5. Harold U. Faulkner, *Politics, Reform and Expansion, 1890-1900.*

6. The generalizations in this and the following paragraphs are drawn largely from Howard H. Quint, *The Forging of American Socialism*, as well as from the works specifically cited.

7. Stow Persons, ed., *The Cooperative Commonwealth*. The 1965 edition,

published by Harvard University Press, contains a short biography of Grönlund by Persons.

8. Edward Bellamy, *Looking Backward, 2000-1887*; Arthur Ernest Morgan, *Edward Bellamy*. For Bellamy's influence, see John Hope Franklin, "Edward Bellamy and the Nationalist Movement"; and Elizabeth Sadler, "One Book's Influence: Bellamy's 'Looking Backward.' " Figures cited are from Franklin, p. 754.

9. Wayland's autobiography is included in a short biographical sketch by A. W. Ricker in J. A. Wayland, *Leaves of Life*; Howard H. Quint, "Julius A. Wayland, Pioneer Socialist Propagandist," and an expanded version in Quint's *American Socialism*, pp. 175-209; George Milburn, "The Appeal to Reason," is harshly critical and detractory.

10. Merle Curti, *The Growth of American Thought*, pp. 605-32; Vernon Louis Parrington, Jr., *American Dreams*; Gerald N. Grob, *Workers and Utopias*; James Dombrowski, *The Early Days of Christian Socialism in America*.

11. James J. Martin, *Men Against the State*, pp. 4-10; "Anarchism," in William D. P. Bliss and Rudolph M. Binder, eds., *The New Encyclopedia of Social Reform*, pp. 41-51, including Victor S. Yarros, "Individualist or Philosophical Anarchism," pp. 41-45, and C. L. Swartz, "Anarchist Communism," pp. 45-50.

12. Martin, *Men Against the State*, pp. 11-94, 202-73, especially pp. 214-18.

13. A contemporary list and discussion of the renewed interest in communitarian experiments during this period appears in Frederick A. Bushee, "Communistic Societies in the United States." See also Kent, "Cooperative Communities," p. 565, and Ralph Albertson, "A Survey of Mutualistic Communities in America." None of these writers pretends that his list is complete.

14. U.S., Department of the Interior, Census Division, *Abstract of the Eleventh Census, 1890*, pp. 12, 37; Work Projects Administration, Washington Writers' Project, *The New Washington: A Guide to the Evergreen State*, p. 73; Johansen and Gates, *Empire*, pp. 246-52, 305-41, provides a standard account of these developments.

15. Jos. D. Weeks, "Report on Trades Societies in the United States," pp. 14-19; Oscar Osburn Winther, *The Great Northwest*, pp. 393-94, 433; Hamilton Cravens, "A History of the Washington Farmer-Labor Party, 1918-1924," pp. 8-9; Robert E. Wynne, "Reaction to the Chinese in the Pacific Northwest and British Columbia, 1850-1910," pp. 208-9; Harriet Ann Crawford, *The Washington State Grange*, pp. 12-17.

16. Eltweed Pomeroy, "The Direct Legislation Movement and Its Leaders"; Crawford, *Washington Grange*, p. 55; Mary W. Avery, *Washington: A History of the Evergreen State*, pp. 214-15.

17. Johansen and Gates, *Empire*, p. 359; Winther, *Great Northwest*, p. 399; Crawford, *Washington Grange*, pp. 78-80, 101-4; Avery, *Washington*, pp. 215-16; Russell Blankenship, "The Political Thought of John R. Rogers."

18. Crawford, *Washington Grange*, pp. 85, 93-94; Donald L. McMurry, *Coxey's Army*, pp. 214-33, 246-47; Blankenship, "Political Thought of Rogers," p. 5, quotes Puyallup residents as saying there were no more than fifty to seventy-five followers; Sadler, "One Book's Influence," pp. 537, 549.

19. B. F. Heuston, *The Rice Mills of Port Mystery*; Sol. S. Wise, *The Light of Eden*; Blankenship, "Political Thought of Rogers," p. 5; E. L. Robinson, *A Common Sense Cooperative System*.

20. Robert J. Hendricks, *Bethel and Aurora*, pp. 3-116; John E. Simon, "Wilhelm Keil and Communist Colonies"; [William Keil], "From Bethel, Missouri, to Aurora, Oregon: Letters of William Keil, 1855-1870."

21. [Keil], "From Bethel to Aurora," pt. 2, pp. 145-46; Clark Moor Will, "The Burial of Willie Keil"; L. R. Williams, *Our Pacific County*, pp. 61-63.

22. Russell Blankenship, *And There Were Men*, pp. 79-94.

23. Roscoe C. Sheller, *Courage and Water*, pp. 23-27.

24. Lottie Roeder Roth, ed., *History of Whatcom County, Washington*, 1:221-33; Lelah Jackson Edson, *The Fourth Corner*, pp. 204-10.

25. James B. Hedges, "Promotion of Immigration to the Pacific Northwest by the Railroads"; Avery, *Washington*, pp. 263-64.

26. Leonard Arrington, *Great Basin Kingdom*, pp. 354, 383-84; *Industrial Freedom*, 4 February 1889; John Ilmari Kolehamainen, "Harmony Island: A Finnish Utopian Venture in British Columbia"; Albertson, "Mutualistic Communities," pp. 419-21; Kent, "Cooperative Communities," p. 642; Robert V. Hine, *California's Utopian Colonies*; Wilbur S. Shepperson, with John G. Folkes, *Retreat to Nevada*.

27. Zebina Forbush, *The Co-opolitan: A Story of the Co-operative Commonwealth of Idaho*, cited in Parrington, *American Dreams*, pp. 119-21.

CHAPTER 2

1. Winther, *Great Northwest*, pp. 421-23.

2. Seattle *Daily Times*, 12 May 1886, hereafter cited as *Times*. Originated in San Francisco in 1882 as the American counterpart of the Karl Marx Red International, the IWA already was shifting from a socialist to an anarchist philosophy. Founder Burnette G. Haskell was at this time organizing the Kaweah Co-operative Colony in the Sierra foothills of California; Hine, *California's Utopian Colonies*, pp. 78-100, provides an account of Haskell and his Kaweah colony; Ira B. Cross, *A History of the Labor Movement in California*, pp. 156-65; Murray Morgan, *Skid Road*, p. 87; Robert E. Wynne, "Reaction to the Chinese in the Pacific Northwest and British Columbia, 1850-1910," pp. 99, 209. By 1887 there were reportedly 2,000 IWA members in Washington Territory, with "white card" (apprentice) divisions in Seattle, Tacoma, and Olympia, and a well-drilled and active "blue card" membership in Seattle that the *Times* perceived was *"designed as the*

revolutionary forces" [*sic*].

3. Seattle *Post-Intelligencer*, 2 October 1919, hereafter cited as *P-I;* Herbert Hunt and Floyd C. Kaylor, *Washington West of the Cascades*, 3:280.

4. Seattle *Daily Call*, 11, 14 November 1885, 5 March 1886; Morgan, *Skid Road*, pp. 93-94; Clarence B. Bagley, *History of Seattle from the Earliest Settlement to the Present Time*, 1:304; Wynne, "Reaction to the Chinese," p. 215.

5. Kathleen Coventon, "History of the Puget Sound Cooperative Colony," pp. 1, 2; *Daily Call*, 28 September, 6, 15 October, 11, 14 November 1885, 22 February, 1 March 1886; Herbert Hunt, *Tacoma, Its History and Its Builders*, 1:364; W. P. Bonney, *History of Pierce County, Washington*, 1:460; C. H. Hanford, *Seattle and Its Environs, 1852-1924*, 1:199.

6. Unidentified penciled manuscript, *ca.* 1914 or after, in possession of Robert Hitchman, possibly written by George V. Smith; *Daily Call*, 23, 28 October 1885, 4, 6, 9, 26 February 1886.

7. *Times*, 10, 13 May 1886; *Model Commonwealth*, 21 May 1886, hereafter cited as *MC*.

8. *MC*, 21 May 1886.

9. *Times*, 24 May 1886.

10. Coventon, "History of PSCC," pp. 14-16; *MC*, 4 June 1886.

11. Unidentified penciled manuscript in possession of Robert Hitchman; Smith quoted in Coventon, "History of PSCC," pp. 12-14; see also *MC*, 19 November 1886; interview with Mrs. W. B. Smith, 10 August 1967; Chicago *Sunday Telegram*, 30 January 1887; interview with Madge Haynes Nailor, 21 July 1967.

12. Smith quoted in Coventon, "History of PSCC," pp. 13-14; Mrs. Beck's letter in *MC*, 26 August 1886.

13. *MC*, 1, 8 July, 2 September, 11 November 1887; Coventon, "History of PSCC," p. 15.

14. *Puget Sound Cooperative Colony*, pp. 17, 31-32, inside back cover.

15. G. M. Lauridsen, A. A. Smith *et al.*, *The Story of Port Angeles*, photograph opposite p. 49; *MC*, Supplement, 13 May, 22 July 1887.

16. Clallam County, Auditor's Office, Articles of Incorporation of the Puget Sound Cooperative Colony, *Records of Clallam County*, file P, 1887-1902, vol. H, class 9; bylaws in *MC*, 13 May 1887.

17. Other members of the first board were Edward D. McKenley, Laura E. Hall, and Alfred E. Huffman of Seattle; William W. Beck, Francis Hinckley, and Philo W. Gallup of Port Angeles; Louis Williams of Portland, Oregon; and John M. Grant of Tacoma, all stockholders. Most of these persons had recently arrived in the Northwest. McKenley was from San Francisco, Huffman from Rockford, Illinois, Beck from Wyoming, Hinckley from Chicago, and Gallup from Greeley, Colorado; *MC*, 1 July 1887. On Sanderson, see Frederic Heath, ed., *Social Democracy Red Book*, p. 115.

18. *Puget Sound Cooperative Colony*, pp. 2-5, 26-27; *MC*, 27 August 1886, 1 July 1887.

19. Clallam County, Auditor's Office, *Records of Clallam County*, book

E, p. 420, and book 2, class 1, p. 7; Norman R. Smith, "Victory: The Story of Port Angeles. . . ," Port Angeles *Evening News*, 17 August 1950.

20. Abraham Lincoln's signature on the document creating the federal reservation prompted a local legend that the President had selected Port Angeles as the "Second National City." For the Lincoln legend, see William D. Welsh, *A Brief History of Port Angeles*, p. 11, the cover of which is dominated by Lincoln's portrait; and Herbert Heywood, "Lincoln's Federal Townsite." On Victor Smith, see Ivan Doig, "Puget Sound's War Within a War."

21. *MC*, 1 July 1887, lists the arrivals by name, home town, and age. The list does not include departures. *MC*, 7 October 1887.

22. Quoted in Earl Clark, "Peninsula Profile—9: Mrs. Madge Nailor Still in Same House Where She Watched Indians as a Girl"; Mrs. Nailor retold this incident many times, including—and in virtually the same words—to the present writer, 31 July 1967. See also Lucile McDonald, "Eyewitness to Peninsula History," p. 2.

23. Smith interview; *MC*, 23 September 1887; Jack Henson, "Co-Operative Colony of 1887 Failed as an Experiment, But Developed Port Angeles."

24. *MC*, 3 June 1887, quoted in Coventon, "History of PSCC," pp. 18-21.

25. *MC*, 23 September, 7 October 1887; the latter issue sets the sawmill potential at 40,000 feet a day rather than 20,000.

26. Ibid.

27. Ibid., 5 August, 23 September, 2, 7 October 1887.

28. Ibid., 27 May, 5 August 1887. One of these arrivals was Peter Kiernan, whose suit against the colony several years later would result in its dissolution.

29. Ibid., 8, 22 July 1887.

30. The Knoff interview which appeared in "a late number of the *Seattle Weekly Times*" has not been located, nor have any copies of such a weekly at that time. Knoff established a successful printing and engraving business in Seattle and became a prominent citizen of the city. Interestingly, C. H. Hanford makes no mention of Knoff's radical past in his short biography, *Seattle and Environs*, 2:729. Knoff's son Alfred, a boy of five when he lived at the colony, also became a Seattle business executive and a civic and club leader; Bagley, *History of Seattle*, 3:482-83.

31. *MC*, 13 May 1887; the Declaration of Principles was published as a supplement to this issue.

32. The bylaws were published in *MC*, 13 May 1887; ibid., 1, 22 July 1887.

33. Bylaws.

34. *MC*, 9 September 1887.

35. Ibid., 9 September, 22 July 1887.

36. Ibid., 8 July, 16 September 1887; election results were printed in *MC*, 30 September 1887. Perhaps it is significant that Mastick received more local votes than any other candidate but a comparably lower percentage of

the proxies—170 and 57, respectively, for a total of 227 votes; he was fifth on the list of total votes behind Smith, Hinckley, McGill, and Sanderson. This might suggest local dissatisfaction with Smith and the original leadership, even though the incumbents were in the strongest position to control proxy votes.

37. Ibid., 7 October 1887.

38. Ibid., 19 August, 30 September 1887.

39. Ibid., 7 October 1887.

40. Gilbert Pilcher, "An Outline of the History of Clallam County, Washington," p. 7; *MC*, 16 March 1888.

41. Letter of E. B. Mastick, Jr., in *MC*, 16 March 1888.

42. Ibid., 30 March 1888.

43. *P-I*, 2 October 1919; Hunt and Kaylor, *Washington West*, 3:280-82; Nailor interview; *A Co-Operative Plan for Securing Homes and Occupations at Port Angeles, Washington*; justice court docket for Port Angeles precinct for 1888-91, in possession of Clallam County Historical Society, p. 3; early correspondence between the Peters is quoted in Coventon, "History of PSCC," pp. 2, 7; *MC*, 12 October 1888.

44. *MC*, 18 October 1888; Henson, "Co-Operative Colony of 1887," lists the officers elected that fall, six of whom were new to the eleven-man board; *Legislative Manual and Political Directory, State of Washington, 1899. . . ,* p. 110; "Thomas Maloney, City Pioneer Dies in Wreck . . . ," unidentified newspaper clipping in possession of Mrs. Nailor; Florence Malony Bowler to the author, *ca.* 1 March 1969.

45. *Puget Sound Cooperative Colony*, p. 23; for an even more glowing description, see Smith's reply to an inquiry in *MC*, 8 October 1886, printed in Coventon, "History of PSCC," pp. 9-12.

46. *MC*, 2 September 1887.

47. Ibid.

48. Photographs of the colony buildings in the possession of Bert Kellogg; *MC*, 4 November 1887.

49. Declaration of Principles.

50. Jack Henson, "Peninsula Profile—6: William J. Ware Saw Birth of City, Has Part in Area's Colorful History"; Hunt and Kaylor, *Washington West*, 2:494; Lucile McDonald, "In Port Angeles—Jack Henson Is Known as the Scribe," p. 11; *MC*, 4 November 1887; Hunt, *Tacoma*, 1:349; Jack Henson, "Ancient Log Cabin Housed Pioneer County Family"; Jessie C. Ayres, "Old Log Cabin Built in 1888 Is Mt. Angeles Road Landmark"; interview of Mrs. L. D. Stewart by Gilbert Pilcher; *MC*, 16 March 1888.

51. For example, on Jack Henson, F. S. Lewis, and Oscar McLaughlin, see McDonald, "In Port Angeles, Jack Henson"; Jack Henson, "Peninsula Profile—25: Gold Rush, First War, Pioneer Days Seen by Mrs. Troy"; Inez McLaughlin, *We Grew Up Together*, p. 2; *MC*, 1 July 1887. Perhaps the Ohio family met a cool reception, for the Fend name does not appear again in reports on colony affairs.

52. *MC*, 22 July, 5 August 1887.

53. Ibid., 27 August 1886.

54. Ibid., 1 July 1887.

55. Ibid., 22 July 1887.

56. Ibid., 1 July 1887.

57. Nailor interview; Henson, "Peninsula Profile—9"; McLaughlin, *We Grew Up*, pp. 40-42; *MC*, 2 July 1886, 23 September 1887.

58. Declaration of Principles; see also *MC*, 2 July 1886.

59. Thomas W. Prosch, "A Chronological History of Seattle from 1850 to 1897," p. 365; Port Angeles *Clallam County Courier*, 14 February 1896; Mrs. Hall was then Mrs. Charles Peters; Henson, "Peninsula Profile—25."

60. Nailor interview; Smith interview; justice court docket, p. 3; "Co-operative Colony at Port Angeles," notes from a letter from Mrs. L. C. [Lois] Smith to Jessie C. Ayres, 5 November 1953, in possession of Mina Saari; "Mrs. Norman R. Smith Dies in California," unidentified newspaper clipping, dated 15 November 1945, in possession of Wilda MacDonald. Mrs. Smith was eighty-five years old at her death and had resided in California for forty years; Hunt and Kaylor, *Washington West*, 3:282; it was George V. Smith's third marriage. For an example of criticism, see Heywood, "Lincoln's Townsite," p. 172.

61. Edna Coventon, quoted in Coventon, "History of PSCC," p. 25.

62. Heywood, "Lincoln's Townsite," p. 172; Henson, "Co-Operative Colony of 1887"; Smith interview; *MC*, 16 March 1888; "The Second National City," in "Proceedings, Port Angeles Community Study," p. 24; Henson, "Peninsula Profile—6."

63. *MC*, 2 July 1886.

64. Ibid., 1 July, 5, 19 August, 11 November 1887; McLaughlin, *We Grew Up*, pp. 5, 19; Port Angeles *Evening News*, 28 November 1953; Smith interview; Nailor interview; Coventon, "History of PSCC," p. 24.

65. *Daily Call*, 6 February 1886; *MC*, 19 August 1887. See *MC*, 5 August, 11 November 1887 for notes on some representative lectures; Putnam quoted in *MC*, 16 September 1887.

66. *MC*, 7, 28 October 1887; McLaughlin, *We Grew Up*, pp. 43-46, gives a loving memory of the Opera House.

67. *MC*, 19 November 1886, 22 July, 17 October 1887; "Co-operative Colony at Port Angeles"; Smith interview; Henson, "Peninsula Profile—6."

68. *MC*, 8 July 1887.

69. Ibid., 18 November 1887.

70. Lauridsen and Smith, *Port Angeles*, p. 60; *MC*, 18 November 1887.

71. *MC*, 21 May 1886, 1, 8 July, 19 August 1887, and others; Declaration of Principles; *Puget Sound Cooperative Colony*, p. 11; Hunt and Kaylor, *Washington West*, 2:494; Port Angeles *Evening News*, 28 November 1953; Lois Smith, "Auntie Mackay, Pioneer Nurse, Described by Former Resident," unidentified newspaper clipping in the possession of Wilda MacDonald; Smith interview.

72. *MC*, 5 August, 2, 16 September, 4 November 1887; "Father" seems

to have had no connotation other than a mark of respect.

73. Coventon, "History of PSCC," p. 20; *MC*, Supplement, 13 May 1887; *MC*, 5, 19 August 1887.

74. *MC*, 19 August, 2 September, 7 October, 4, 18 November 1887, 18 October 1888; Clallam County, Superior Court, file 871, Peter F. Kiernan vs. The Puget Sound Co-operative Colony; Frederick P. Miletich, "The Historical and Economic Geography of Port Angeles, Washington," p. 44; Port Angeles *Evening News*, 28 November 1953.

75. *MC*, 2 September 1887.

76. Ibid., 22 July, 2 September 1887; see also ibid., 15 July 1887, quoted in Coventon, "History of PSCC," pp. 23-24.

77. E. W. Wright, ed., *Lewis and Dryden's Marine History of the Pacific Northwest* ..., p. 364; Gordon R. Newell, *Ships of the Inland Sea*, pp. 126, 136, 158, 203, 210; Lauridsen and Smith, *Port Angeles*, pp. 55-56, gives slightly different dimensions for the *Angeles*.

78. *MC*, quoted in Lauridsen and Smith, *Port Angeles*, p. 56; this was Central Elementary School; Henson, "Co-Operative Colony of 1887"; McLaughlin, *We Grew Up*, p. 5.

79. Lauridsen and Smith, *Port Angeles*, p. 56; *Puget Sound Cooperative Colony*, pp. 8-12.

80. Bylaws.

81. *Puget Sound Cooperative Colony*, p. 8; pieces of scrip in possession of Wilda MacDonald; [William D. Welsh], "Welsh Rarebits"; justice court docket, pp. 5, 6, 7-11, 19-20, 116; no record of an appeal appears in the dockets of the Clallam County superior court.

82. Quoted in Lauridsen and Smith, *Port Angeles*, p. 52.

83. The meaning of "foreman" is not clearly explained. Possibly there was one foreman for the company, Maloney perhaps; possibly the reference is to the several foremen of different departments and jobs. The singular form of the word is used throughout the statement of the plan; Lauridsen and Smith, *Port Angeles*, p. 54.

84. *MC*, 5 July 1889, quoted in ibid., p. 59.

85. Justice court docket, p. 116; the corner of Front and Laurel streets was the site of the Opera House; Clallam County, Superior Court, file 83, George Fletcher vs. The Puget Sound Co-operative Colony, file 85, Peter Peterson vs. The Puget Sound Co-operative Colony.

86. Bylaws; *MC*, 18 October 1887; Clallam County, Auditor's Office, platbook 1, pp. 1, 3.

87. *MC*, 16 March 1888; Clallam County platbook 1, pp. l, 3.

88. Clallam County platbook 1, pp. 5, 12; *MC*, 3 January 1890; this is not necessarily the first appearance of the advertisement, for few issues from the previous months have been located; locations of these properties can be discerned with some difficulty on the "Map of Port Angeles, Washington," compiled by Norman R. Smith in 1891.

89. Lauridsen and Smith, *Port Angeles*, p. 58; "Secretary's Report," 15 September 1890.

90. "Secretary's Report"; Clallam County, Superior Court file 871.

91. Smith, "Victory," 18 August 1950; from Smith's autobiography and the account of the wage system, this would appear to refer to the fall and winter of 1888-89, but the events that follow occurred the next winter.

92. King County, Superior Court, file 7924, L. T. Haynes . . . vs. Thomas Maloney . . . ; Smith, "Victory," 18 August 1950.

93. Smith, "Victory," 18 August 1950; Haynes faction quotation from King County, Superior Court file 7924.

94. Lauridsen and Smith, *Port Angeles*, p. 57; Miletich, "Geography of Port Angeles," p. 44; Clallam County, Superior Court file 871; Clallam County, Superior Court, file 764, Puget Sound Co-operative Colony vs. V. Whittington; *MC*, now *The Commonwealth*, 3 January 1890; Port Angeles *Evening News*, 28 November 1953; McLaughlin, *We Grew Up*, p. 4; Smith interview; Nailor interview.

95. Lauridsen and Smith, *Port Angeles*, pp. 64-86; Welsh, *Port Angeles*, pp. 12-14; Thomas H. Bradley, *O'Toole's Mallet*, is a record of the auction including an introductory speech by Bradley which is probably the first written history of Port Angeles.

96. Welsh, *Port Angeles*, pp. 14-15.

97. Lauridsen and Smith, *Port Angeles*, p. 61.

98. Clallam County, Superior Court, file 829, May I. Smith, . . . vs. Puget Sound Co-operative Colony. . . .

99. Clallam County, Superior Court file 871.

100. Ibid.; most of this information is from the "First Report of Receiver," filed 8 February 1894.

101. Clallam County, Superior Court file 871.

102. Ibid.

103. Ibid.

104. Henson, "Co-Operative Colony of 1887."

105. Welsh, *Port Angeles*, p. 12.

106. Several members of the Mastick family were active at Home community; Heath, *Red Book*, pp. 115-16; *Clallam County Courier*, 14 February 1896; *Souvenir of the Fifth Legislature of the State of Washington; Industrial Freedom*, 22 May 1900; Hunt and Kaylor, *Washington West*, 2:494-97; *Legislative Manual and Political Directory*, 1899, pp. 110-11; Florence Malony Bowler to author, *ca.* 1 March 1969. On Smith's candidacy, see Charles E. Laughton Papers, N. Soderberg to Laughton, n.d., Lyman E. Wood to Laughton, 10 March 1891, and other letters.

CHAPTER 3

1. Henry Demarest Lloyd Papers, G. E. Pelton to Lloyd, 14 December 1897; photocopies of all items cited from the Lloyd Papers are in University

of Washington Library, Seattle.

2.   Much information in these and the following pages is from G. E. Pelten [sic], "Historical Sketch of B. C. C.," *Industrial Freedom*, Supplement, *ca.* 5 November 1898; *Industrial Freedom* hereafter cited as *IF; Coming Nation*, 29 February 1896, hereafter cited as *CN*; Quint, *American Socialism*, p. 357. Microfilm of *Coming Nation* was loaned by the Wisconsin State Historical Society, Madison.

3.   Photograph in possession of Florence Pelton Clark, Seattle; *Who's Who in New England*, 3:782; *Brief Biographies, Maine*, p. 157; F. A. Winslow, "Naturalist at Age of 2, Norman Lermond Never Quit Nature Study."

4.   Lloyd Papers, Pelton to Lloyd, 25 May 1895.

5.   *IF*, 7 May 1898; *CN*, 14 March 1896; letters from Lermond suggesting the organization appeared in *CN*, 28 December 1895, 21 March 1896; the call with signers' names appears in *CN*, 11, 18 July 1896; N. W. Lermond, "Short History of the Brotherhood."

6.   Lloyd Papers, Norman Wallace Lermond to Lloyd, 25 April 1896.

7.   Ibid.; Chester McArthur Destler, *Henry Demarest Lloyd and the Empire of Reform*, p. 381; Caro Lloyd, *Henry Demarest Lloyd, 1847-1903*, 2:59-60.

8.   *CN*, 1 August, 10 October 1896.

9.   In ibid., 25 April 1896. A copy of the constitution is in the Harry E. B. Ault Manuscripts, University of Washington Library, Seattle; hereafter cited as Ault MSS.

10.   The constitution as proposed provided for only seven officers and seven departments, with the industrial and exchange departments one; *CN*, 12 September 1896. An amendment voted upon simultaneously with the constitution created the documents described here; *CN*, 10 October 1896.

11.   *IF*, 25 June 1898.

12.   Lloyd Papers, Lermond to Lloyd, 21 September 1896; *CN*, 10 October 1896. On Parsons, see Arthur Mann, "Frank Parsons: The Professor as Crusader," or a slightly modified version in Mann's *Yankee Reformers in the Urban Age*, pp. 126-44.

13.   Destler, *Lloyd*, pp. 281-83; Lloyd, *Lloyd*, 2:59-60; Lloyd Papers, Lermond to Lloyd, 25 April, 16 July 1896, 26 November 1897, Frank Parsons to Lloyd, 12 December 1896; *CN*, 23 January 1897, 11 February 1899; Joseph R. Buchanan, *The Story of a Labor Agitator*, pp. 47, 259; *IF*, 18 February, 18 March 1899.

14.   *CN*, 17 October, 5 December 1896, 23 January, 6 February, 10 April 1897, 2 February 1898; *IF*, 14 May 1898; on Taylor, see B. O. Flower, *Progressive Men, Women, and Movements of the Past Twenty-Five Years*, p. 68; on Miss Mason, see William McDevitt, "Un-lost Horizon: Shangri-La on Puget Sound" (September-October 1950), p. 9; on White, see *CN*, 18 April 1896.

15.   Ray Ginger, *The Bending Cross*, pp. 72-73, 191-93; McAlister Coleman, *Eugene V. Debs*, pp. 166-70; Eugene V. Debs, "How I Became a Socialist"; Lloyd Papers, Lermond to Lloyd, 25 April 1896; Ira Kipnis, *The*

American Socialist Movement, 1897-1912, p. 50; *CN*, 23 January 1897. Ginger implies that Debs never accepted the post of organizer, but his name appears as such in the printed copy of the constitution in the Ault MSS and in *CN*.

16. Reports of the convention, including Debs's and Parsons' speeches, are given in *CN*, 3 July 1897; Quint, *American Socialism*, pp. 288-94; Kipnis, *Socialist Movement*, pp. 50-54; Ginger, *Bending Cross*, p. 195; Bernard J. Brommel, "Debs's Cooperative Commonwealth Plan for Workers." Statements of principles and constitutions appear in *CN*, 17 July 1897, and *Social Democrat*, 1 July 1897. For contemporary comment, see Ray S. Baker, "The Debs Co-operative Commonwealth." Nathan Fine, *Labor and Farmer Parties in the United States*, p. 190; H. Wayne Morgan, *Eugene V. Debs*, p. 18.

17. *CN*, 17 July 1897, 29 January 1898; New Whatcom *Reveille*, 9 December 1897; *IF*, 7 May 1898; Debs as a hero is evident from numerous references in *IF*, and from my interview with Florence Pelton Clark, 20 January 1966. The SDA convention is recounted in Quint, *American Socialism*, pp. 310-16.

18. H. W. Halladay, "Equality Colony"; Ault MSS, "You Can't Change Human Nature"; "The Social Democracy of America," contains references by several newspapers to Washington as if it were the chosen state.

19. The advantages of Washington are noted occasionally in *CN* during the fall of 1897; for example, 7 August 1897; Lloyd Papers, Lermond to Lloyd, 31 August 1897; Baker mentions Rogers in "Debs Co-operative Commonwealth"; local unions suggesting sites are listed in *CN*, 25 September 1897; Pelton, "Historical Sketch."

20. Clark interview, 11 February 1966.

21. Pelton, "Historical Sketch"; E. L. Robinson, *A Common Sense Co-operative System*; the Buckley colony is described in *CN*, 4, 25 September, 30 October 1897.

22. Skagit County, Auditor's Office, Land Contract 27357, Deed Records, book 3, pp. 592-94; Pelton, "Historical Sketch"; warranty deed, 30 December 1897, in Skagit County Abstract and Trust Company, Abstract of Title 2393, p. 31, in possession of Mr. and Mrs. R. E. Peterson; Skagit County, Auditor's Office, Trust Deed 27755, Deed Records, book 35, pp. 150-52.

23. McDevitt, "Un-lost Horizon" (March-April 1950), pp. 6, 7; Skagit County, Auditor's Office, Agreement 27633, Leases and Agreements, book 3, pp. 312-14; Ault MSS, "The Hatchery" and "The Gardener"; Clark interviews, 20, 26 January 1966; Skagit County, Auditor's Office, Trust Deed 28475, Deed Records, book 35, pp. 383-85; *IF*, 14 May 1898; deed, 1 June 1898, in Abstract of Title 2393, pp. 53, 77.

24. Halladay, "Equality Colony"; *CN*, 11 December 1897; Edward Bellamy, *Equality*; William McDevitt, whose recollections are not always reliable, wrote a half-century later that the colonists had asked Bellamy to name the colony and that the author had suggested the title of his recent book—McDevitt, "Un-lost Horizon" (March-April 1950), p. 6; *IF*, 12

November 1898, 1 November 1901; *Young Socialist*, November 1899, p. 6; hereafter cited as *YS*; *Reveille*, 15 December 1897, listed the members thus: "E. F. Nolan, recently of Alabama, is president of the colony. Z. S. Ferris, late of California, is secretary, and G. E. Pelton, who was the man who selected this site and brought the colony here, is general agent. Other members of the colony are: H. R. Horton of Iowa, John Helm, of Montana; Alexander Pugh, of Missouri; Mr. Blakely, of Kitsap County; Mr. Dunckel, Carrie E. Lewis [*sic*], C. Sinnot and A. Lewis, of Edison; H. Halliday [*sic*], Mr. Weston, Mr. DeWolf, Mr. Johnson, Mr. Peak, H. Hand, Mr. Gifford and Mr. Calvenger [*sic*, doubtless B. F. Clevenger]." A month earlier, 14 November, Pelton had listed the members on hand as: C. E. Lewis, A. R. Lewis, of Washington; Z. C. Ferris, E. F. Nolan, of California; Alexander Pugh, Missouri; Ernest Marquart, Illinois; Manley Dunckel, South Dakota; John Helme, Montana; C. F. DeWolfe, Oregon; H. J. Hand, Idaho; G. E. Pelton, Maine; C. Sinnott, Washington; H. R. Horton, Nebraska; H. W. Halladay, Kansas. J. E. Peek of Oregon and L. L. Gifford of Colorado were said to be only a few days out and traveling together by teams; *CN*, 11 December 1897. These men, with several wives and children, and despite discrepancies in spelling and home states, may be considered the original "pioneers" of Equality.

25. *CN*, 30 November, 4, 11 December 1897; Lloyd Papers, Pelton to Lloyd, 14 December 1897; Halladay, "Equality Colony."

26. Oliver P. Darr, "Equality To-day," *IF*, Supplement, *ca.* 5 November 1898; Lloyd Papers, Lermond to Lloyd, 26 November 1897, Pelton to Lloyd, 14 December 1897; George W. Quimby to H. W. Halladay, 5 December 1897, and R. B. Bow to B. F. Clevenger, 24 December 1897, Freeland Colony, Vertical File 72, University of Washington Library; hereafter cited as Freeland File; numerous issues of *CN* for the winter of 1897-98; *Reveille*, 15 December 1897.

27. Clark interviews, 20 January, 11 February, 21 March 1966; *CN*, 19 March 1898. The "train" may have been only a special car or reduced group rates. Railroad companies were engaged in rate wars in their rivalry to carry passengers to new western settlements and the Yukon gold fields; BCC members had been advised that if they joined forces in their migration, special group rates would be available. See a letter from F. D. Festner in *CN*, 27 November 1897.

28. Equality colonists' views toward the war are expressed occasionally throughout 1898 in *IF*; see also Ault MSS, "Equality." Their comments on the Alaska gold rush occasionally appear in *IF*; see also Ault MSS, "You Can't Change Human Nature."

29. W. C. B. Randolph, "The Future of the Movement," *IF*, Supplement, *ca.* 5 November 1898; McDevitt, "Un-lost Horizon" (July-August 1950), p. 7; interview with Rita Savage Malsbary, 3 December 1965, and Clark interview, 11 February 1966, referred respectively to their grandmother and mother.

30. *IF*, 7 May 1898; Clark interview, 20 January 1966; letters appearing in *IF* from Herman Studer, Kansas, 21 May 1898, J. S. Powers, Denison,

Texas, 25 June 1898, and Isaac H. Keves, Oregon, 25 June 1898.

31. *CN*, 26 February 1898; Mount Vernon *Argus*, 19 May 1899; hereafter cited as *Argus*; Ault MSS, "Equality" and "The Preacher"; an agreement in Freeland File refers to the building as the "Junior order hall"; interview with Mrs. Clinton D. Halladay, 18 February 1968; *CN*, 29 January, 11, 18 December 1897, 29 January, 19 February, 23 April 1898.

32. *IF*, 7 May, 10 June, 30 July, 31 December 1898; Lloyd Papers, Lermond to Lloyd, 26 November 1897; *CN*, 20 November 1897, has a detailed description of these "exchange checks," and later issues tell of their purchase by BCC members; *Searchlight* (September-October 1951), p. 10, has a picture of the scrip.

33. *IF*, 7, 14, 21 May 1898; McDevitt, "Un-lost Horizon" (March-April 1951), p. 7.

34. Ault MSS, "General Headquarters"; Halladay, "Equality Colony"; Clark interview, 20 January 1966; interview with Catherine Pulsipher, 23 April 1966; Freeland File, H. W. Halladay *et al.* to trustees of the BCC, 15 April 1898; McDevitt, "Un-lost Horizon" (September-October 1950), p. 9, (March-April 1951), p. 7; *IF*, 14 May 1898, discusses the essential differences between persons at Edison, Equality, and the Lewis tract; see also Bige Eddy, in *IF*, 7 May 1898; *IF*, 21 May 1898.

35. *CN*, 23 April 1898; Lloyd Papers, Lermond to Lloyd, 25 April 1896; McDevitt, "Un-lost Horizon" (September-October 1950), p. 9; Good Friday of 1898 fell on 6 April; the date of this meeting is unknown, but it probably was in the early part of April; Freeland File, H. W. Halladay *et al.* to trustees of the BCC, 5 April 1898—a petition including a resolution unanimously passed at an assembly of fifty Equality members on that same date. The relation in time between this meeting and the previously described joint meeting is not clear; obviously, if it followed the general meeting, the Good Friday allusion is a fabrication; Halladay, "Equality Colony"; *IF*, 25 June 1898.

36. Letters of H. W. Halladay, Dennis McCoy, Chas. H. Swigart, Wm. McDevitt, in *IF*, 9 July 1898.

37. Letters of Candee and J. R. Fox in *IF*, 9 July 1898; Freeland File, letter of unidentified person to Lermond, 12 July 1898.

38. *IF*, 25 June 1898; *CN*, 3 October 1898.

39. *IF*, 6 August, 24 September 1898; William Alfred Hinds, *American Communities and Co-operative Colonies* (1908 ed.), p. 533; McDevitt, "Un-lost Horizon" (September-October 1950), p. 10; *CN*, 3 October 1898; Clark interview, 20 January 1966.

40. Quoted in Kent, "Cooperative Communities," p. 622; *IF*, 24 September, 24 December 1898, 7 January 1899.

41. *Who's Who in New England*, pp. 782-83; Winslow, "Naturalist at 2"; Dorothy M. Burnham to the author, 1 April 1966; "Famed Shell Collection Acquired by College"; Albert Whitmore to the author, 23 March 1966; Ellis Spear to the author, 1 February 1966.

42. McDevitt, "Un-lost Horizon" (September-October 1950), p. 10; *YS*,

February 1900; her resignation, dated 10 October 1898, is in Freeland File; *Times*, 2 February 1901; *IF*, 10, 24 September, 15, 29 October 1898, 1 April 1899, 27 November 1900 *passim*; *Argus*, 2 October 1903; *Catalogue for 1901-1902 and Announcements for 1902-03 of the University of Washington*; Robert de Roos, "An Interview with William McDevitt, LL. M."; Richard Donovan, "Life with San Francisco: McDevitt and the Enormous Room"; Lucy Robins Lang, *Tomorrow Is Beautiful*, p. 44; San Francisco *Chronicle*, 10 June 1959.

43. *IF*, 10, 24 September, 1, 22 October, 24 December 1898, 14 January, 18 February 1899.

44. Ault MSS, "General Headquarters"; Halladay, "Equality Colony." No records of incorporation for either the BCC or Equality Colony have been found in the Skagit County auditor's office, nor could they be found in the office of the Secretary of State, Olympia. Records of the superior court of Skagit County refer to the BCC as an "unincorporated association." Skagit County, Superior Court, file 4823, R. H. Young . . . vs. H. W. Halladay . . . ; Freeland File, Equality Colony letterhead on letter dated 8 October 1899 and ballots; *IF*, 10 September 1898 *passim*.

45. *IF*, 25 June, 3 September 1898, 22 April 1899.

46. Ibid., 22 October 1898; ibid., Supplement, *ca*. 5 November 1898. The story of Harmony Colony unfolds from scattered items in the following newspapers: *IF*, 1 October 1898-11 March 1899; Chehalis *People's Advocate*, 1 October 1897, 22 April 1898-14 October 1899; Chehalis *Bee-Nugget*, 6 January-25 August 1899. A reprint of the prospectus, "About Harmony Colony," appeared in *People's Advocate*, 17 February 1899; Lewis County, Auditor's Office, Harmony Cooperative Association to the Public, file 12461, Miscellaneous Records 4, p. 410; Harry Swofford to the author, 11 March 1969. For a more detailed account of Harmony, see Charles P. LeWarne, "Communitarian Experiments in Western Washington, 1885-1915," pp. 271-79.

47. *IF*, 18 June, 3 September 1898; see also 25 June, 2 July 1898; A. C. Whiteside, "Among the Socialists at Edison."

48. In the 1900 and 1902 general elections, Skagit County gave Socialist candidates just under 5 percent of the total votes. In Samish precinct where Equality is located, the percentage fell from approximately 18 to 13 percent. Moreover, at least two-thirds of the county's Socialist vote came from outside Samish precinct from voters who were probably little affected by the colonists. Among all candidates of the two Socialist parties on the ballots in 1900, 1902, and 1904, only seven were or had been members of Equality. Thus, besides their failure to capture Washington for socialism, the Equality colonists were politically ineffective in other respects. Official returns in *Argus*, 16, 23 November 1900, 21 November 1902. For a different assessment of the political effectiveness of Equality and other colonies, see Paul B. Bushue, "Dr. Hermon F. Titus and Socialism in Washington State," for example, p. 19. Quotation from Halladay, "Equality Colony."

49. Darr, "Equality To-day"; *P-I*, 18 March 1898; *IF*, 6 May, 11 June

1898, 1 November 1901; "Equality Colony"; Ault MSS, "Equality Colony" and "The General Assembly"; McDevitt, "Un-lost Horizon" (July-August 1950), p. 9.

50. Ault MSS, "The General Assembly"; tape-recorded interview with Inza Barry by June Larrick, 23 February 1966; Skagit County, Superior Court, file 4823, "Application for the Appointment of a Receiver."

51. [Bige Eddy], "Musings of a Mossback," 27 May 1899; Clark interview, 11 February 1966; Ault MSS, "The Pioneer."

52. *CN*, 5 June, 3 July, 21 August 1897, 5, 25 March 1898; *IF*, 14 May 1898, 3 June 1899; bylaws, *IF*, 25 June 1898; Clark interview, 20 January 1966; Freeland File contains twenty-four completed membership forms, differing slightly from one another and having different dates; *Reveille*, 11 March 1899; *Argus*, 17 March 1899.

53. *P-I*, 18 March 1898; *IF*, 14 May, 16 July 1898; Darr, "Equality To-day"; Kent, "Cooperative Communities," p. 618; Hinds, *American Communities* (1902 ed.), p. 398; letter from A. A. Wardall in *Co-operator*, December 1903, p. 12.

54. *IF*, 14 May 1898; Catherine Pulsipher, "Do You Remember Equality Colony?" poem appearing in the column, "Skagit—Sonnets and Satire," in a Mount Vernon newspaper, late 1963 or 1964, clipping in possession of Emma Herz Peterson.

55. "Un-lost Horizon" (May-June 1950), pp. 7, 9; Malsbary interview; interview with Gladys Ault Gray, 1 April 1966.

56. *CN*, 2, 9 October, 27 November 1897; Malsbary interview; Halladay interview, 4 December 1965; *IF*, 2 July 1898; interviews with Mr. and Mrs. Sam L. Finfrock, 25, 29 March 1966; Ault MSS, "Equality"; interview with Albert E. Lieseke, 20 March 1966; interview with Ella Lieseke Merlich, 1 July 1968.

57. *IF*, 7, 14 May 1898, 28 January, 20 May 1899; Whiteside, "Among the Socialists"; Walter O. Griggs in *IF*, 20 May 1899; the neighbor quoted in Worth W. Caldwell, "The Equality Colony," p. 29; McDevitt, "Un-lost Horizon" (July-August 1950), p. 7.

58. *IF*, 24 September 1898; letter of William Lieseke, 10 April 1924, quoted in Ernest S. Wooster, *Communities of the Past and Present*, p. 48.

59. Clark interview, 11 February 1966; Ault MSS, "The Pioneer"; Albert Lieseke interview; Pulsipher interview; *Reveille*, 3 December 1902, 6 December 1905.

60. *IF*, 4, 18, 25 February, 11 March 1899.

61. Ibid., 20 May 1899.

62. See an early prospectus quoted in Lermond, "Short History"; *CN*, 7 August 1897.

63. *CN*, 4 September, 18, 25 December 1897.

64. *IF*, 14 May 1897, 30 July, 6 August 1898, 27 November 1900; Hinds, *American Communities* (1908 ed.), p. 532, quoting *IF* of an unspecified date.

65. McDevitt, "Un-lost Horizon" (July-August 1950), p. 3; see also

bylaws; Freeland File, copies of five labor contracts, dated 1905; Worth Wilson Caldwell, "Rise and Fall of the Equality Colony, Stronghold of Power, Then Satan's Nest . . . "; Caldwell, "Equality Colony," p. 28.

66. *IF*, 25 June 1898 *passim*.

67. Ibid., 21 May 1898.

68. Bylaws; *IF*, 14, 21, 27 May 1898, 4 February, 4 March 1899, 1 November 1901.

69. Pelton's comment in *CN*, 20 October 1897; *IF*, 4 February 1899 *passim*; *Argus*, 14 September 1900, 2 September 1904; Clark interviews, 20 January, 11 February 1966; *Argus*, 21 July 1899.

70. Albertson, "Mutualistic Communities."

71. *IF*, 7 May 1898; Darr, "Equality To-day."

72. *IF*, 7, 14 May 1898; Darr, "Equality To-day"; letter from W. J. Spillman, in *IF*, 11 June 1898; *Argus*, 14 October 1898.

73. Emma Herz Peterson interview, 28 November 1965; Mrs. R. E. Peterson interview, 23 April 1966; *IF*, 25 June 1898, 11 November 1901.

74. Ault MSS, "The Gardener"; *IF*, 1 November 1901; Caldwell, "Equality Colony," p. 28.

75. Ault MSS, "The Gardener"; on Swigart, see John William Leonard, ed., *Who's Who in Engineering*, p. 2041; Darr, "Equality To-day"; *IF*, 1 November 1901; Clark interview, 11 February 1966; [Eddy], "Musings of a Mossback," 27 May 1899, refers to Lewis' "exclusive" imagination.

76. "Prospectus," *IF*, 16 July 1898; Darr, "Equality To-day"; *IF*, 13 August 1898; Caldwell, "Equality Colony," p. 28; *Argus*, 9 February 1906; *Reveille*, 8 February 1906.

77. Daughters of the American Revolution of the State of Washington, "Family Records and Reminiscences of Washington Pioneers," 1:202-3; Lucile McDonald, "Early Life Was Tough on the Skagit," pp. 2-3; George Savage's diary (actually reminiscences) quoted in Catherine Savage Pulsipher, "Notes on the Equality Colony at Bow, Washington"; *IF*, 21 May, 9 September 1898; Darr, "Equality To-day"; "Prospectus," in *IF*, 16 July 1898; Pulsipher interview.

78. *IF*, 6 August 1898-4 March 1899, 1 November 1901; *Argus*, 23 September 1898, 5 May 1899; Freeland File, letter of Dave Hammack to A. K. Hanson, 15 January 1906, requests return of mill machinery borrowed by D. H. Barry "several years ago"; "Plat of Equality Colony Townsite, May, 1899," *IF*, 17 June 1899; F. L. Horning, "A Hearty Welcome," p. 14.

79. *IF*, 13 May 1899; Freeland File, agreements with Morrison and Wright, with Kasch and Hewitt, and with T. J. Oakes; *Reveille*, 20 October 1904. Lumber production continued in the region. A Marysville firm operated a contemporary mill at Blanchard, bringing logs through colony property. Later, near the colony mill site, the Bloedel-Donovan Company built and operated a mill known, appropriately, as the Colony Mill; Kramer A. Adams, *Logging Railroads of the West*, p. 149; R. E. Peterson interview.

80. Freeland File, bill of sale for the *Progress*; [Eddy], "Musings of a Mossback," 27 May 1899; *IF*, 7, 14 May, 2, 30 July, 6 August 1898; Ault

MSS, "The Captain"; interview with John W. Savage, 9 February 1966; the cannery hopes are mentioned in Whiteside, "Among the Socialists," and elsewhere.

81. Quotation from *IF*, 30 July 1898; reply mentioned in *IF*, 6 August 1898; Ault MSS, "The Captain"; *IF*, 1 November 1901.

82. Darr, "Equality To-day"; *IF*, 7 May 1898, 25 February 1899, 1 November 1901. Sixty-five years later, Mrs. Clinton D. Halladay still owned several pieces of this furniture, plain, well-built, and durable.

83. Joseph Adams, "What Have You Found in Equality Colony?"; *IF*, 13 August 1898, 1, 22 April 1899, 1 November 1901.

84. June Burn, "Puget Soundings: A Strange Chapter in Puget Sound History"; Clark interview, 20 January 1966; Caldwell, "Rise and Fall." A reporter who interviewed former colonists, Caldwell estimated that colony members lived for about one-third the cost of persons in neighboring towns. *IF*, 7 May, 13 August 1898, 18 February 1899, 1 November 1901.

85. *IF*, 4 March 1899, 27 November 1900.

86. "Equality Colony," p. 17; *CN*, 7 August 1897.

87. *IF*, 3 May 1898, 15 April 1899, 1 November 1901; Halladay, "Equality Colony"; *CN*, 5 March 1898; *Argus*, 9 September 1898. In 1901 the colony received $1,100 from the Seattle and Montana Railroad Company for two strips of land through the property; Skagit County, Superior Court, file 3802, Seattle and Montana Railroad Company, Petitioner, vs. Myron W. Reed . . . Respondents.

88. *CN*, 28 December 1895; *Reveille*, 24 June 1906; Lloyd Papers, Lermond to Lloyd, 26 November 1897, Pelton to Lloyd, 14 December 1897; petition in Freeland File; Ault MSS, "The Preacher."

89. *IF*, 7, 27 May, 14 July, 17 September 1898, 1 November 1901; Ault MSS, "Equality"; Freeland File, agreement with S. M. Butler, 15 April 1898; McDevitt, "Un-lost Horizon" (September-October 1950), pp. 9-10.

90. McDevitt, "Un-lost Horizon" (September-October 1950), p. 9; Marvin Sanford, "The Story of Freeland," p. 7; *IF*, 31 December 1898, 1 November 1901.

91. McDevitt, "Un-lost Horizon" (July-August 1950), p. 8; *Reveille*, 26 October 1899; on Boomer, see Everett *Commonwealth*, 24 July 1913, and Lauridsen and Smith, *Port Angeles*, pp. 251-52; Eddy's column ran in *IF*, 31 December 1898-17 June 1899; *CN*, 23 April 1898; *IF*, 22 October 1898; on Kaufman, see Crawford, *Washington Grange*, pp. 146, 164, 216, 332.

92. Ault MSS; on the significance of Ault, see Robert L. Friedheim, *The Seattle General Strike*, especially pp. 47, 51, 52, and obituaries in the *P-I* and the *Times*, 6 January 1961. See also Mary Joan O'Connell, "The Seattle Union Record, 1918-1928: A Pioneer Labor Daily."

93. *IF*, 18 February, 22 April, 27 May 1899; *YS*, November 1899, p. 3; Ault MSS, "Lewiston."

94. *Reveille*, 30 April, 1, 6 May 1902; Sanford, "Story of Freeland," p. 7; O'Connor, *Revolution in Seattle*, p. 287, states that *Industrial Freedom* became a monthly after February 1901 until it ceased publication in

December 1902. *Whidby Islander*, 15 December 1902.

95. Darr, "Equality To-day"; Clark interview, 24 March 1966; Gray interview; Ault MSS; photographs in possession of the Seattle Museum of History and Industry and Mrs. Gray; *IF*, 7, 14, 21 May 1898; Pulsipher interview; letter of Alfred C. Eastman in *IF*, 9 July 1898.

96. Interview with Frank Hoehn, 5 November 1966; *IF*, 1 November 1901; Sarah Ward Temple to A. McDonald, 10 April 1899, in *IF*, 3 June 1899.

97. Darr, "Equality To-day"; *IF*, 7, 14, 21, 28 May, 23 July 1898, 4 February, 13 May 1899; Hoehn interview; *P-I*, 14 May 1898; Clark interview, 20 January 1966. .

98. *IF*, 21 May, 6 August 1898, 18 March, 3, 24 June 1899; Clark interview, 20 January 1966; Kent, "Cooperative Communities," p. 618.

99. Adams, "What Have You Found?"; *IF*, 9 July, 13 August 1898, 14 January 1899, 1 November 1901; interview with Mrs. Albert Anderson, 21 November 1965; Darr, "Equality To-day."

100. *IF*, 14, 28 January, 25 February 1899; *YS*, December 1899, p. 7; Darr, "Equality To-day"; photographs in possession of the Seattle Museum of History and Industry and Emma Peterson; Albert Lieseke interview.

101. *IF*, 14 May 1898; Ault MSS, "General Headquarters"; Adams, "What Have You Found?"

102. *IF*, 15 April 1899, 1 November 1901; Adams, "What Have You Found?"; Whiteside, "Among the Socialists."

103. Caldwell, "Rise and Fall," and "Equality Colony," p. 27; *IF*, 7, 14 May, 24 September 1898, 4, 25 February 1899.

104. McDevitt, "Un-lost Horizon" (July-August 1950), p. 8; Harry Ault, "The Colony Kids," *YS*, May 1900, p. 2.

105. *IF*, 7, 28 May, 11 June 1898, 25 February 1899; Malsbary interview; *Argus*, 8 December 1899 *passim*; Burn, "Puget Soundings," p. 7.

106. *IF*, 28 May, 9, 16 July, 6 August 1898; Darr, "Equality To-day"; Clark interview, 11 February 1966; Gray interview.

107. *IF*, 24 September, 1, 8 October 1898, 28 January 1899; Darr, "Equality To-day"; Clark interview, 24 March 1966; Gray interview; Albert Lieseke interview; interview with Inza Joslyn Barry, 23 February 1966; *Argus*, 24 November 1905.

108. *IF*, 7 January 1899; Gray interview was similar to other attitudes expressed; Malsbary interview; Savage interview, 9 February 1966; Clark interview, 24 March 1966; *YS*, February 1900, p. 5, April 1900, p. 8.

109. Savage interview, 9 February 1966; Clark interview, 24 March 1966; Gray interview; Pulsipher interview; Ault MSS, "The Hatchery."

110. *YS*, December 1899, p. 3, April 1900, p. 7; *IF*, 28 May, 4 June, 6 August 1898.

111. *YS*, November 1899, p. 4, February 1900, p. 5, April 1900, p. 6; Ault, "The Colony Kids."

112. Ault MSS, "The Quartette," and the dance program; Adams, "What Have You Found?"; Malsbary interview; Clark interview, 11 February 1966;

IF, 7 May, 11 June 1898, 27 May 1899; *Argus*, 11 August 1899; [Eddy], "Musings of a Mossback," 27 May 1899.

113. *IF*, 3 September 1898, 27 May 1899; *YS*, April 1900, p. 6; Adams, "What Have You Found?"; [Eddy], "Musings of a Mossback," 27 May 1899; Ault MSS, "The Quartette"; Clark interview, 11 February 1966.

114. Ault MSS, "The Quartette."

115. *IF*, 17 December 1898, 4, 18 February 1899; Clark interview, 11 February 1966.

116. *YS*, April 1900, p. 2. In Ault MSS is a penciled memorandum, "Walk to Bellingham to hear Bryan"; *Argus*, 6 April 1900; *Reveille*, 5, 26 October 1899, 14, 28 September, 12 October 1902, 23 June 1905.

117. Ault MSS, "The Hatchery"; *IF*, 7 May 1898, 4, 18 February, 20 May 1899; Raymer's later role confirmed by owner of Raymer's Old Book Store, Seattle, 29 November 1965.

118. Gray interview; *IF*, 3 September 1898; Clark interview, 11 February 1966; McDevitt, "Un-lost Horizon" (January-February 1951), p. 5.

119. *YS*, November 1899, p. 6; *IF*, 29 April, 20 May 1899.

120. *IF*, 10 December 1898; Clark interview, 11 February 1966.

121. Clark interviews, 11 February, 24 March 1966; Gray interview; R. E. Peterson interview; Skagit County, Auditor's Office, Register of Deaths; *YS*, April 1900, p. 6; Hoehn interview, 5 November 1966; *Argus*, 16 December 1898, 17 November 1899; *IF*, 14 May 1898, 20 May 1899.

122. Pulsipher, "Notes on Equality"; Clark interview, 11 February 1966; *IF*, 18, 25 March, 3 June 1899; Darr, "Equality To-day"; Savage interview, 9 February 1966.

123. Lloyd Papers, Lermond to Lloyd, 21 September 1896; Lermond, "Short History," p. 2.

124. *IF*, 7 May 1898.

125. Adams, "What Have You Found?"; see also *IF*, 4 February 1899 *passim*; A. K. Hanson, quoted in Hinds, *American Communities* (1902 ed.), p. 397; "Equality Colony," p. 17; Helen L. Young, "A Western Utopia."

126. *IF*, 4 March, 25 June, 16, 23 July, 6 August 1898; Clark interview, 20 January 1966; Adams, "What Have You Found?"; Barry interview; Hoehn interview; Gray interview; Caldwell, "Rise and Fall"; colony official quoted in Hinds, *American Communities* (1902 ed.), p. 397. The author has found no indication of Roman Catholic members.

127. *IF*, 1 November 1901. There were discrepancies in these figures; that same year the colony reported assets of $75,000 with liabilities of $1,000. See Hinds, *American Communities* (1908 ed.), pp. 533-34.

128. *Reveille*, 1 May 1902; letter of E. B. Ault with editorial comment, ibid., 6 May 1902; Ault's later observations in Ault MSS, "General Headquarters."

129. Wardall's comments in *Co-operator*, December 1903, p. 12; this is the first mention of a flour mill or cheese factory; Freeland File, letter dated 22 June 1904.

130. Freeland File contains minutes of various meetings of the general

assembly during 1905 and 1906. Freeland Colony on Whidbey Island had been established a few years earlier. See Theodor Hertzka, *Freeland*.

131. Hertzka, *Freeland*, p. xxi; on Hertzka's influence, William D. P. Bliss and Rudolph M. Binder, eds., *The New Encyclopedia of Social Reform* . . . , p. 571.

132. Hertzka, *Freeland*, pp. 96-97, 137.

133. [Alexander Horr] , "The Freeland Movement," pages unnumbered, a thirteen-page introduction to the 1904 United States edition of Ransom's translation of Hertzka's *Freiland vereines*. This introduction was also issued as the September 1904 issue of *Freeland* magazine, with Alexander Horr as author; *CN*, 11 January, 12 September 1896.

134. Horr's BCC application blank in Freeland File; Lang, *Tomorrow Is Beautiful*, p. 288; Emma Goldman, *Living My Life*, pp. 349-50, 516; *Discontent*, 11 December 1901; [Horr], "The Freeland Movement"; Mc-Devitt, "Un-lost Horizon" (March-April 1951), p. 8, incorrectly identifies Horr as the American translator of the Hertzka work.

135. Freeland File, application blanks; Lang, *Tomorrow Is Beautiful*, p. 42; *Argus*, 30 December 1904; photograph of the Cooper Union notice, perhaps from a magazine, in Marvin Sanford, "Freeland, Home and Equality," p. 5; the meeting date is not clear. Upon joining Equality, Horr asked for an immediate leave of absence.

136. *Argus*, 17, 24 February, 28 July, 8 September 1905; application blanks for several of these persons are in Freeland File, as are letters inquiring about membership during this period.

137. Freeland File contains a copy of the proposed constitutional changes running in parallel columns with the old constitution dated for submission to the membership on 20 July 1905; ibid., unidentified newspaper clipping indicating that the new constitution was adopted on 5 September 1905; ibid., Kingsmill Commander to A. K. Hanson, 30 November, 1905.

138. Sanford, "Freeland, Home and Equality," p. 5; Wooster, *Communities*, p. 18; Frederick A. Bushee, "Communistic Societies in the United States," p. 636; the practice is briefly spelled out in a proposed constitution in [Horr] , "The Freeland Movement," upon which the Skagit County model was probably based.

139. Skagit County, Superior Court file 4823; *Reveille*, 26 April 1907.

140. *Argus*, 31 March, 28 July, 8 September 1905; lease, 6 September 1905, in Abstract of Title 2393, p. 53; Wooster, *Communities*, p. 48; Skagit County, Superior Court file 4823.

141. Letter dated 1 August 1905, Skagit County, Superior Court, Chattel Mortgages, and Agreements, file 4813, I. E. Shrauger and E. P. Barker . . . vs. M. P. Hurd and Willard Brickey . . . ; *Argus*, 10 November 1905.

142. Freeland File, application blank and other information on Commander, also Commander to Hanson and Hart, 28 November 1905, Ould to "Dear L. [C.] and Comrades," 7 December 1905. The correspondence gives further indication of the personal animosity, physical fights, accusations, and threats occurring in the colony.

143. *Argus*, 29 December 1905, 12 January 1906; the official transcript of this case has not been located by the Skagit County clerk's office; Skagit County, Superior Court file 4823.

144. Freeland File, minutes of general assembly meetings of 16 December 1905, 1, 11, 16, 20, 22 January, 1, 9, 19, 20 February, 5 March 1906; Burn, "Puget Soundings," p. 7; Skagit County, Superior Court file 4823.

145. Skagit County, Superior Court file 4823; *Argus*, 9 February 1906; *Reveille*, 8 February 1906.

146. Wooster, *Communities*, p. 47.

147. Freeland File, minutes of 19 February, 5 March 1906; these are the last minutes in the file.

148. *Argus*, 2 March 1906; Skagit County, Superior Court file 4823.

149. Skagit County, Superior Court file 4823; *Argus*, 23 March 1906.

150. On Ferris, see *Argus*, 2 February 1906; Skagit County, Superior Court file 4823; biography of Peth in *An Illustrated History of Skagit and Snohomish Counties*, p. 604.

151. *Argus*, 16 August 1907; Skagit County, Superior Court, file 5597, John J. Peth and Mary J. Peth, his Wife . . . vs. G. E. Pelton . . . ; Mr. and Mrs. R. E. Peterson interview.

152. Goldman, *Living*, p. 446; San Francisco *Chronicle*, 24, 27 December 1908, 16, 19 January 1909, 30 July 1916, 23 November 1917, 27 October 1947; San Francisco *Examiner*, 27, 31 October 1916, 3, 9 March, 24 December 1917; Alexander Horr, *Fabian Anarchism*; Alexander Horr, "Freeland in a Nutshell"; Lang, *Tomorrow Is Beautiful*, pp. 42–46, 289; McDevitt, "Un-lost Horizon" (March-April 1951), p. 8.

153. Bellamy, *Equality*, p. 351.

CHAPTER 4

1. *IF*, 25 June 1898.

2. King County, Superior Court, file 31138, John Collins vs. The Fidelity Trust Company of Seattle, A Corporation, and H. S. Connor and James P. Gleason.

3. Hanford, *Seattle and Environs*, 3:617-18; newspaper clipping, Edmond S. Meany File, Northwest Collection, University of Washington Library, Seattle; various deeds of the Fidelity Trust Company are in Island County, Auditor's Office, Deeds Records.

4. Interview with R. A. Pierson, 27 January 1968; *Whidby Islander*, 15 February 1901, hereafter cited as *WI*; the editors omitted an "e" in the spelling of Whidbey; Marvin Sanford, "The Story of Freeland," p. 5; *CN*, 20 November 1897; interview with Ernest Lieseke, 8 August 1968; Island County, Superior Court, Civil Case 661, Emma Graham vs. James P. Gleason. . . .

5. Island County, Auditor's Office, Articles of Incorporation of the Free Land Association, Corporations File 3384; also included as the first article of the bylaws of Freeland [*sic*] Association, printed in *WI*, Supplement, 1 February 1901.

6. Bylaws.

7. Articles of Incorporation; *IF*, 24 April, 17 September 1900; bylaws; *WI*, 15 November 1901.

8. *WI*, 15 February 1901.

9. F. Hindle, "The Rochdale Plan," *WI*, 1 August 1901; a contemporary standard argument for the Rochdale plan was George Jacob Holyoake, *The History of the Rochdale Pioneers*, a copy of which was in the Freeland Colony library, Freeland Co-operative Association Papers.

10. Marvin Sanford, "Freeland, A Rochdale Town," pp. 3-4; stock ledger, 1900-1901, in possession of Ernest Lieseke; *IF*, 17 September 1900; *WI*, October 1900, 15 July 1901; Pierson interview, 27 January 1968.

11. *WI*, 15 February 1903; advertisement in ibid., 1 October 1902.

12. Ibid., 15 June 1901.

13. Freeland Co-operative Association Papers, tape-recorded interview with Ernest Lieseke by Steven Uthoff and Fred Smith, 13 April 1968. *WI*, 15 December 1902, 15 February 1903. On the *Bessie B.* and other boats, see *WI* throughout 1901 and 1902.

14. *WI*, 1 May 1901; Ernest Lieseke interview, 8 August 1968; Hunt and Kaylor, *Washington West*, 3:341; stock ledger, 1900-1901; "Island County: A World Beater," p. 20.

15. *WI*, 1 March 1901, 15 April, 1 August 1902.

16. *IF*, 29 January, 1 May, 1 June 1901; Pierson interview, 27 January 1968; Ernest Lieseke interview, 8 August 1968; Merlich interview; Albert Lieseke interview; *WI*, 1 February, 1 March, 15 May 1901, 1 March 1902; many from the South Dakota group apparently did not remain at Freeland long.

17. *WI*, 1 March 1901; see Island County, Auditor's Office, Platbook 2, pp. 21-23.

18. *WI*, 15 August 1902.

19. Ibid., 15 January 1901.

20. Ibid.

21. Ibid., 2 December 1902, 1 April 1903; Freeland Co-operative Association Papers, tape-recorded interview with Austin Marshall by Steven Uthoff and Fred Smith, 13 April 1968.

22. *WI*, 15 May, 2 December 1902, 15 July 1903; photograph in possession of Mr. Pierson; Marshall interview, 13 April 1968.

23. *WI*, 1, 15 September 1902, 15 February 1903; photograph, in possession of Mr. Pierson, taken while this building was under construction.

24. *WI*, 1-15 January 1902, 1-15 January, 1 February 1903.

25. Ibid., 1 November 1901, 1 September, 15 December 1902, 1 February 1903.

26. Marvin Sanford, "DeForest Sanford, June 11, 1871-November 30, 1956."

27. *WI*, October 1900.

28. Ibid., 1 January, 1 March 1901, and thereafter; 1 June, 1 August, 1 December 1902.

29. Ibid., 15 January, 1 September 1901, and others.

30. *Discontent*, 5 February 1902; *WI*, 1, 15 October 1901.

31. *WI*, 15 September, 1 October 1901.

32. Ibid., 1 October, 1 November 1901, 1-15 January 1902.

33. Ibid., 1-15 January, 15 March, 1 June, 1 December 1902; *IF*, 1 April, 1 June 1902; *Discontent*, 5 February, 9 April 1902.

34. *WI*, 1, 15 April 1903.

35. Stock ledger, 1900-1901; Sanford, "DeForest Sanford."

36. *IF*, 29 January 1901; this socialist self-image is apparent from the interviews cited with Ernest Lieseke, Mr. Marshall, Mr. Pierson, and Mrs. Merlich.

37. *WI*, November 1900, 1 February, 15 November 1901, February-April 1902, 1, 15 January 1903.

38. Ibid., 15 February 1902.

39. Ibid., 15 May, 15 September, 1 October 1902; stock ledger, 1900-1901.

40. Coupeville *Island County Times*, 3 September 1902; Everett *Commonwealth*, 24 July 1913; Pierson interview, 27 January 1968; Freeland Co-operative Association Papers, book list, and William Lieseke's diary, 18 July, 7 August, 26 October 1915, 6, 20 February 1916.

CHAPTER 5

1. *CN*, 21 August 1897.

2. Heath, ed., *Red Book*, pp. 58-59; hereafter cited as *Red Book*; the first issue of the *Social Democrat* was that of 1 July 1897, hereafter cited as *SD*; Quint, *American Socialism*, pp. 58-59, 285-93, 300-302.

3. An unidentified New York *Journal* reporter quoted in the *New York Times*, 1 July 1897.

4. Debs quoted in the *New York Times*, 22 June 1897; Ray S. Baker, "The Debs Co-operative Commonwealth"; Declaration of Principles and Constitution, printed in *CN*, 17 July 1897, and *SD*, 1 July 1897.

5. Quint, *American Socialism*, pp. 285-88; *New York Times*, 30 June 1897.

6. *SD*, 15 July, 1 August 1897; *CN*, 14 August 1897.

7. *CN*, 14 August 1897; Cyrus Field Willard, "Autobiography," chap. 14, pp. 18-19; John W. Leonard, ed., *Who's Who in America . . . 1898-1899*,

p. 339; Richard J. Hinton, *John Brown and His Men*, pp. 201-6; Quint, *American Socialism*, pp. 303-4; James C. Malin, *John Brown and the Legend of Fifty-six*, pp. 449-50; Clifton K. Yearley, Jr., *Britons in American Labor*, p. 220. The International was created in 1864, and Hinton had first come to the United States about 1851.

8. Arthur Ernest Morgan, *Edward Bellamy*, pp. 247, 250, 261, 263, 270-71, 273; Willard, "Autobiography," chap. 15, pp. 1-2; W. E. S., "In Memoriam—Cyrus Field Willard," pp. 140-41; John Hope Franklin, "Edward Bellamy and the Nationalist Movement," p. 751.

9. Edward Bellamy Papers, Cyrus Field Willard to Bellamy, 3 August 1897; Willard, "Autobiography," chap. 14, p. 19.

10. Leonard, ed., *Who's Who in America . . . 1899-1900*, p. 73; *CN*, 14 August 1897; Quint, *American Socialism*, p. 304.

11. *CN*, 21 July, 11 September 1897.

12. *Red Book*, pp. 58-61; *CN*, 21 August 1897; Quint, *American Socialism*, p. 304; *SD*, 23 June 1898; Willard, "Autobiography," chap. 14, pp. 19-20.

13. Baker, "Debs Co-operative Commonwealth," p. 539; *SD*, 23 September, 7 October 1897 *passim*; Quint, *American Socialism*, p. 305; *CN*, 21 August, 2, 9, 16, 23 October, 11 December 1897, 8 January 1898; *Red Book*, p. 61; see also *SD*, 2 June 1898; Spokane *Chronicle* quoted in *CN*, 27 November 1897.

14. Alice Hyneman Sotheran, "Reminiscences of Charles Sotheran as Pioneer American Socialist," in Charles Sotheran, *Horace Greeley and Other Pioneers of American Socialism*, p. xxxv; *Red Book*, p. 60; Quint, *American Socialism*, pp. 307-10.

15. *Red Book*, pp. 61-65; *SD*, 16 June 1898; Quint, *American Socialism*, pp. 310-15; Ginger, *Bending Cross*, pp. 197-98.

16. *Red Book*, pp. 65-67; *SD*, 16 June 1898; Quint, *American Socialism*, pp. 314-15; Pelton, "Historical Sketch."

17. Quint, *American Socialism*, pp. 313-15; Ginger, *Bending Cross*, p. 198; Willard, "Autobiography," chap. 14, pp. 21, 27.

18. *SD*, 16 June 1898; the final issue of the *Social Democrat* was that of 7 July 1898; Quint, *American Socialism*, pp. 315-17; throughout his discussion of SDA factionalism, Quint puts forth the thesis that the colonizationists were basically Populist and nativist oriented, while the political activists were grounded in Marxist class-struggle doctrine; see especially p. 309. *CN*, 2 July 1898; quotation from Cyrus Field Willard, "As It Is Today: History of the Co-operative Brotherhood . . ."; *Red Book*, p. 68.

19. Laurence Grönlund, "Socializing a State"; *SD*, 16, 23 June 1898; Quint, *American Socialism*, pp. 317-18.

20. Willard, "As It Is Today."

21. Willard, "Autobiography," chap. 14, p. 25, chap. 15, pp. 11-14; Willard, "As It Is Today"; on Iris, Colorado, see Muriel Sibell Wolle, *Stampede to Timberline*, p. 193.

22. Willard, "Autobiography," chap. 14, pp. 25-26, chap. 15, pp. 5-8.

23. Bremerton *Sun*, 12 August 1937; *Times*, 12 March 1898; Willard,

"Autobiography," chap. 15, p. 8; *IF*, 27 October 1898.

24. Willard, "Autobiography," chap. 15, pp. 8-11; *IF*, 27 October 1898; Kitsap County, Auditor's Office, Deeds and Agreements, file 29563, vol. Z, pp. 586-88.

25. Charter in the office of the secretary of state, Topeka, Kansas. Quint, *American Socialism*, p. 306; *SD*, 28 April 1898. The charter, although referring to "agriculture and other industries," refers specifically to neither mining nor bonding power. Willard, "As It Is Today."

26. King County, Auditor's Office, file 3625, Articles of Incorporation of the Co-operative Brotherhood.

27. *IF*, 27 October 1898; Willard, "Autobiography," chap. 15, p. 10.

28. Bremerton Public Library, manuscript of interview with Henry W. Stein; Katherine Stein Anderson, "Burley"; Bremerton *Sun*, 25 December 1935; Iva Luella Buchanan, "Economic History of Kitsap County, Washington, to 1889," pp. 247-52; Willard, "Autobiography," chap. 15, p. 10.

29. Willard, "As It Is Today"; Willard, "Autobiography," chap. 15, pp. 13, 15, and elsewhere; *IF*, 19 November, 3 December 1898.

30. *IF*, 3, 17 December 1898, 28 January 1899; Willard, "Autobiography," chap. 15, pp. 16-17.

31. *IF*, Supplement, *ca.* 5 November 1898; ibid., 17 December 1898, 21 January 1899; *The Co-operator*, January 1903, hereafter cited as *Co-op*.

32. *IF*, 3, 31 December 1898; Willard, "Autobiography," chap. 15, pp. 18-20.

33. *IF*, 22, 29 October, 17, 31 December 1898, and supplement *ca.* 5 November 1898; the Co-operative Brotherhood column ran from 19 November 1898 to 28 January 1899; the men appointed were Ed Pelton, David Burgess, and Alexander Pugh.

34. Willard, "Autobiography," chap. 12, p. 17.

35. [Eddy], "Musings of a Mossback," 28 January 1899.

36. Card in Kitsap County Historical Association, Bremerton; Willard, "Autobiography," chap. 15, pp. 16-17; Stein interview manuscript.

37. Willard, "Autobiography," chap. 15, pp. 15-16.

38. Ibid., pp. 18-27, 39-40.

39. Ibid., p. 22; "A Backward Glance O'er Travelled Roads."

40. Willard, "Autobiography," chap. 15, pp. 27, 32-39.

41. W. E. S., "In Memoriam," pp. 140-41; San Diego *Union*, 18 January 1942; Willard, "Autobiography," chap. 15, p. 41.

42. *Co-op*, 16 June, 14 July 1900, 9 January, 1 June 1901; *New York Times*, 21 December 1901; Willard, "Autobiography," chap. 15, pp. 28-29, 35, 41; Katherine Stein Anderson, lifelong Burley resident, recalled that a person whose name she did not remember had lost colony money in mining investments. She did not believe, however, that this was Borland. Interviews with Mrs. Anderson, 26 January 1966, 1 July 1969.

43. *The Co-operative Brotherhood... Full Statements of Plans and Purchases*; the entrance fee was soon raised to five dollars. "Official Notices," *Co-op*, 6 April 1901, and others.

44. *Co-op*, 30 June, 13 October 1900, 28 December 1901.

45. *IF*, Supplement, *ca.* 5 November 1898; a copy of the contract for Duncan Pearce, dated 4 October 1900, is among the documents in Kitsap County, Superior Court, file 3059, M. T. Bruce . . . vs. The Co-operative Brotherhood . . . ; W. E. Copeland, "The Co-operative Brotherhood and Its Colony," p. 320; Tacoma *Ledger*, 2 January 1900, hereafter cited as *Ledger*.

46. *CN*, 10 June 1898; *Co-op*, 20 April 1901.

47. W. P. Borland, "The Emancipation of Industry," p. 105; Anne Shannon Monroe, "The Co-operative Brotherhood of Burley, Washington"; W. E. Copeland refers to about 120 members in "The Co-operative Brotherhood," p. 404. Slightly later ("Co-operative Brotherhood and Its Colony," p. 320), Copeland refers to "some three hundred members in good standing, of whom about thirty reside at Burley, some with and some without their families."

48. Borland, "Emancipation of Industry," p. 104; *Co-operative Brotherhood*; Copeland, "Co-operative Brotherhood and Its Colony," p. 319; *IF*, Supplement, *ca.* 5 November 1898; *Co-op*, December 1903.

49. *Co-op*, September 1902, May, September 1903; Copeland, "Co-operative Brotherhood and Its Colony," p. 319. On deaths of elderly residents, S. P. Leep, *Co-op*, 22 September 1900; W. E. Copeland, ibid., May 1904; Carl Zwicker, ibid., April 1903; A. L. Whiteside, ibid., June 1903; for one week of illnesses, see *Co-op*, February 1903; diary of Roland Eugene Muirhead, 11, 12 April 1900. Katherine Anderson does not agree that many were aged or infirm, reasoning that they could not have cleared land or done the work they did if they had been; interview, 1 July 1969.

50. Kitsap County, Superior Court file 3059, exhibit C, Deed of Trust, 2 January 1899; "Deed of Trust: How the Co-operative Brotherhood Secures Collective Ownership," *IF*, Supplement, *ca.* 5 November 1898; Copeland, "Co-operative Brotherhood and Its Colony," pp. 318, 322. The basic difference between the two deeds was the inclusion in the earlier of the three Equality colonists as trustees; in the second deed these men had been replaced; *Co-operative Brotherhood*; *Co-op*, 9 February 1901.

51. For the amendments, see *Co-op* throughout the winter and spring of 1901; for criticism, see letter of Clarence Clowe, ibid., 27 April 1901.

52. Ibid., February, April 1903; diary of Alonzo A. Wardall, 3 September 1903; the lease was printed in *Co-op*, October 1903.

53. Diary of Wardall, Richard C. Berner to Cedric A. Wardall, 19 August 1960. This letter is based on these diaries, which Wardall kept from 1863 to 1918. Clipping from the Milwaukee *Sentinel* in the diary for 1903; *Co-op*, July, October 1903; quotation from diary of Wardall, 2-6 September 1903.

54. Diary of Wardall, 26-29 March, 17-31 December 1904; Wardall regularly used the symbol # to denote dollars. Kitsap County, Auditor's Office, Articles of Incorporation, file 27851.

55. Copeland, "Co-operative Brotherhood and Its Colony," pp. 317-18.

56. *IF*, 3 December 1898, 28 January 1899; *Co-op*, 22 September 1900, June 1903; Willard, "Autobiography," chap. 15, pp. 16-17; *Co-op*, 30

December 1899; "'Looking Backward' at Burley 'Dream' Colony . . . ,"
Ledger, 5 August 1940; Borland, "Emancipation of Industry," pp. 104-5.

57. *Co-op*, September, November, December 1902; Co-operative Brotherhood ledger, 1 July 1900 to 30 June 1901, in possession of Katherine
Anderson.

58. *Co-op*, November 1902, March 1903.

59. A description of the sawmill operation is given in "Burley Pen
Pictures: November at Burley," *Co-op*, December 1903.

60. *Co-op*, June 1906; Kitsap County, Superior Court, file 2168,
Co-operative Brotherhood vs. Allen Shingle Company.

61. *IF*, 3 December 1898, 28 January 1899; *Co-op*, 30 October 1899,
October, December 1902; Copeland, "Co-operative Brotherhood," p. 404.

62. *IF*, 3 December 1898; Willard, "Autobiography," chap. 15, p. 20;
Co-op, 30 June, 27 October 1900, September, November 1902, January,
April 1903, May 1904, June 1906; Anderson interview, 26 January 1966;
Patricia Granger, "The Co-operative Colony at Burley, Kitsap County," *ca.*
1936.

63. "Burley Pen Pictures: Clearing the Land," *Co-op*, June 1903.

64. Copeland, "Co-operative Brotherhood and Its Colony," p. 318.

65. Ibid. Commander's obituary in Tacoma *News-Tribune*, 17 May 1965;
Co-op, October 1902, July 1903.

66. *Co-op*, 22 December 1900, 25 January, 9 February 1901, September
1902, September 1903; "Burley Pen Pictures," appeared through most of
1903; *WI*, 15 July 1902; *People's Press* of Albany, [n.d.], quoted in *Co-op*,
September 1902.

67. *Co-op*, October 1903, June 1906; this is the last issue of the
Co-operator known to this writer; Kitsap County, Superior Court file 3059.

68. Granger, "Co-operative Colony," p. 4; on Rader, see Will A. Steel and
Albert Searl, *Steel and Searl's Legislative Souvenir Manual for 1895-96*, p.
110; *Co-op*, November 1902, February, March 1903. On Hubbard, see
Soundview, October 1902, p. 17. The admiration was mutual; *The Philistine*,
October 1905, pp. 157-58. The last issue of *Soundview* in the apparently
complete file in the University of Washington Library is dated September
1908. No mention is made that this copy is the final edition.

69. *Co-op*, 4 August 1900.

70. Monroe, "Co-operative Brotherhood"; Copeland, "Co-operative
Brotherhood and Its Colony"; Copeland, "Co-operative Brotherhood";
Borland, "Emancipation of Industry"; Hinds, *American Communities* (1902
ed.), pp. 390-96; Charles E. Buell, *Industrial Liberty*, pp. 95-100; Buell is
described in Leonard, *Who's Who in America . . . 1903-05*, p. 198.

71. Diary of Muirhead, 4-12 April 1900; *Co-op*, September 1903, May
1904.

72. *Co-op*, 20 April 1901.

73. Anderson interview, 26 January 1966; interviews with Leola E. Stein,
22, 23 August 1966; Granger, "Co-operative Colony," p. 4; *Co-op*, 20 April
1901; Copeland, "Co-operative Brotherhood and Its Colony," pp. 318-20; a

photograph held by the Kitsap County Historical Association confirms that
the hotel dormitory was indeed "rough."

74. Copeland, "Co-operative Brotherhood and Its Colony," p. 320;
"Burley Pen Pictures: Dinner at the Hotel," *Co-op*, May 1903; *Co-op*, 23
February 1901.

75. "Burley Pen Pictures: Dinner."

76. *Co-op*, 29 September 1900, August 1902, April 1903; on the
vegetarian community, see ibid, 25 August 1900; *WI* quoted in Stewart H.
Holbrook, "The Co-operators of Burley Lagoon."

77. "Burley Pen Pictures: Our Social Life," *Co-op*, July 1903; interviews
with Sam L. Finfrock, 25, 29 March 1966; letter in *Searchlight*, May-June
1950, p. 21.

78. Jessie Brewster, "Burley Pen Pictures: A Burley Sunday," *Co-op*,
August 1903.

79. On the band, see *Co-op*, June-November 1900, quotation from 9
June; Shepperson, *Retreat to Nevada*, pp. 149-50.

80. *Co-op*, February, May 1903, May 1904; Bremerton Public Library,
manuscript of interview with Mary Corporan [*sic*].

81. See "Burley Pen Pictures: Our Social Life," *Co-op*, July 1903, and
various issues of *Co-op*; Granger, "Co-operative Colony," p. 7; *IF*, 19
December 1898; *Co-op*, 7 July, 15 December 1900, August, December 1902,
March 1903; "The Fourth of July at Burley."

82. *Co-operative Brotherhood*; Buell, *Industrial Liberty*, p. 97; Joseph
Asbury Johnson, "The Spirit of Humanity," quoted in Buell, *Industrial
Liberty*, p. 99.

83. *Co-op*, July, November 1903, May 1904; Copeland, "Co-operative
Brotherhood and Its Colony," p. 320; "Burley Pen Pictures: Social Life";
Anderson, "Burley."

84. James Dombrowski, *The Early Days of Christian Socialism in
America*, p. 94; Quint, *American Socialism*, pp. 103-41; Kingsmill Commander, "William Ellery Copeland"; Willard, "Autobiography," chap. 15, p.
19; *Co-op*, 2 October 1900; Granger, "Co-operative Colony," p. 3; Bremerton
Sun, 25 December 1935; Bremerton Public Library, manuscript of interview
with M. L. Fenton; diary of Wardall, 31 March 1904.

85. Anderson interview, 26 January 1966; as late as 1914, marriages were
being performed by the Rev. Ellis; Kitsap County, Auditor's Office, Register
of Marriages, Index of Marriages, 1891-1915, p. 65; Pierce County, Superior
Court, Probate File 16089, In the Matter of the Guardianship of Arthur Blake
Ellis, an incompetent, and Probate File 17377, In the Matter of the Estate of
Arthur Blake Ellis, deceased.

86. Willard, "Autobiography," chap. 15, p. 29.

87. Anderson, "Burley"; Minutes Book, pp. 42-49, 68-69; meetings of 18
July, 5 September 1901, 16 August 1903 and others, School Board Records
of District 12, in possession of the Kitsap County Historical Association;
Patricia Granger to Hubert LaDue, 21 November 1936, appended to Granger,

"Co-operative Colony," p. 10; Copeland, "Co-operative Brotherhood and Its Colony," p. 318.

88. Minutes Book, p. 41, and meetings of 5 May 1900, 12 February, 3 April, 18 July 1901, 13 November 1903; *Co-op*, 6 October, 1 December 1900; School Board Records of District 12, F. D. Newberry to A. L. Whiteside, 31 August 1901, and receipt for advertisement in the Seattle *Daily Times*, dated September 1903; comment on Simmons from *Co-op*, October 1903.

89. *Co-op*, back cover, any issue, 1903; ibid., 20 October 1900; Stein interview manuscript.

90. *Co-op*, August 1903; Stein interview manuscript.

91. *Co-op*, July 1903; Bagley, *History of Seattle* 3:722-23; Austin Edwards Griffiths, "Great Faith: Autobiography of an English Immigrant Boy in America, 1863-1950," p. 206; Margaret V. Sherlock, "The Recall of Mayor Gill."

92. *Co-op*, back cover, any issue, 1903.

93. Ibid., June 1906; Kingsmill Commander, "On Memory's Wall," *Co-op*, June 1906; Edmond S. Meany, *History of the State of Washington*, p. 324n.

94. Kitsap County, Superior Court file 3059.

95. Ibid.

96. Ibid.; on Pitt, see Joe Pitt, "Navy Yard District Citizen Tells of Old Times."

97. Kitsap County, Superior Court file 3059.

98. Port Orchard Chamber of Commerce, *South Kitsap County, State of Washington*; Doris Russell, "South Kitsap History Traced"; Buchanan, "Economic History," pp. 247-51.

99. Henry W. Stein, "Highway to Touch Historic Ground: Site of Old Colony at Burley to Come Into Its Own"; see also Anderson, "Burley."

CHAPTER 6

1. In addition to numerous books and articles cited elsewhere in this chapter, see popular accounts in Lambert Florin, *Western Ghost Town Shadows*, pp. 145-49; Corinne Jacker, *The Black Flag of Anarchy*, pp. 136-38; Stewart H. Holbrook, "There Was No Place Like Home"; Howard M. Brier, *Sawdust Empire*, pp. 198-201.

2. Albertson, "Mutualistic Communities," p. 417; George H. Allen, "Inside Workings of Anarchistic Colony Are Revealed . . ."; Kingsmill Commander, "At Home with the Anarchists"; diary of Muirhead, 13 April 1900; *Ledger*, 25 September 1901; Pierce County, Clerk's Office, Deeds, 3:373; Pearl Engle and Jeanette Hlavin, eds., "History of Tacoma Eastern

Area," p. 27; J. W. Gaskine, "The Anarchists at Home, Washington," p. 916; Macie Govan Cope to the author, 3 December 1971.

3. Allen, "Anarchist Colony"; diary of Muirhead, 15 April 1900; Verity quoted in Gaskine, "Anarchists," p. 916.

4. Verity quoted in Gaskine, "Anarchists," pp. 916-17; Verity refers to the seller as a Tacoma banker, although he had once told a visitor that the seller was a Tacoma anarchist; diary of Muirhead, 15 April 1900. A copy of the deed has not been located. Verity's account does not note the total price or the cost per acre, but says payments were due every sixty days; Muirhead understood that the price was $7.00 an acre with payments due every ninety days.

5. S[iegfried] Clyde, "A Sketch of Home, Its Past and Its Present"; interview with Siegfried Clyde, 23 July 1968.

6. Clyde, "Sketch of Home"; E. E. Slosson, "An Experiment in Anarchy," p. 780; Gig Harbor *Peninsula Gateway*, 8 February 1946; diary of Muirhead, 13 April 1900; Allen, "Anarchist Colony"; Verity to Muirhead, 13 January 1915, on microfilm with Muirhead's diary; Mrs. Cope to the author.

7. Allen, "Anarchist Colony"; diary of Muirhead, 13 April 1900.

8. Allen, "Anarchist Colony"; Slosson, "Experiment," shows pictures of the first two houses, pp. 780, 781, 783; citing the 1900 census report as his basis, Slosson computed the quotient at five acres per capita, making allowances for pasturage, wild lands, and lands producing export crops.

9. Allen, "Anarchist Colony"; Verity quoted in Gaskine, "Anarchists," pp. 916-17; Pierce County, Auditor's Office, Corporations File 116811, Articles of Incorporation and Agreement of the Mutual Home Association.

10. *Discontent*, 6 June 1900.

11. The author has found no copy of bylaws, although they are mentioned in the Articles of Incorporation. The original subscribers included the above officers and Delana Verity, Kenneth Verity (their son), B. F. Odell, Annie Odell, Francis M. Seigmund, Sylvia Allen, W. J. King, Eliza King, Hattie Thomson, M. D. Penhallow, J. W. Geithman, and Ella Wren. Later election results in *Discontent*, 30 January 1901, 15 January 1902; *Demonstrator*, 13 January 1904, 1 February 1905, 17 January 1906, 16 January 1908; *Agitator*, 5 January 1911.

12. Verity quoted in Gaskine, "Anarchists," p. 917; *Demonstrator*, 11 May 1904, 17 May 1905.

13. Verity quoted in Gaskine, "Anarchists," p. 916; *CN*, 28 March 1896; Murray Morgan, *The Last Wilderness*, pp. 104-5; *Discontent*, 4 January 1899; files of the *New Era* have not been located.

14. Diary of Muirhead, 12 April 1900; *Discontent*, 12 October 1898; interview with David Dadisman, 23 July 1968. David Dadisman recalled that the only house besides those of the three founders and his father was that of J. E. Martin.

15. Pierce County, Auditor's Office, Deeds, 140:596, 141:640. The additional twenty-four acres is described differently in the two deeds; first as

a lot, the second time as a fractional part of a section; both references seem to indicate the same parcel of land; Pierce County, Auditor's Office, Platbook 9, p. 75, Deeds, 150:365; 157:104; 171:218, 206, 552; Pierce County, Auditor's Office, General Index of Grantees, 7:796; *Discontent*, 6 June 1900; Mrs. A. F. Cotterell, "Memoirs of Home, An Account of the Pioneers"; *Demonstrator*, 15 July 1903; interview with Evadna Cooke, 16 July 1968; interview with Lewis Haiman, 2 August 1968; interview with Mrs. Bertram Bruenner, 2 July 1969.

16. Gaskine, "Anarchists," pp. 918, 919; Morgan, *Last Wilderness*, 105-6; Radium LaVene, "There Was No Place Like Home," pt. 1, p. 1; *Discontent*, 4 January 1899.

17. The intent of the name is discussed by a later editor in *Discontent*, 19 February 1902; Oliver A. Verity, "Something About Discontent"; *Discontent*, 11 May 1898, 4 January 1899, 10 July 1901.

18. Goldman, *Living*, p. 224; Stewart H. Holbrook, "Home Sweet Home, the Anarchists of Joe's Bay," 5 December 1937; *Discontent*, 13 July 1898.

19. Goldman, *Living*, pp. 224, 244; *Discontent*, 18 May, 8 June 1898, 7 June 1899; *Demonstrator*, 5 January 1907; Emma Goldman, "Donald Vose: The Accursed," pp. 353-54; Bruenner interview; Cotterell, "Memoirs of Home," 4 October 1934; Clyde interview; Goldman mentions Home peripherally in her autobiography, but says nothing of her visits.

20. D. Stanton Hammond to the author, 20 May 1968; *Who Was Who in America*, 1:872; Morgan, *Last Wilderness*, pp. 105-6, asserts that the two men arrived at Home together on 11 May 1898 and soon after began to publish *Discontent*, a statement that is inconsistent with items on Morton appearing in *Discontent*; see below.

21. *Discontent*, 25 April, 2 May 1900.

22. Diary of Muirhead, 17 April 1900.

23. *Discontent*, 19 June 1901; Cotterell, "Memoirs," 17 May 1934; Dadisman interview, 23 July 1968; interview with Radium LaVene, 22 June 1968.

24. *Discontent*, 9 January, 6 March, 14, 28 August, 11 September 1901; United States, District Court, District of Washington, file 1914, United States of America, Plaintiff, vs. Charles L. Govan, Defendant, FRC No. 77443, Accession No. 62a400, Federal Records Center, National Archives, Seattle; Tacoma *Evening News*, 21, 28 August 1901; hereafter cited as *News*.

25. Sidney Fine, "Anarchism and the Assassination of McKinley"; Goldman, *Living*, p. 296. On Czolgosz, see Robert J. Donovan, *The Assassins*, pp. 82-107.

26. *Ledger*, 7, 9, 12 September 1901.

27. *News*, 10, 11, 12, 14 September 1901.

28. *Ledger*, 14 September 1901.

29. New Whatcom *Reveille*, 13, 15, 29 September, 6, 9 October 1901; *Asotin County Sentinel*, quoted in *Ledger*, 4 October 1901; *P-I*, 11 September 1901.

30. *Discontent*, 18 September 1901; Hoehn interview; *Ledger*, 9, 15

September 1901; Bureau of Immigration Report, August 1918, quoted in U. S. Congress, House of Representatives, Subcommittee of the Committee on Immigration and Naturalization, *Communist and Anarchist Deportation Cases, Hearings*, 66th Cong., 2nd sess., 21-24 April 1920, "Digest of Cases Deported on U. S. Transport 'Buford'" (Washington, 1920), p. 105.

31. Quoted in *Ledger*, 15 September 1901.

32. Ibid., 17, 21 September 1901.

33. Ibid., 7, 15, 23 September 1901; *Discontent*, 18 September 1901. Not all anarchists shared Morton's denunciation of the assassination, however; see Fine, "Anarchism and Assassination," pp. 794-99.

34. *Ledger*, 14 September 1901; Holbrook, "Home Sweet Home," pt. 2, p. 3; Dadisman interview, 23 July 1968; LaVene, "No Place," pt. 2, p. 1.

35. *Discontent*, 2 October 1901; *Ledger*, 30 September 1901.

36. *Discontent*, 6 November 1901; Richard Bremner, "Editor's Introduction," in Anthony Comstock, *Traps for the Young*, pp. xiii-xiv, xxvii.

37. *Ledger*, 23, 25, 26 September 1901; *Discontent*, 13 November, 13 December 1901; LaVene, "No Place," pt. 2, p. 1.

38. Diary of Muirhead, 15 April 1900; photograph of Adams in possession of Mrs. Cooke; *Soundview*, June 1905, p. 64; Adams' article, "A Healthy Comparison," was reprinted in *Discontent*, 2 April 1902; about half of the article quoted a pamphlet by Rachel Campbell entitled *The Prodigal Daughter. Ledger*, 9 March 1902; *Discontent*, 19 March 1902.

39. *Discontent*, 19 March 1902, describes the trial and also includes comments from the *News* and the Tacoma *Sun-Democrat*; U.S., Circuit Court, District of Washington, Western Division, file 846, United States vs. J. E. Larkin and J. W. Adams, FRC No. 74723, Accession No. 62a379, Federal Records Center, National Archives, Seattle.

40. *Discontent*, 16 January 1901, 19, 26 March 1902; *Ledger*, 15, 17 July 1902; U.S., Circuit Court, District of Washington, Western Division, file 847, United States vs. Lois Waisbrooker, FRC No. 74723, Accession No. 62a379, Federal Records Center, National Archives, Seattle. The judge, however, suspended payment of the fine. On Mrs. Waisbrooker's earlier career, see James C. Malin, *A Concern about Humanity*, pp. 116-32.

41. *Discontent*, 1 January, 5, 26 February 1902.

42. *Ledger*, 25 September 1901, 8, 10 March 1902; Dadisman interview, 23 July 1968; *Discontent*, 30 April 1902.

43. *Discontent*, 23, 30 April 1902; *Ledger*, 8, 10 March 1902.

44. Sam H. Nichols, comp., *Session Laws of the State of Washington, Eighth Session, 1903*, p. 52; *House Journal, Eighth Legislature of Washington . . .* , pp. 61, 247, 340, 514, 593, 1244-45; Zechariah Chafee, Jr., *Government and Mass Communications: A Report from the Commission on Freedom of the Press*, I:372.

45. Dadisman interview, 23 July 1968; diary of Philip C. Van Buskirk, 15 May 1902; *Discontent*, 30 April 1902, was the final issue; *Demonstrator*, 11 March 1903, was vol. 1, no. 1. Seventy years later Home residents enjoy noting that although Lakebay remained the post office for the area, the

building was moved to Home in the 1960s; Gaskine, "Anarchists," p. 919.

46. *Discontent*, 12, 26 February 1902.

47. Ibid., 11 May 1898, 17 April 1899, 9 January 1901; "An Anarchist Experiment Station"; "Some Disadvantages of Anarchism," p. 3103; Commander, "At Home"; diary of Wardall, 4 September 1903; Herbert Bashford, "Troubles of a Tolstoi Colony"; Slosson, "Experiment"; diary of Muirhead, April 1900.

48. *Demonstrator*, 11 March 1903, 7, 12 December 1904; *Discontent*, 19 April, 25 May 1898, 19 April 1899, 11 September 1901. The recollection of general tolerance was borne out by every person interviewed who lived at Home.

49. Gaskine, "Anarchists," p. 920; Bashford, "Troubles of a Tolstoi Colony"; E. E. R. [Emma E. Rader], "The Em-Bossed at Home"; *Discontent*, 17 July 1901; LaVene, "No Place," pt. 1, p. 1; *Demonstrator*, 18 December 1907.

50. Lang, *Tomorrow Is Beautiful*, p. 50. The schoolhouse doubled as a community center, and children who remained at Home longer than Mrs. Lang do not recall such pictures nor the Fourth of July she describes when a party of young people forcibly replaced these pictures with American heroes. *Discontent*, 11 November 1899, 10 July, 13 November 1901; *Demonstrator*, 18 November 1903, 6 December 1905, 18 April, 21 November 1906, 6 November 1907; see ibid., 4 July 1906, for a more conventional Fourth of July celebration; the Christmas celebration is described in *Agitator*, 1 January 1911.

51. *Demonstrator*, 29 July 1903; Haiman interview; Cooke interview, 16 July 1968; Haffer interview; interview with Mimi Pritchard, 2 July 1969.

52. William D. P. Bliss and Rudolph M. Binder, eds., *The New Encyclopedia of Social Reform* . . . , p. 484.

53. Diary of Van Buskirk, 2 June 1902.

54. *Soundview*, November 1903, p. 152; Rader quotation from *Soundview*, August-September 1903, p. 11; for a representative article by Adams, see *Soundview*, June 1905, pp. 42-44; *Demonstrator*, 11 May 1904, 4 January, 5 April, 16 September 1905, 21 November 1906; Macdonald, *Fifty Years of Freethought*, 2:341.

55. Slosson, "Experiment," p. 782; Haiman interview; diary of Muirhead, 14 April 1900; *Demonstrator*, 3 April 1907; Bashford, "Troubles of a Tolstoi Colony"; diary of Van Buskirk, 24 May 1902.

56. Diary of Van Buskirk, 18 May 1902; Slosson, "Experiment," p. 782; Haiman interview.

57. Penhallow quotation from *News*, reprinted in *Discontent*, 11 September 1901; *Demonstrator*, 4 August 1907; Slosson, "Experiment," p. 782; diary of Muirhead, 12 April 1900; Cooke interview, 16 July 1968. The first church has appeared in very recent years.

58. Cooke interview, 16 July 1968; *Demonstrator*, 29 April, 27 May, 17 June, 30 December 1903, 13, 27 January 1904, 14 April 1906; diary of Muirhead, 15 April 1900; Berthe Knatvold, "Where Individual Liberty

Rules"; *Soundview*, November, 1904, p. 32; Elmer T. Clark, *The Small Sects in America*, pp. 148-50.

59. *Discontent*, 11 September 1901, and others; questionnaire in Freeland File 72, University of Washington Library, Seattle. Underlining is Allen's.

60. Diary of Muirhead, 15 April 1900; *Demonstrator*, 1, 8 April 1903, 8 June 1904, 19 February 1908; *Agitator*, 1 July 1911; Pierce County, Superior Court, civil file 31050, Oscar Engvall, Plaintiff, vs. John Buchie . . . Defendants; LaVene interview; LaVene, "No Place," pt. 2, p. 17; Haiman interview; Bruenner interview.

61. Commander, "At Home," p. 4; Dadisman interview, 23 July 1968; *Discontent*, 20 June, 15 August 1900, 3 April, 8 May, 31 July 1901, 12, 19 February 1902; *Demonstrator*, 16 August 1905, 2 May 1906; LaVene interview.

62. *Discontent*, 19 April, 27 September 1899; diary of Muirhead, 13 April 1900.

63. Gaskine, "Anarchists," p. 919; Slosson, "Experiment," p. 783. Slosson did not visit these communities but gathered his information from H. G. Byers of the University of Washington, who did visit; Meany, *History of Washington*, p. 323n; Cooke interview, 16 July 1968, and others; *Agitator*, 1 May, 15 October 1911.

64. Cooke interview, 24 July 1969; *Discontent*, 26 April 1899, 16 October 1901; *Demonstrator*, 17 June, 16 September 1903; LaVene interview; Haiman interview; Bruenner interview.

65. *Discontent*, 19 April 1899, 22 May 1901, 30 April 1902; *Demonstrator*, 11 March 1903, 15 March 1905; *Agitator*, 15 November 1910; Bureau of Immigration report quoted in *Communist and Anarchist Deportation Cases*, p. 105.

66. *Demonstrator*, 13 January 1903; diary of Van Buskirk, 13 April 1900; Clyde interview; *Agitator*, 15 January, 15 February, 15 May 1911, 15 May 1912; Bruenner interview; LaVene interview; *Discontent*, 26 February 1902.

67. *Discontent*, 20 July 1898, 26 June 1901; *CN*, 19 June, 23 October 1897; *Demonstrator*, 1 June, 7 December 1904, 17 April 1907; diary of Muirhead, 16 April 1900; LaVene interview; Bruenner interview; Pritchard interview; Gaskine, "Anarchists," p. 921; Holbrook, "Home Sweet Home," 19 December 1937.

68. LaVene, "No Place," pt. 1, p. 8; see also pt. 2, p. 6; Joë Kapella [*sic*], "The Famous House in a Tree," in LaVene, "No Place," pt. 2, pp. 2-3; Cooke interview, 16 July 1968; Holbrook, "Home Sweet Home," 12 December 1937; *Demonstrator*, 2 May 1906.

69. *Discontent*, 31 July 1901.

70. Diary of Muirhead, 12 April 1900; diary of Van Buskirk, 22 May 1902; Robert D. Monroe, ed., "Sailor on the Snohomish; Extracts from the Washington Diaries of Philip C. Van Buskirk"; "Some Disadvantages of Anarchism," p. 3103; *Discontent*, 11 December 1901.

71. Rader, "The Em-Bossed at Home," p. 17; Stewart H. Holbrook, "Brook Farm, Wild West Style"; Knatvold, "Individual Liberty."

72. Diary of Muirhead, 14 April 1900; *Demonstrator*, 11 March 1903; *Co-op*, February 1903.

73. Cooke interview, 16 July 1968; *Demonstrator*, 18 March, 18, 29 April, 27 July, 23 September 1903, 13, 27 January, 11 May 1904, 14 April 1906; LaVene interview; LaVene, "No Place," pt. 2, pp. 11-12; Mrs. Hazzard later was prosecuted in a sensational trial after one of her patients died from malnutrition. Seattle *Town Crier*, 10 February 1912 *passim.*

74. *Demonstrator*, 25 April 1903, 3 February, 16 March 1904; *Discontent*, 19 February 1902; diary of Van Buskirk, 23, 29 May 1902.

75. *Demonstrator*, 15 July, 30 December 1903, 15 February 1905.

76. *Demonstrator*, 14 September, 1904, 1 November 1905; Hammond to the author, 20 May 1968; James F. Morton, Jr., *The Curse of Race Prejudice*; this pamphlet is an extension of a talk given at the Alhambra Theater in New York on 21 January 1906; *Who Was Who in America*, 1:872.

77. *Discontent*, 8 January 1902; *Demonstrator*, 29 June 1904, 1 February, 5 April, 17 May, 19 July 1905, 18 July 1906; *Agitator*, 1 November 1911.

78. Lang, *Tomorrow Is Beautiful*, pp. 30, 48-52; Macdonald, *Fifty Years*, especially, 2:381-83; William Z. Foster, *History of the Communist Party of the United States*, pp. 124, 184; Elizabeth Gurley Flynn, *I Speak My Own Piece*, pp. 213, 248; Tacoma *News-Tribune*, 7 November 1939; Holbrook, "Home Sweet Home," 12, 19 December 1937. The autobiographies of Mrs. Flynn and Haywood do not mention visiting Home, although both wandered in the Northwest in these days and may well have visited. William D. Haywood, *Bill Haywood's Book*; LaVene, "No Place," pt. 2, p. 11; Bruenner interview; Kapella, "The Famous House in a Tree," p. 3; see also Harry Hibbard Kemp, *Tramping on Life*, and *More Miles*; Morgan, *Last Wilderness*, p. 111; "Home Colony Photographs," *Washington Library Letter*, 24 May 1963; Muirhead to Verity, 10 March 1915, and Muirhead to George Shepperson, 30 May 1957, microfilm appended to the diary of Muirhead; William Z. Foster, *From Bryan to Stalin* and *Pages from a Worker's Life*; Haiman interview; LaVene interview.

79. *Encyclopedia Brittanica* (1955 ed.), 11:855; Robert L. Beisner, "'Commune' in East Aurora," *American Heritage*, February 1971, pp. 72-77, 106-9; *Demonstrator*, 22 April 1903.

80. *Demonstrator*, 22 April 1903, 21 June 1905; for Rader's account, see *Soundview*, July 1903, pp. 68-71; [Elbert Hubbard], "Heart to Heart Talks with Philistines by the Pastor of His Flock."

81. *Agitator*, 1 January 1911; *Discontent*, 13 July 1898, 25 January 1899, 26 December 1900, 17 April 1901; *Demonstrator*, 4 November 1903, 12 October 1904, 16 January, 20 November 1907.

82. *Demonstrator*, 9 March 1904; Cotterell, "Memoirs," 12 July 1934.

83. *Discontent*, 19 September, 19 December 1900, 22 January 1902; *Demonstrator*, 13 April 1904, 5 April, 18 October 1905. Most spring issues

for any year of the *Demonstrator* give news and scores of the baseball team; Dadisman interview, 23 July 1968; LaVene interview.

84. Diary of Muirhead, 15 April 1900; Dadisman interviews, 23 July, 2 August 1968, and others; Cotterell, "Memoirs," 12, 19 July 1934.

85. See *Discontent*, 1 July 1903, and Henry C. Hanson, "Child Freedom," for discussion of education; *Demonstrator*, 22, 29 April 1903; Allen's comments in *Discontent*, 28 November 1900; comment on rules from Bashford, "Troubles of a Tolstoi Colony"; Cotterell, "Memoirs," 17 May 1934; Dadisman interview, 23 July 1968; comment on the teacher from "Some Disadvantages of Anarchism," p. 3104.

86. Dadisman interview, 23 July 1968; *Discontent*, 21 June 1899, 5 September 1900, 2 April 1902; *Demonstrator*, 11 March 1903; *Agitator*, 1 January 1911. This building, converted to a private residence, still stands in 1974. This writer has found no evidence that the curriculum at Home was unconventional, despite insinuations in Tacoma newspapers.

87. Quotation from *Discontent*, 3 July 1901; Cotterell, "Memoirs," 12, 19 July 1934; LaVene interview; Jacques Cattell, ed., *American Men of Science*, 3:3119; Bruenner interview. Some "children of Home" that the author has met or has learned about include, besides those mentioned in these paragraphs: a longtime Port Orchard real estate broker, a Los Angeles businessman, a Seattle educator and musician, the owner of a Seattle foundry corporation, a Home resident who prospered in poultry marketing and land investments, the longtime owners and operators of the Home Telephone Company, and the wives of a Boeing Company executive, a prominent Seattle physician, and a well-known Seattle labor attorney.

88. *Demonstrator*, 11 March, 10, 17 June, 15 July 1903, 13 April 1904, 20 November 1907.

89. William John Burns, *The Masked War*, pp. 62-91; Doug Welch, "Home Colony Now Dreams of Yesteryear."

90. Quoted in Welch, "Home Colony Dreams."

91. Burns, *Masked War*, pp. 84, 92. The accuracy of the Burns narrative is betrayed not only by the antics described and the florid language used, but by reference to the population of Home as about 1,200 (p. 65) and by two sequential reports, one dated "Sunday, November 15th, 1910" and the following dated "Monday, November 14th, 1910" (pp. 86-87).

92. Welch, "Home Colony Dreams"; *Communist and Anarchist Deportation Cases*, p. 123; Knatvold, "Individual Liberty"; Burns, *Masked War*, pp. 92-93.

93. *Discontent*, 4 December 1901; Goldman, "Donald Vose," pp. 353-54; Foster, *Worker's Life*, p. 208; Lang, *Tomorrow Is Beautiful*, p. 80.

94. Foster, *Worker's Life*, p. 209; Goldman, *Living*, pp. 545, 550-51; Goldman, "Donald Vose," pp. 354-57; Lang, *Tomorrow Is Beautiful*, pp. 77-79. The Foster and Lang accounts, both by persons claiming to have been present, give slightly different accounts of how Vose was detected, although both claim it happened by accident. Foster, however, asserts that suspicions about Vose had been growing.

95. Lang, *Tomorrow Is Beautiful*, p. 91; LaVene, "No Place," pt. 2, p. 14; Pritchard interview; Foster, *Worker's Life*, p. 209; Goldman, "Donald Vose," p. 357.

96. Morton's comment in *Demonstrator*, 2 August, 1 November, 6 December 1905, 2 May 1906; Swartz, "Anarchistic Communism," in Bliss, *New Encyclopedia of Social Reform*, p. 50. The author is indebted to Carolyn Ashbaugh of Sac City, Iowa, whose research on Lucy Parsons confirms the intensity of the struggle among the Chicago anarchists for the control of the movement and the newspaper. Letter to the author, 5 May 1973.

97. *Demonstrator*, 7 February, 20 June 1906.

98. Ibid., 3 July 1907; Swartz, "Anarchistic Communism," p. 50; Ashbaugh to the author.

99. *Demonstrator*, 18 December 1907; 9 February 1908, is the last issue of the file in the archives of the Washington State University Library, Pullman, which was complete for previous years; it is the last issue listed in Walter Goldwater, *Radical Periodicals in America, 1890-1950: A Bibliography with Brief Notes*, p. 11.

100. *Agitator*, 1 December 1911; *Discontent*, 26 February 1902; Foster, *From Bryan to Stalin*, p. 59; *Demonstrator*, 2 August 1905; LaVene interview; Haiman interview; Cooke interview, 16 July 1968. Jay Fox, "I Was at Haymarket," pp. M5, M7.

101. Haiman interview; *Agitator*, 1 February 1912.

102. *Agitator*, 15 November 1910, 1 March 1911; London's letter in ibid., 1 June 1911; see also the letter of Wm. C. Owen, ibid., 1 April 1911.

103. Various issues of *Agitator* during 1910-12; see especially, 1 January, 15 March, 4 April 1911; a subscription blank is appended to diary of Muirhead, microfilm.

104. *Agitator*, 1 March, 1 July, 1 November 1911, 15 January 1912.

105. Lang, *Tomorrow Is Beautiful*, p. 49; Foster's columns in *Agitator*, 15 April-15 August 1912; Foster, *History*, p. 117; Foster, *From Bryan to Stalin*, p. 59.

106. *Agitator*, 1 October 1912; *Syndicalist*, 1 January, 15 March, 1 April 1913.

107. *Syndicalist*, 1, 15 March, 15 April 1913; 15 September 1913 is the last issue in the complete file in the University of Washington Library; it is also cited as the final issue in Goldwater, *Radical Periodicals*, p. 42.

108. Foster, *Worker's Life*, p. 208; Lang, *Tomorrow Is Beautiful*, p. 49; Foster, *From Bryan to Stalin*, p. 57n; Foster states the title of the poem as "Holiness" and the author as McClintock.

109. LaVene interview; Haiman interview; Lang, *Tomorrow Is Beautiful*, p. 49; *New York Times*, 2, 6, 7, 19 September 1961.

110. Verity to Muirhead, 13 January 1915, appended to diary of Muirhead; *Ledger*, 23 August 1911; Haiman interview; Bruenner interview.

111. *Agitator*, 1 July 1911; *Ledger*, 23 July 1911; Pierce County, Superior Court, Criminal File 21902, State of Washington vs. Adrian Wilbers.

Because Wilbers' case was taken to the superior court from the justice court sitting at Longbranch, the records are readily available; the other cases were similar in nature.

112. Pierce County, Superior Court file 21902; *Ledger*, 23 July, 25 August 1911.

113. *Ledger*, 26 August 1911, 19 January 1912; Tacoma *News*, 25 August 1911, 18 January 1912; Pierce County, Superior Court file 21902; Tacoma *Evening Times*, 17, 18, 19 January 1912.

114. *Ledger*, 23 July, 31 August 1911; *News* quoted in *Agitator*, 15 November 1911; Wilbers' quotation from *News*, 18 January 1912; Tacoma *Times*, 15 January 1912; *Agitator*, 15 September 1911.

115. See dance notice, *Agitator*, 15 January 1912, for example of fund raising; Cooke interview, 16 July 1968; Haiman interview; Verity to Muirhead, 13 January 1915, appended to Muirhead diary.

116. Cooke interview, 16 July 1968; Haiman interview; Haffer interview.

117. LaVene, "No Place," pt. 2, pp. 7, 13-14; *News*, 15, 16 January 1912; Tacoma *Times*, 15, 17 January 1912; *Ledger*, 16 January 1912; *Agitator*, 1 July 1911.

118. *Agitator*, 1 July 1911.

119. Ibid.

120. Pierce County, Superior Court, Criminal File 21895, State of Washington vs. Jay Fox; the specific law quoted from Nichols, comp., *Session Laws*, p. 1183.

121. Tacoma *Tribune*, 24, 27 August 1911; *News*, 24 August 1911.

122. *Agitator*, 1 September, 15 October, 1 November 1911, 1 January 1912; Pierce County, Superior Court file 21895.

123. Following his suicide in 1958, the Tacoma *News-Tribune* called Nolte one of the most colorful of the old-time Tacoma attorneys, 27 January 1958; Tacoma *Spectator*, 18 February 1902; *News*, 10, 11, 12 January 1912; Tacoma *Times*, 10, 11, 12 January 1912; *Ledger*, 11, 12 January 1912.

124. *Ledger*, 12 January 1912.

125. *News*, 12 January 1912.

126. Pierce County, Superior Court file 21895.

127. *Ledger*, 12, 13 January 1912; *News*, 12, 13 January 1912; Pierce County, Superior Court file 21895.

128. Pierce County, Superior Court file 21895; *Ledger*, 7 February 1912; *News*, 7 February 1912; *Agitator*, 15 February 1912.

129. *Agitator*, 1 September, 1 November 1912; *Syndicalist*, 1, 15 March 1913; the series ran in *Agitator*, February-April 1912.

130. *Syndicalist*, 15 January, 1 March 1913; the league also published a ten-page pamphlet on the case, *The Free Speech Case of Jay Fox*; Pierce County, Superior Court file 21895; Ernest Lister Papers, James J. Anderson to Lister, 15 May, 3 June 1915, Lister to Anderson, 21 May 1915.

131. Lister Papers, A. O. Burmeister to Lister, 9 June 1915, Burmeister to Zeighaus [*sic*], 9 June 1915, marked "personal" (Irwin W.

Ziegaus was the governor's secretary); W. O. Chapman to Lister, 10 June 1915, Fred G. Remann to Lister, 27 July 1915, Anderson to Lister, 3 September 1915.

132. Tacoma *Tribune*, 27 July, 11, 12 September 1915; Lister Papers, Anderson to Lister, 3 September 1915, J. G. Brown to Clarence Parker, 3 August 1915, Lister to Anderson, 7, 11 September 1915; pardon, dated 11 September 1915; *Ledger*, 12 September 1915.

133. O'Connor, *Revolution in Seattle*, pp. 110, 127; Theodore Draper, *The Roots of American Communism*, p. 322; Draper doubts that Fox was a member of the Communist party, p. 446n; Foster, *History*, p. 185; Bruenner interview; Welch, "Home Colony Dreams"; "Only Memories Remain of Home Colony's Past . . ."; Stewart H. Holbrook, "Anarchists at Home," p. 437; Terry Pettus, "Sixty Years a Union Man," pp. 4, 7.

134. J. C. Harrison, "One Picture of Home Colony."

135. Pierce County, Superior Court, Civil File 41264, State of Washington . . . vs. Jay Fox . . . , and Civil File 43388, Oscar Engvall . . . vs. Anna Haiman . . . .

136. Amended articles filed 25 June 1909, with the Pierce County Auditor, copy in abstract of title 63341, Tacoma Title Company, in possession of Mrs. Cooke; Verity to Muirhead, 24 January 1916, appended to Muirhead's diary. The Joe's Bay Trading Company applied to the court to determine which set of officers they should pay rent due on tidelands. Pierce County, Superior Court, Civil File 41569, Joe's Bay Trading Co. . . . vs. Jay Fox . . . ; Pierce County, Superior Court file 43388. In answer to the original complaint, the defendants emphasized that they had successfully managed the affairs and purposes of the association and that the plaintiffs composed a previously uninterested group that had never participated in affairs until beginning their recent harassment; Pierce County, Superior Court, file 40242, E. B. Berger . . . vs. Lewis Haiman . . . ; a contempt charge against Jay Fox was dismissed.

137. Clyde interview.

138. Quoted in *Communist and Anarchist Deportation Cases*, pp. 105-6.

139. Ibid.; Pritchard interview.

140. *Communist and Anarchist Deportation Cases*, pp. 121-30; *I.W.W. Deportation Cases*. U.S., Congress, House Committee on Immigration and Naturalization, Hearings, 27-30 April 1920, "Reports in the Cases of Various Aliens Transferred from Seattle, Wash., and Other Points to Ellis Island, N. Y. for Deportation, and Thereafter Released," 66th Cong., 2nd sess., 1920, pp. 56-64, lists forty-one persons from Seattle under detention at Ellis Island. None of these are names recognizable to this writer as former residents of Home or of other Puget Sound colonies.

141. Clyde, "Sketch"; Holbrook, "Home Sweet Home," 19 December 1937; Holbrook, "Anarchists at Home," p. 437.

142. Jack Ryan, "No Place Like Home"; Leila Allen Edmunds, subject of the article, has since died.

CHAPTER 7

1. Margaret Marshall, "The Solitary Settler at Hunter's Bay"; interview with Mrs. Vance Coder, 23 June 1969; Ray S. Spencer to the author, 22 April 1969.

2. Wooster, *Communities*, p. 138; Robert L. Tyler, *Rebels of the Woods*, pp. 206-7.

3. Edgar Cheporov and Pyotr Yashchenko, "1922 Seattle Commune Thrives in Russia," introduction by J. M. McClelland, Jr.

4. Albertson, "Mutualistic Communities," p. 425.

5. Cooke interview, 16 July 1968; Hoehn interview.

6. Hoehn interview; *Co-op*, December 1903. "Maddenism" refers to Edwin C. Madden, a post office official whom radicals held responsible for the alleged suppression of their newspapers.

7. Bushee, "Communistic Societies," p. 649; Julia Elizabeth Williams, "An Analytical Tabulation of the North American Utopian Communities by Type, Longevity, and Location," pp. 15-16; Rosabeth Moss Kanter, *Commitment and Community*, p. 245.

8. *Ledger*, 30 September 1901.

9. McDevitt, "Un-lost Horizon" (March-April 1951), p. 9.

10. Quint, *American Socialism*, p. 91: [Paul Tyner], "Under the Rose: 'Bellamy Colonies,'" pp. 528-29.

11. Kanter, *Commitment and Community*, pp. 2, 65-66, 75-125. Kanter's six "commitment mechanisms" are underlined in the text. This short discussion does scant justice to her systematic analysis of these mechanisms.

12. Alexander Trachtenberg, ed., *The American Labor Year Book, 1917-1918*, pp. 336-39; *IF*, 27 November 1900; Bellingham *Reveille*, 4 December 1901, 6 December 1905, 17 March 1907 *passim*; Marvin Sanford to the author, 30 June 1969; Quint, *American Socialism*, pp. 169-70; San Francisco *Chronicle*, 12 January, 11 November 1912, 10 June 1959; Tacoma *Times*, 19 January 1912; Harrison, "One Picture of Home Colony."

13. James Weinstein, *The Decline of Socialism in America, 1912-1925*, pp. x-xi, 102.

14. Everett *Commonwealth*, 24 July 1912; O'Connor, *Revolution in Seattle*, pp. 110, 287-89; Sanford to the author, 30 June 1969; Tacoma *News-Tribune*, 17 May 1965.

15. U.S., District Court, Western District of Washington, Southern Division, file 2439, United States vs. W. H. Kaufman, FRC No. 74883, Accession No. 62a379, Federal Records Center, National Archives, Seattle; *Demonstrator*, 6 December 1905; O'Connor, *Revolution in Seattle*, pp. 160-61.

16. San Francisco *Chronicle*, 30 July 1916; San Francisco *Examiner*, 27, 31 October 1916, 23 November, 24 December 1917.

17. *New York Times*, 17 December 1970; George Arthur, "Utopia/ Limited"; on two recent Washington communes, see Sara Davison, "Open Land: Getting Back to the Communal Garden . . . ," and Robert C. Blethen, "A Northwest Commune 'Trip.'"

18. William Hedgepeth, *The Alternative*, p. 164.

19. Kanter, *Commitment and Community*, pp. 5-7; "The American Family; Future Uncertain." Of much written about recent communal activity, the author has also found useful Ron E. Roberts, *The New Communes*, and Herbert A. Otto, "Communes: The Alternative Life-Style."

Bibliography

MANUSCRIPTS

The University of Washington Library, Seattle, holds the Harry E. B. Ault manuscripts, the Freeland Co-operative Association Papers (including the William Lieseke diary), and materials in Freeland Colony Vertical File 72, as well as the diaries of Alonzo A. Wardall and Philip C. Van Buskirk. The University of Washington also has a microfilm of relevant portions of the diary of Roland E. Muirhead, the original being at the Edinburgh University Library, Edinburgh, Scotland. The Edward Bellamy Papers are at Houghton Library, Harvard University, Cambridge, Massachusetts, and the Henry Demarest Lloyd Papers (microfilm edition, 1970) are at the State Historical Society of Wisconsin, Madison. Copies of the autobiography of Cyrus Field Willard are in the Olive Kettering Library, Antioch College, Yellow Springs, Ohio, and the Houghton Library. The Willard autobiography and the Lieseke, Wardall, Van Buskirk, and Muirhead diaries are included in the alphabetical listing below.

GOVERNMENT DOCUMENTS

Records in the appropriate county offices contain much information on the colonies and colonists of this study. Deeds, incorporation-papers, various civil and criminal proceedings, and receivership records have been particularly useful. The papers of Governor Ernest Lister and Acting Governor Charles E. Laughton are in the Archives and Records Center, Olympia, Washington. The Secretary of State, Topeka, Kansas, furnished a copy of the charter of the Co-operative Commonwealth Company. Records of federal court proceedings are in the Federal Records Center, National Archives, Seattle. Published government documents include state legislative records, federal immigration hearings, and census reports. All such materials used are fully cited in the footnotes.

BOOKS, ARTICLES, PAMPHLETS,
AND MISCELLANEOUS UNPUBLISHED MATERIALS

Adams, Joseph. "What Have You Found in Equality Colony?" *Industrial Freedom*, 16 June 1899.

Adams, Kramer A. *Logging Railroads of the West.* Seattle: Superior Publishing Co., 1961.

Albertson, Ralph. "A Survey of Mutualistic Communities in America." *Iowa Journal of History and Politics* 34:375-444.

Allen, George H. "Inside Workings of Anarchistic Colony Are Revealed . . ." Tacoma *Daily Ledger*, 7 January 1912.

"The American Family: Future Uncertain." *Time*, 28 December 1970, p. 36.

"An Anarchist Experiment Station." *Independent* 54:708-9.

Anderson, Katherine Stein. "Burley." Typewritten MS in possession of Kitsap County Historical Association, Bremerton, Wash.

Arrington, Leonard J. *Great Basin Kingdom: An Economic History of the Latter-day Saints, 1830-1900.* Cambridge, Mass.: Harvard University Press, 1958.

Arthur, George. "Utopia/Limited." *Helix*, 16 January 1969, pp. 6-7.

Ault, Harry. "The Colony Kids." *Young Socialist* 1 (May, 1900):2.

Avery, Mary W. *Washington: A History of the Evergreen State.* Seattle: University of Washington Press, 1961.

Ayres, Jessie C. "Old Log Cabin Built in 1888 is Mt. Angeles Roadmark." Port Angeles *Evening News*, May 1953. Clipping in possession of Wilda MacDonald.

"A Backward Glance O'er Travelled Roads." *Co-operator*, September 1903, pp. 23-27.

Bagley, Clarence B. *History of Seattle from the Earliest Settlement to the Present Time.* 3 vols. Chicago: S. J. Clarke Publishing Co., 1916.

Baker, Ray S. "The Debs Co-operative Commonwealth." *Outlook* 56:538-40.

Ballinger, Richard A., and Arthur Remington. *Remington & Ballinger's Annotated Codes and Statutes.* Seattle and San Francisco: Bancroft-Whitney, 1910.

Bashford, Herbert. "Troubles of a Tolstoi Colony: How the Individualists of 'Home' on Puget Sound Got Into Difficulty with the Government." San Francisco *Sunday Examiner, Magazine, ca.* 1902. Clipping in possession of Evadna Cooke.

Beisner, Robert L. "'Commune' in East Aurora." *American Heritage*, February 1971, pp. 72-77, 106-9.

Bellamy, Edward. *Equality.* Appleton Dollar Library ed. New York and London: D. Appleton-Century, 1934. 1st ed., Boston: D. Appleton, 1897.

——. *Looking Backward. 2000-1887.* Modern Library ed. New York: Random House, 1951. 1st ed., Boston: Ticknor, 1887.

Bestor, Arthur E. *Backwoods Utopias: The Sectarian and Owenite Phases of Communitarian Socialism in America, 1663-1829*. Philadelphia: University of Pennsylvania Press, 1950.

——. "Patent Office Models of the Good Society: Some Relationships between Social Reform and Westward Expansion." *American Historical Review* 58:505-26.

Blankenship, Russell. *And There Were Men*. New York: Alfred A. Knopf, 1942.

——. "The Political Thought of John R. Rogers." *Pacific Northwest Quarterly* 37:3-13.

Blethen, Robert C. "A Northwest Commune 'Trip.'" Seattle *Times Magazine*, 19 April 1970, pp. 8-9.

Bliss, William D. P., and Binder, Rudolph M., eds. *The New Encyclopedia of Social Reform*. . . . New ed. New York and London: Funk and Wagnalls, 1908.

Bonney, W. P. *History of Pierce County, Washington*. 3 vols. Chicago: Pioneer Historical Publishing Co., 1927.

Borland, W. P. "The Emancipation of Industry." *Pacific Monthly* 4 (1904):101-6.

Bradley, Thomas H. *O'Toole's Mallet: Or The Resurrection of the Second National City of the United States of America*. 2nd ed. Seattle: Calvert Co., 1894.

Bremner, Richard. Editor's Introduction to *Traps for the Young*, by Anthony Comstock. John Harvard Library ed. Cambridge, Mass.: Harvard University Press, 1967.

Brewster, Jessie. "Burley Pen Pictures: A Burley Sunday." *Co-operator*, August 1903, p. 11.

Brief Biographies, Maine: A Biographical Dictionary of Who's Who in Maine, 1926-1927. Lewiston, Me.: Lewiston Journal Co., 1926.

Brier, Howard M. *Sawdust Empire: The Pacific Northwest*. New York: Alfred A. Knopf, 1958.

Brommel, Bernard J. "Debs's Cooperative Commonwealth Plan for Workers." *Labor History* 12:560-69.

Buchanan, Iva Luella. "Economic History of Kitsap County, Washington, to 1889." Ph.D. dissertation, University of Washington, 1930.

Buchanan, Joseph R. *The Story of a Labor Agitator*. New York: Outlook Co., 1903.

Buell, Charles E. *Industrial Liberty: Our Duty to Rescue the People of Cuba, Porto Rico, and the Philippine Islands from That Greatest of All Evils—Poverty*. Plainfield, N.J., 1943.

"Burley Pen Pictures." *Co-operator*, May 1903; pp. 17-18; June 1903, pp. 19-21; July 1903, pp. 17-20; December 1903, pp. 17-20.

Burn, June. "Puget Soundings: A Strange Chapter in Puget Sound History." *The Puget Sounder*, August 9, 1935, pp. 1, 7.

Burns, William John. *The Masked War: The Story of a Peril That Threatened the United States by the Man Who Uncovered the Dynamite Conspirators and Sent Them to Jail.* New York: George H. Doran, 1913.

Bushee, Frederick A. "Communistic Societies in the United States." *Political Science Quarterly* 20:625-64.

Bushue, Paul B. "Dr. Hermon F. Titus and Socialism in Washington State." Master's thesis, University of Washington, 1967.

Caldwell, Worth W. "The Equality Colony: A Far Western Experiment That Cured Fifty Thousand Persons." *Sunset,* February 1924, pp. 27-29.

_____. "Rise and Fall of the Equality Colony, Stronghold of Power, Then Satan's Nest . . . ." Bellingham *Sunday Reveille,* 1 October 1922.

Catalogue for 1901-1902 and Announcements for 1902-1903 of the University of Washington. Seattle: Metropolitan Press, 1902.

Cattell, Jaques, ed., with Garrison Catell and Dorothy Hancock. *American Men of Science: A Biographical Dictionary.* 5 vols. 10th ed. Tempe, Ariz.: Jaques Cattell Press, 1961.

Chafee, Zechariah, Jr. *Government and Mass Communications: A Report from the Commission on Freedom of the Press.* 2 vols. Chicago: University of Chicago Press, 1947.

Cheporov, Edgar, and Yashchenko, Pyotr. "1922 Seattle Commune Thrives in Russia." Introduction by J. M. McClelland, Jr. Longview *Daily News,* 11-12 November 1967.

Clark, Earl. "Peninsula Profile—9: Mrs. Madge Nailor Still in Same House Where She Watched Indians as a Girl." Port Angeles *Olympic Tribune,* 4 March 1949.

Clark, Elmer T. *The Small Sects in America.* Rev. ed. New York and Nashville, Tenn.: Abingdon Press, 1949.

Clyde, S[iegfried]. "A Sketch of Home, Its Past and Present." Typewritten MS copied from the Gig Harbor *Peninsula Gateway,* 4 July 1947, in Tacoma Public Library.

Coleman, McAlister. *Eugene V. Debs: A Man Unafraid.* New York: Greenberg, 1930.

Commander, Kingsmill. "At Home with the Anarchists." *Co-operator,* October 1903, pp. 4-6.

_____. "On Memory's Wall." *Co-operator,* June 1906, pp. 1-4.

_____. "William Ellery Copeland." *Co-operator,* May 1904, pp. 3-5.

The Co-operative Brotherhood . . . Full Statement of Plans and Purposes. N. p., *ca.* 1899. Pamphlet in possession of Mrs. Katherine Anderson.

Copeland, W. E. "The Co-operative Brotherhood." *Arena* 28 (1902): 403-5.

_____. "The Co-operative Brotherhood and Its Colony." *Independent* 55:317-23.

Corporan [*sic*], Mary. Interview MS, n.d., in Bremerton, Wash., Public Library.

Cotterell, Mrs. A. F. "Memoirs of Home: An Account of the Pioneers." Vaughn *Peninsula Citizen.* Clippings of seven of the ten articles in the series, 26 April-11 October 1934, in possession of Evadna Cooke.

Coventon, Katheleen. "History of the Puget Sound Cooperative Colony." Typewritten MS, 1939, photocopy in University of Washington Library, Seattle.

Cravens, Hamilton. "A History of the Washington Farmer-Labor Party, 1918-1924." Master's thesis, University of Washington, 1962.

Crawford, Harriet Ann. *The Washington State Grange, 1889-1924: A Romance of Democracy*. Portland, Ore.: Binfords and Mort, 1940.

Cross, Ira B. *A History of the Labor Movement in California*. Berkeley: University of California Press, 1935.

Curti, Merle. *The Growth of American Thought*. New York and London: Harper and Brothers, 1943.

Darr, Oliver P. "Equality To-day." *Industrial Freedom*, Supplement, *ca.* 5 November 1898.

Daughters of the American Revolution of the State of Washington. "Family Records and Reminiscences of Washington Pioneers." 34 vols. Vol. 1 compiled by Julia McCormick Moyer, 1927-28. University of Washington Library, Seattle.

Davison, Sara. "Open Land: Getting Back to the Communal Garden . . . ." *Harper's Magazine* 240:91-102.

Debs, Eugene V. "How I Became a Socialist." *Comrade* 1:146-48.

deRoos, Robert. "An Interview with William McDevitt, LL. M." *Quarterly Newsletter of the Book Club of California* 19:75-83.

Destler, Charles McArthur. *American Radicalism, 1865-1901; Essays and Documents*. New London: Connecticut College Press, 1946.

_____. *Henry Demarest Lloyd and the Empire of Reform*. Philadelphia: University of Pennsylvania Press, 1963.

Doig, Ivan. "Puget Sound's War Within a War." *The American West* 8:22-27.

Dombrowski, James. *The Early Days of Christian Socialism in America*. New York: Columbia University Press, 1936.

Donovan, Richard. "Life with San Francisco: McDevitt and the Enormous Room." San Francisco *Chronicle*, 26 March 1942.

Donovan, Robert J. *The Assassins*. New York: Harpers, 1955.

Dos Passos, John. *Nineteen Nineteen*, in *U. S. A.* Boston: Houghton Mifflin, 1946.

Draper, Theodore. *The Roots of American Communism*. Compass Books ed. New York: Viking Press, 1963.

[Eddy, Bige.] "Musings of a Mossback: Independent Comment on Current Conditions by a Dyed-in-the-Wool Calamity Howler." *Industrial Freedom*, 31 December 1898-17 June 1899.

Edson, Lelah Jackson. *The Fourth Corner: Highlights from the Early Northwest*. Bellingham, Wash.: Cox Brothers, 1951.

Egbert, Donald Drew, and Persons, Stow. *Socialism and American Life*. 2 vols. Princeton, N.J.: Princeton University Press, 1952.

Engle, Pearl, and Hlavin, Jeanette, eds. "History of Tacoma Eastern Area." N.p., *ca.* 1954. Mimeographed pamphlet.

"Equality Colony." *Co-operator*, September 1902, pp. 17-18.

"Famed Shell Collection Acquired by College." *The Colby Alumnus*, 15 October 1945, p. 12.

Faulkner, Harold U. *Politics, Reform and Expansion*, 1890-1900. Harper Torchbooks ed. New York, Evanston, Ill., and London: Harper Row, 1963.

Fenton, M. L. Interview MS, n.d., in Bremerton, Wash., Public Library.

Fine, Nathan. *Labor and Farmer Parties in the United States*. New York: Rand School of Social Science, 1928.

Fine, Sidney. "Anarchism and the Assassination of McKinley." *American Historical Review* 60:777-99.

Flower, B. O. *Progressive Men, Women, and Movements of the Past Twenty-five Years*. Boston: New Arena, 1914.

Flynn, Elizabeth Gurley. *I Speak My Own Piece: Autobiography of "The Rebel Girl."* New York: Masses and Mainstream, 1955.

Foster, William Z. *From Bryan to Stalin*. New York: International Publishers, ca. 1937.

_____. *History of the Communist Party of the United States*. New York: International Publishers, 1952.

_____. *Pages from a Worker's Life*. New York: International Publishers, 1939.

"The Fourth of July at Burley." *Co-operator*, August 1903, pp. 17-19.

Fox, Jay. "I Was at Haymarket." *Our World*, 27 April 1951, pp. M5, M7.

Franklin, John Hope. "Edward Bellamy and the Nationalist Movement." *New England Quarterly* 11:739-72.

The Free Speech Case of Jay Fox. New York, 1912. Pamphlet in Northwest Collection, University of Washington Libraries, Seattle.

Friedheim, Robert L. *The Seattle General Strike*. Seattle: University of Washington Press, 1964.

Gaskine, J. W. "The Anarchists at Home, Washington." *Independent* 78:914-22.

Ginger, Ray. *The Bending Cross*. New Brunswick, N.J.: Rutgers University Press, 1949.

Goldman, Emma. "Donald Vose: The Accursed." *Mother Earth* 10:353-57.

_____. *Living My Life*. 1 vol. ed. New York: Alfred A. Knopf, 1934.

Goldwater, Walter. *Radical Periodicals in America, 1890-1950 . . . .* New Haven, Conn: Yale University Library, 1966.

Granger, Patricia. "The Co-operative Colony at Burley, Washington." Typewritten MS, ca. 1936, in Kitsap County Regional Library, Bremerton, Wash.

Griffiths, Austin Edwards. "Great Faith: Autobiography of an English Immigrant Boy in America, 1863-1950." Typewritten MS in University of Washington Library, Seattle.

Grob, Gerald N. *Workers and Utopia: A Study of Ideological Conflict in the American Labor Movement, 1865-1900*. Evanston, Ill.: Northwestern University Press, 1961.

Grönlund, Laurence. *The Cooperative Commonwealth*. Ed. by Stow Persons. Cambridge, Mass.: Harvard University Press, Belknap Press, 1965. 1st ed., Boston: Lee and Shepard, 1884.

_____. "Socializing a State." *Progressive Thought*, October 1900, pp. 15-22.

Halladay, H. W. "Equality Colony: A Brief History Showing Our Objects and Present Condition—Cooperative Colonies Are Not All Failures." *Industrial Freedom*, 1 November 1901.

Hanford, C. H. *Seattle and Its Environs, 1852-1924.* 3 vols. Chicago and Seattle: Pioneer Historical Publishing Co., 1924.

Hanson, Henry C. "Child Freedom." *Agitator*, 1 March 1911.

Harrison, J. C. "One Picture of Home Colony." Letter to *Solidarity* dated 23 January 1915. Reprint in possession of Radium LaVene.

Haywood, William D. *Bill Haywood's Book: The Autobiography of William D. Haywood.* New York: International Publishers, *ca.* 1929.

Heath, Frederic, ed. *Social Democracy Red Book.* Progressive Thought no. 10. Terre Haute, Ind.: Debs Publishing Co., 1900.

Hedgepeth, William. *The Alternative: Communal Life in New America.* New York, Toronto, and London: Macmillan, 1970.

Hedges, James B. "Promotion of Immigration to the Pacific Northwest by the Railroads." *Mississippi Valley Historical Review* 15:183-203.

Hendricks, Robert J. *Bethel and Aurora: An Experiment in Communism as Practical Christianity with Some Account of Past and Present Ventures in Collective Living.* New York: Press of the Pioneers, 1933.

Henson, Jack. "Ancient Log Cabin Housed Pioneer County Family." Port Angeles *Evening News*, 29 March 1952.

———. "Co-operative Colony of 1887 Failed as an Experiment, but Developed Port Angeles." Port Angeles *Evening News*, 28 November 1953.

———. "Peninsula Profile—6; William J. Ware Saw Birth of City, Has Part in Area's Colorful History." Port Angeles *Evening News*, 5 February 1949.

———. "Peninsula Profile—25; Gold Rush, First War, Pioneer Days Seen by Mrs. Troy." Port Angeles *Evening News*, 25 June 1949.

Hertzka, Theodor. *Freeland: A Social Anticipation.* Trans. by Arthur Ransom. London: Chatto and Windus, 1891; New York: Freeland Printing and Publishing, 1904.

Heuston, B. F. *The Rice Mills of Port Mystery.* Chicago: C. H. Kerr, 1891.

Heywood, Herbert. "Lincoln's Federal Townsite." *Overland Monthly*, 2nd ser., 23:171-73.

Hindle, F. "The Rochdale Plan." *Whidby Islander*, 1 August 1901.

Hinds, William Alfred. *American Communities.* Rev. ed. Chicago: C. H. Kerr, 1902.

———. *American Communities and Co-operative Colonies.* 2nd rev. ed. Chicago: Charles H. Kerr, 1908.

Hine, Robert V. *California's Utopian Colonies.* Rev. ed. New Haven, Conn., and London: Yale University Press, 1966.

Hinton, Richard J. *John Brown and His Men: With Some Account of the Roads They Traveled to Reach Harper's Ferry.* New York: Funk and Wagnalls, 1894.

Holbrook, Stewart H. "Anarchists at Home." *American Scholar* 15:425-38.

———. "Brook Farm, Wild West Style." *American Mercury* 57:216-23.

_____. "The Co-operators of Burley Lagoon." Portland *Oregonian*, 20 November 1957.

_____. *Far Corner: A Personal View of the Pacific Northwest*. New York: Macmillan, 1952.

_____. "Home Sweet Home, the Anarchists of Joe's Bay." Portland *Sunday Oregonian, Magazine*, 5, 12, 19 December 1937.

_____. "There Was No Place Like Home." Portland *Oregonian*, 14, 15, 16 January 1958.

Holyoake, George Jacob. *The History of the Rochdale Pioneers*. London: George Allen and Unwin, Ltd.; New York: Charles Scribner's Son, [ca.] 1893.

"Home Colony Photographs." *Washington Library Letter*, 24 May 1963.

Horning, F. L. "A Hearty Welcome." *Co-operator*, May 1903, pp. 13-15.

Horr, Alexander. *Fabian Anarchism: A Fragmentary Exposition of Mutualism, Communism and Freeland*. San Francisco: Freeland Printing and Publishing Co., 1911.

_____. "Freeland in a Nutshell." Reprint from *Lucifer*, n.d., in possession of Labadie Collection, University of Michigan, Ann Arbor.

[_____]. "The Freeland Movement." Introduction to the United States edition of Hertzka, *Freeland* (New York, 1904); also issued as the September 1904 issue of *Freeland* magazine, a copy of which is in the Hoover Institute on War, Revolution, and Peace, Stanford, Calif.

House Journal of the Eighth Legislature of the State of Washington . . . . Spokane: Inland Printing Co., 1903.

[Hubbard, Elbert.] "Heart to Heart Talks with Philistines by the Pastor of His Flock." *Philistine* 18:65-98.

Hunt, Herbert. *Tacoma, Its History and Its Builders: A Half Century of Activity*. 3 vols. Chicago: S. J. Clarke, 1916.

_____, and Kaylor, Floyd C. *Washington West of the Cascades: Historical and Descriptive, the Explorers, the Indians, the Pioneers, the Modern*. 3 vols. Chicago, Seattle, and Tacoma: S. J. Clarke, 1917.

An Illustrated History of Skagit and Snohomish Counties: Their People, Their Commerce and Their Resources, with an Outline of the Early History of the State of Washington. N.p.: Interstate Publishing Company, 1906.

Island County: A World Beater. Everett, Wash.: F. B. Hawes, n.d.; reprint, *ca.* 1967.

Jacker, Corinne. *The Black Flag of Anarchy: Antistatism in the United States*. New York: Charles Scribner's Sons, 1968.

Johansen, Dorothy O., and Gates, Charles M. *Empire of the Columbia: A History of the Pacific Northwest*. 2nd ed. New York, Evanston, Ill., and London: Harper and Row, 1967.

Johnson, Joseph Asbury. "The Spirit of Humanity." In Buell, *Industrial Liberty*, pp. 98-100.

Kanter, Rosabeth Moss. *Commitment and Community: Communes and Utopias in Sociological Perspective*. Cambridge, Mass.: Harvard University Press, 1972.

Kapella [*sic*], Joe. "The Famous House in a Tree." In LaVene, "There Was No Place Like Home," pt. 2, pp. 2-3.

[Keil, William]. "From Bethel, Missouri, to Aurora, Oregon: Letters of William Keil, 1855-1870." Trans. by William G. Bek. *Missouri Historical Review* 68:23-41, 141-53.

Kemp, Harry Hibbard. *More Miles: An Autobiographical Novel.* New York: Boni and Liveright, 1926.

———. *Tramping on Life: An Autobiographical Narrative.* Garden City, N.Y.: Garden City Publishing Co., 1922.

Kent, Alexander. "Cooperative Communities in the United States." U.S. Department of Labor *Bulletin* 6:563-646.

Kipnis, Ira. *The American Socialist Movement, 1897-1912.* New York: Columbia University Press, 1952.

Klamroth, L., and Randolph, W. C. B. "Co-operative Colony at Edison." Seattle *Times*, 6 August 1898.

Knatvold, Berthe. "Where Individual Liberty Rules: Small Community Near Tacoma Where Every Person Knows Only Their Own Laws; No Question Asked or Answered at Home Colony, Where Recluses Farm Lands." Tacoma *Tribune*, 17 August 1913.

Kolehainen, John Ilmari. "Harmony Island: A Finnish Utopian Venture in British Columbia." *British Columbia Historical Quarterly* 5:111-23.

Lang, Lucy Robins. *Tomorrow Is Beautiful.* New York: Macmillan, 1948.

Lauridsen, G. M., Smith, A. A., *et al. The Story of Port Angeles, Clallam County, Washington: A Historical Symposium.* Seattle: Lowman and Hanford, 1937.

LaVene, Radium. "There Was No Place Like Home." 2 pts. Mimeographed MS, 1945.

Legislative Manual and Political Directory, State of Washington 1899 . . . . Tacoma: Central News Company, 1899.

Leonard, John W., ed. *Who's Who in America: A Biographical Dictionary of Living Men and Women of the United States, 1899-1900.* Chicago: A. N. Marquis, 1899. *1903-1905.* Chicago: A. N. Marquis, 1903.

———. *Who's Who in Engineering: A Biographical Dictionary of Contemporaries, 1925.* 2nd ed. New York: A. N. Marquis, 1925.

Lermond, N. W. "Short History of the Brotherhood." *Industrial Freedom*, 7 May 1898.

LeWarne, Charles P. "Communitarians in Western Washington, 1885-1915." Ph.D. dissertation, University of Washington, 1969.

Lieseke, William. Diary, 1915-16. In Freeland Co-operative Association Papers, University of Washington Library, Seattle.

Lloyd, Caro. *Henry Demarest Lloyd: 1847-1903, A Biography.* 2 vols. New York: G. P. Putnam's Sons, 1912.

"'Looking Backward' at Burley 'Dream' Colony: Dad Fenton Tells of Troubles of Those Who Tried to Live Bellamy Concept." Tacoma *Sunday Ledger*, 5 August 1940.

McDevitt, William. "Un-lost Horizon: Shangri-La of Puget Sound." *Searchlight*, 8 installments running serially from March-April 1950 to May-June 1951.

Macdonald, George E. *Fifty Years of Freethought: Being the Story of the 'Truth Seeker' with the Natural History of Its Third Editor.* 2 vols. New York: Truth Seeker Co., 1931.

McDonald, Lucile. "Early Life Was Tough on the Skagit." Seattle *Sunday Times, Charmed Land Magazine*, 18 October 1964.

———. "Eyewitness to Peninsula History: Since 1887, Madge Nailor Has Observed and Participated in the Development of Port Angeles and Vicinity; Now She Works to Help Preserve the Records of the Past." Seattle *Sunday Times, Magazine*. 30 October 1960.

———. "In Port Angeles—Jack Henson Is Known as the Scribe." Seattle *Sunday Times, Magazine*, 23 December 1962.

McLaughlin, Inez. *We Grew Up Together.* Seattle: L. and H. Printing, *ca.* 1959.

McMurry, Donald L. *Coxey's Army: A Study of the Industrial Army Movement of 1894.* Americana Library ed. Seattle and London: University of Washington Press, 1968. 1st ed., Boston: Little, Brown and Co., 1929.

Malin, James C. *A Concern about Humanity: Notes on Reform, 1872-1912, at the National and Kansas Levels of Thought.* Lawrence, Kan.: published by the author, 1964.

———. *John Brown and the Legend of Fifty-Six.* Philadelphia: American Philosophical Society, 1942.

Mann, Arthur. "Frank Parsons: The Professor as Crusader." *Mississippi Valley Historical Review* 37:471-90.

———. *Yankee Reformers in the Urban Age.* Cambridge, Mass.: Harvard University Press, Belknap Press, 1954.

Marshall, Margaret. "The Solitary Settler at Hunter's Bay: 'Grandpa' Wilson Is Last Remaining Resident of Lopez Island Religious Colony." Seattle *Sunday Times, Magazine*, 4 December 1955.

Martin, James Joseph. *Men Against the State: The Expositers of Individualist Anarchism in America, 1827-1908.* DeKalb, Ill.: Adrian Allen, 1953.

Meany, Edmond S. *History of the State of Washington.* 1909 ed. New York: Macmillan, 1946.

Milburn, George. "The Appeal to Reason." *American Mercury* 23:359-71.

Miletich, Frederick P. "The Historical and Economic Geography of Port Angeles." Master's thesis, University of Washington, 1954.

Mitchell, Marlene. "Washington Newspapers, Territorial and State; a Bibliography and Checklist." Master's thesis, University of Washington, 1964.

Monroe, Anne Shannon. "The Co-operative Brotherhood of Burley, Washington: How Will It All Work Out? The Years Will Tell." Seattle *Post-Intelligencer*, 17 June 1900.

Monroe, Robert D., ed. "Sailor on the Snohomish: Extracts from the Washington Diaries of Philip C. Van Buskirk." MS, 1957, in possession of Mr. Monroe, Seattle.

Morgan, Arthur Ernest. *Edward Bellamy.* New York: Columbia University Press, 1944.

Morgan, H. Wayne. *Eugene V. Debs: Socialist for President.* Syracuse, N. Y.: Syracuse University Press, 1962.

Morgan, Murray. *The Last Wilderness.* New York: Viking, 1955.

____. *Skid Road: An Informal Portrait of Seattle.* Revised paperbound ed. New York: Viking, 1962.

Morton, James F., Jr. *The Curse of Race Prejudice.* New York: James F. Morton, Jr., *ca.* 1906.

Muirhead, Roland Eugene. Diary, 1900, with appended papers. Edinburgh University Library, Edinburgh, Scotland. Microfilm copy, University of Washington Library, Seattle.

Neuberger, Richard L. *Our Promised Land.* New York: Macmillan, 1938.

Newell, Gordon R. *Ships of the Inland Sea: The Story of the Puget Sound Steamboats.* 2nd ed. Portland, Ore.: Binfords and Mort, 1960.

Nichols, Sam H., comp. *Session Laws of the State of Washington. Eighth Session, 1903.* Tacoma: Allen and Lamborn Printing Co., 1903.

Nordhoff, Charles. *The Communistic Societies of the United States: From Personal Visit and Observation . . . .* London: John Murray, 1875.

Noyes, J. H. *History of American Socialisms.* Philadelphia: Lippincott, 1870.

O'Connell, Mary Joan [Sister Maria Veronica, S.N.J.M.]. "The Seattle Union Record, 1918-1928: A Pioneer Labor Daily." Master's thesis, University of Washington, 1964.

O'Connor, Harvey. *Revolution in Seattle: A Memoir.* New York: Monthly Review Press, 1964.

"Only Memories Remain of Home Colony's Past: Original Searchers for Freedom Have Departed, but Misty Tales of Their Reputed Eccentricities Still Talked About." Unidentified newspaper clipping, *ca.* 1943, Tacoma Public Library.

Otto, Herbert A. "Communes: The Alternative Life-Style" *Saturday Review,* 24 April 1971, pp. 16-21.

[Parker, Adele.] "Cooperative Colonies in the State of Washington." Typewritten MS, 1936-37, in Washington State Library, Olympia.

Parrington, Vernon Louis, Jr. *American Dreams: A Study of American Utopias.* Providence, R. I.: Brown University Press, 1947.

Pelten [*sic*], G. E. "Historical Sketch of B. C. C." *Industrial Freedom,* Supplement, *ca.* 5 November 1898.

Perlman, Selig, and Taft, Philip. *History of Labor in the United States, 1896-1932.* Vol. 4, *Labor Movements.* New York: Macmillan, 1935.

Pettus, Terry. "Sixty-Four Years a Union Man." *Our World,* 16 February 1951, pp. 4, 7.

Pilcher, Gilbert. "An Outline of the History of Clallam County, Washington." MS, n.d., in Washington State Library, Olympia.

Pitt, Joe. "Navy Yard District Citizen Tells of Old Times." *Daily News Searchlight,* 21 June 1930. Microfilm copy in Kitsap County Miscellany, Washington State Library, Olympia.

Pomeroy, Eltweed. "The Direct Legislation Movement and Its Leaders." *Arena* 16:29-43.

Port Orchard Chamber of Commerce. *South Kitsap County, State of Washington.* Port Orchard: n.p., 1922.

Powderly, Terence V. *Thirty Years of Labor, 1859-1889 . . . .* Rev. ed. Philadelphia: published by the author, 1890.

Prosch, Thomas W. "A Chronological History of Seattle from 1850 to 1897." MS, *ca.* 1900, in possession of Seattle Historical Society.

Puget Sound Cooperative Colony. Milwaukee: Ellery W. Ellis, *ca.* 1887; facsimile reproduction, Seattle: Shorey Book Store, 1965.

Pulsipher, Catherine Savage. "Do You Remember Equality Colony?" A poem appearing in the column, "Skagit—Sonnets and Satire," in an unidentified Mount Vernon, Wash., newspaper, late 1963 or 1964; clipping in possession of Emma Herz Peterson.

_____. "Notes on the Equality Colony at Bow, Washington." Typewritten MS, 1966, in possession of C. P. LeWarne.

Quint, Howard H. *The Forging of American Socialism: Origins of the Modern Movement.* American Heritage Series ed. Indianapolis, New York, and Kansas City: Bobbs-Merrill, 1964.

_____. "Julius A. Wayland, Pioneer Socialist and Propagandist." *Mississippi Valley Historical Review* 35:585-606.

R[ader], E[mma] E. "The Em-Bossed at Home." *Soundview* 2 (April, 1903):17.

Randolph, W. C. B. "The Future of the Movement." *Industrial Freedom,* Supplement, *ca.* 5 November 1898.

Roberts, Ron E. *The New Communes: Coming Together in America.* Englewood Cliffs, N.J.: Prentice-Hall, 1971.

Robinson, E. L. *A Common Sense Cooperative System: A Practical Plan of Cooperation with Arguments in Its Support . . . .* Cave Mills, Tenn.: The Coming Nation, 1896.

Roth, Lottie Roeder, ed. *History of Whatcom County, Washington.* 2 vols. Chicago and Seattle: Pioneer Historical Publishing Co., 1926.

Russell, Doris. "South Kitsap History Traced." Port Orchard *Independent,* special 75th anniversary ed., 1963.

Ryan, Jack. "No Place Like Home: Once a Land of 'Anarchy, Sin,' Home Notes Anniversary Quietly." Tacoma *News-Tribune,* 10 February 1966.

Sadler, Elizabeth. "One Book's Influence: Bellamy's 'Looking Backward.'" *New England Quarterly* 17:530-55.

[Sanford, Marvin.] "DeForest Sanford, June 11, 1871-Nov. 30, 1956." San Francisco *Evening Lamp,* June 1957, pp. 5-12.

_____. "Freeland, A Rochdale Town." *Searchlight,* September-October 1949, pp. 3-4.

_____. "Freeland, Home and Equality." *Searchlight,* January-February 1950, pp. 5-6.

_____. "The Story of Freeland." *Searchlight,* November-December 1949, pp. 5-7.

"The Second National City. Port Angeles." In "Proceedings, Port Angeles Community Study." MS, Port Angeles Public Library, Port Angeles.

Shannon, David A. *The Socialist Party of America: A History*. New York: Macmillan, 1955.

Sheller, Roscoe. *Courage and Water: A Story of Yakima Valley's Sunnyside; A Factual Story of the Founding, Development and Growth of the Unique and Unusual City of Sunnyside, Washington, Located in the Heart of the Famous Yakima Valley*. Ed. by Joseph P. Lassoie. Portland, Ore.: Binfords and Mort, 1952.

Shepperson, Wilbur S., with John G. Folkes. *Retreat to Nevada: A Socialist Colony of World War I*. Reno: University of Nevada Press, 1966.

Sherlock, Margaret V. "The Recall of Mayor Gill." *Pacific Monthly* 26:116-30.

Simon, John E. "Wilhelm Keil and Communist Colonies." *Oregon Historical Quarterly* 36:119-53.

Slosson, E. E. "An Experiment in Anarchy." *Independent* 55:779-85.

Smith, George Venable. *A Co-operative Plan for Securing Homes and Occupations at Port Angeles, Washington*. Port Angeles: Tribune-Times Job Printing, 1893; facsimile reprint, Seattle: Shorey Book Store, 1965.

[Smith, Lois.] "Auntie Mackay, Pioneer Nurse, Described by Former Resident (A Friend on Memory's Trail)." Unidentified newspaper clipping, n.d., in possession of Wilda MacDonald.

Smith, Norman R. "Map of Port Angeles, Washington," 1891.

_____. "Victory: The Story of Port Angeles by the Son of Victor Smith, founder of This City." Port Angeles *Evening News*. 58 installments running serially from 12 June to 22 August 1950; clippings collected in portfolio, University of Washington Library, Seattle.

"The Social Democracy of America." *Literary Digest* 15:274-77.

"Some Disadvantages of Anarchism." *Independent* 54:3103.

Sotheran, Alice Hyneman. "Reminiscences of Charles Sotheran as Pioneer American Socialist." In Charles Sotheran, *Horace Greeley and Other Pioneers of American Socialism*. New York: M. Kennerley, 1915, pp. ix-xxxiv.

Souvenir of the Fifth Legislature of the State of Washington. Tacoma: E. M. Jeancon and F. A. Sauvageot, 1897.

Steel, Will A., and Searl, Albert. *Steel and Searl's Legislative Souvenir Manual for 1895-1896*. Seattle: Koch and Oakley Publishing Co., 1895.

Stein, Henry. Interview MS, n.d., in Bremerton, Wash., Public Library.

Stein, Henry W. "Highway to Touch Historic Ground: Site of Old Colony at Burley to Come into Its Own." Tacoma *News-Tribune*, 25 June 1925.

Stewart, Mrs. L. D. MS of interview by Gilbert Pilcher, *ca.* 1937, in Washington State Library, Olympia.

Swartz, C. L. "Anarchist Communism." In Bliss and Binder, eds. *The New Encyclopedia of Social Reform*.

Trachtenberg, Alexander, ed. *The American Labor Year Book, 1917-1918*. New York: Rand School of Social Science, 1918.

Tyler, Alice Felt. *Freedom's Ferment: Phases of American Social History from the Colonial Period to the Outbreak of the Civil War*. Harper Torchbooks ed. New York, Evanston, Ill., and London: Harper and Row, 1962.

Tyler, Robert L. *Rebels of the Woods: The I. W. W. in the Pacific Northwest*. Eugene: University of Oregon Press, 1967.

[Tyner, Paul.] "Under the Rose: 'Bellamy Colonies.'" *Arena* 21:528-29.

Van Buskirk, Philip C. Diary, 1851-1902. University of Washington Library, Seattle.

Verity, Oliver A. "Something about Discontent." *Discontent*, 13 November 1901.

Wardall, Alonzo A. Diary, 1863-1918. University of Washington Library, Seattle.

Warren, Sidney. *Farthest Frontier: The Pacific Northwest*. New York: Macmillan, 1949.

Wayland, J. A. *Leaves of Life: A Story of Twenty Years of Socialist Agitation*. Girard, Kan.: Appeal to Reason, 1912.

Webber, Everett. *Escape to Utopia: The Communal Movement in America*. New York: Hastings House, 1959.

Weeks, Jos. D. "Report on Trades Societies in the United States." U. S., Congress, House, *Miscellaneous Documents*, 47th Cong., 2nd sess., vol. 13, pt. 20.

Weinstein, James. *The Decline of Socialism in America, 1912-1925*. New York and London: Monthly Review Press, 1967.

Welch, Doug. "Home Colony Now Dreams of Yesteryear: Fiery Anarchists Long Gone from What Was Once Most Notorious Radical Center." Seattle *Post-Intelligencer*, 20 December 1942.

[Welsh, William D.] "Welsh Rarebits: The Colony Script [*sic*] . . . Mushroom Wages . . . Then Came Disaster . . . ." Unidentified clipping in possession of Mina Saari.

W. E. S. "In Memoriam—Cyrus Field Willard." *Theosophical Forum* 22:140-41.

Whiteside, A. L. "Among the Socialists at Edison." Seattle *Post-Intelligencer*, 18 May 1898.

Who Was Who in America: A Companion Volume to Who's Who in America. Vol 1: *1897-1942. Biographies of the Non-Living with Dates of Death Appended*. Chicago: A. N. Marquis, 1943.

Who's Who in New England: A Biographical Dictionary of Leading Living Men and Women of the States of Maine, New Hampshire, Vermont, Massachusetts, Rhode Island and Connecticut. Vol. 3. Chicago: A. N. Marquis, 1938.

Will, Clark Moor. "The Burial of Willie Keil." *The Sou'Wester* 3(Winter 1968):63-65.

Willard, Cyrus Field. "As It Is To-day: History of the Co-operative Brotherhood . . . ." *Industrial Freedom*, Supplement, *ca*. 5 November 1898.

_____. Autobiography. MS, *ca.* 1938. Copies in Antioch College Library, Yellow Springs, Ohio, and Houghton Library, Harvard University, Cambridge, Mass.

Williams, Julia Elizabeth. "An Analytical Tabulation of the North American Utopian Communities by Type, Longevity, and Location." Master's thesis, University of South Dakota, 1939. Includes Lee Emerson Deets, "Amercan Idealistic Community Experiments," a paper delivered to the Sociological Society of America in 1931.

Williams, L. R. *Our Pacific Coast.* Raymond, Wash.: Raymond *Herald,* 1930.

Winslow, F. A. "Naturalist at Age of 2, Norman Lermond Never Quit Nature Study . . . ." Boston *Sunday Globe,* 7 June 1925.

Winther, Oscar Osburn. *The Great Northwest: A History.* 2nd ed. New York: Alfred A. Knopf, 1952.

Wise, Sol. S. *The Light of Eden: Or, A Historical Narrative of the Barbarian Age, a Scientific Discovery.* Seattle: S. Burg, 1896.

Wolle, Muriel Sibell. *Stampede to Timberline: The Ghost Towns and Mining Camps of Colorado.* Boulder: University of Colorado Press, 1949.

Wooster, Ernest S. *Communities of the Past and Present.* Newllano, La.: Llano Colonist, 1924.

Work Projects Administration, Washington Writers' Program. *The New Washington: A Guide to the Evergreen State.* Rev. ed. Portland, Ore.: Binfords and Mort, 1950.

Wright, E. W., ed. *Lewis and Dryden's Marine History of the Pacific Northwest* . . . . Reprinted ed. New York: Antiquarian Press, 1961.

Wynne, Robert E. "Reaction to the Chinese in the Pacific Northwest and British Columbia, 1850-1910." Ph. D. dissertation, University of Washington, Seattle, 1964.

Yarros, Victor S. "Individualist or Philosophical Anarchism." In Bliss and Binder, ed., *The New Encyclopedia of Social Reform.*

Yearley, Clifford K., Jr. *Britons in American Labor: A History of the Influence of the United Kingdom Immigrants on American Labor, 1820-1914.* Baltimore: The Johns Hopkins Press, 1957.

Young, Helen E. "A Western Utopia." *The Dilettante* 2 (May 1900): 17-21.

INTERVIEWS

Anderson, Mrs. Albert. Seattle. 21 November 1965, 18 February 1968.

Anderson, Katherine Stein. Burley. 26 January 1966, 1 July 1969.

Barry, Inza Joslyn. Atascadero, Calif. 23 February 1966 (interview tape recorded by Mrs. June Larrick).

Bruenner, Mrs. Bertram. Seattle. 2 July 1969.

Clark, Florence Pelton. Seattle. 20 January, 7, 11 February, 21 March 1966.

Clyde, Siegfried. Home. 23 July 1968.

Coder, Mrs. Vance. Anacortes, Wash. 22 July 1969.

Cooke, Evadna. Seattle. 16 July, 2 August 1968, 24 July 1969.

Corporan [*sic*], Mary. Interview manuscript, undated, in Bremerton, Wash., Public Library.

Cunningham, Miskel. Seattle. 23 September 1973.

Dadisman, David. Home. 23 July, 2 August 1968.

Fenton, M. L. Interview manuscript, undated, in Bremerton, Wash., Public Library.

Finfrock, Mr. and Mrs. Sam L. Edmonds, Wash. 25, 29 March 1966.

Gray, Gladys Ault. Walla Walla, Wash. 1 April 1966.

Haffer, Virna. Tacoma. 6 August 1968.

Haiman, Lewis. Home. 2 August 1968.

Halladay, Mrs. Clinton D. Seattle. 4 December 1965, 18 February 1968.

Hoehn, Frank. Ephrata, Wash. 5 November 1966.

LaVene, Radium. Los Angeles. 22 June 1968.

Lieseke, Albert. Port Orchard, Wash. 20 March 1966.

Lieseke, Ernest. Freeland. 8 August 1968. A second interview tape recorded by Steven Uthoff and Fred Smith, 13 April 1968, is in the Freeland Co-operative Association File, Manuscripts Division, University of Washington Library, Seattle.

Malsbary, Rita Savage. Sedro Woolley, Wash. 3 December 1965.

Marshall, Austin. Freeland. 13 April 1968. Interview tape recorded by Steven Uthoff and Fred Smith is in the Freeland Co-operative Association File, Manuscripts Division, University of Washington Library, Seattle.

Merlich, Ella Lieseke. Cottage Grove, Ore. 1 July 1968.

Nailor, Madge Haynes. Port Angeles. 31 July 1967.

Peterson, Emma Herz. Seattle. 16, 28 November, 16 December 1965. At Equality Colony site, 23 April 1966.

Peterson, Mr. and Mrs. R. E. Bow, Wash. 23 April 1966.

Pierson, R. A. Everett, Wash. 27 January 1968. At Freeland, 8 August 1968.

Pritchard, Mimi. Seattle. 2 July 1969.

Pulsipher, Catherine Savage. Sedro Woolley, Wash. 23 April 1966.

Savage, John W. Seattle. 7, 9 February 1966.

Smith, Mrs. W. B. Port Angeles. 10 August 1967.

Stein, Henry. Interview manuscript, undated, in Bremerton, Wash., Public Library.

Stein, Leola E. Portland, Ore. 22, 23 August 1966.

Stewart, Mrs. L. D. Manuscript of interview by Gilbert Pilcher, *ca.* 1937, in Washington State Library, Olympia.

The owner of Raymer's Old Book Store. Seattle. 29 November 1965.

An early resident of Home who requested that she not be identified was interviewed at Purdy, Wash., in September 1968.

NEWSPAPERS

Bremerton *Sun*, 1935 ____.

[Burley] *The Co-operator*, 1898-1906.

Burley *Soundview*, 1902-8.

Chehalis *Bee-Nugget*, 1883-1938.

Chehalis *People's Advocate*, 1892-1902.

Chicago *Evening Telegram*, 1882-86.

[Chicago] *The Syndicalist*, 1913.

[Coupeville] *Island County Times*, 1891-1959.

[Equality] *Industrial Freedom*, 1898-1902.

[Equality, Spokane, and Lewiston, Ida.] *Young Socialist*, 1899-1904.

Everett *Commonwealth*, 1911-17.

Gig Harbor *Peninsula Gateway*, 1917 ____.

[Greensburg, Ind., Tennessee City, and Ruskin, Tenn.] *Coming Nation*, 1893-1903.

[Home] *The Agitator*, 1910-12.

[Home] *The Demonstrator*, 1903-8.

[Home] *Discontent, Mother of Progress*, 1898-1902.

[Langley and Freeland] *The Whidby Islander*, 1900-1903.

Mount Vernon *Argus*, 1891 ____.

New York Times, 1851 ____.

[Port Angeles] *Clallam County Courier*, 1895-1902.

Port Angeles *Evening News*, 1916 ____.

Portland *Oregon Journal*, 1902 ____.

Portland *Oregonian*, 1861 ____.

San Diego *Union*, 1868 ____.

San Francisco *Chronicle*, 1865 ____.

San Francisco *Examiner*, 1865____.

Seattle *Daily Call*, 1885-86.

Seattle *Daily Times*, 1886 ____.

[Seattle and Port Angeles] *The Model Commonwealth*, 1886-89.

Seattle *Post-Intelligencer*, 1876 ____.

Seattle *Town Crier*, 1906-24.

Tacoma *Daily Ledger*, 1883-1937.

Tacoma *Evening News*, 1881-1919.

Tacoma *News-Tribune*, 1883 ____.

Tacoma *Spectator*, 1901-2.

Tacoma *Times*, 1903-49.

Tacoma *Tribune*, 1907-18.

[Terre Haute, Ind., and Chicago] *Social Democrat*, 1897-98.

Whatcom, New Whatcom, and Bellingham *Reveille*, 1883-1922, 1923-26.

Index

The following abbreviations are used:

BCC   Brotherhood of the Co-operative Commonwealth
CB   Co-operative Brotherhood
FLA   Free Land Association
IF   *Industrial Freedom*
IWW Industrial Workers of the World
MHA Mutual Home Association
PSCC Puget Sound Co-operative Colony
SDA Social Democracy of America
WI   *Whidby Islander*

Billingsley, Annie, 76, 88
Birch Bay, Wash., 84, 85
Births, 23, 39, 170
Blacksmith: at PSCC, 23, 24; Pritchett, 33; PSCC property leased for, 50; at Equality, 63-64, 79, 85, 95-96; at Burley, 140, 150; Pearce, 155; tools at Burley, 165; at Glennis Colony, 168; Odell, 170
Blair family, 177
Blakely Island, Wash., 228
Blanchard, Wash., 62, 73, 84
Blavatsky, Mme. H. P., 132
Bliss, William D. P., 57, 207
Blockhouse, Wash., 75
Bloedel-Donovan Company, 258
Blumer, Jacob, 180
Boats: at PSCC, 41-42; and Industrial Brotherhood, 69; at Equality, 86, 98; at Freeland, 118-19; to Olalla, 137; at Burley, 156, 160, 168; built by Home founders, 169; of Capt. Lorenz, 169, 181; at Home, 176, 177, 179, 192; on Home excursion, 194; at Gourley colony, 227; runs planned, 230; Ault and Hoehn boat trip, 232; usable at high tide, 233. *See also* names of individual boats
Boeing Company, 278
Bohlman, S. H., 164, 165
Bolshevik Revolution, 228-29
Boomer, George E., 88, 239
Borland, Wilfred P.: as SDA official, 130-31, 136; life, 132-33; and Willard's departure, 143-44; later life, 144; gives Burley population figures, 145; on Burley insurance program, 146; *Co-operator* editor, 152; article by, 154; as journalist, 163; and Burley funds, 267
Boston, Mass.: in *Looking Backward*, 6; newspaper on Lermond, 69; Hinton in, 131; Willard in, 131-32; Theosophical Society in, 132; Copeland born in, 159
Boston University, 59
Bow, Wash., 94, 105
Bowle, Richard, 194
Boyd, W. B., 107
Braams Scheuer, P. A., 154
Brickey, Willard, 107
Brickmaking, 24, 40, 47, 78, 150
Brocchi, Dalmiro, 157
Brook Farm, Mass., 5, 195
Brotherhood of Locomotive Firemen, 132
Brotherhood of the Co-operative Commonwealth: emergence and plans, 55-56; Lermond and, 56-60, 68-69; organizational steps of, 57-59, 64, 252, 256;

constitution, 57-59, 67-68, 112, 252; officers, 59-60, 73, 108; and SDA, 60, 129, 133; and Debs, 60-61; interest in Washington State, 61-62; establishes Equality, 62-63; headquarters at Edison, 65, 80, 92; national character of, 66; Equality and Edison rivalry, 67-70; and Harmony Colony, 71; membership rules, 74; colony problems, 78; and funds for mill, 83; colonization plans, 86, 114; emblem, 87; newspapers, 87-88; scrip, 93-94; mail volume, 94; Junior BCC attempted, 96; donations to, 98; and Christian Socialists, 100; Freeland movement officials joined, 104; changes under Horr, 105-6; financial problems, 108; dissolution, 110-11; objectives, 112; effect on Washington socialism, 112, 238; Daniels in, 115; Burley separate from, 141; and railroad rates, 254
Brown, J. G., 219
Brown, John, 131
Bruce, M. F., 164
Bryan, William Jennings: 1896 presidential campaign, 10, 55, 57, 59, 60, 216; visits Whatcom, 98
Buckley, Wash., 11, 62
Buell, Charles E., 154, 158, 163
Buffalo, N. Y., 132, 177-78
Burgess, David: editor of *IF*, 88; Equality principal, 95; visits Freeland, 126; as writer, 127, 239; in politics, 238; and CB board, 267
Burley Colony, 129-67; and SDA, 61, 129-36; and Equality, 71, 232; CB, 107, 138-39; Commander from, 108, 232; Stevens from, 115; selection of site, 136-38; settlement, 139-42; factions at, 141-44, 235-36; membership, 144-46; government of, 146-48; industry and agriculture, 148-51, 230, 236; Circle City, 149, 154-55, 166; publications and publicity, 151-54, 239; social aspects of, 154-63, 232; decline and receivership, 164-67, 232; relations with Home, 168, 192, 194, 196, 203, 232; Tacoma local of CB, 176-77; farming in area, 234. *See also* Co-operative Brotherhood; Social Democracy of America; Willard, Cyrus Field
Burley Mercantile Rochdale Association, 148
Burlington Railroad, 32
Burmeister, A. O., 219
Burns Detective Agency, 203-4
Burns, William J. (detective), 203, 205
Burns, William (union official), 140

Rader, L. E., 153, 163, 189, 197, 200
Radicals: and BCC, 55; bookstores, 69, 98; and Equality, 87, 97, 98, 112; in New York, 105; and McKinley assassination, 124-25; and radical press, 125, 182, 184, 231, 239-40; Freeland, 127; and Burley, 157, 162, 163; and Home, 177, 185, 188, 194, 198, 199, 216, 220, 223, 224-25; in Pierce County, 181; and World War I, 198, 223; Vose's contacts with, 204; ahead of their time, 226; colonists as, 231; in Washington, 239, 240, 241, 242; of 1960s, 240-42. *See also* individual radical persons, groups, newspapers
Railroads: effect on Washington, 9, 10; and labor, 9, 15, 122, 123; encourage colonization, 13; at PSCC, 21, 29; and Ware, 32; and selection of colony sites, 37, 62; arrival of colonists, 64, 75, 76, 254; and Equality, 82, 85, 86; in FLA charter, 115; SDA proposal, 133
Railway Times, 129, 132
Rappites, 5
Raymer, Charles D., 98
Real estate promotions: at PSCC, 30, 44-47, 49, 50-51, 230; and origins of Freeland, 114-15; in Rochdale plan, 117; Sanford and, 125; changed Home, 224
Recalls, 116, 163
Receiverships: at PSCC, 41, 46, 48-52; at Equality, 108, 109-11; at Burley, 164-66; of MHA, 221-22
Recreation: at PSCC, 38; at Equality, 80, 90, 94-99; at Burley, 157, 162; Home picnics, 191, 194, 197; real estate developments, 224; neighbors in, 234
Reed, Myron W., 60, 66, 100
Reformation, 4
Reform movements: and communitarian tradition, 3-8, 235; in Washington, 3, 9; after Civil War, 5; discussed in *IF*, 87-88; discussed at Burley, 152, 157, 162-63; discussed in *Discontent*, 175; discussed in *Independent*, 186; agitation and, 216-17; colonists' influence in, 239-40; of 1960s, 240-42. *See also* individual reforms, individual reformers; Radicalism
Reincarnation, 12, 190
Reitman, Ben L., 199
Religion: religious communitarianism, 4, 235; and Keil colony, 11; and Davis colony, 12; at PSCC, 36; agnosticism, 36, 101; atheism, 36, 120-21, 207; at Equality, 65, 100-101; at Freeland,

120-21; at Burley, 158-60; free thought, 173, 198, 207; at Home, 175, 182, 188, 190, 198, 207, 226; at Gourley colony, 227-28, 229; in communes of 1960s, 241-42; mentioned, 231. *See also* individual religious groups
Republican party, 9, 30, 53, 125
Revolution: as viewed by communitarians, 4, 59, 158; Russian (1905), 188; Mexican, 209; Bolshevik, 228-29
Rice Mills of Port Mystery, The, 10
Rights of individuals: stressed by anarchists, 7; violated at Haymarket, 38-39; in Hertzka's Freeland scheme, 104; of colonists, 130; and *Discontent*, 174-75; in *Agitator*, 209
Roads: at Equality, 67; at Freeland, 115, 121-22; through Burley, 167; at Home, 191
Robins, Bob, 197
Robinson, E. L., 11, 62
Rochdale cooperatives: Wardall as organizer, 103, 147-48; Wardall at Equality, 103; described, 116-17; at Freeland, 117, 126, 128; at Burley, 148; Home Grocery Co., 191
Rochester, Junius, 19
Roestel, Paul, 214
Rogers, John R., 10, 11, 61, 87
Roman Catholics: PSCC and, 36, 42; at Equality, 101, 261; priest on anarchy, 178; mentioned, 174
Ronald, J. T., 19
Root houses, 81, 109, 149
Roycroft Community, 194, 199-200
Rubenstein, Ida, 198
Rubenstein, Mike, 198
Ruble, W., 56
Ruskin Colony, B.C., 13
Ruskin Colony, Tenn.: short history, 7; colonists from, 60, 194, 233; *Coming Nation*, 87; SDA officials visit, 133
Russia: revolutionists of 1905, 188; colonists at Home, 208; Foster's death, 211; communes in, 228-29

Sadler, Kate, 198
St. Louis, Mo.: G. V. Smith visits, 20; Sanderson in, 21, 53, 238; Henson in, 32; Populist convention, 57; BCC meeting, 57; SDA local union, 133
Sales of products: at Equality, 82, 85, 86, 90; at Freeland, 119; at Burley, 143, 149, 153, 166; at Gourley colony, 228; mentioned, 230. *See also* Land; Markets
Salvage, George K., 107
Samish Bay, Wash., 63